THE CIVILIZATION OF THE AMERICAN INDIAN SERIES

A CATALOG
OF MAYA HIEROGLYPHS

Published in co-operation with The Carnegie Institution of Washington

UNIVERSITY OF OKLAHOMA PRESS : NORMAN

A CATALOG OF MAYA HIEROGLYPHS

By J. ERIC S. THOMPSON

BY J. ERIC S. THOMPSON

A Catalog of Maya Hieroglyphs (Norman, 1962)
Maya Hieroglyphic Writing: An Introduction (Norman, 1960)
Thomas Gage's Travels in the New World (ed.) (Norman, 1958)
The Rise and Fall of Maya Civilization (Norman, 1954, 1966)
Excavations at San José, British Honduras (Washington, 1939)
Mexico before Cortez (New York, 1933)
Archaeological Investigations in the Southern Cayo District, British Honduras
(Chicago, 1931)
Ethnology of the Mayas of Southern and Central British Honduras
(Chicago, 1930)
Maya History and Religion (Norman, 1970)

INTERNATIONAL STANDARD BOOK NUMBER: 0–8061–0520–8

LIBRARY OF CONGRESS CATALOG CARD NUMBER: 62–13347

My days among the Dead are past;
Around me I behold,
Where'er these casual eyes are cast,
The mighty minds of old:
My never-failing friends are they,
With whom I converse day by day.

. . . .

My hopes are with the Dead; anon
My place with them will be,
And I with them shall travel on
Through all futurity;

—ROBERT SOUTHEY

PREFACE

My dependence on the work of Hermann Beyer, William Gates, and Günter Zimmermann is very apparent and is gratefully acknowledged both here and in the body of the book. There is no call to list those who have brought to light hieroglyphic texts, for their name is legion, but I feel it incumbent on me to pay my thanks to four men who between them have found and recorded such a high proportion of those texts. Those four are Teobert Maler, Alfred Maudslay, Sylvanus Morley, and Alberto Ruz, and, typifying the international character of Maya glyphic research, they are of four nationalities.

A number of my colleagues have sent to me for inclusion in this catalog new texts, some of them unpublished, which have come to light in the past two or three years. For their generosity I wish to thank E. Wyllys Andrews, Henry Berlin, William Coe, José Luis Franco, Ian Graham, Pierre Ivanoff, César Lizardi, Alberto Ruz, Linton Satterthwaite, Edwin Shook, G. L. Vinson, and Gordon Willey. Ralph Roys has been a tower of strength in my many perplexities.

I have spoken in the introductory chapter of the patience and skill of Miss Avis Tulloch in preparing the splendid drawings of glyphs. Her cheerful collaboration has been invaluable. To Miss E. K. Wakeford, of the Saffron Walden Literary and Scientific Institution, I am more than grateful for the ceaseless vigilance with which she rode herd on colons and periods; for such mavericks as there may be—and I fear they are numerous—the blame is mine. Mr. and Mrs. Michael Swan, of Ashdon, compiled the tables of distributions of affixes. Finally, a word of gratitude to Mrs. Annie Wright, gifted with the uncanny knack of making elevenses at 9:15 whenever preparation of the catalog was particularly irksome.

J. Eric S. Thompson

Harvard
Ashdon, Saffron Walden
Essex, England

CONTENTS

PLATES

DRAWINGS OF GLYPHS

A CATALOG
OF MAYA HIEROGLYPHS

INTRODUCTION

A CATALOG OF MAYA HIEROGLYPHS is the second of four volumes on Maya hieroglyphic writing which, in my optimism, I once planned. The first of the tetralogy was *Maya Hieroglyphic Writing: An Introduction,* published by the Carnegie Institution of Washington in 1950 and republished, with a second preface, by University of Oklahoma Press in 1960. In my original plan the second volume was to have been a commentary on the Maya Dresden codex, but soon after the first volume appeared, I reluctantly concluded that the glyph catalog would have to precede the commentary.

The magnitude of the task had more than daunted me, and, in starting on the easier commentary, I had shirked my duty. Still, it is never too late to don sackcloth and apply the ashes of repentance, although I confess to having done penance far longer than I had anticipated when I laid aside the commentary.

"Those things having been done," as in the schoolboy's translation of an ablative absolute from Caesar's Gallic wars, I plan to follow this volume with the commentary on the Maya Dresden codex. Lastly, although now ten years nearer Charon's ferry, I still hope to write the fourth volume, mindful that four is the number the Mayas associated with a man's life work.

Two catalogs of Maya glyphs have already been published, those of Gates (1931) and Zimmermann (1956), but both are confined to glyphs in the three surviving Maya hieroglyphic codices, namely, the above-mentioned Dresden codex and the Madrid and Paris codices.

Gates' work, *An Outline Dictionary of Maya Glyphs with a Concordance and Analysis of Their Relationships,* assigned numbers to 296 main signs and to 112 "minor elements," but in some cases (for example, the month glyphs Ch'en, Yax, Zac, and Ceh) glyphs which differed only in their affixes were assigned separate numbers, and some "minor elements" are included also among the major signs. Moreover, minor elements did not retain their numbers when they were attached to main signs. The work was derived from the card catalog of codical glyphs prepared about A.D. 1900 by C. C. Willoughby, at the instance of Charles Bowditch, a wealthy Bostonian and pioneer of work in Maya hieroglyphs. Gates (1932b), in paying tribute to Willoughby's part, quotes him as saying, "It took me two years to do it, and you [Gates] have copied it in eight days."

Beyer (1933) deals very harshly with the dictionary. Much of his criticism is well justified and constructive, but political enmities played their part in giving the discussion a bitter taste. Gates, it is true, produced a dictionary which because of its unsystematic nature was not as useful as it might have been, but Beyer's criticism was of minutiae, not of the general plan, and, I, page-like, having trodden boldly in the footsteps of this good King Wenceslas, appreciate his difficulties and regard Beyer's blasts as too wintry.

Zimmermann's *Die Hieroglyphen der Maya-Handschriften* is a splendid contribution. It is well arranged and the system of assigning numbers to all elements of a compound glyph and indicating the positions of affixes by periods and colons is admirable. Indeed, the system I have followed is largely an imitation of the Zimmermann system. I am agreeably surprised at the lack of misprints and mix-ups in numbers.

In the system of numbering first used by Zimmermann (1953) numbers were assigned as follows: 1–99 for affixes; 100–199 for portraits of gods and parts of the body; 200–299 for animal heads; 300 onwards for main (geometric) signs. I had pointed out in 1952, when the scheme was first broached, that those short numerical sequences would not allow the system to be expanded to include the more variable glyphs on the monuments, and I urged much greater flexibility in numbering. Yet, only the numbers 1–99 were allotted to the affixes in the final scheme (Zimmermann, 1956), and portraits started with number 100.

With the publication of the 1953 paper, I realized that my numbers could not be squeezed into Zimmermann's categories. In the end I had 370 affixes, whereas Zimmermann had allowed only 100 places for that group, and my glyphs corresponding to his portrait category would have exceeded the 100 places he allotted to them. Reluctantly, I was forced to abandon his numeration. I give (pp. 399–403) a concordance of his numbers and mine.

In its final form, Zimmermann's catalog comprised 83 affixes and 200 main signs including animals and portraits, together with some variant forms, lettered *a* and *b*, to which I have assigned separate letters. I regret that it was not possible to make my catalog conform to this fine work of scholarship.

COMPILATION OF THE PRESENT CATALOG

The present catalog comprises 370 affixes (1–370); 356 main signs other than portraits but including animals (501–855); 88 portraits (1000–1087), a group which will certainly be expanded when the series is completely studied; and 48 in the dubious "purgatory" group (1300–1347). These total 862 signs.

The first step in preparing the catalog was to obtain photographs, published or unpublished, of as many inscriptions as possible, together with photostats of the very careful drawings by Miss Annie Hunter (in Maudslay, 1889–1902) of many of the texts at Quiriguá, Copán, Palenque, Yaxchilán, and other sites. Were there any doubt, the drawings of Miss Hunter were checked against photographs. Colleagues and other institutions engaged in Maya research were most kind and helpful in supplying photographs. Indeed, a surprising number of new texts were brought to light in the gestatory years. These photographs and photostats, together with Hermann Beyer's careful drawings of texts at Chichén Itzá and near-by sites, were cut up text by text, and all legible glyphs, other than those of known calendric values (day and month signs, period glyphs, glyphs of the lunar series, etc.), were mounted on cards, each main sign being assigned a separate card.

These cards, of gray cardboard, measure 23.5 cm. long by 18.5 cm. wide. The photographs and drawings were pasted down the left side of each card, often with a certain overlapping, so that each sheet held eighteen to twenty glyphs, all of which, as already noted, represented the same main sign. Where no photograph or photostat was available, the reference was written in abbreviated form with note on the affixes, if any. In the case of some of the commonest glyphs, such as Imix with 611 entries and Cauac with 472 entries, a dozen or more cards were needed.

Immediately to the right of each photograph or drawing is written the monument reference, as in the last column of the present catalog. Following that are noted in roughly descriptive terms the two to four glyphs which immediately precede the glyph in question on the monument. There follows a / to indicate the position of the glyph being catalogued, and after that there is a brief description of the two or three glyphs which immediately follow on the monument. Finally, the Maya date to which the glyph is referable forms the last entry on the extreme right of the card. The examples of each main sign were numbered after the cards were completed. A typical entry (on sheet 300) reads: 115. Yaxchilán L.9,B1. 1 Eb 20 Yaxkin; jade, lunar postfix / hooked nose; 3 B.I. katuns; jaguar. (9.14.4.11.12) 1 Eb 20 Yaxkin.

The purpose in listing the associated glyphs is, of course, to make it easy to identify clauses. I had hoped that the record of the accompanying date might uncover glyphs associated with special days or with time intervals, such as the 819-day count. In these objectives I was disappointed, but more careful scrutiny may yet yield results. I had intended to give the earliest and latest dates of the occurrence of each main sign and the site at which, according to present data, the glyph first appears.

Pressure to complete the catalog caused the abandonment of that arrangement, but the data can be obtained from the information given, although, admittedly, not without some trouble.

Much time was spent in comparing questionable drawings with photographs and vice versa. Unfortunately, many texts had to be discarded because of their weathered condition or because available photographs were unsatisfactory. This was particularly true of inscriptions of the northern Petén, where the limestone used for stelae erodes easily. An extreme instance of this occurred at El Palmar, Quintana Roo, where I was able to scratch lines with my thumbnail on the surfaces of stelae which had been in contact with the ground, and where one could quickly rub away a surface with a hard-bristled brush. Several sites in that northern part of the Central area produced not a single non-calendrical glyph. Poor photographs also reduced the number of glyphs available for study. Among those blameworthy I count myself, for I am confident that good photographs taken in artificial light of Stela 1, Cobá would add to our knowledge of glyph distribution. I photographed the monument with indifferent success thirty-four years ago.

Poor stone and poor photography distort the picture of glyphic distribution. For that reason it is gratifying that recent work at Tikal has helped to fill the Petén lacuna.

Glyphs in the three surviving hieroglyphic codices were not entered on the gray cards. Instead, I depended for those glyphs and their occurrences first on the Gates' dictionary, and later, after its publication in 1956, on the Zimmermann catalog; it seemed an unnecessary waste of time to do again what those two had already done. Nevertheless, I checked their assignments before using them, and very occasionally my reading of a glyph differed from that of one or the other of my predecessors. When more than eight occurrences of a compound appeared, I sometimes refer the reader to the Gates' entries. I much appreciate the help I obtained from the earlier cataloguers.

New texts which came to light after the conclusion of this first stage, and a few texts, largely those on pottery, which I had overlooked were not entered on the gray cards but were transcribed directly into the catalog. The gray cards will eventually find a home where they will be available for study.

The second stage was to convert the data assembled on the gray sheets into a catalog. This involved examining one by one all entries for a given glyph and translating it into the arithmetical formula, which, following Zimmermann's scheme, is used here as explained on page ooo. This proved to be a tedious task of inordinate length. In very many cases drawings had to be compared a second time with photographs, principally to make sure that affixes had been correctly delineated; where no illustration accompanied an entry, reference had to be made to the original source. Much time was spent poring over diminutive photographs of weathered glyphs; affixes were particularly troublesome, largely because of the small space they occupy, but also, to some extent, because some draughtsmen of glyphs assumed that the affixes were largely meaningless fripperies and therefore called for no particular care in transcribing them.

Identification of such damaged specimens from indifferent photographs can hardly be objective. Indeed, decision whether to accept, query, or reject an identification must on occasions have depended on passing mood or the flow of gastric juices. Users of the catalog should bear in mind the subjectivity of my approach, and be prepared to re-examine my very fallible identifications before drawing any conclusions. I make no doubt that were I to reclassify the more badly damaged glyphs, I would reach quite a few decipherments different from those now listed; certainly there would be many changes in the employment of query marks, and more would be added than deleted.

On the other hand, as the catalog progressed, I learned more readily to identify damaged glyphs; could I do the work again, assuredly some compounds then passed over would be recognized, but to set coulter and share to plow afresh more deeply would be unbearable. Only a complete remaking of the catalog would eliminate errata in compilation and transcription—and sometimes in the watches of the night I have feared their number is legion. They must be left to flourish like charlock amid the wheat.

Because the subjective element is dominant and errata cannot be eliminated, the student must regard this catalog as a guide rather than as an immutable compilation; most certainly he should consult the source to satisfy himself that he agrees with each reading before using it. It is because of this element of subjectivity in the approach that I have used the indefinite article before *Catalog* in the title of this publication.

Even before the work of arranging the glyphs on gray cards was concluded, Miss Avis Tulloch, then staff artist of the Department of Archaeology of the Carnegie Institution of Washington, started on the long task of drawing, first, affixes, and then main signs as I selected them. The moment is opportune to express my deep appreciation of Miss Tulloch's skill and, above all, her patience in heeding my arbitrary changes, reshufflings, and even reconstructions of glyphic elements deriving at times from the eye of faith.

For reasons already noted, I was unable to use the Zimmermann numbers. I started by grouping and numbering affixes according to their resemblances one to another. Unfortunately, as the work progressed, new affixes appeared, and some of those obviously belonged with groups already placed in the sequence. To renumber once the catalog had been started hardly commended itself because of the virtual certainty that such shifts would introduce errors. Consequently, I abandoned any serious attempt to group either affixes or main signs by design, probably an impossible task in any case.

SEPARATION OF AFFIXES FROM MAIN SIGNS

The distinction between main sign and affix is not always clear. Generally, in cases of doubt I have followed Beyer's dictum (1934) that "affixes of bilateral symmetry with vertical axis in the superfix . . . always adjoin their main signs with their bases." That definition eliminated a number of elements from the list of affixes, although they might seem to be used more often as affixes than as main signs. Glyph 679, the "forward" sign, is a case in point. It appears far more frequently on the monuments of the Central area as an affix than as a main sign in its own right. Yet it fails to qualify as an affix, for it does not lie with its base to the main sign when it is prefixed to the left. Moreover, in the texts of Chichén Itzá it usually functions as a main sign. Accordingly, after first treating this "forward" sign as an affix, I renumbered it and promoted it to main-sign status.

As a corollary to Beyer's rule, one can say that normally a main sign which is bilaterally symmetric does not change its axis when it is attached to the left of another main sign. Nevertheless, bilaterally asymetric main signs can change their axis on being attached to the left of another main sign if details of the glyph might be lost by lateral compression or elimination. Glyphs 565, 612, and 613 fall into this category. To be completely logical, one could claim that these signs are really affixes although almost invariably used as main signs, but such a classification would be pedantic. In only one of the 97 occurrences of Glyph 613 in the codices is it affixed to another main sign, but in that one case the glyph is rotated 90 degrees so that its base adjoins the main sign to which it is attached. Common sense is against classifying Glyph 613 as an affix on the strength of this single rotation to serve as an affix.

Consideration of shape is very helpful in distinguishing affixes from main signs. Generally a main sign is as high as it is wide; an affix, because of the restricted space it occupies, is usually about twice as wide as it is tall. This, in turn, has an interesting corollary: affixes which do not easily lend themselves to a square shape are usually doubled when they become main signs, particularly if there is no superfix to reduce the vertical distortion. Affixes 25, 75, and 110 are cases in point. This is a matter of aesthetics, not of any rule of writing; without doubling there is grotesque distortion. Conversely, when a main sign, normally as tall as it is wide, has to be compressed to do duty as an affix, the consequent distortion may be overcome by doubling the sign. Affixes 178, 200, 254, and 287 are examples of this process. Beyer (1926) pointed out many years ago that doubling a sign normally does not affect the meaning, and all the evidence of the glyph catalog supports his conclusion, yet some students of Maya glyphs give a repeated sound value to these doubled signs. In fact, doubling of an element serves as a warning to us that the doubled sign, if affixed to the main sign, is probably a main sign serving as an affix, and, if the doubled sign serves as a main glyph, it is a warning to us that the sign is doubled because it is an affix promoted to fill a place for which it is not normally well shaped. The baktun (528–528) glyph is a rare exception to the rule.

The assignment of separate numbers to the affixes just mentioned rather than label them as Glyphs 534, 528, 503, 687, and 503 variant is largely because I suspect that these signs vary their meanings on becoming affixes. The Cauac sign (528) doubled becomes the baktun glyph, but doubled to form an affix (200), its meaning or meanings are surely something quite different. Similarly, Glyph 534 has a set of meanings which I suspect are absent when the glyph becomes an affix (178). Furthermore, a few hand signs carry separate numbers as main signs and affixes (e.g., 671 and 219; 713 and 217). To have placed them all in the category of main signs when the catalog was half-completed would have called for much rearrangement and danger of errors creeping in with the rearrangement. This is the excuse for retaining two or three other duplications (e.g., Affix 183 and Main sign 546; Affix 181 and Main sign 683) which crept in unobserved.

At the present stage of glyphic research it is better to be overcareful in distinguishing elements. For that reason I have assigned different numbers to a few glyphic elements which may well be variants of another sign. Again, these are principally in the group of affixes. They include Affixes 51 and 53, 89 and 92, 125 and 128, 107 and 280, and 202 and 288. I have kept these separate because it is easier to merge them at some future date than to separate them were I to combine them now and later evidence indicate they are separate entities. Affixes 82 and 83, I am almost completely convinced, are variants of the same sign because the hatching and comb infix which alone distinguish them appear to be interchangeable in other contexts (see Glyphs 669*a* and *b* and 568*a* and *c*).

On the other hand, some resemblances probably arise from convergence. Affixes 40 and 302 almost certainly fall in that group. Affix 60, clearly a knot, and Affix 145, a hank of cotton cloth or thread, are sometimes hard to separate if the knot is thick and "floppy" and the hank is thin. Convergence therefore is another reason for assigning separate numbers to elements until one is certain that one is merely a variant of another.

Some affixes, like most main signs, can be broken down into two or more separate elements. For instance the katun affix (28) could equally well be written 25.528.25 or, when some elision has taken place, 25.528. However, as this affix is a separate entity with a known function, it is clearly advisable to treat it as a whole and assign it its own number. Once one started breaking down glyphs into their component elements, there would be no end to it. For instance, Glyph 528, the Cauac sign, just mentioned, would have to be given three numbers—one for the "bunch-of-grapes" infix and two for the two elements composing the lateral infix. Moreover, as there is variation in the infixes of the Cauac glyph, the component numbers would shift according to where and when each particular glyph was carved or painted. To give significance to every stroke or simple element in a sign would be as dangerous as to regard our "E" as signifying "F" and a minus sign. In assigning separate numbers to some glyphs with infixes (e.g., 502), but not to others (e.g., 561), I have been wholly and unrepentently subjective.

Quite rarely, two affixes are fused in arrangements which probably respond to the caprice of the draughtsman. Variant 2 of Affix 57 is an example. Here elements 57 and 125 have been fused. The fused affix appears beneath a Kayab glyph which normally has both those elements as separate postfixes; the unusual fusion would have been perfectly comprehensible to any Maya reader. Similarly, Variant 3 of Affix 128 is a most unusual fusion of Affixes 128 and 168 which occurs on Altar G1, Copán. The arrangement is 282.128[168]:561. The occurrence on the nearly contemporaneous Altar T, Copán, of the compound 282.128:168: 561 makes it certain that the above interpretation is correct. Again, the Maya reader would have no difficulty in reading this queer arrangement; as they are also comprehensible to the modern student, I have not assigned separate numbers to such fused signs.

One must try to steer a fair course between "splitting" and "lumping."

If there is a danger of multiplying signs by overcautious splitting, there is also a danger of lumping together distinct signs. In one or two cases (e.g., Glyphs 790 and 791) I may have done that, but in such cases I have tried to warn the reader. Among affixes the forms illustrated for numbers 77, 121, and 165 may not belong together, but all are rare, and the student can check the occurrences and reach his own conclusion.

I have dwelt on the above matters at some length partly to underline my warning of the subjectivity of the approach.

COMMENTS AND TABLES

Comments on glyphs and information on their incorporation in clauses is somewhat haphazard. I had originally purposed to have quite full comments and to refer to all clauses. The decision to restrict such comment was made with reluctance, but one must cut one's coat to the cloth that the loom of time allows one. In defense, I wish to make clear that such information can be extracted from the gray cards which eventually will be at the disposal of students. Interpretations of glyphs proposed by fellow students are not included in the comments unless they are beyond dispute; their introduction would distort the purpose of the catalog and introduce polemics.

Cross-references indicate listing of the glyph in question under a different heading. Some of the entries are duplicates, but in many cases the combination is listed only once. Accordingly, the cross-references amplify the range of a particular glyph and clarify its associations. An occurrence of a glyph which is recorded only in the tabulation of another glyph is not included in the grand total of glyphs. Were such cross-references to be included, the grand total would be increased by perhaps 200.

The tables which show the main signs with which each prefix and postfix occurs should be used with care. It sometimes happens that an affix is prefixed or even postfixed to a main sign which, in turn, is joined to the main sign being tabulated. It is not always obvious in such cases whether the affix belongs with the first or second main sign. I decided, therefore, to enter such affixes only under the second main sign, leaving it to the user of this catalog to exercise his own judgment whether to divorce affix and main sign or leave the marriage undisturbed.

AFFIXES AS MAIN SIGNS

Many affixes on occasions function as main signs. All such occurrences are tabulated in the same way as the regular main signs, the letters M.S. appearing after the number of the affix to denote this change in status. Naturally, affixes, on rising to become main signs, attract their own affixes—smaller fleas upon their backs to bite 'em. The count of affixes serving as main signs is added to the grand total of that category.

PORTRAIT GLYPHS

The portrait glyphs are not in the catalog although drawings of most of them (Nos. 1000–1084) are given. The reasons for this eclectic treatment are:

1. With a few possible exceptions the portrait glyphs do not function as do the regular main signs, for in most of their appearances they lack affixes or main signs affixed; such elements as are affixed appear to serve as titles or indicators of function. An example of this is the caan, "sky," sign (561) frequently prefixed to the portrait glyph of the long-nosed god, the Chacs of Yucatán (Glyph 1030) for reasons set forth under Glyph 561.

2. The inclusion in the catalog of all appearances of these portrait glyphs would have further delayed this long-overdue publication. Cataloguing of portrait glyphs is very time consuming, for mild weathering, which may not seriously affect the legibility of normal main signs, can play havoc with the identification of a portrait glyph.

3. The portrait glyphs will be discussed in a general survey of Maya religion which I intend to make.

GLYPHS ON POTTERY

Inclusion in the catalog of glyphs painted, carved, or stamped on pottery presented certain difficulties principally because of the doubt as to how many of such texts had any meaning. For instance, several common glyphs appear on pottery with certain affixes with which they are never paired on the monuments or in the codices. These compounds found only on pottery might correspond to changes in subject matter, but it is equally possible—and, indeed, more probable—that some of these new pairings of affix with main sign derive not from the need to express some new idea, but merely from the artist's wish to produce a well-balanced and aesthetically pleasing arrangement. Should that be so, listing of such associations of affix with main sign might be highly misleading. Yet, the compiler can hardly suppress a series of texts because he suspects they may be meaningless. One must include such texts, but with a warning to the student that many of them may convey an aesthetic rather than a legible message.

With thought to such considerations I have included in the catalog readily available texts on pottery, but I have not tried to search out rare or unpublished examples, and I have omitted glyphs which are repeated to form a decorative feature, as on many Copador vessels and nearly all Mayoid polychrome of the Ulloa Valley. I have also excluded glyphs on a tecali vase and a carved pottery vessel in the Bliss collection and on a piece of mother-of-pearl in a private collection (Covarrubias, 1957, pl. 53), all of which are of very questionable authenticity.

A striking feature of glyphic texts on pottery is the considerable copying from one vessel to another, as first pointed out by Longyear (1952, p. 64; fig. 24) in the case of the famous quetzal vase of Copán and a vase Gann excavated from a mound near the west bank of the Río Hondo.

Certain glyphs were much favored by the decorators of pottery and are repeated over and over again. The opening glyph of the quetzal vase, just noted, is a case in point. This compound 229.617, usually with 126 postfixed, appears on several pieces of pottery from Uaxactún, and on vessels from Pusilhá, Caracol, Holmul, near the Río Hondo, Q. R., on the quetzal vase, which almost surely was not made at Copán, and on a carved brown-ware vase found at San Agustin Acasaguastlán, but probably made at Copán. Here the distribution is heavily weighted in favor of the eastern Petén and contiguous territories, perhaps because that area contains most Classic sites of the Central area which have been excavated. In one or two cases inaccurate delineation of the compound favors the supposition that the artist was copying elements he did not understand, and that there was no obligation to reproduce them with care so that they would be legible to those who could read.

The compound 60 or 61.77:585, the quincunx sign with affixes was another favorite with painters. This appears on vessels from Uaxactún, Caracol, Holmul, Pusilhá, Peto, Nebaj, Río Hondo in the Motagua Valley, Copán, and the conch god vase in the Bliss collection. With different affixes the glyph appears on vessels or sherds from Benque Viejo, Uaxactún, unspecified location in the Petén, Huehuetenango (surely an import), Palenque (I.S. pot), and Chama, and on a vessel from the Fenton collection.

The serpent segment (565) is another favorite of the decorators of pottery, and is also found on objects of jade, obsidian, and shell.

The monkey head with hand before it (220.755) is a compound found only on pottery. In addition to the five examples listed, other heads painted on pottery almost certainly represent monkeys, although they are too stylized to be catalogued as such. This same compound is almost certainly recognizable among elements which Longyear (1952, fig. 19*d*, *k, l*) groups to form his Glyph Motif C of Copador polychrome. In this same Motif C category is a long-beaked bird with a sort of curl emerging from the base of the beak. This compound (319?.236 M.S.) appears on pottery from the Petén–British Honduras area and the Río Hondo tributary of the Motagua Valley. These two compounds may once have been painted on pottery to convey a meaning, but they certainly finish on Copador pottery as purely decorative motives.

The fish (738) is also a common glyph on pottery, ranging from Chilib, Yucatán, to Mexicanos, El Salvador, although the examples in those two localities were surely not of local manufacture.

It is surely significant that among the glyphs particularly favored by potters and apparently copied from one pot to another are those of a monkey, a fish and a bird, glyphs easily recognized by the illiterate.

Nevertheless, a glyph occasionally may refer to the scene painted below it on a vessel. For instance 210 M.S. 110 (conch shell) appears above a painting of God N wearing a conch shell, as noted by Lothrop *et al.* (1957:257) whereas the compound 63:210 M.S. is once (Dresden 41*b*) the glyph of God N. On the other hand, the conch-god vase from Caracol has a picture of God N with conch on back, but there is no conch glyph, and the same is true of other occurrences of this god on pottery. However, the design on the vessel from Caracol includes a fish with the head of the fish god (Glyph 1011), and among the glyphs above is 738, the fish glyph. Nevertheless, if a reference was intended, Glyph 1011 would have been better than 738.

In such quite rare cases of apparent agreement between glyph and design, I would be inclined to suppose that the artist chanced to know a glyph which had a connection with the scene, and inserted it in what was otherwise a decorative pattern, for the decorators of the best pottery were presumably the artists who painted murals, usually with glyphic texts, to the designs of the priests. Several appearances of the fish glyph above scenes which contain no fish and, conversely, the numerous appearances of God N, the conch god, without accompanying glyphs of that deity or of conch shells argue against these texts' being explanatory. However a greater knowledge of the meanings of the glyphs is needed to validate this conclusion.

The painted Initial Series jar from Uaxactún has errors which suggest that the artist was not copying a prepared drawing. Apart from the errors in calculation (three corrections are needed to produce a proper I.S. date), there are several errors in details of glyphs which show the artist's ignorance of his subject and which could hardly have appeared had this been a careful copy of a priest-astronomer's drawing. There are indications (e.g., the codical Chicchan head for 9 with the probable Glyph A) that the artist used a codex in preparing his design, but did not follow it slavishly.

In contrast, the unique vessel from Palenque with carved Initial Series carries a carefully prepared text with correct Initial Series and a correctly recorded entry of a base in the 819-day count. This was esoteric knowledge surely beyond the ken of a decorator of pottery, and one can only conclude that the artist was following a careful drawing supplied by his sacerdotal employer.

Aside from this most unusual piece, pottery which shows most evidence of carrying functional glyphs is carved brown-ware. Examples of this ware are widely scattered from Alta Verapaz to El Salvador, but on distributional and epigraphic evidence there is little reason to doubt that this most attractive pottery was made in or near Copán. The ware is most common at that site, and certain of the glyphs found on it are compounds otherwise confined to the texts on Copán monuments.

Carefully delineated and often somewhat unusual glyphs occur in low relief on rectangular tetrapod stands of pottery found in the vicinity of Cobán, but which, on the strength of the glyphs one would suppose to have been made on or near the banks of the Pasión or lower Chixoy. The glyphic plaques were mold-made.

In concluding this brief survey of glyphs on pottery, one might note as perhaps significant that glyphic texts which are or are most likely to be functional are carved or stamped and date from the closing stage of the Tepeu phase of the Classic period; painted glyphs on pottery which give more indications of being ornamental are associated largely with an earlier stage of the Tepeu phase.

GLYPHS ON JADE, OBSIDIAN, AND SHELL

In contrast to the glyphic texts painted on pottery, many of those incised in small objects of jade and other polished stone, obsidian, shell, and bone are functional and seem to cover the same subjects as the stelae and other monuments of the Classic period. For instance, the shell plaques from Piedras Negras (Morley, 1937–38, Vol. III, pp. 169–73) carry a series of dates, three of which appear on stelae at this same site, and several of the associated glyphs are compounds found only in the territory or "state" of Piedras Negras.

Two jades from the sacred cenote at Chichén Itzá and another, now in the Metropolitan Museum of Art, bear dates in the Maya calendar which give every indication of having been engraved in the Central area under the direction of specialists in the Maya calendar. A fourth, from

Tzibaanche and now in the British Museum (Beyer, 1932), has a minor error suggestive of careless copying of the original drawing. A plaque of a basalt-like stone from near the Río Michol, Chiapas, also carries a calendric inscription (Berlin, 1955).

Other texts on jewelry are not calendric but appear to have meaning. In several instances unusual glyphs allow us to locate the area in which the work of incising them was done. For instance, the large jade head now in the British Museum and said to have come from near Copán (Maudslay, 1889–1902, Vol. I, pl. 32 and pp. 44 and 47) has a text which without doubt was incised in the neighborhood of Palenque, and, indeed, the head itself is in Palenque style. Jade earplugs and a sting ray found at Palenque have glyphs of local types indicating that they were incised locally. There is a considerable body of material for recognizing centers of manufacture by local glyph styles.

DEDUCTIONS ON THE NATURE OF MAYA WRITING

As previously noted, there are in this catalog 492 main signs, including portraits and those in the dubious class, and 370 affixes. The slight duplication of main signs by affixes would reduce this grand total of 862 to perhaps 825 or even 800 signs. Future research, as indicated, may further reduce this total by confirming that certain signs are merely variants of others. On the other hand, the future will certainly bring to light more texts, and these will almost surely contain some signs not now in the catalog. All in all, the figure of 750 seems reasonably conservative for the total of Maya signs with all duplications and variations eliminated. Portraits of deities are included in the total on the grounds that at least some of them have other values. For examples, portraits of deities can represent the numbers 1 to 13. Again, in some inscriptions, particularly those of Yaxchilan, the portrait of the goddess of the moon (*u*) may stand for the possessive *u*. There are also cases in which portraits replace other main signs or even affixes.

In comparison with this total of 750 Maya signs, the total of Egyptian symbols excluding ligatures and numbers is 604, and the hieroglyphic symbols listed in Gardiner's *Egyptian Grammar* reach 734 (Diringer,

1948:196); in Ptolomaic times they ran into thousands. It has been said that no pictographic or ideographic script can manage with less than 500 to 600 signs, and numbers may easily run very much higher, as in the case of Chinese. On the other hand, the number required for a syllabary may drop to around 100 or less.

In considering the total of Maya glyphs as possible evidence of the nature of the writing, one must bear in mind the limited range of subjects covered by the surviving texts. To the best of our knowledge, several subjects which might have required special glyphs—the trading accounts of a Maya merchant or the tribute list of a Maya ruler are examples—are not represented in what has been somewhat grandiloquently termed the *corpus inscriptionum mayarum*. Moreover, the coverage of subjects in the surviving divinatory almanacs is not exhaustive; warfare, fishing, building, birth, and marriage are not represented. Yet each subject probably had its own glyphs which have not come down to us.

In any case, the total of approximately 750 surviving glyphic elements rules out a syllabic origin for Maya writing, and, in passing, I should say that, as far as I can see, there is no equivalent to the determinatives of Egyptian script. There remains the possibility that the Maya system was originally ideographic and pictographic, but in time changed to syllabic (the possibility that it became alphabetic can be safely ignored).

The best evidence for or against a transition might be found in an examination of the most frequent signs, up to a hundred, perhaps, as that is the approximate number of signs required for a syllabary. The test must be confined to main signs and affixes used as main signs for frequencies of affixes have not been calculated.

Thirty-three main signs appear more than one hundred times. Together, they account for 6,849 entries, a little over 55 per cent of the grand total of 12,425 for all main signs and affixes used as main signs, but excluding portrait glyphs. In descending order of frequency these are:

Glyph No.	Name	Frequency
501	Imix	611
528	Cauac	472

544	Kin	425
526	Caban	355
561	Sky	354
736	Death	266
756	Bat	264
533	Ahau	254
683	Moon	237
668	God B's Gl.	207
758	Xul	201
671	Manik hand	196
757	Jog with cross	185
669	Death fist	182
521	Uinal	178
585	Quincunx	169
747	Vulture	167
506	Kan	161
17	Yax	161
751	Jaguar	159
573	Hel	159
548	Tun	156
552	Crossed bands	154
565	Serpent segment	137
568	Sacrifice	136
586	Hatched dot	123
648	Kaz	123
510	Lamat-Venus	117
764	Chicchan snake	114
667	Inverted fist	114
713	Flat hand	109
567	Good tidings	102
507	Spotted Kan	102

The next seventeen most numerous main signs or affixes used as main signs are Nos. 613, 740, 513, 670, 563, 672, 515, 743, 612, 19, 518, 765, 614,

679, 504, 281, and 738, with a total of 1,435 entries ranging from 97 down to 75. Together, these fifty glyphs should represent many of the commonest syllables or opening consonant and verb if the Maya did have some such system. They account for a little over 66 per cent of the total entries. Presumably, the commonest affixes would function in a similar way were there some such system, but, in that case, one wonders why the Maya continued to differentiate between affix and main sign.

The occurrences of calendric glyphs functioning as such are not listed in the catalog except for a single collective entry. Thus *Imix* (501), the first day of the Maya sacred almanac, is easily the commonest glyph exclusive of its calendric appearances. Next commonest is *Cauac* (528) which is a day sign and also the *haab* or year sign. There follow *ƙin* (544), sign for sun and day, and then *Caban* (526), "earth," another day sign.

Thus, the four commonest glyphs in non-calendric usage come from the ranks of calendric signs, and no less than thirteen of the thirty-three commonest signs listed above are from the calendric series. Of the remainder, two (vulture and Jaguar) are of considerable ritualistic importance, five (death, sacrifice, good tidings, kaz [evil, misfortune], and caan [sky]) represent abstract ideas, and one (668) is used only as the name glyph of a deity.

If these listed signs also have phonic values, one must conclude that Maya terms which were already established as of great ritualistic importance happened also to be chosen for their phonic values. To judge by what happened in the development of writing in the Old World and what happened in the growth of rebus writing in ancient Mexico (Thompson, 1958), one might reasonably expect to learn that the Maya developed an acrophonic system (use of a sign to represent the sound with which it begins). Let us test this against three or four of the commonest Maya glyphs.

The commonest Maya glyph in non-calendric contexts, as we have noted, is *Imix*. This or *Imox* is its name in all Maya calendars except Pokomchi (not a lowland tongue) which uses *Mox*. Accordingly, if this day sign was used acrophonically, its values should be *im* or, less probably, *mi* or *mo. Im* is an almost sterile root in Yucatec and Chol, the two lowland Maya languages or dialects almost certainly closest to the Maya spoken by those who inscribed the hieroglyphic texts of the Classic and proto-Classic periods (Chontal probably belongs in this category, but there are no good vocabularies of Chontal, and, in any case, it is very close to Chol and to Yucatec). *Mi* is almost equally sterile, for it is the start of only two roots in Yucatec and of about eight in Palencano Chol, but most of these are of terms unlikely to appear in hieroglyphic texts. *Mo* are the opening letters of a number of words in Yucatec and Chol, but in an acrophonic system it would be more logical to use "Mol" to represent the sound *mo*. Moreover, the appearances of Imix in the codices do not seem to be relatable to actions or situations covered by words beginning with *mo*. It is clear, therefore, that if *Imix* has a phonic value, it was not obtained by acrophony.

The names of three of the five most numerous signs (*Cauac, Caban,* and *Caan*) commence with the same syllable, *ca*. There are a number of important Maya words which start with *ca*, but certainly not enough to require three of the five commonest signs to represent them. Here also, then, the evidence is against any acrophonic system.

Actually, the evidence is convincing that the *Caban* and *Caan* signs represent respectively earth and sky or—with *al* postfix—on high (*caanal*) in nearly all their appearances in the codices; in the case of *Cauac* the situation is somewhat more complicated, for it is reasonably certain that in addition to being a symbol for rain and thunderstorms, it is also a symbol for divine, as pointed out in the discussion of the glyph. Landa assigns to it the phonic value *cu*.

Frequency and sound values do not match, but in an acrophonic system it might be more sensible to use easily depicted and identified objects: e.g., axe, *baat,* for *ba;* footstep, journey, *be;* vase, *bok,* for *bo;* and so on. There is no evidence of any such system among the Mayas.

Evidence for a system of acrophony seems to be nonexistent, but there are a number of instances of glyphic elements, particularly affixes, serving as parts of speech. Among these are the signs for *il, al, te, tun,* and *oc,* but no real evidence has been presented for supposing that these signs could stand for less than the complete phonic value; *tun,* for example, never stands for *t* or *tu.*

The distribution of glyphs between stelae and codices has direct bearing on the problem of a possible syllabic system in Maya writing. Some glyphs are common on the monuments, but rare or unknown in the codices, and glyphs common in the codices are unknown on the monuments. For instance, the jaguar glyph (751), the vulture glyph (747), the bat glyph (756), and the Chicchan snake glyph (764) are common glyphs on the monuments, but occur only rarely or not at all in the codices. Conversely, the glyphs for good tidings (567) and for evil or misery (648) are frequent in the codices, but quite unknown on the monuments.

The explanation here is surely variation in subject matter. Seemingly, there are no divinatory almanacs on the monuments, and therefore the glyphs which give the results of divination are absent. On the other hand, the rituals commemorated on the monuments may well have called for the frequent representations of jaguars, bats, and vultures, since all three have associations with sacrificial rites in Maya tradition and ceremony. Note, for example, how frequently the bat glyph is associated with the sacrifice glyph (568). The bat and jaguar glyphs have definite associations and combinations with affixes which never occur in the codices. The pomp and circumstance of the sacrificial rituals commemorated on the stelae had no place in the simple divinatory almanacs for farming, hunting, and bee-keeping, and therefore the glyphs which reflect such observances are absent from the codices.

On the other hand, variation of subject matter should affect only slightly or not at all glyphs employed in a phonetic system, for if the bat glyph has, let us suppose, the sound value *ba,* it should be needed as frequently in one sort of text as another. Certainly, in English one might reasonably expect as many words incorporating *ba* in a treatise on divinity as in a book on climate or the history of boxing. Therefore, absence of glyphs frequent in texts of one kind from texts of another kind is a strong argument against any sort of truly phonetic writing. Here I would emphasize that rebus writing, known to have been used by the Mayas to some extent, is not a true phonetic writing, for it deals with whole words, not syllables or letters of the alphabet.

Examination of the typical Maya glyph compound comprising main sign and generally prefix and postfix—sometimes three or four elements all together—can inform us on the nature of Maya writing. Affixes, as is well established, can serve as main signs, and, more rarely, main signs can become affixes; but, with two or three exceptions, shifts from main sign to affix and vice versa are not common. This rarity of interchange argues against a syllabic writing, for should such elements have phonic values, they should be freely interchangeable, for the whole point of a syllabic writing is that one puts the parts together, as in playing anagrams, without any restriction on sequence except the need to make sense. Yet that is precisely what one cannot do with Maya compounds. The bat (for *ba*) glyph is always a main sign; it is nearly always the middle of the sandwich, as though to indicate few words began with *ba*. The same is true of nearly all the main signs. Moreover, so few main signs are joined together that one must assume, if there was a phonetic system, that the sounds represented by, let us suppose, two common glyphs such as Imix and Kin, never appeared together in glyphic texts.

The distribution of affixes throws further light on this problem. Those which appear as both prefixes and postfixes number 125, whereas no less than 197 are recorded only as prefixes, and there are 48 which occur only as postfixes. Even these figures do not correctly picture the restrictions on the use of affixes, for some of that group of 125 which can be prefixed or postfixed are far more frequent in one position than the other. For example, Nos. 1 and 12 are overwhelmingly used as prefixes; Nos. 23 and 181, on the contrary, almost always serve as postfixes. Here then that flexibility inherent in a system of syllabic writing is again absent, for it is hard to believe that large numbers of syllables can appear only at the beginning of words, never at their ends.

Moreover, in spoken Yucatec, suffixes are far commoner than prefixes, especially with verb stems; and, on the assumption that main signs correspond to stems, this usage should call for many more postfixes than prefixes in the written texts. Yet, as we have seen, the contrary is the case; there are many more prefixes than postfixes.

Lowland Maya is strongly monosyllabic. Page one of the *Chilam Balam of Chumayel* (Roys, 1933) has 142 words, of which 64 are monosyllabic, 51 disyllabic, 23 are trisyllabic, and four are tetrasyllabic. Actually, 20 of these words are increased by one syllable because they carry the plural suffix *ob*. On the other hand, few Maya hieroglyphs consist of a single sign; most have a prefix and postfix or even three or four affixes. The glyph compounds do not pair with the written word if one assumes a syllabic writing.

Affixes for which widely accepted translations exist help to explain this discrepancy. It is clear that words which are independent in the spoken language become affixes of the glyphs corresponding to the words with which they are associated. Thus, adjectives (e.g., the colors, the glyph for "great") become affixes of the words they qualify, and the same is true of prepositions (e.g., the locative *ti* and the possessive *u*), of adverbs (*ox* used in the sense of "highly"), and of numerical classifiers. The incorporation of such separate words in a glyph compound helps to account for the rather low proportion of simple glyphs without affixes. Speech particles (e.g., *al, il, te*) also are identifiable as affixes.

The positions of affixes of known meaning generally reflect spoken Maya on the assumption that the order of reading is prefix—main sign—postfix. This is the same sequence as in reading complete glyph blocks and is, I think, generally accepted. Some system must have been followed if there was a phonic system or utter chaos would have ensued, but order of reading is of far less importance if the writing is largely ideographic. Color affixes are prefixed to main signs just as color adjectives precede the words they qualify in spoken Maya; the locative affix *ti* is prefixed to the main sign or can be postfixed to the verb to which it belongs (e.g., *at* 5 Ahau or count forward *to*); *al* and *il* are usually postfixed to the main sign for they are generally suffixes in speech (e.g., *caanal, ahauil*); we find *te* as a prefix when it is used as a numerical classifier (e.g., *uac te Zotz'*, fourth day of month Zotz') or postfixed as in the glyph for the god Bolonyocte).

In passing, the use of affixes to represent speech particles calls for a word. At first thought a compound such as *caanal* written as the glyph (561) for *caan* with *al* (Affix 23) postfixed appears to be on the borders of syllabic writing; yet, so far as present knowledge goes, such signs were never used syllabically. There is, for instance, no evidence that the affix *te* could represent the opening letters of such words as *tem, ten, tep'*, or *tet* which have no connection with *te* except that of containing the same sound.

It is of interest to note the range of affixes found with the four most frequent signs already discussed: Imix (501), Cauac (528), Kin (544) and Caban (526). They occur respectively with 83 prefixes and 38 postfixes; 88 prefixes and 51 postfixes; 49 prefixes and 28 postfixes; and 49 prefixes and 33 postfixes. If the view, already advanced, is correct, that these four glyphs are most frequent primarily because of their importance in ritualistic life (calendar, cosmology, and rites) and not for phonetic reasons, it follows that the affixes associated with them are probably of the classes noted above and are not elements in some syllabic system. Indeed, most of the identifiable affixes occur with all four of these signs. For comparison, one might note the affixal associations of four glyphs which from their positions at the starts of sections in divinatory almanacs of the Dresden codex give every indication of being verbal forms, so-called glyphs of action (Thompson, 1950, pp. 264–68). These are Glyphs 552, 565, 667, and 669. They occur respectively with 40 prefixes and 23 postfixes; 38 prefixes and 17 postfixes; 8 prefixes and 7 postfixes; and 30 prefixes and 21 postfixes. Here, then, there is a considerable drop in affixes even when one takes into account the lower frequency of these signs. Yet, if these signs are phonetic, in contrast to the largely ideographic nature adduced for the Imix group, one might reasonably expect an increase of affixes with them. Prefixes again outnumber postfixes by nearly two to one.

The prefix of one glyph is sometimes postfixed to the preceding glyph in a clause (e.g., Affix 59 in Beyer, 1937, figs. 36 and 32–35, or Affix 25 in Beyer, 1937, figs. 32, 35, and 33, 34, 36–38. Also Affix 200 prefixed to Gl. 747 instead of postfixed to the preceding Gl. 756 on Quiriguá F, B9). Such shifts are completely out of order if, as has been claimed for two of these affixes, the elements are syllabic.

Very rarely a prefix and postfix are paired. Affix 168 (Ben-Ich sign) is always a prefix, never a postfix and never a main sign. Quite frequently, but by no means always, where Affix 168 is prefixed to a sign, Affix 130 is postfixed. As this pair occurs with some frequency with glyphs of known meaning and function (e.g., the day sign Ahau when used to mark the end of a katun), a search for particles of speech which are often paired as prefix and suffix of a noun (Ahau is a noun) might identify this pair. As a demonstration of research technique, it is worth bearing in mind that the demonstrative *le* is one such possibility, for it is acompanied by a suffix (e.g., *pek,* "dog," *le peka,* "this dog," *le peko,* "that dog," and *le peke,* "that distant dog"). Conceivably, Affix 130 represents the particle *e,* a very common suffix in Yucatec speech, although in Palencano Chol the demonstrative pronoun *hini* is not coupled with a suffix. This, however, is an aside, for the present purpose is not to offer tentative decipherments, but to review how the catalog can be used as an aid to understanding the nature of Maya writing.

In conclusion, the observation of an earlier writer bears repeating. It is rather generally agreed that the inventors and users of the Maya script spoke a lowland Maya not very different from present-day Yucatec, Chol, or Chontal. With the speech of the users known and even accompanying pictures in the codices to indicate subject matter, it is difficult to understand why a succession of students of half a dozen nationalities has failed, despite nearly a century of effort, to solve what should be a relatively simple problem if the claim that the writing is a true phonetic system is correct.

For the present I see no compelling reason to discard the belief that Maya glyphs are part ideographic, but part rebus writing; that they are influenced by ritualistic and mythological contexts, but in some respects, as in elements for speech affixes, come closer to orthodox standards of true writing. In short, we are confounded by an unsystematic hodge-podge of slow growth (Thompson, 1950; 1959). Hodgepodges, of course, lack either keys or locks to fit them.

For those who share my pleasure in anniversaries, this catalog was completed in this year of Grace 1960, just one baktun (528.528 in the catalog), the equivalent of 364 of our years, after Bishop Diego de Landa wrote his account of the Maya calendar and hieroglyphs.[1]

[1] The time has come, with the start of a second baktun, to end the abuse of Bishop Landa for his destruction of Maya hieroglyphic books. His critics, of whom I was one, fail to take into account the events which led to that sad happening. Those were the investigations at Mani and elsewhere into recrudescences of paganism which revealed many cases of the sacrifice of children, some of them baptized Christians, in conditions of great savagery. Landa knew that to stamp out such barbarities it was essential to destroy the paraphernalia of the paganism that inspired it. We, four centuries removed from those events, in sorrow at the loss of the books, may overlook the slaughter of innocents which provoked the action. The accounts of those sacrifices do not make pleasant reading; Landa was on the spot when the confessions were made.

HOW TO USE THIS CATALOG

IN THIS CATALOG OF MAYA GLYPHS the numbers 1 to 500 are reserved for affixes; 501 to 999 for main signs; 1000 to 1299 for portraits of gods and perhaps individuals; and above 1300 for a small group of glyphs of uncertain delineation or dubious origin.

Main signs and such affixes as function also as main signs are arranged in sequence. At the head of each sign appear a drawing of the glyph, its number, and also, in many cases, a name by which it can be easily recognized. Some of these names—those of the days, for instance—are well established, but others are arbitrary and given merely to facilitate recognition. Some of the names in this second category are derived from Beyer (Glyph 565 "Serpent segment" is among these); other names I have coined. For example, Glyph 684 is called "Toothache," not because it has any connection with that affliction, but because the glyph is tied up in a piece of cloth knotted at the top like the old-fashioned comic pictures of children with toothache. In other cases the name seems to apply to the object portrayed, but with no claim that it necessarily does represent that object. Glyph 685 is termed "Pyramid," and it is quite likely that it does in effect represent a pyramid with stairway; it is less probable that Glyphs 537, 538, and 542 represent the god Xipe.

The line in parentheses below this gives, on the left, the number of examples of the glyph which have been identified (including those queried). However, in the case of glyphs with calendrical associations—Glyph 526, the day sign Caban, for instance—the numerous occasions on which a glyph functions within the established framework of the calendar are not entered or counted. Following on this same line is an entry, "Sheet numbers so-and-so." The numbers refer to the gray cardboard sheets on which the photographs and drawings of the glyphs are mounted, together with information on the two or three glyphs before, and the same number after, each occurrence, and also the date with which it is associated and where it is to be found. These sheets from which the catalog was compiled eventually will be deposited where they are readily accessible to students. If the glyph appears in the codices, the numbers assigned to it by Gates (1931) and Zimmermann (1956) in their catalog of codical glyphs are noted.

There follow the entries of all known appearances of the glyph. The left column gives the number assigned each entry on the gray cardboard sheets. These serve as a ready reference, but their value is chiefly for future users of the work cards. In the middle of the line appears an asterisk which refers to the glyph in question; its use directs the eye more easily to the main sign with its clustering affixes. Numbers, if present, between the reference column on the extreme left and the asterisk are the affixes prefixed or (if above 500) the main signs prefixed, or joined to left or above, to the main sign under discussion. If the prefix is to the left, its number is followed by a period; if it is above, its number is followed by a colon. Similarly, the numbers, if any, between the asterisk and the last column giving the name of the site are those of affixes which are postfixed or to main signs which are postfixed or joined, to right or below, to the main sign under discussion. Here a period before the number indicates that it is to the right of the main sign in question; a colon before a number similarly indicates that its position is below the main sign. If there are two or more affixes in the same relationship to the main sign, the number farthest from the affix is the outer affix. For instance, 1.16.60:*.93:24:125 signifies that Affixes 1 and 16 are to the left of the main sign with Affix 1 on the extreme left and Affix 60 is above. Affix 93 is to the right and Affix 24 is below with Affix 125 underneath it.

Brackets show that the number they enclose is infixed, and, occasionally, the asterisk itself may be in brackets to indicate that the main sign under discussion is itself infixed. Infixing is referable to the number immediately to the left.

Essentially, the system is that of Zimmermann (1956), and it is a pleasure to acknowledge the derivation. I was in the process of developing a somewhat similar system, but when Zimmermann's method was first announced, in 1952, I abandoned my efforts along those lines in favor of his superior method.

Brackets indicate that the glyphic element corresponding to the number or to the asterisk thus enclosed is infixed in the preceding glyphic element. Occasionally, the main sign is doubled or trebled, and in such cases the periods or colons separating the asterisks allow the reader to reconstruct the arrangement. Thus, *:*.* would indicate the main sign tripled in the form of a pyramid.

Arrangement of occurrences of a glyph is: firstly, examples without any affixes; secondly, those with prefixes, for the most part in ascending order with illegible examples last; thirdly, those with numerical coefficients only expressed as prefixes; fourthly, those with postfixes only, again, arranged in ascending order. Numbers are given in Roman letters.

When I first started to compile the catalog, I arranged the sequence according to the numerical position of the first affix, but, later, realizing that the second affix was probably more important than the first in many cases, I changed to a rather eclectic arrangement according to which affix I thought most important. For instance, Affix 1, the *u* bracket, in most cases is a grammatical particle to express the possessive, and has no effect on the meaning of the main sign. Accordingly, I shifted to an arrangement under which an entry such as 1.86:* would be listed not with number 1 but in the position assigned to number 86. On the other hand, it was not advisable to rearrange those main signs already catalogued because of the danger of errors in numbers or punctuation which each rearrangement entails. Accordingly, the arrangement is not standardized. Were I starting afresh, I would distinguish between outer and inner affix. The former separates one side or one end of the inner affix from the perimeter of the glyph block. The inner affix is often more closely related to the main sign than is the outer affix. Future research may show this relationship to be invariable.

The right-hand column gives in contracted form, as explained below, the location of each glyph on monument or in codex. Several examples of the same combination of main sign and affixes are listed together only if they are from the same site. In a few instances of eight or more examples of the same combination in a codex, Gates' listing (1931) is given in lieu of the regular pagination.

In transcription of texts the catalog system can be used, substituting only the number of the main sign for the asterisk of the catalog. The use of bold face to mark the main sign is not recommended, for it is unsightly and distracting to the eye. It is also unnecessary, for the addition of "af" to a main-sign number used as affix or of "ms" to the number of an affix used as a main sign clarifies dubious cases. For instance, an imaginary compound transcribed as 59.679af:281ms:23 leaves no doubt of the arrangement. In case of doubt as to which element is the main sign, omission of "af" or "M.S." conveys the writer's uncertainty.

Fellow epigraphers, of your charity do not improve this system; confusion will outweigh gain and tinkered pans soon leak.

CONTRACTIONS AND
ELIMINATIONS USED

Acasaguastlán	San Agustin Acasaguastlán
af	Attached to a number indicates use as an affix
Aguas Cal.	Aguas Calientes
Aguatec.	Aguateca
Alt.	Altar
Alt. Sac.	Altar de Sacrificios
Amel.	La Amelia
B. Viejo	Benque Viejo
Balak.	Balakbal
Balustr.	Balustrade
Beyer	H. Beyer, 1937, text figures
Bonam.	Bonampak
Br.	British
Bur.	Burial
Calak.	Calakmul
Capt.	Captives
Carac.	Caracol
Cart.	Cartouche
Cent.	Central
Chinkul.	Chinkultic
Col.	Column
Coll.	Collection

Comal.	Comalcalco
Cop.	Copán
C.R.	Calendar Round
Crt.	Court
Cross	Tablet of the Cross
Cyl.	Cylindrical
D.	Dresden Codex
D.N.	Distance Number, alias Secondary Series
Dzib.	Dzibilchaltún
E.	East
Fig.	Figure
Fol.	Tablet of the Foliated Cross
Found.	Foundations
Frag.	Fragment
Gl., Gls.	Glyph or glyphs
Guat.	Guatemala
Gxiie etc.	Gordon, 1902, plate XII, XIII
H.S.	Hieroglyphic Stairway
Honrad.	La Honradez
Horiz.	Horizontal
Inscr.	Tablets of the Inscriptions
I.S.	Initial Series
Intro.	Introductory
inv.	Inverted
L.	Lintel
Lint.	Lintel. Form used when L. might cause confusion
Lt.	Left
M.	Codex Madrid at start of reference
M.	Middle following name of site
M. Cow	Mountain Cow
Md.	Mound
Mid.	Middle
Miscell.	Miscellaneous
Moral.	Morales
M.S.	Main sign
MSS	Miscellaneous sculptured stone
Mur.	Mural
Mus.	Museum
Nar.	Naranjo
Neg.	Negative. The following number is the old filing

	number, Department of Archaeology, Carnegie Institution of Washington
96 Gl.	Tablet of the 96 Glyphs
N.	North
Oxkin.	Oxkintok
Pab.	El Pabellon
P	Personified. After number or asterisk
P.	Codex Paris
Pal.	Palenque, at start of reference
Pal.	Palace, following name of site
Pan.	Panel
P.E.	Period Ending
Ped.	Pedestal
Pil.	Pilaster
Pl.	Plate
P.N.	Piedras Negras
Pusil.	Pusilhá
Q. Roo	Quintana Roo
Quir.	Quiriguá
R.	Río
Rev.	Review
Rm.	Room
Rt.	Right
Ruz 1 and 2	Tablets also called "del palacio" and "Los Esclavos." See Ruz 1952 and 1952a
S.	South
S.	San or Santa, before Spanish Christian name
Salv.	El Salvador
Sanct.	Sanctuary
Sarcoph.	Sarcophagus
Scribe	Tablets of the Scribe from basement of the Tower. (Palacios 1937). Also from Temple 21.
Seib.	Seibal
Serp.	Serpent
Sq.	Square
St.	Stela
Str.	Structure
Sub.	Subterranean
Sun	Tablet of the Sun
Sup.	Support

T.	Temple
Tab.	Tablet
Tamar.	Tamarandito
Thr.	Throne
Tik.	Tikal
Tort.	Tortuguero
Tzend.	Tzendales
Uaxac.	Uaxactún
Up.	Upper
v	attached to number or asterisk indicates variant
Var.	Variant
Vert.	Vertical
W.	West
Xcalum.	Xcalumkin
Xlabpak	Santa Rosa Xlabpak
Yax.	Yaxchilán

The kind of monument—stela, altar, or lintel—is not stated where, as at Copán, all monuments are numbered or lettered in a single sequence. Such monuments are listed as Cop.B, Cop.S, not Cop.St.B, Cop.Alt.S. In sites, such as Piedras Negras, where stelae, altars, lintels, thrones, and miscellaneous sculptures each has its own series, stelae are designated by number only; other cases of monuments have their corresponding contractions before the number. Thus P.N.3 refers to Stela 3 at that site, P.N.Alt.3 to the altar with that number, and P.N.,L.3 to the monument invariably referred to as Lintel 3, although it is now commonly agreed that at Piedras Negras these were probably wall tablets rather than lintels.

At Quiriguá no designation of type of monument is given except for the huge zoomorphs found in front of the original zoomorphs O and P. These are called Alt.O and Alt.P.

Nomenclature of hieroglyphic texts at Palenque is in indescribable confusion. It is a pity a numerical sequence for all texts has not been adopted.

Lettering of columns on monuments usually follows Morley, 1920 and 1937–38.

AFFIXES

GLYPH 7 M.S.
(1 Example)

1. 74: * Cop. vase Longyear 16n

GLYPH 8 M.S.
(1 Example; Sheet 360)

1. 230. *:247? Beyer 534

GLYPH 17 (Yax) M.S.
(161 Examples; Gates' Glyph 70; Zimmermann's Glyphs 249 1344)

	a	b	
134.	*af.	*	M. 65b
161.	45:	*	Dos Pozos H.S.2, B3
120.	59.	*:87	"At the Yaxche" D. 67b
121.	59.	*:87	"At the Yaxche" P. 16b
48–82.	74:	*	Variant for South in M. 35 times
154.	115?.74:	*	M. 61c
17–47.	134.74:	*.134	South in D. 20 times; in M. 11 times
83.	134.	*.134	M. 58b
112.	172.74:	*	D. 57a
113.	181?.74:	*	M. 87a
117^1.	85:	*.165	D. 60b
84–111.	130:	*.181	M. 65a–72b (32 times)
114.	VI.130:	*	M. 67b
115.	VII.130:	*	M. 67a
116.	XIII.130:	*	M. 66b
1–5.	144:	*.281	D. 18c; 19c; 27b; 46e; 50f
6.	144:	*:281	P. 7c
7–11^2.	144:	*.544	M. 91a (twice); 99b (thrice)
12^2.	VII.144:	*.544	M. 92a
13–15^2.		*:544	M. 66b; 105c; 109a? all in pictures
16^2.		*:544.181	M. 100b
135, 136.	166.	*	M. 69b; 71b
145^3.	VI.	*:219	D. 48b
146, 147.	VI.168:	*:219	D. 34c; 48c
148.	VI.168:	*:219	M. 42c
149.	VI or VII.168:	*:219	P. 10b
150, 151.	VI:168:	*:219.130	P. 4d; 9b
152.		*:219:178	P. 8d
137.	137.192.	*	D. 56b

118, 119.	207.	*:24	M. 81c (twice)
160.	218:	*	Tik. 31, C20
157.	224.98.	*vert.	D. 53b
139–41.	236:	*	P. 8c (twice); 9d
124–29[3].	1.327:	*	M. 20a; b; c (each twice)
130[3].	1?:327:	*	D. 61b
133[3].	25.327:	*	D. 31a
131, 132[3].	513af.327:	*	D. 70c; 73a
153.	544:23.	*.136	D. 38c
138.	15.683:	*	D. 49c
154.	IX.	*	M. 95d
122.		*:87	Yaxche tree P. 16b
123.		*:87	Yaxche tree M. 95d
158, 159.		*:88	Tik. 3., H16; H18
156.		*:98	D. 56b
142–44.		*:614af	M. 58c; 59c (twice)

[1] Apparently a completion compound to be read with the adjacent katun glyph; it appears to correspond to the 218–575 compound of the stelae.

[2] In these compounds found only in Codex Madrid it is highly probable that careless workmanship led to the substitution of the kin sign (544) for the Kan cross (281) which it resembles.

[3] In these 327–17 M.S. compounds, the top of Glyph 17 is cleft, the snake-like affix rising from the cleft.

The 17 M.S.–219 compounds are also entered under Glyph 671 for it is impossible to be sure which is the affix and which the main sign. One might also treat the compound as a separate glyph, particularly since it appears to be the name glyph of a deity.

GLYPH 19 M.S.
(83 Examples; Gates' Glyph 345; Zimmermann's Glyph 1310)

82, 83.		*[95]	Holmul bowl lid, pl. 24
1.	1.	*	D. 48d
2, 3.	1.	*	M. 87b; 107c
4–10.	1.	*:25	D. 24a; 46e; 48e; 49e; 50d; e; f.
11–18.	1.	*:25	M. 20b; 38c; 41a; 81c; 87b; 106c; 108c; 109a
19[1].	1.	*.25	M. 81c

[41]

20–24.	1.	*:59	D. 17b (twice); 18b (thrice)
25.	1.	*:130	D. 17c
26.	1.	*:?	M. 87b
27.	10.	*.59	D. 16c
28.	23:	*	D. 39c
29, 30.	25.	*	M. 22c; 100c
31–59.	25.	*:25	M. 91c; d; 93a; b; d; 94a; b; c; d (twice); 95c; d; 97c (thrice); 98d (twice); 99b (twice); c (twice); d; 100b; c; 101a; b; 103c; 104a; 106c
60.	25.	*.25	M. 108a
61–65.	59:	*	M. 17a; 94c (twice); 95c (twice)
66.	1.59:	*	M. 17a
67–70.	1.91:	*	D. 4c (thrice); 5c
71.	181.	*:25	M. 83b
72.	190.	*:25	M. 73b
81.	202inv:95:	*	Holmul bowl lid, pl. 24
73.		*:25	M. 17a
74–76.		*:59	D. 16c; 17b; c
77.		*:59	M. 94c
78.		*.62	D. 18c
79.		*.116	M. 64b
80.		*:130:116	D. 46 (Muan)

[1] Glyph 19 is in vertical position.

To this affix when used as a main sign in the codices I have assigned the meaning *koch*, "divinely sent punishment or disease" (Thompson, 1958).

GLYPH 21 M.S.
(8 Examples; Gates' Glyph 346; Zimmermann's Glyph 1310a)

1.	1.	*:25	D. 58a
2.	17.	*	D. 39a
8.	32:	*:?	Tamar. H.S. 2, E15

5.	59.	*	D. 37b
3.	130.	*.116:62	D. 62
6.	207.	*:47	M. 85c
4.		*:60	R. Amarillo. Alt. 1, J1
7.		*.61	Pusil. tall cyl. jar

Nos. 5 and 6 are accepted by Zimmermann and Gates as my Glyph 163. Number 6 substitutes for the usual glyph for south. Both have the spiral as an important element.

GLYPH 23 (al) M.S.
(18 Examples; Gates' Glyph 324; Zimmermann's Glyph 79)

18.	1:	*	Tort. 6, A10
10.	15.125:	*:25:23	Beyer 138
11.	15.125:	*.25:?:?	Beyer 139
1–4.	66:	*	D. 8b; 15b; 27a; 39b
5, 6.	66:	*	P. 3b; P. 10b?
14–17.	66:	*	M. 22b; 50c; 59c; 65a
7.	74:	*	M. 46a
13.	299:?:	*	M. Cow 2, A3
12.	VI:	*?:?	Quir. P, P3
8, 9.		*:130	Pal. House A, Balustr. A3, B3

The details of Affix 66 vary somewhat from one codex to another. Those in Codex Madrid may be Affix 136 doubled. No. 18 might belong with the 579 glyph to their left, but this would be a most unusual arrangement.

GLYPH 24 (il) M.S.
(2 Examples; Gates' Glyph 600; Zimmermann's Glyph 80)

1.	35.12:	*:23	Beyer 185
2.	126:23:	*:*	Beyer 97

GLYPH 25 (comb) M.S.
(22 Examples; Sheet 360; Gates' Glyph 322; Zimmermann's Glyph 81)

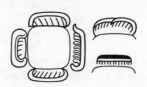

18[1].		*:*	D. 7c
4, 5.	1.	*:*:130	D. 10b (twice)
7.	1.	*:*:*.?	M. 52c
6.	1?.	*:*	M. 95a
1.	12:	*:23	Beyer 537
8[2].	47.	*	M. 2a
2, 3.	60.	*:23	Beyer 131; 132
9[2].	190.	*	M. 2a
10[2]–12[2].	190.	*.181	D. 44b; 45b (twice)
13, 14.	190.	*.181	D. 36a; 45b
15–17.	207.	*:130	D. 12a; 13a (twice)
19.	VII.	*:*:130	M. 95a
20.		*:*.130	D. 25a
21.		*:*.130	M. 70a
22.		*:*:130	M. 95a

[1] Surrounded with oval of dots.
[2] In vertical position. All others are horizontal.

GLYPH 35 M.S.
(1 Example)

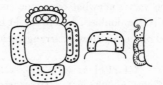

1.	53.	*	Beyer 535

GLYPH 50 M.S.
(1 Example)

1.	204.44:	*:24	Cop. Md. 2 reused stone

GLYPH 55 M.S.
(11 Examples)

1–5.	59.	*	Beyer 648–650; 677; 678
6, 7.	59:	*	Beyer 687; 690
8, 9.	59.	*	Beyer 688; 689. Postfix 178 to right
10, 11.	59.	*	Uxmal Ball Crt. E. ring; W. ring

Glyph 55 as main sign falls into the prefatory class. It broadens out to the normal shape of a main sign. As noted, postfix 178 which is a permanent part of the glyph as a suffix is placed to the right in examples 8 and 9.

GLYPH 58 M.S.
(17 Examples; Sheets 365, 366; Gates' Glyph 67; Zimmermann's Glyph 20)

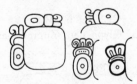

14[1], 15.		*	M. 43b; 47a
10.	1:	*?:25:130:89	P.N. 12, D2
4.	13.	*:683i	Beyer 488
1.	16:	*:102	Cop. A, A12
2.	16:	*:130	Yax. L. 15, G2
3.	16?:	*:23	Quir. P, P6
6, 7.	125:	*?	Beyer 171, 172

8.	125.	*?	Beyer 173
5.	131:	*	Tonina 31, Gl. 13
12.	204.44:	*or 59:24	Cop. Md. 2 reused stone
11.	VI:	*:?:136?	Quir. P, P3
13.	?:	*?:59	P.N. Alt. Support B3
9.		*:126	Beyer 487
16.		*.149	D. 36c
17[1].		*:196	M. 43a

[1] In vertical position.

Numbers 14 and 17 appear to have attached to them the number 7, but I believe this is merely due to lack of space and poor layout.

GLYPH 59 (ti) M.S.
(7 Examples; Sheets 365, 366; Gates' Glyph 612; Zimmermann's Glyph 72)

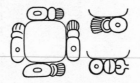

3.	I:	*:89	Pusil. D, E4
7.	II:	*:126	Pusil. D, C10
2.	230.	*:47	Beyer 486
1.	230.	*:126	Beyer 485
5.	VI:	*:*	Quir. P, P3
6.	VI:	*:23?:134	Quir. P, P3
4.		*.181	Beyer 489

GLYPH 60 M.S.
(3 Examples; Gates' Glyph 689; Zimmermann's Glyph 58)

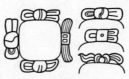

1.	128:	*:23	Normal form of Glyph F of lunar series
2.	168:	*:23?	Carac. 6, D13
3.	168:	*:*:130?	Quir. P, Cart. 3

GLYPH 62 M.S.
(2 Examples; Gates' Glyph 324.4; Zimmermann's Glyph 73)

1.	23:	*:23	M. 52b
2.		*:23	M. 90b

GLYPH 74 (Down Balls) M.S.
(6 Examples; Gates' Glyph 325; Zimmermann's Glyph 75)

1.	1.	*:*	D. 27a
6.	16:	*:129?	Tik. L. 2, H14
2.	25.	*:*	D. 28a
3.	?.	?:*	D. 25a
4.	?.	*	M. 92a
5.		*:23	M. 46a

GLYPH 77 (Bird Wing) M.S.
(1 Example)

1.	*:*:145?	Pusil. D, E8

GLYPH 78 M.S.
(1 Example)

1.	1.85.	*	D. 73c

Affix 85 might equally well be the main sign and 78 a postfix.

GLYPH 80 M.S.
(1 Example; Gates' Glyph 403; Zimmermann under Glyph 86)

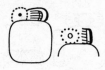

1.	59.	*:87	D.36c

The glyph clearly means "at the wooden enclosure" with Glyph 80 corresponding to enclosure. The Maya word which corresponds most closely to this is *dz'ul*. *Dz'ulbal* is an arbor; *dz'ulche* is a wooden enclosure. *Cololche* and *macanche* are other terms for a wooden enclosure.

GLYPH 82 M.S.
(9 Examples)

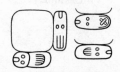

1.	1:	*:126?	M. Cow Alt. 2, C2
7.	122.59:	*:117	Quir. J, H6
5, 6.	122.175:	*:117	Quir. J, E7; C12
2.	12.131:	*	Tonina Alt. 52, Gl. 10
8.	200:	*:200	Tik. L. 2, A12
9.	588.588:	*.130?	Pal. Ruz 1, O7
3.	679.166Var.?:	*	Nar. 29, G16
4.	XII:1:128	*?	Calak. 89, B8

GLYPH 84 M.S.
(3 Examples; Gates' Glyph 701; Zimmermann's Glyph 77 [in part])

1.	166.	*:98	D. 72b
2.	166.	*:98:25	M. 35c
3.	172	*:*:98	P. 5b

Number 2 is included here for comparative reasons. On size and arrangement it has greater claims to be the main sign.

GLYPH 92 M.S.
(3 Examples; Sheet 360)

1, 2.	53.	*:*	Beyer 531; 532
3.	?.35:	*	Beyer 533

The affix here used differs somewhat from the standard 92 form. Its recognition as a variant of 92 was made by Beyer (1937:113) and is not open to serious question.

GLYPH 95 (Black) M.S.
(10 Examples; Gates' Glyph 68; Zimmermann's Glyph 22)

1-5[1].		*	M. 43a; b (twice); c
			(twice)
6.	1.	*:140	D. 53b
7.	15.	*?:23	D. 53b
8.		*.87	D. 31c. Ekche tree.

[49]

9.		*:96	Variant for month Uo.
			D. 48c; 62; 63
10.		*.265	M. 37b

[1] The glyph in horizontal position and the black edging is not shown. Numbers appear above these, but probably have no connection with them.

GLYPH 99 M.S.
(1 Example; Gates' Glyph 403; Zimmermann's Glyph 86)

1.	59.	*	M. 109c

GLYPH 103 M.S.
(16 Examples; Sheet 360; Gates' Glyph 323; Zimmermann's Glyph 61)

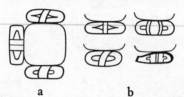

a   b

13.		*	Copador pottery. Longyear 16a
7.	1.79:	*:60?:?	Cop. U, S2
1.	24:	*:12.	Beyer 536
14.	74:	*	Salvador vase. Longyear 160
12.	99:	*	Pal. Site X
2–5.	145:	*:136	Beyer 526–29
6.	145.	*:136	Beyer 530
10.	511.196:	*	M. 82a
8, 9.		*:276	M. 100d (twice)
11.		*:?	M. 82a
15.	125:	*:125	Papa, Alta Verapaz. Vase
16.	125:	*:129	Papa, Alta Verapaz. Vase

GLYPH 109 (Red) M.S.
(11 Examples; Gates' Glyph 66; Zimmermann's Glyph 20)

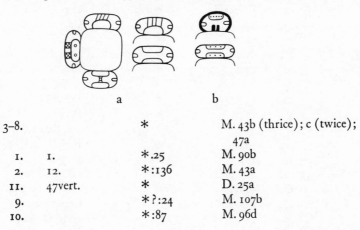

		a	b
3–8.		*	M. 43b (thrice); c (twice); 47a
1.	1.	*.25	M. 90b
2.	12.	*:136	M. 43a
11.	47vert.	*	D. 25a
9.		*?:24	M. 107b
10.		*:87	M. 96d

Numbers appear to be attached to Nos. 3–7, but I think that is merely a matter of crowding and bad arrangement.

GLYPH 110 (Bone) M.S.
(40 Examples; Sheets 289, 290; Gates' Glyph 321; Zimmermann's Glyph 32)

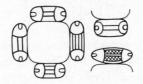

23.		*	M. 28d
24.		*:*	P. 9b
8.		*:*	Beyer 115
10, 11[1].	1.	*.*:8	Beyer 117, 118
3[1].	32?:	*	Cop. H.S., Frag. Gxiig
19.	?:44	*	Pal. Ruz 1, C6
25–27.	49:	*	M. 10c; P. 16, 17c
28.		*.49	P. 21d (pictorial inversion)
31.	49:	*.181	P. 7d
29, 30.	1.49:	*	D. 36a; 40b
35.	109:49:	*	M. 36a
14.	59:	*:*.?:11?	Cop. H.S., Frag. Gxiij
13.	74:	*:74	Cop. A, H1

15.	74:	*:130?	Cop. 13, F6
21.	74:	*:142	Calak. 51, D3
1.	IV.74:	*:142	Cop. G', C6
7.	74:	*:?	Carac. 16, A19
17.	74:	*:?	Cop. D, B8
36.	87.	*	M. 59b
2.	115:	*	Cop. T. 11, E door, S pan. A2
12.	136:44v?:	*	Beyer 119
37.	181:	*:?	P. 2c
4[2].	235:	*:142	Pal. Ruz 2, F3
20.	287:	*	P.N., L. 2, K'3
32.	287:	*	D. 57b
33, 34.	172.287:	*	D. 46d; 58c
6[1].	590?.	*	Yax. L. 10, E7
16.	13.590:	*	Cop. 13, E8
5.	1.?:	*:130	Quir. D, A23
18.	1:?:	*	Cop. 3, A8
22.	1.?:	*	Iturbide stone, B4
38.	III.	*:*:47	M. 88c
39.	?:	*:131 or 130	Cop. H.S. Gxiid
40.	?:	*	Tik. jade B4
9.		*:*:71	Beyer 116

[1] Affix 110 placed in a vertical position.
[2] Affix 235 may belong with the adjacent Caban sign.

The compound 287–110 is of interest because, as noted by Morley and Lizardi, Affix 287 replaces the dog ? head in Glyph B of the lunar series, but the dog head with 110 Postfix is a very common glyph. The example at Piedras Negras of 287:110 is an interesting link between that city and Codex Dresden.

GLYPH 112 (Flint Knife) M.S.
(20 Examples; Sheet 357; Gates' Glyph 18.1; Zimmermann's Glyph 31)

1–6.	44 or 138:	*	Beyer 171; 173; 175–178
7, 8.	44 or 138:	*	Beyer 172, 174
9.	49:	*	D. 23b

10–19.	49:	*	M. 38c (4 times); 42a; 43a (5 times)
20.	1.49:	*	D. 58

The distribution of this affix as a main sign is of interest. Although it is generally identified as flint knife, one might note that it appears on Dresden 23b in a context of food offerings. Nos. 7 and 8 have an unusual outline.

GLYPH 136 M.S.
(8 Examples; Gates' Glyphs 323.2 & 324.6; Zimmermann's Glyph 1370)

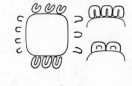

1–3.	114.	*:23	M. 92b (thrice)
4–6.	114.	*:*:23	M. 91c (thrice)
7.		*:*:23	M. 61b
8.		*:*:103	M. 78a

GLYPH 145 M.S.
(6 Examples; Gates' Glyph 422; Zimmermann's Glyph 46)

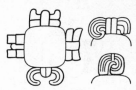

5.	42:	*	Arenal polychrome vase
2, 3.	58.	*:103	M. 100d (twice)
1.	109.	*	D. 39b
6.	204?:	*.106?	Dos Pozos H.S. 2, B3
4.		*:87	M. 92a

As a main sign this glyph of a hank of cloth is the symbol of the old goddess, patroness of weaving in the codices. The two examples of the Classic period do not seem to have associations with that deity.

[53]

GLYPH 146 M.S.
(4 Examples; Gates' Glyph 323.5; Zimmermann's Glyph 36)

1-4.   *.103.116   M. 85c; 87c (thrice)

GLYPH 149 M.S.
(2 Examples; Gates' Glyph 343; Zimmermann's Glyph 84)

1.	58.	*	D. 36c
2.	I.1.90:	*	D. 47f

GLYPH 153 M.S.
(3 Examples; Zimmermann's Glyph 1353)

1.	III.	*:23	D. 9a
2.	III.	*:23	P. 2d
3.		*?.181	Coba 1, A18

Note the same combination of the number 3 with 153 occurs with Glyph 526. The 153–501 compound seems to be especially associated with the date 13.0.0.0.0 4 Ahau 8 Cumku. Entry 3 above is also associated with that date.

GLYPH 155 M.S.
(3 Examples)

2.		*	Gl. of 8th lord of nights
1.	229.	*	Uaxac. vase, Smith 80q'
3.	234?.?:	*	Halal N. Lint. C

Beyer has demonstrated that this glyph represents the arched body of a snake. The example from Halal appears to show a snake's head at each end. Compare with the background of Tikal, Temple 4, Lintel 3. The glyph normally shows little resemblance to its source.

GLYPH 163 M.S.
(3 Examples; Gates' Glyph 339; Zimmermann's Glyph 70b)

1.	90.	*.24	M. 93c
2.	194?.	*:140	P. 3c
3.	194?.	*:?	D. 18a

GLYPH 166 M.S.
(11 Examples; Gates' Glyph 3a; Zimmermann's Glyph 27)

1.	58.	*:103	D. 48d. Zac Akab (Barthel)
2.	58.	*:?	M. 14b
3.	114	*:23	P. 18b
4–9.	114.	*:24	M. 107c (6 times)
10.	114.	*:276	M. 40a
11.	114.	*.126:276	D. 44b

GLYPH 173 M.S.
(5 Examples)

2.	1:	*:*	Beyer 611
4.	12.72:	*.61:178	Xcalum. I.S. build., lt. col. A4
5.	74:	*:*:47v?	Dzibil. 9, C1
1.	74:	*:4	P.N. Thr. 1, D′
3.	74:lines: 606:23.74: lines:	*[606] or *	Half-period glyph

In the half period glyph, 173 is often an affix. No. 5 appears to function as a half period glyph but Glyph 606, normally an essential element of that glyph, is absent, as are the lines or bars at the top. In this example and in No. 1 the doubled elements are joined base to base.

GLYPH 179 M.S.
(1 Example)

1.	1.	*	Pal. T. 18 stucco

GLYPH 181 (Moon) M.S.
(3 Examples)

1.	number.or:217.	*.23 or 82	Gl. D of lunar ser.
2.	1 or 204.or:	*	Gl. C of lunar ser.

variable:217.

3.   *.IX   Coba 20, A13. Unusual
Gl. A

In Examples 1 and 2, Glyph 181 seems to be postfixed to Glyph 217, but the value of each compound is known, and clearly the moon sign is the key element. It is really Gl.683 cut in half because of lack of space. This is certainly true of the unusual example of Gl.A on Coba 20. Glyphs B and A are squeezed into one block and Gl.683 is sliced in half to form Gl.181. There is considerable variability in composition of Gls. C and D. The student should consult specialized studies on the lunar series.

GLYPH 184 M.S.
(3 Examples)

1.   74:   *:130?   P.N., L. 3, D''
2, 3.   35??:   *:35??   Beyer 360, 361

GLYPH 186 M.S.
(1 Example; Gates' Glyph 359.3; Zimmermann under 1302)

1.   149:   *   M. 70a

Zimmermann classifies this as Glyph 1302.

GLYPH 188 M.S.
(32 Examples; Sheets 249, 250)

9.	125.	*:69	Pal. H.S., C2
30.	130?:	*	Rossbach coll. Lothrop, 1936a
17.	145:	*	Yax. 7, D3
11, 14, 15, 16.	145.	*:87	Yax. 21, G4; L.52, H4; L. 58, E1; L. 2, J1
5.	53.168:	*	Pal. Inscr. E. N11
4.	53.168:	*:130	Pal. Inscr. E. J8
6.	53?.168:	*?	Pal. Inscr. M. F10
10.	59.168:	*	Yax. 12, D2
21, 23, 26.	59.168:	*	P.N., L. 3, H1; Z2; L. 2, W10
22, 24.	59:168:	*	P.N. 3, F5; 15, B1
20.	59:168:	*:*	P.N. Thr. 1, H'3
25.	59:168:	*:130	P.N. 8, W1
32.	59.168:	*	Bonam. 2, C2
18.	59:168:	*:130?	Yax. 6, C6
27.	59.168:?	*?	P.N.1, J17
28.	103.168:	*:24?	Poco Uinic 3, B20
2.	113.168:	*	Pal. Fol. O7
8.	113v:168:	*	Pal. 96 Gl. C6
7.	113?:168:	*:130	Pal. Inscr. W. S8
12.	?.168:	*	Yax. 11, E1
31.	?.168:	*	P.N. cenote jade
1.	19?.168:		Cop. T. 11, W. door A2
19.	?:168:	*	P.N. Thr. 1, Z6
13.	168?:	*	Yax. L. 47, F4
29.	244?:168:	*	Tort. 1, A4
3.	1.181?:142.	*:130	Pal. Fol. E6

The distribution of Affix 188 used as a main sign is of interest. With two exceptions all occurrences are confined to the Usumacinta Valley and Chiapas. The glyph appears in distinctive clauses at Yaxchilán and Piedras Negras.

GLYPH 190 M.S.
(4 Examples; Gates' Glyph 435; Zimmermann's Glyph 33)

1, 2.	*.181	M. 97a (twice)
3.	*.196 or 181	M. 96d
4.	*.?	M. Cow celt

GLYPH 192 M.S.
(3 Examples; Gates' Glyph 431; Zimmermann's Glyph 1306)

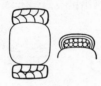

1–3.	137.	*:*	D. 51b; 52b; 55a

Another example of the doubling of an affix when it serves as a main sign.

GLYPH 210 (Univalve shell) M.S.
(6 Examples; Sheets 360, 361; Gates' Glyph 362; Zimmermann's Glyph 757)

5.	63:	*	Glyph of God N.D. 41b
1.	75:	*:59	Beyer 610
2.	?.44?:	*:59	Uaxac. sherd 3506
3.	1017 or 1016.?:	*	Tik. 3, C5
4.		*	D. 56b
6.		*.110	Bliss vase Cat. 133. God N.

GLYPH 216 M.S.
(2 Examples)

1.	25.?:	*	Aguatec. 7, G3
2.	34:	*:130	Aguatec. 1, A8

See remarks under Glyph 514.

GLYPH 227 (seated man) M.S.
(13 Examples; Gates' Glyph 125; Zimmermann's Glyph 100)

1.		*	D. 58b
2, 3.		*	M. 18b; 88c
4, 5.		*.*	D. 22c; 68a
6.		*.*	M. 59c
7.	I.	*.736.736	M. 36d
8, 9.	172?.	*	D. 24c; 47e
10.	IV.	*	D. 49f
11, 12.	IV.	*	P. 11b; 22a?
13.	?.	*	P. 5b14

In the doubled glyphs, the little men are seated back to back. Note that on D.68a the glyph is above a picture in two Chacs seated back to back, one in dry weather, the other in the rain.

GLYPH 233 M.S.
(3 Examples; Gates' Glyph 744; Zimmermann's Glyph 47)

2.	544?:	*	P.N., L. 2, E′1
3.	561?:	*	Quir. G, F′8
1.		*:23	D. 57b

The head from Piedras Negras is, apparently, that of an animal whose paws support a superfix which may be the kin sign.

GLYPH 236 M.S.
(21 Examples; Sheets 394, 435)

21.		*	Uaxac. mural G3
1.		*	Xcalum. N. build. Frag. G
13.	1.	*?	Holmul tripod bowl, Gl. 26
11.	60.	*[542 horiz.]	Uaxac. sherd 3506
19.	99.	*	Hondo, Guat. bowl. Seler
10.	165?.	[*] animal jaws	Beyer 424
17.	213.	*	Uaxac. sherd 3124, Gl. 12
14, 15.	319?.	*	Q. Roo blowgun bowl Gls. 7, 8
20.	319?.	*	Poctun tripod bowl
16.	319?.	*	Cop. Quetzal jar Gl. 7
18.	319?.	*	Hondo, Guat. bowl. Seler
12.	?	*	El Encanto 1, D15
4–9.		[*] animal jaws:59	Beyer 200; 201; 420–23
3.		[*] animal jaws.59	Beyer 202
2.		*:?	Xcochkax jamb fragment

Various birds not easily identifiable. The peculiar loop over the long beak of what may be a humming bird entered as 319? probably represents copying by pottery painters of a design originating with a single artist. Number 19 has a feather (99) balanced on top of the beak, a pleasant touch.

GLYPH 237
(6 Examples; Sheet 436)

1.		*.shaggy head	Cop. K, M2
2, 3.		*.shaggy head	Pal. Ruz 1, L14; P6
4.		*.youthful head	Cop. H.S., Step E
5.		*.shaggy head:?	Cop. 2, C5
6.		*.shaggy head:60?	Yax. L. 22, A2

The heads, save No. 4, are reminiscent of those of the jaguar. All show a canine projecting from the corner of the mouth. There are black (hatched) areas around the mouth of Nos. 1, 5, and 6, and No. 6 has a large black superorbital area. On the whole, I am inclined to think the animal whose eye is being pecked out by the bird (a vulture?) is the dog. Can this glyph have any connection with *col ich,* "tear out the eye," which is frequent in occurrence in the Books of Chilam Balam and in the Ritual of the Bacabs?

GLYPH 238 M.S.
(2 Examples; Gates' Glyph 324.2.1.; Zimmermann's Glyph 28)

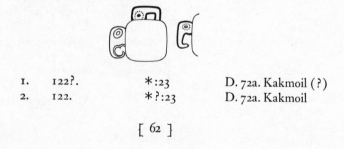

1.	122?.	*:23	D. 72a. Kakmoil (?)
2.	122.	*?:23	D. 72a. Kakmoil

Affixes

The reading of this compound as Kakmoil, "pertaining to Kakmo," is suggested by the fact that the glyph is followed in one case by the drought glyph and in the other by the death-tun compound. Kinich Kakmo, "sun-face-fire-parrot," was the name of the sun god at Izamal.

GLYPH 239 M.S.
(6 Examples; Sheet 291)

3.	89.	*	El Cayo L. 1, D12
1.	168?:	*.59:23?	Alt. Sac. 4, C5
2.	168?:	*.?:23?	Alt. Sac. 5, C12
4, 6.	IX.	*	Cop. 2, B7; H′, D2b
5.	IX:	*	Cop. 3, A7

It is not certain that all six examples represent the same glyph. The three with coefficients of 9 have been discussed by Morley (1920), but note that it is now established (Thompson, 1944) that the initial series of Copán 3 does have a month sign.

GLYPH 248 M.S.
(4 Examples)

1[1].		*.*	Uaxac. I.S. vase, Gl. 13
2[2].		*:*	Chama. Carey vase, G4
3.	33.	*:178	Uaxac. sherd 3124
4[2].		*:99?	Chama. Carey vase, C2

[1] The main sign is on its side, and to it the narrower normal Affix 248 is attached, also on its side.
[2] Simplified forms of Affix 248.

GLYPH 250 M.S.
(2 Examples; Gates' Glyph 392; Zimmermann's Glyph 1375)

| 1. | | * | D. 21a |
| 2. | 59: | * | D. 57a |

GLYPH 251 M.S.
(2 Examples; Gates' Glyphs 363 and 390)

| 1. | | * | P. 10b24 |
| 2. | | *.23:210 | D. 53b |

The identifications are not beyond question.

GLYPH 263 M.S.
(2 Examples; Sheet 360)

| 1. | | *:* | Beyer 619 |
| 2. | 1. | *:23 | Beyer 620 |

GLYPH 268 M.S.
(2 Examples; Gates' Glyph 19.35.1; Zimmermann's Glyph 1313)

| 1, 2. | | *:* | D. 53b; 54b |

GLYPH 281 (Kan Cross) M.S.
(74 Examples; Sheets 207–10; Gates' Glyph 69; Zimmermann's Glyph 23)

49, 50.		*	M. 43c, 47a
69.		*	P.N. bowl. Coe Fig. 6od
33.		*[?]	Uaxac. sherd 4856
8, 11, 12.	12.	*:23	Yax. Str. 44, S.E. step X2;
			L. 32, A9; 20, E6
16.	12:	*:23	Yax. L. 10, D2
42.	12.	*:23?	Bonam. Rm 1, bottom
39.	16.?:	*	Uaxac. sherd 3506
62.	17:	*	D. 18c (ill)
64.	17:	*	M. 66b (ill)
57.	17.	*	M. 110b
58–61.	144:17MS.	*	D. 18c; 19c; 27b; 46e; 50f
63.	144:17MS:	*	P. 7c
52.	24.	*:?	M. 108c
25–29.	32:	*:59?	Carac. 6, F15; D22, F24; 1,
			E3; H3
71–73.	33.	*	Carac. 3, D13a; D18a; D20a
74.	33?.	*:23	Carac. 3, A18a
65.	52?.	*	Yax. L. 10, E2
54.	59.	*.87	D. 31c "at the kanche tree"
67.	86:	*:130	Tort. 6, G5
48.	115.	*:24(inv.)	M. 87b
37.	116.	*:265	Chama. Carey vase, D1
23.	167:	*:23	Jonuta 2, A3
31.	168:	*.88	Beyer 483
24.	168?:	*?	Uaxac. 12, B3
14.	48.214:	*:178?	Pal. Fol. C14
46.	225.214:	*:23?	Pal. Fol. Balustr. H1
47.	225?.214?:	*:23	Pal. Cross Bal. H1
17.	229.	*:23	Yax. L. 46, G''3
41.	229:	*:23	Bonam. Rm. 1, bottom
56.	250:	*	M. 27d
53.	VIII or IX:	*:23	M. 43a
44.	?.	*:110	Uaxac. 14, back
20.	?:	*.136:23?	Seib. 3 in hand

70.	?.	*:23	Tort. 7, A3
13.	?:	*:23	Yax. L. 54, B2
2, 3, 4.		*:23	Cop. T. 11, S.E. pan. B2; H, C2; H.S. frag.
5, 6.		*:23	Pal. Cross, S15; Sun, P4
9.		*:23	Yax. Str. 44, S.E. step, V3
43, 64.		*:23	Bonam. Rooms 1 & 2
30.		*:23	Ixlu Alt. of 2, C5
21.		*:23	Cancuen, Alt. 1, A4
35.		*:23	Xculoc Mid. Lint., J
51.		*:23	P. 8b
34.		*.23	Xculoc N. Lint., C
1.		*.23	Cop. A, F3
19.		*.23?	P.N. L. 2, A'2
66.		*.23?	Acanceh tomb mural
22.		*:23?	Nar. 22, H15
40.		*:23?	Uaxac. sherd 3982
18.		*:23:IX	P.N. 12, D4
15.		*:47?:23	Yax. L. 6, B6
32.		*:23:103	Beyer 481
10.		*.16?.229:23 [188]	Yax. L. 35, X1
55.		*.85:87	D. 48f
7.		*:98	Quir. D, D20
36.		*.116:142v	Nebaj. Fenton vase
45.		*?:116	Cop. ball crt. marker
68.		*.173?	Acanceh tomb mural
38.		*:255v.?	Chama. Carey vase

The Kan cross was the symbol for yellow in Yucatán at the time of the Spanish conquest, but there are some grounds for supposing that it was previously the symbol for turquoise. It is probably a symbol for "precious," and it certainly has close associations with water (Thompson, 1950, 275–76).

Of interest are the 17–281 compounds in the codices, often with Prefix 144, which I do not believe to be numerical. There seems little doubt that these compounds represent offerings—green precious objects is one possibility. It is even possible that the symbol stands for *balche,* the Maya mead, a ritualistic name for which is *yax ha,* "uncontaminated water." It should be noted that in Codex Madrid the kin sign replaces the Kan cross in this compound. The substitution of kin for kan sign found also with head forms has been discussed by Gates, 1931, 71, 95. In this connection it is of interest to note that the people of Lerma, on the Campeche coast, call a stool *kinche,* although they are well aware that in Yucatán it is called *Kanche* (R. H. Thompson, 1958, 74).

The very frequent appearance of Affix 23 as a postfix is strong confirmatory evidence of the correctness of the sound value *al* assigned this element by Barthel (1952, 48), for the terminal *al* is commonly joined to color names—*chacal, zacal, kanal* when these are used adjectivally. In addition, one can make the deduction that the Maya of the Classic period who developed the glyphs used a similar termination.

Glyph 281 is one of those borderline cases, for it might equally well be classified as a main sign. It is placed in the affix group to keep it with the other color signs. Moreover, it is a common infix.

GLYPH 283 M.S.
(6 Examples; partly Gates' Glyph 340; partly Zimmermann's Glyph 1359)

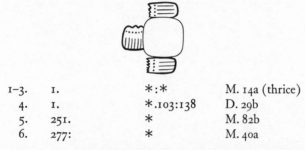

1–3.	1.	*:*	M. 14a (thrice)
4.	1.	*.103:138	D. 29b
5.	251.	*	M. 82b
6.	277:	*	M. 40a

This sign is placed among the affixes because its axis is variable and because when it stands by itself as a main sign it may be doubled. It is distinguished from Glyph 610 by its ragged edge. Both Zimmermann and Gates group together my Glyphs 610 and 283, and it may well be that the categories I suggest are not justified.

GLYPH 287 M.S.
(1 Example)

1.	1.187:	*	Symbolic form of Glyph B of lunar series Affixes 11 or 204 may replace Affix 1

It has long been known that Glyph 287 as main sign is the symbolic form of Glyph 758 (jog with Infix 7). For discussion see Lizardi 1941.

See under Glyph 560.

GLYPH 352 M.S.

(1 Example)

1.   *:47   Pusil. slab-footed tripod
bowl. Br. Mus.

OCCURRENCES OF AFFIXES AS PREFIXES
OF MAIN SIGNS

(Italics indicate that the affix is infixed)

1. 19, 21, 23, 25, 58, 59, 74, 78, 82, 95, 103, 109, 110, 112, 149, 173, 179, 188, 227, 236, 263, 283, 287, 501, 502, 503, 504, 506, 507, 510, 512, 513, 515, 516, 518, 520, 521, 526, 527, 528, 530, 532, 533, 534, 535, 537, 539, 540, 542, 544, 548, 552, 555, 556, 557, 558, 561, 563, 565, 568, 570, 573, 576, 580, 581, 582, 585, 586, 590, 592, 598, 601, 602, 604, 606, 607, 612, 613, 619?, 624, 625, 630, 633, 634, 637, 638, 639, 642, 644?, 646, 648, 650, 657, 662, 663, 665, 667, 668, 669, 670, 671, 674, 676, 678, 679?, 682, 683, 684, 685?, 687, 689, 702, 705, 709, 710, 712, 713, 714, 715, 723, 733, 736, 740, 742?, 743, 747, 751, 752, 756, 757, 758, 759, 761?, 764, 765, 767, 768, 769, 773, 774?, 780, 785, 788, 793, 806, 812, 833, 848, 855, 1301, 1307, 1342
2. 510, 528, 563, 595, 644, 683?
3. 506, 519?, 526, 528, 535, 563, 573, 580, 606, 624?, 671, 676, 712, 713, 744, 754?, 757, 758, 788
4. 503, 520?, 521, 528, 533, 561, 563, 575, 585, 683, 733, 738?, 751, 764, 769
5. 528
6. 520?, 683?
7. 561, 765
8. 548, 679?
9. 501?, 528
10. 506, 601, 648, 669, 715, 759
11. 59, 501, 503, 504, 506?, 518, 519, 520, 521, 526, 528, 529, 533, 539, 542, 544,

548, 563, 573, 586, 606, 624, 630, 644, 645, 658, 669, 670, 671, 678, 684, 710, 712, 713, 714, 740, 743, 747, 751, 757, 758, 764, 788, 834, 1319

12. 24, 25, 82, 120, 173, 281, 501, 504, 506, 507, 510?, 512, 513, 515, 516, 520, 521, 524, 526, 528, 529, 533?, 534, 537, 542, 544, 547, 548, 552, 559, 561, 563, 568, 569, 570, 573, 580, 585, 586, 592, 600, 602, 622, 626, 638, 646?, 651, 663, 669, 671, 673, 683, 685, 689, 690, 709?, 710, 711, 712, 713, 715, 738, 740, 741, 742, 743, 745, 747, 751, 756, 757, 758, 764?

13. 58, 110, 501, 501v, 502, 503, 504, 507, 510?, 526, 528, 530, 533, 544, 548, 552?, 556, 561, 563, 565, 573, 580, 581, 585, 586, 589, 601, 607, 619?, 625, 630, 648, 667, 669, 670, 671, 683, 695, 711, 712, 736, 740, 743, 747, 757, 758, 764

14. 526, 561, 668, 736, 765

15. 23, 95, 533, 534, 561, 567, 667, 668, 671, 682, 683?, 736

16. 58, 281?, 501, 510, 513, 516, 518, 521, 526, 528, 546, 552, 561, 565, 569?, 580, 586, 596?, 671, 683, 703, 707, 712, 713, 738, 743, 744, 751, 756?, 758, 759, 760, 765, 844, 856?

17. 21, 281, 506, 510?, 521, 524, 526, 528v, 528, 534, 544?, 548, 552, 558, 563?, 565, 575, 577, 578?, 580, 585, 613, 668, 671, 676, 736, 740?, 743, 744?, 756, 856, 1347

18. 501?, 563, 565, 585?, 586, 692, 695

19. 188?, 501, 517?, 528, 545?, 561, 565, 568, 603, 604, 648, 658v, 666, 670, 671, 686, 712, 713?, 756, 769

20. 558

21. 32, 526, 528, 557, 559, 573, 575, 580, 586, 601, 657?, 660, 683, 738, 741, 756, 758, 764

23. 17, 19, 24, 62, 173, 501, 503, 505, 515?, 526, 528, 534, 544, 552inv, 561inv, 565, 566, 585, 647, 663, 668, 676, 683, 684, 713, 756, 759, 765, 806

24. 103, 281, 501, 521, 526, 529, 533, 534, 544, 548, 561, 668, 669, 670?, 683, 713, 731, 736, 743?, 748, 756, 757, 758

25. 19, 74, 216, 501, 502, 503, 506, 507, 512, 513, 520, 526, 528, 533, 534, 537, 544, 548v, 552, 561, 565, 567, 573, 582, 583?, 585, 586, 592?, 601, 604?, 611?, 612, 613, 616, 626, 648, 668, 669, 673, 683, 688, 711, 736, 741?, 743?, 752, 757, 762, 764, 797, 812, 815

27. 501, 506, 537, 542, 585, 627, 635

28. 548, 672, 747

29. 563

30. 613

31. 573, 613

32. 110?, 281, 511, 515, 521?, 526, 528, 553, 561, 562, 568, 570, 585, 643, 670, 695, 716, 744?, 747, 751, 756, 758, 827, 843, 1339

33. 248, 281, 506, 544, 561, 568, 611, 755, 758, 765

34. 216, 675, 683

35. 24, 92, 184??, 501, 510?, 526, 528, 533, 553, 560, 561, 568, 570, 575, 597, 598, 669, 670, 683, 684?, 702?, 713, 750, 756, 759, 765

36. 511, 553, 560?, 562, 569, 570, 716, 747, 750, 756, 764, 778, 793
37. 511, 518, 562, 793
38. 511, 518, 528?, 553, 560, 562, 565, 566, 568, 569, 570, 683?, 692, 716, 743?, 756, 778?, 793
39. 528?, 552, 560
40. 503, 504, 516?, 560, 561?, 566, 569, 570, 606, 747, 756?, 778, 793
41. 553, 562, 568?, 747?
42. 145, 746
43. 528, 530?, 533?, 542?, 716, 793
44. 44, 58, 110, 112, 210?, 501, 502, 524, 544, 556, 560, 561, 563, 565, 568, 580, 586, 606, 624, 669, 671, 683?, 686, 686v, 744, 751, 761, 786, 853, 1030j
45. 17, 501, 575, 709, 747, 777?
46. 501, 675
47. 25, 109, 544, 552, 565, 582, 632, 670, 715, 727, 791
48. 281, 504, 515, 528, 538, 542, 561, 565, 573, 617, 747, 764, 790
49. 110, 112, 573, 578, 666, 746, 790
50. *684*, 713
51. 501, 528, 545, 561, 565, 612, 747
52. 281?, 503, 568, 741, 751
53. 35, 92, 188, 586, 666, 669, 670, 673, 747, 765, 1313
55. 528 and Beyer figs. 683–685
56. 563?, 568
57. 515, 528, 582?, 683, 710, 747
58. 145, 149, 166, 501, 503, 504, 506, 512, 518, 521, 526, 528, 528v, 529, 533, 534, 544, 548, 552, 553, 558, 565, 572?, 573, 580, 598, 624, 625, 632, 648?, 668, 671, 673, 682, 683, 713, 736, 742, 743, 744, 756, 764, 765, 769
59. 17, 19, 21, 80, 82, 99, 110, 188, 250, 281, 501, 502, 504, 507, 509, 512, 513, 516, 518, 520, 521, 522, 526, 528, 533, 534, 537, 542, 544, 545, 548, 552, 557, 561, 562, 563, 565, 567, 568, 570, 573, 575, 578, 583, 585, 586, 590, 613, 663, 668, 669, 670, 671, 673, 679, 683, 684, 712, 713, 731, 733, 737, 743, 745, 746, 747, 748?, 755, 756, 769, 777, 807, 815, 832, 849, 856
60. 25, 236, 501, 515, 521?, 524?, 528, 537?, 539?, 542, 552, 561?, 565, 568, 577, 585, 586, 587, 669, 671, 713, 738, 744, 751, 754?, 756, 757, 758, 762, 788, 844, 851
61. 501, 502, 521?, 528, 533, 565, 568, 585, 586, 644, 657, 683, 708?, 737, 738, 741?, 743, 756, 757?, 758?, 770
62. 501, 507, 513, 526, 527, 528, 533, 544, 548, 552, 557, 558, 565, 573, 585, 604, 611, 613, 713, 731, 756, 758
63. 210, 501, 548, 626, 790, 792
64. 528, 544, 548, 626, 759, 790, 792, 823
65. 507, 542?, 552, 579, 751, 756?, 757, 769
66. 23
67. 565, 598, 601, 607, 642, 679

68. 501, 544, 548, 552, 586, 592, 593, 671, 683, 744, 746, 1334
69. 610, 612?, 613
70. 528, 537, 544, 552, 668, 755
71. 548, 612, 674, 738
72. 173
73. 585, 612
74. 7, 17, 23, 110, 173, 184, 281, 501, 504, 506, 507, 508?, 513?, 521, 528, 534, 537, 539, 542?, 544, 552, 556, 557, 558, 564, 565, 575, 585, 586, 594, 612, 613, 616, 617, 624, 626, 655, 667, 669, 671, 672, 676?, 679, 683, 685, 690, 695, 712, 713, 724, 738, 743, 744, 747, 752, 755, 756, 757, 762, 771, 793, 1314?
75. 210
76. 528, 534?, 575
77. 501, 506?, 575, 585, 748
78. 506, 513, 514, 516, 521, 534, 585, 606?, 674?
79. 103, 513, 530, 534?, 614, 620, 621, 628, 679, 683, 758?, 781
80. 614, 733?
81. 504, 513, 565
82. 738?, 743
83. 756?
84. 501, 506, 512, 513, 521, 526, 528, 544, 546, 559, 561, 564, 611, 663, 712?, 738, 744, 756, 785, 807, 810
85. 17, 501, 528, 561, 573, 611, 613?, 663, 702, 744, 759
86. 503, 506?, 513?, 517, 519, 521, 526, 528, 538, 545, 548, 561, 578, 610, 611, 657, 666, 671, 704, 708, 746, 756, 769, 777?, 1321, 1322
87. 110, 501, 502, 506, 507, 512, 515, 518, 526, 528, 530, 532, 533, 542, 548, 561, 585, 600, 613, 670, 683?, 744?, 755, 757, 758
88. 501?, 671, 819
89. 239, 501, 504, 510, 528, 560, 561, 575, 585, 606, 607, 625, 630, 653, 666, 670, 712, 740?, 744?, 747, 757?, 758
90. 149, 163, 513, 521, 526, 528, 537, 544, 548, 552, 580, 608, 663, 668, 671, 682, 685, 736, 757, 791, 829
91. 19, 501, 526, 528, 552, 558, 565, 663, 671, 682, 791
92. 501, 515, 528, 532, 537, 544, 552, 558, 561, 565, 585, 598, 625, 669, 751, 757, 769?, 825?
93. 543, 577, 589, 607, 666, 670, 672, 682, 683, 710, 758, 764
94. 501, 626
95. 501, 511, 526, 528, 538, 539, 540, 544, 546?, 552, 559, 561, 565, 568, 572, 595, 632, 668, 671, 712, 743, 747, 748?, 756, 756, 769, 792
96. 526, 563, 585, 591, 604, 613, 663, 669, 682, 796
97. 521, 561
98. 17, 569, 670
99. 103, 236, 663, 703
100. 573, 585

101. 585, 764, 1303, 1304
102. 507, 533, 552, 565, 683, 743?, 756
103. 188, 502, 503?, 506?, 516, 530, 545, 613, 683, 744, 750
104. 731
105. 714
106. 501?, 528
107. 504, *671*?
108. 698?, 764
109. 110, 145, 501, 504, 506, 507, 510, 526, 528, 542, 544, 552, 561, *570*, 572, 578, 582, 595?, 610, 612, 613, 624, 668, 669, 671?, 683, 698, 736, 744, 755, 756, 757?, 758, 759, 765, 800, 815
110. 502, 504, 512, 519, 526, 533, 536, 552, 559, 560, 566, 568?, 570, 575, 580, 595, 606, *671*, 694, 742, 748, 749, 758
111. 539
112. 548?, 558, 581, 624, 671, 757, 758
113. 188, 188v, 534?, 545, 561, 610, 707, 740, 752, 757, 765
114. 136, 166, 501, 532, 566, 572?, 627
115. 17?, 110, 281, 501?, 506, 510, 512?, 515, 521, 528, 544?, 552, 556, 557, 561, 563, 573, 585, 586, 593, 601, 610, 648, 663, 667, 671?, 673, 726, 734, 735, 738?, 744?, 746, 747?, 752?, 756, 761, 765, 843
116. 281, 501, 504, 528, 561, 585, 612, 666?, 671, 738, 744, 751, 757, 764, 814, 815, 1321
117. 502, 506, 507, 518, 521, 526?, 528?, 529, 531, 533, 534, 535, 600, 707?, 747, 756, 757, 764
118. 501, 528, 561, 563, 582, 597?, 607?, 746, 758, 764
119. 501, 510, 575
120. 506, 590?, 739?, 747?, 755, 792
121. 501, 502, 713, 750?, 757
122. 82, 238, 503, 504, 506, 510, 512, 516?, 518, 521, 526, 528, 529, 533, 534, 538, 544, 546, 552, 561, 562, 563, 582, 583, 594, 595, 624, 642, 666, 669, 670, 675?, 683, 698?, 712, 713, 733, 738, 741?, 743, 747, 756, 757, 764, 765, 785, 820, 1020, 1030, 1035, 1064
123. D.36b col. 2, Gl. 1
124. 501, 528, 533?, 548, 597, 612, 733, 738, 744
125. 23, 58, 103, 188, 503, 504, 513, 518, 526, 530, 533, 544, 552, 561, 563, 565, 568, 606, 607, 617, *630*, 638, 644, 669, 670, 671, 679, 683, 689, 745, 747, 751, 755, 756, 758, 759?, *778, 828, 831*
126. 24, 501, 502, 504, 506, 513, 516, 521, 528, 530, 533, 534, 552, 561, 564, 565, 578, 582, 585, 586, *588*, 598, 606?, 607, 616, 670, 671, 679, 683, 712, *714*, 738, 741, 746, 751, 756, 758, 759, 761
127. 548, 679?, 769?
128. 60, 82, 548, 561, 579, 586, 609, 630, 683, 740, 744?, *751*?, 764
129. 513, 520, 524, 528, 552, 561?, 578?, 592, 596, 647?, 669, 675, 709, 712, 740?, 755?

130. 17, 21, 501?, 506, 507, 510, 513, 520, 521, 528, 534, 539, 544, 565, 572, 588, 593?, 621, 626, 663, 667, 668, 669, 671?, 682, 683?, 816
131. 58, 82, 528?, 669?, 683?, 743?, 747
132. 565?, 741?, 769, 820?
133. 501, 502, 561?, 669, 683, 759
134. 17, 526, 533, 554, 575, 595, 638, 671, 749
135. 501, 544, 545, 561, 573?, 757?
136. 110, 501, 506, 533, 534, 544, 547, 548, 561, 586, 589, 591, 595, 606, 626, 636, 679, 687, 713?, 716?
137. 17, 501, 533, 561
138. 112
140. 765
141. 557, 593, 758
142. 188, 501, 544?, 580, 613, 633, 671?, 740, 745, 793
143. 506, 544?
144. 17, 281, 542
145. 103, 188, 542, 561, 565, 578, 582?, 585, 612, 613
146. 501, 528, 533, 537, 542, 552
147. 1059
148. 506?, 683
149. 186, 533, 534, 601, 608, 687
150. 507, 528, 529, 630, 683?, 744, 746?, 747, 756
151. 515?, 528, 561, 575, 586, 634, 713
152. 568?, 751
153. 501, 515, 526, 544, 563, 612, 666, 758
154. 695, 819
155. 506, 526, 533?, 544?, 552, 595, 609, 670, 756?
156. 506, 526
157. 548, 671
158. 528
159. 582
160. 561
161. 521
162. 501, 506
163. 526, 544, 595, 669
164. 747
165. 236?, 590, 622, 627, 644, 681?, 759
166. 17, 82, 84, 501, 528, 561, 564, 758, 765
167. 281, 605
168. 17, 60, 188, 239?, 281, 501, 502, 504, 505, 506, 507, 510?, 511, 512, 513, 516, 518, 520?, 521?, 526, 528, 529, 533, 544, 547, 548, 552, 553, 559, 560, 561, 562, 563, 564, 565, 566, 569, 570, 573, 575, 585, 590, 593, 606, 609, 612, 613, 621, 626, 632, 661, 663, 669, 671, 672, 673, 679, 683?, 684, 692, 700, 703, 716, 733,

738, 741, 743, 744, 747, 751, 752, 753, 754, 756, 757, 758, 764, 769, 778, 793, 849, 1303, 1304

169. 518
170. 561, 562, 713
171. 544, 765
172. 17, 84, 110, 227?, 505?, 521, 526, 533, 544, 548, 559, 561, 567, 573, 609, 648, 663, 682, 736, 800
173. 506, 528, 1300, 1301
174. 501, 520, 529, 530, 532, 565, 671, 709, 751
175. 82, 528, 561, 566
176. 528, 585, 751?, 757?
177. 501, 506?, 507, 518, 528, 536, 585, 837
178. 501, 506, 521?, 534, 544, 573, 626, 669, 671, 679?, 683, 711, 713, 738, 746, 756, 769
179. 503, 684
180. 684?, *1004*
181. 17?, 19, 110, 188?, 506, 507, 520, 521, 526, 533, 534?, 542, 548, 552, 557, 561, 565, 578?, 582, 585, 586, *588*, 619, 630, 632, 640, 648, 663, 667, 682, 684, 687, 701, 713, 744?, 746, 755?, 758, 806, *1025*
182. 501
183. 528, 544
184. 528, 539, 544, 585, 594, 624, 671, 713, 738, 744, 752, 757, 762
185. 519, 522
186. 537, 585, 712
187. 287, 513, 516, 520, 521, 522, 526, 544, 586, 743, 746, 758
188. 502?, 685, 741?, 764?, 774, 777
189. 561?
190. 19, 25, 501?, 506, 526, 528, 682, 758, 794, 1030*l–n*
191. 528, 563?, 565?, 606, 713
192. 17, 501, *512*, 526, 561, 601, 663
193. 501
194. 163?, 501, 526?, 548?, 671
195. 502
196. 103, 501, 513, 514, 586, 666?
197. 512, 515, 598?, 754, 843
198. 506, 507, 539, 600?, 671, 758?
199. 506, 533?, 552
200. 82, 501?, 507, 515, 528
202. 188?, 501, *515*, 528, 544, 559, 586, 630, 635, 669, 679?, *683*, 743, 756, 764
203. 501, 536?, 540, 548, 592, 628, 683, 1340
204. 50, 58, 501, 504, 515, 519, 526, 528, 533, 534, 535, 539, 544, 563, 565, 568?, 573, 575, 578?, 582, 586?, 598, 602, 606, 609, 624, 644, 669, 671, 676, 678?, 683, 712, 713, 714, 741, 743?, 743, 747, 756?, 757, 758, 764, 768

205. 501, 522, 526, 528, 532, 533, 561?, 565, 573, 585?, 644, 671, 747, 757
206. 561?, 580?, 626, 769?
207. 17, 19, 25, 501, 515, 521, 537, 544, 548, 558, 563, 601, 613, 663, 671, 790
208. 614
209. 575
210. 533, 563, 613, 785?
211. 506?, 558, 590, 628, 669, 670, 738
212. 764
213. 236, 501, 528, 533?, 679?, 751, 758?, 788
214. 281
216. 528, 568
217. 501, 515, 526, 528, 542, 544, 558, 575?, 621, 624, 748
218. 17, 501, 528, 532, 544, 561, 575, 585
219. 501, 521, 528, 532, 534, 544, 558, 561, 563, 757?
220. 501, 502, 511?, 513, 514, 520, 534, 544, 561?, 587, 683, 743, 755, 758, 765, 769?
221. 501, 515, 521, 526, 544, 567
222. 561, 578
223. 629
224. 17
225. 281, 713
226. 501, 541, 764
227. 510 inv., 542 inv., 561, 736
228. 501, 504, 506, 507, 512, 515, 518, 520, 521, 528, 544, 548, 552, 565, 568, 573, 586, 592, 595, 607, 622, 630, 646, 669?, 683, 700, 712, 713, 741, 751?, 756, 758, 764, 768, 1326
229. 155, 281, 501, 502, 526, 528, 533, 547, 563, 565, 568, 580, 585, 586, 608, 616, 617, 622, 661, 683, 712, 738, 743, 746?, 747?, 751?, 753, 755?, 758, 764?, 821, 1315, 1327
230. 8, 59, 501, 516, 521, 573, 580, 585?, 683, 710, 757
231. 502, 565, 568?
232. 526?, 535?, 606, 624, 669?, 678, 713, 756, 758, 764
233. 501, 562, 613, 808, 817, 847
234. 558, 561, 731, 736?, 751, 757, 758
235. 110
236. 17, 512, 528, 548, 561, 736, 745?, 746, 747, 751
237. 521, 819
238. 501, 522, 528, 531, 548, 552, 561?, 573, 585, 667, 668, 669, 686, 736, 747?
239. 594, 756
240. 632, 747
242. 515
243. 516
244. 188, 521, 522
245. 561, 572?, 624, 748

247. 526
248. 501, 518, 690, 743?, 768
249. 526, 683
250. 281, 526
251. 283, 558, 663
253. 513
256. 526
257. 528, 624
258. 528, 669?
259. 568
260. 600?
261. 528
262. 528
263. 528
264. 528
265. 501, 528, 580?, 747
266. 568
267. 544, 548, 612, 613, 648
268. 544, 548, 765
269. 533, 553, 586
270. 533, 736, 747
271. 506, 537, 683
272. 546
274. 552
275. 552
277. 283, 663?, 664?, 679
278. 553, 672, 673?, 683
279. 524, 582, 673, 746?, 747?
280. 582
281. 501, 513, 528, 577, 583, 668, 671, 684, 742, 743, 751, 756, 757, 790
282. 561, 616, 751
283. 526, 537, 552, 558, 563, 586, 613, 682, 731, 758
284. 561, 609
286. 561, 670
287. 110, 528?, 560, 561, 757?
288. 529, 613, 746
290. 548
291. 552, 553, 585?, 600?, 683, 744?, 755?
294. 561
296. 552, 585, 613, 671
297. 529
298. Seating. With months in codices.
299. 23, 521, 528, 549, 562, 683

300. 573
303. 568
304. 568
307. 1329
310. 683, 743?, 747?, 751?
311. Probably misdrawing of reversed Affix 351.
312. 695
313. 561
315. 673, 824
316. 774?
317. 671, 755?
318. 671
319. 236, 671, 722?
320. 683
322. 756
323. 751, 758?
324. 585?, 629
325. 510, 526
326. 544, 683, 731
327. 17, 627
328. 770
329. 578
330. 783
331. 575?, 738
332. 738
333. 501, 738, 744, 757, 1323
334. 741
335. 743
336. 1330
338. 751
339. 832
340. 824
341. 596, 743
343. 828
344. 756
345. 533
346. 521
347. 1332
348. 793
351. 774
353. 750
354. 833
355. 561, 741?

356. 1331
357. 563, 586
359. 522, 528, 575, 744?, 849, 850
361. 528
364. 569
366. 854
367. 561, 1343
369. 501
370. 528

Numerals attached to these glyphs usually as prefixes; rarely as postfixes: 17, 23, 25, 58, 59, 82, 110, 149, 153, 227, 239, 281, 501, 502, 503, 504, 506, 507, 510, 511, 513, 514, 515, 516, 518, 519, 520, 521, 522, 524, 526, 528, 530, 533, 534, 537, 538, 540, 542, 544, 546, 548, 552, 558, 559, 560, 561, 563, 565, 567, 568, 570, 573, 575, 577, 580, 582, 585, 586?, 592, 593, 597, 601, 606, 607, 610, 612, 613, 616, 617, 623, 626, 628, 629, 630, 632, 638, 648, 656, 667?, 668, 669, 670, 671, 672, 676, 677, 678, 680, 683, 685, 687, 696, 703, 714, 731, 736, 739, 740, 741, 743, 744, 746, 747, 748, 750, 751, 755, 756, 757, 758, 759, 764, 765, 766, 769, 785, 798, 800, 801, 804, 807, 820, 825, 826, 831, 850, 852, 855, 1050, 1308, 1309, 1316, 1317, 1319

OCCURRENCES OF AFFIXES AS POSTFIXES OF MAIN SIGNS

1. 112, 501, 502, 507, 526, 580, 592, 595, 623, 632, 669, 709?, 715, 736, 756?, 805, 812
2. 506, 528, 642, 669?, 671, 679, 695?, 745, 756
3. 710
4. 173, 501, 504?, 513, 514, 516?, 528, 546, 585, 600, 685, 710, 712?, 744, 756
6. 544
7. 528?, 570?, 625?, 639?, 756
8. 110, 501, 506, 520, 527, 534?, 544, 548, 552, 570?, 586, 638, 662?, 669, 679, 703?, 736
9. 568, 578, 821
10. 648
11. 110?, 563
12. 103, 501, 503, 504, 510, 526, 528, 544?, 573, 578, 580, 586?, 683, 713, 738, 743, 743inv., 819?, 1072
13. 502, 523?, 736
15. 667?, 683?, 736
16. 281?
17. 510, 557, 582, 585, 671?, 682, 764
18. 501, 565, 586
19. 510, 522, 528, 568, 583, 586, 627, 634, 666, 667, 671?, 731, 736, 772
21. 533, 551, 573, 586
22. 573
23. 23, 24, 25, 58, 59?, 60, 62, 74, 95, 136, 153, 166, 233, 238, 239?, 251, 263, 281, 501, 502, 504, 508, 510, 513, 515, 516, 520?, 521?, 522, 526, 528, 533, 534, 535,

537, 538, 539, 544, 548, 552, 553?, 554, 555, 558, 561, 562, 563, 566, 568, 570, 571, 573?, 583, 585, 586, 589, 595, 598, 599, 600, 602, 606, 608, 609, 610, 613, 617, 618, 626, 630, 632, 646?, 659, 663, 665, 667, 668, 669, 670?, 671, 679, 682, 683, 685, 691, 713, 715, 731, 733, 736, 738, 740, 741, 744, 746, 747, 748, 756, 757?, 758, 764, 765, 790, 793, 807, 824?, 834, 1305, 1307, 1308?, 1340

24. 17, 50, 58, 109, 163, 166, 188?, 281Inv, 501?, 503, 504, 506, 507, 510, 518, 521, 526, 528, 530, 533, 534, 535, 537, 542, 544, 546?, 548, 552, 553, 558, 562, 565, 568, 570, 573, 577, 580inv., 585, 586, 606, 607, 624, 625, 626, 634, 642, 644, 645, 648, 657?, 667, 668, 669, 670, 671, 683, 687, 692?, 712, 713, 731, 734, 735, 736, 740, 747, 755, 757, 758, 773, 781?, 791, 799?

25. 19, 21, 23, 58, 84, 109, 501, 502, 506, 512, 515, 516, 521, 532, 533, 541, 542, 548, 552, 557, 558, 563?, 573, 582, 585, 586, 589, 590, 601, 602, 612, 622, 626, 630, 638, 648, 669, 671, 679, 682, 714, 736, 743, 747, 751, 756, 757, 758, 759, 813, 1327

26. 622

27. 501, 533?, 534, 547?, 568?, 573, 590, 662, 757

30. 692

32. 536, 677, 1001

33. 528?

34. 501, 581?

35. 184??, 510, 513, 526, 558, 561, 565, 568, 575, 590?, 597, 669, 714

36. 561, 597

40. 526, 561, 563, 580

43. 597

47. 21, 59, 110, 281?, 352, 521, 523, 526, 552, 563, 565, 582, 588, 610, 613, 616, 663, 667, 671, 683, 686, 723, 731, 747, 758, 812

48. 513, 515, 528, 570, 585, 740, 769?

49. 110

50. 580?

53. 542, 684, 690?, 743, 748, 765?

54. Used with period glyphs in D.N., 548

55. 533?

56. 513, 618, 741, 757, 773

57. 506, 513, 516, 528, 669, 740, 743, 744, 774

58. 524, 744, 833

59. 19, 58, 210, 236, 239, 281?, 504, 506?, 513, 515, 516, 518, 544, 548, 556, 563, 567, 568, 575, 578, 580, 586, 597, 606, 607, 610, 613, 614, 633, 644, 648, 670, 671, 673, 679, 684, 686, 712, 731, 738, 741, 747, 751, 758, 761, 765, 787, 843, 846, 1334

60. 21, 103?, 237?, 501, 504, 506, 511?, 528, 544, 548, 552, 553?, 565, 583, 604?, 626, 630, 671, 673, 731?, 743, 756?, 757

61. 21, 173, 527, 604, 605, 660, 683, 713

62. 19, 21, 515, 552?, 561, 563, 669, 679, 763

65. 501, 586?, 609, 679, 758?
67. 580, 616
69. 188, 513?, 514, 565, 616
70. 552, 619, 755
71. 110, 501, 669, 756
74. 110, 502, 506, 508, 511, 516?, 522, 552, 561, 595, 606, 654, 668?, 669, 670, 672, 673, 679, 738, 751, 774
75. 744?
77. 520, 568?, 585, 622, 738, 747
79. 743
81. 504, 712
82. 503, 504, 516, 520?, 528, 533, 535, 544, 548, 562, 563, 565, 568?, 573, 604?, 671, 683?, 712, 713
83. 528
84. 521?, 727
85. 281, 744, 757, 759
86. 568?, 671, 751, 756?
87. 17, 80, 95, 109, 145, 188, 281, 501, 506, 513?, 515, 520, 526, 528, 542, 544, 548, 556, 558, 563, 568, 572, 583?, 586, 587, 592?, 600, 626, 646, 651, 670?, 671, 682, 683, 703, 710, 714, 746, 747?, 756?, 765, 1030*l–m*
88. 17, 281, 501, 526, 529, 532, 534, 540, 565, 573, 588, 630?, 644, 670, 671, 684?, 695, 710, 733, 743, 757, 785, 819
89. 58, 59, 513, 578?, 579?, 751, 758?, 1302
90. 528, 548
92. 501, 544, 569, 586, 733?
93. 589, 607, 710
96. 95, 511, 544, 556, 580, 586?, 758, 765
97. 501
98. 17, 84, 281, 741
99. 248?, 582
102. 58, 501, 504, 521, 533, 534, 547, 561, 565, 568, 570, 580, 586, 610, 658, 668, 671, 683, 709, 710, 713?, 717, 733, 738, 739, 741?, 743?, 743, 756, 757, 760, 761, 1309
103. 136, 145, 146, 166, 281, 283, 512?, 516, 518?, 520, 521, 526, 528, 533, 534, 536, 544, 548, 552, 558, 561, 573, 586, 590, 602?, 625, 652, 663, 668, 670, 671, 679, 682, 683, 733, 736, 738, 747, 751, 757, 758, 759, 765, 799, 1326
104. 501, 503, 506, 510?, 532, 795
106. 145?, 501, 503, 526, 757, 761
108. 764?
109. 683, 798
110. 210, 281, 502, 563, 590, 595, 673, 710, 721, 736, 748, 758
111. 683
112. 528, 561, 758

113. 534, 572?, 580, 733, 750
114. 502, 528, 533, 539, 604?, 630, 648?, 670, 713?
115. 526?, 614, 663
116. 19, 21, 146, 281, 501, 505, 506, 510, 511?, 512, 515, 518, 523, 526, 528, 532?, 533, 534, 537?, 544, 545, 546, 548, 552, 556, 559, 561, 566, 573, 575, 582, 586, 593, 597?, 598, 616, 620, 621, 625, 644, 662, 671, 679, 684, 690, 692, 700, 705, 713, 726, 734, 735, 741?, 743, 746, 747, 748, 750, 756, 757, 758, 765, 818, 825, 1317
117. 82, 515, 528, 561, 565, 585, 592, 604, 669, 679, 695?, 741, 747?, 751?, 765
118. 515
119. 510, 1311?
120. 670, 738, 739
121. 532, 563?, 586?, 616?, 713, 714?, 746
122. 504, 548, 561, 563, 565, 583, 586, 666 inv., 669, 671, 675, 712, 740
125. 103, 501, 504, 506, 515, 518, 522, 526, 527, 528?, 533, 539, 541, 544, 548, 556?, 559, 561?, 570?, 575, 585, 588, 593?, 617, 632?, 644, 670?, 671, 679, 683, 684, 710?, 712, 740, 741, 747, 750?, 756, 757, 758, 769, 815, 821
126. 58, 59, 82?, 166, 502, 506?, 507, 511, 512, 513, 514, 515, 516, 520, 521, 522?, 526, 528, 532, 540, 548, 552, 561, 563 inv., 572, 575, 578, 582, 585, 586, 588, 602, 607?, 609, 616, 617, 644, 667, 669, 670, 671, 683, 684, 700, 712, 713, 714, 733?, 738, 740, 743, 747, 755, 756, 757, 758, 769, 821, 843, 1326
127. 512
129. 103, 552, 679, 816
130. 17, 19, 23, 25, 58, 60?, 82, 110, 184?, 188, 216, 501, 502, 503, 506, 511, 512?, 513, 515, 516, 518, 519, 520, 521, 526, 528?, 529, 532, 533, 534, 539, 542, 544, 547?, 548, 551, 552, 559, 560, 561, 562, 563, 564, 565, 566, 567, 569?, 570, 573, 574, 575, 580, 585, 586, 588, 590, 592, 593, 594, 604, 607, 608, 609, 612, 616, 617, 621, 626, 630, 644, 663, 667, 668, 669, 670, 671, 672, 678, 679, 682, 683, 687, 689, 708, 710, 713, 714, 716, 731, 733?, 736, 738, 740, 743, 745, 747, 750, 752, 754, 756, 758?, 764, 765, 769, 776, 778, 793, 821?, 1304?
131. 110?, 511, 513, 586, 644, 670, 765?
133. 502, 845
134. 17, 59, 520, 533, 554, 575, 749
135. 515, 561, 652, 679, 748?, 765, 795
136. 17, 58?, 103, 109, 281, 501, 503, 506, 511, 515, 521, 526, 528, 533, 542, 544, 548, 565, 573, 579, 582, 585, 588?, 593?, 604?, 606, 608, 626, 632, 634, 671, 695, 710, 713, 715, 736, 743, 754, 756, 757, 758, 1312, 1328
137. 501, 504
138. 283, 561, 610?, 648, 673, 682, 714, 765
139. 552, 602, 617, 624, 630, 650, 670, 752
140. 95?, 163, 501, 506, 518, 526, 528, 544, 561, 569?, 570, 597, 611, 632, 644, 648, 670, 671, 682, 704, 731, 736, 751, 757, 856
141. 589?, 607?, 670, 671, 698?, 756?

142. 110, 281, 501, 502, 503, 506, 507, 511, 512, 513, 516, 517, 521, 522, 526, 528, 536, 542, 544, 548, 549, 552, 560, 561, 563, 565, 568, 570, 578, 583, 585, 595, 596, 602, 609?, 610, 617, 630, 669, 670, 672, 683, 684, 687, 692, 710, 713, 735, 743, 744, 747, 751, 757, 758?, 762, 771, 772, 793, 823, 1313
143. 730
145. 77?, 552, 561, 585, 601, 673, 751, 819
146. 667
148. 501, 504, 738, 744
149. 58, 608, 731
150. 501, 751?, 764?
151. 503?, 528, 532
153. 518?
155. 526, 586, 669
160. 741?
163. 542
165. 17, 575, 671?, 713, 748?, 759
173. 281?, 528, 546?, 565, 586?, 606, 1028
174. 528
175. 561?
177. 507, 553, 756
178. 173, 248, 281?, 501, 502, 503, 504, 506, 507, 515, 520, 521, 526, 528, 530, 532, 533, 537, 544, 546, 548, 552, 556, 558, 560, 561, 563, 565, 570, 573?, 575, 582, 586, 588, 594, 602, 607, 616, 624, 630, 644, 669, 670, 671, 672, 676, 679, 683, 684, 692, 695, 711, 713, 736, 740, 741, 743, 745, 747?, 751, 756? 758?, 764?, 765?, 769, 1300
179. 539, 544
180. 512, 513, 528, 644
181. 17, 25, 59, 190, 501, 502, 506, 507?, 511, 512, 513, 515, 516, 520, 526, 528, 529, 532, 533, 534, 539, 542, 544, 546, 550, 557, 559, 561, 562, 563, 565, 572, 573, 582, 585, 586, 588, 590, 592, 593, 601, 603, 604, 606, 610, 614, 616, 622?, 629, 630, 634, 644, 668, 669, 671, 672, 679, 683, 684, 692, 693, 695, 701, 713, 715, 736, 738, 740, 743, 744, 746, 747, 750, 756, 757, 758, 759, 765, 769, 781, 812, 1314, 1339
184. 506, 516?, 522, 561, 594, 671, 774, 1322
186. 544, 558, 585, 592?, 671, 736, 758
187. 501, 528, 544, 598
188. 281, 501, 514, 528, 580, 608, 671, 684, 747, 751?, 758, 765
190. 687?
192. 501, 558, 756?
195. 502, 673
196. 58, 190, 528, 597
200. 82, 200?, 540, 573?, 756
201. 644

202.	528, 533, 585, 586
203.	501, 512, 548, 586, 645
204.	657?
205.	512, 586, 602, 679
207.	526?, 671
210.	251
213.	533?, 751
215.	683
216.	501, 721
217.	522, 526, 528, 544, 580, 684, 740, 750
219.	17, 528, 553, 585, 604, 630, 673, 679, 715, 756
220.	741, 840
221.	501
226.	512
227.	552, 648, 743
228.	528, 544, 556?
229.	281, 528, 689, 819
230.	502
232.	528, 561
236.	504
240.	740
241.	504, 518, 558, 617, 671
245.	520?, 521, 526, 561, 630?
246.	526, 573, 585, 607, 670?, 683, 713?, 740, 745, 758, 769, 1314
247.	8?, 526, 644?
248.	501, 606
250.	526, 610
251.	526, 663, 758
252.	526, 528
254.	515, 533?, 548, 570, 586, 616, 670, 683, 1082
255.	281, 503, 528, 672, 740, 751
257.	527
260.	526, 528, 744?, 758, 787?
265.	95, 281
268.	533
269.	533
273.	544, 679
276.	103, 166, 501, 552, 667, 671, 682?, 734, 735, 811?
277.	533?, 552, 610?
279.	582, 627, 683, 743?, 747?, 757
280.	744
281.	173?, 506, 528, 544
283.	526, 528, 668

285. 561, 669?
287. 657
288. 536, 578, 669?, 672
289. 533
291. 562?, 604
292. 552, 585?
293. 552, 561
295. 552, 826
301. 580, 686
302. 605, 713, 832
305. 526
306. 679
308. 526, 663, 667, 757?
309. 526, 663
314. 526, 578, 588, 682?
316. 671
321. 641
326. 510, 544
330. 783
335. 743
337. 732
339. 832
342. 746
349. 756
350. 756, 757, 764?
357. 772
358. 528
360. 518?, 522, 528, 569, 617
362. 529
363. 544
365. 561, 670
368. 528

MAIN SIGNS

501-856

GLYPH 501 (Imix)
(611 Examples; Sheets 1–20; Gates' Glyph 1; Zimmermann's Glyph 1321)

22, 34, 36.	*	Cop. 2, B6; C; A4; H′′, C2
45, 50, 57, 406.	*	Pal. Fol. G3; Inscr. W. J3; 96 Gl. J4; Fol. Sculpt. stone A6
71, 72, 95.	*	Yax. L. 25, M2; U2; 19, A8
97.	*	P.N., L. 3, C′2
123.	*	Jonuta 2, A4
124.	*	Comitán 1, B2
142, 143.	*	Bonam. Rm. 1 (twice)
150.	*	Chajcar pottery box
211.	*	Beyer 615
213.	*	Chama. Carey vase
240, 241.	*	M. 27b (twice)
323, 324.	*	D. 53b; 54b
325.	*	P. 16b
58.	*[95]	Pal. House A, Mid. door
407.	*[95]horiz.	Pusil. slab-foot tripod bowl

595.	1.	*	Chajcar carved vase. Diesel-dorff 1926–33
126.	1.	*:60	Comitán 1, A1
73, 80, 86, 173.	1.	*:102	Yax. L 41, D3; 18, A9; 15, A3; L. 8, E1
76, 85, 89.	1:	*:102	Yax. Str. 44, Mid. step; L. 45, R2; L. 10, D2
61.	1:	*[528?]:130	Pal. H.S., D3
202, 203, 237.	1.	*.187	Beyer 45; 264; 265
23.	1.	*.187:23	Cop. F, B6
192.	1:27:	*:23	Beyer 254
193.	1.27:	*:23	Beyer 255
68.	1:	*	Quir. P. Cart. 12
594.	1?.	*:?	Uxmal tecali vase, D1
29.	1:503.	*:106v	Cop. H.S., Frag. A
157.	11.?:	*[95].528?:116	P.N., L. 3, P1
145.	12.	*	Bonam. Rm. 1
144.	12.	*:140	Bonam. Rm. 1
159.	12.	*:528	Bonam 1, H2
206.	12.136:	*	Beyer 268
134.	12:248:	*	Xcalum. S. build. W. pan.
151.	12.248:	*:140v	Xcocha frag.
92.	12.698:	*	Yax. L. 18, D4
194.	12?.27.	*:23	Beyer 256
59.	V?.265:25:	*	Pal. House C Sub.
40.	13.	*:60	Uxmal 1, A1
200.	13.	*:60	Beyer 262
397, 398.	13.	*:65	Uxmal Col. Alt. A1; rim
41.	13.60:	*	Kuna L. 1, C6
1.	13v.60:	*	Cop. U, T3
591.	13.	*	Kabah mask trunk A1
235.	13.	*:187	Beyer 43
402.	13.503.	*P:12	Pal. 96 Gl. G6. D.N. intro. gl.
275.	16.	*	P. 18
396.	16.	*:125?	Cop. 10, H4
276.	16.	*:140	D. 65a
102.	16?.	*[95]:34:?	P.N., L. 2, J'2
118.	head.18?:	*	Nar. 8, E4
399.	19.	*	Carac. conch god vase
306.	*.19:	*	M. 35b
210.	23.	*	Beyer 393

99.	24:60v.	*	P.N. Thr. 1, D'3
139.	24inv.	*P	Cop. Quetzal vase
47.	25.	*	Pal. Sun O14
136.	25:	*	Chama. Carey vase
112.	25:	*	Nar. 24, E18
104.	25:	*.?:142	Bonam. 1, O1
103.	25?.	*.4:178	P.N., L. 7, U1
405.	25:	*.*	Uaxac. sherd 5021
335[1].	*.25:	*	Cop. H''
336[1].	*.25:	*	Pal. Tower Scribe 2, D3
337, 341, 349[1].	*.25	*	Quir. A, D11; D, D22; Str. 1, R'
343, 344, 352, 353, 355, 359, 276, 377[1].	*.25:	*	Yax. L. 25, A4; L. 56, L2; L. 15, C5; L. 17, K1; L. 33, H12; 11, U4; 23, D16; 6, C10
389, 394[1].	*.25:	*	Carac. 17, A5; 18
380, 381, 408, 409[1].	*.25:	*	Bonam. 2, G6; I4; Rm. 1; Rm. 2
382[1].	*.25:	*	Seib. 7, B9
383[1].	*.25:	*	Nar. 8, F10
386[1].	*.25:	*	Tonina 7, D4
366[1].	*.25:	*:142	Yax. L. 13, F5
388[1].	*:142.25:	*:142	Jonuta 1, B4
348[1].	*:142.25:	*:142	Yax. 12, D6
368[1].		*P:25	Yax. L. 46, J''1
351[1].	1000.*.25:	*	Yax. L. 41, C4
362[1].	1000.*:25:	*P:142	Yax. L. 43, D3
410[1].	1000.*.25:	*	Bonam. Rm. 2
378[1].	*:196.25:	*	P.N. 12, Captive 8
78[1].	*.25:	*:136	Bonam. Rm. 2
391[1].		*?:25	Caracol Alt. 12, I5
403.	25:	*.*	Nebaj. Fenton vase
354[2].	*:25:	*	Yax. Str. 44, Mid. step C8
332, 333[2].	*.25:	*	Cop. A, F10; H.S. Step S
346[2].	*.25:	*	Yax. L. 27, D2
379[2].	*.25:	*	P.N. 23, L7
345[2].	*:142.25:	*:142	Yax. L. 27, G2
392, 393[2].	*:142.25:	*:142	Caracol Alt. 12, 1, 13; 2, 14
360, 364, 373[3].	*.25:	*	Yax. 11, A'8; 15, E2; 13, G4
369[3].	*:25:	*	Yax. 11, H1
361, 375[3].	*:142.25:	*:142	Yax. 20, C2; 23, B16
372[3].	*:142.25?:	*:142	Yax. 1, E14

363, 367[4].	*.25:	*	Yax. L. 43, D3; L. 38, D3
338–340,	*.25:	*	Quir. D, A19; A24; D19;
347, 350.			Str. 1, G'; frag.
371.	*:25:	*	Yax. 7, D5
395.	*.25:	*	Calak. 9, I6
401.	*.25:	*	Bonam. Rm. 2
309.	25:	*.*	P.N. Drum frag.
385.	*?.25:	*	Tonina 42
334.	*?.25:	*	Cop. C, C2
331.	*P:142.25:	*:142	Cop. U, V1
342.	*:142.25:	*:142	Quir. Alt. O, P1
358.	*:142.25:	*	Yax. 18, D6
384.	*:142.25:	*:142	Tonina 20, B4
357.	1000:*.25:	*	Pal. House A, frag.
356.	1000.*.25:	*	Yax. 11, S3
365[1].	*.203:	*	Yax. L. 2, Q1
370[1].	*.203?:	*	Yax. 11, C16
49.	*.203:	*:142	Nebaj. Fenton vase C4
96[3].		*.204P	Yax. 19, D2
137.	35v.	*	Uaxac. sherd 1202
7.	44:	*	Cop. A, B12
212.	45.60?:	*	Uxmal, Monjas capstone
125.	46.92:	*	Tik. L. 2, B6
253.	51.	*.?	M. 92a
9.	58.77:	*[95]	Cop. J, C4
74.	58.	*.181:23	Yax. L. 17, A4
79.	58.	*[95]:34	Yax. L. 37, R3
114.	58.	*[95]	Nar. 23, H15
195.	58:27:	*.23	Beyer 257
272.	58.552:	*	D. 50f
243.	59.	*	P. 16b
214.	IX.59:27:	*	Beyer 47
215.	IX.59:	*	Beyer 48
387.	60?	*	Dos Pilas H.S. 1, F8
220.	61.	* on side	Uaxac. I.S. vase
245.	62.	*	D. 51a
247.	62.	*:136	D. 38b
244.	II.62.	*	D. 52a
307.	62?:	*:*.104	M. 26b
242.	63:	*	D. 69
12.	68:	*?.23	Cop. J., W. 18
121.	74:	*:221?	Tik. L3, E4
120.	?.74:?:	*	Tik. L3, F3

292.	VII.84:	*	M. 35c
293.	I.84?:	*	D. 32b
291.	VII.85:	*	D. 48f
296.	87:	*	M. 96c
604.	88:	*[95]	Dos Pilas H.S. 2, D8
116.	89.?:	*.?	Nar. 13, G6
153.	528:116.89.89:	*	Quir. C, D7
196, 197.	89:	*	Beyer 258, 259
199.	89:?:	*	Beyer 261
201.	89.	*:148	Beyer 263
100.	92.	*	P.N. 15, C15
198.	92.	*	Beyer 260
287, 288.	96.	*:140	D. 66a; 68a
289.	96.	*:137	D. 72b
290.	96:	*.181	D. 73c
282.	96:	*	D. 61a
283, 284.	96.	*	D. 40c; 73a
588.	1.96:	*	Chama bat vase. Seler
285, 286.	IX.96:	*	D. 33a; 35a
14.	106?:	*[95]	Cop. J, E45
264, 265.	109.	*	D. 35a; 56a
266–270.	109.	*:140	D. 39b; 71c; 72a; 72c; 73a
271.	109.	*:24	D. 66b
42.	115?.	*:276	Acanceh tomb mural
27.	114.119:	*:34?	Cop. H.S. frag.
141.	118.	*:276	Br. Mus. vase. Bushnell & Digby
175.	119.	*.187	Pal. T. 18, stucco
98.	121.60v:	*	P.N. Thr. 1, F′5
108.	126.135?:	*	Cancuen Alt. 1, E1
11.	130?:	*P:125	Cop. J, W6
238.	133.	*:102	Beyer 51
239.	133:	*.102	Beyer 52
222.	133:669b.	*	Beyer 235
204.	135:	*	Beyer 266
107.	135?:	*	Seib. 12, A7
263.	136.	*:140	M. 11a
277.	IX.136:V:	*	Beyer 49
305.	137.192:	*	D. 73c
205.	142:	*	Beyer 267
278.	146:	*:505	M. 59b
39.	153.220:	*	Cop. 23, I1
119.	153.?:	*	Nar. 35, D9

162.	153.220:	*	Pal. Cross, C1
167.	153:683.217:	*:142	Quir. C, B6
404.	153.683:221:	*	Quir. F, B16
411–564.	162:	*.506	154 examples in codices
	or 162:506.	*	
310, 311.	194.162:506.	*	D. 67b; 68a
312.	11.162:506.	*	M. 22d
317–319.	166:	*	M. 10a; 11a; 12a
18.	168:	*:130	Cop. P, A9
37.	168:	*?:71	Los Higos 1, D11
322.	168:1016.	*	P. 16e
38.	87?.168:	*?	Los Higos 1, D4
155.	174:	*	Pal. T. 18, stucco
43.	174:	*	Yax. L. 37, S7
304.	177:	*.?	M. 37c
161.	182.	*	Yax. L. 32, H1
60.	190?.?:	*	Pal. H.S., C1
300.	193.178:	*	M. 59b
106.	200?:	*	Seib. 7, B6
101.	200?.?:	*[95]	P.N., L. 2, J2
84.	202.	*	Yax. 20, E5
93.	204.	*:102	Yax. L. 46, F''5
152b.	203?.588:	*.203	Mam shell figure
110.	205:	*	Nar. 24, A9
15.	205?.	*	Cop. 9, D4
168.	205?:220:	*	Quir. J, C8
251, 252.	207.51:	*	D. 70; 73a
250.	207:	*	D. 61
249.	XIX.207:	*	D. 61
46.	207.91.528:	*	D. 12a
122.	213:	*.181	Tik. Alt. V, Gl. 15
164.	217.	*	Pal. Sun, N1
2.	217.	*:142	Cop. U, S3
294, 295.	217:	*	M. 96c (twice)
165.	217.?:	*?	Pal. Inscr. W., L1
163.	11.217:25:	*	Pal. Cross, E2
178.	?.217:	*?	Pal. Cross, Balustr. A2
597, 612.	218:	*.181	Tik. 31, D23
169.	218?:	*	Quir. P, Cart. 2
176.	219.	*:142	Aguas Cal. 1, D3
44.	219:	*	D. 62
316.	219:506.	*	M. 25a

16.	219.1000:	*:23	Cop. P, E11
17.	1000:219?:	*[9?]	Cop. P, B8
221.	220?.	*:570:178	Tort. 6, F2
174.	220.?:	*	Yax. 11, E1
48.	226:	*.181	Pal. Inscr. M, H9
236.	228.	*.187	Beyer 44
138.	229.	*.27	Uaxac. sherd 3122
589.	229?:	*.18	Ikil L. 1, B
55.	230.221?:	*[528].130	Pal. Ruz 1, N11
254.	233:	*	D. 52b
279.	238.	*	D. 32a
280.	238.	*:140	M. 11b
605.	333.1:248:	*:24?	Dos Pilas, 2, D2
607.	333.11:	*:?	Aguatec. 2, D1
13.	265.	*	Chama. Carey vase
90.	281.12:	*:23:25	Yax. L. 10, E6
601, 602.	369:	*[95]	Dos Pilas H.S. 2, B1; A6
402.	13.503.	*P:12	Pal. 96 Gl. G8. D.N. intro.
308.	504:124v.	*:140	D. 65a
565–586.	506.or:	* or *.or:506	22 examples in M. (Gates 4.15, 4.15a)
315.	506^5?.	*^{5}:*.506	P. 17e
314.	506.	*:104	M. 94d
313.	506.	*:136	D. 43b
298.	558.	*:104	M. 94d
299.		*.558:192	M. 93d
321.	558.	*:612af	M. 92d
94.	563af.	*:188	Yax. L. 46, H''2
281.	567.238:	*	D. 67b
598.	VI:19.568:	*.181:88?	Tort. 6, F12
140.	586:	*.563	Cop. Quetzal vase
224, 230.	1.586:25:	*	Beyer 32; 38
227, 228.	12.586:25.	*	Beyer 35; 36
190.	12.586:27:	*	Beyer 252
191.	12?.586:	*.27	Beyer 253
226.	13.586:25:	*	Beyer 34
229.	13.586:205:	*	Beyer 37
231–234.	228.586:25:	*	Beyer 39; 41; 42; 33
225.	228.586:25?:	*	Beyer 40
216.	602:126.	*:25?	Pal. Fol. Sculpt. stone A10
330.	611.	*	M. 47a
328, 329.		*.611	M. 46a; 47a

63, 64, 129, 130.	767.	*	Pal. H.S., D6; Tower Scribe; Fol. Bal. L2; Cross Bal. L2
172.	12.666	[*]:142	Yax. L. 10, C4
400.	92.1:666	[*]	Pal. Inscr. W. P11
166.	666	[*]:87	Pal. Death, H3
217.	?.666	[*]:87	Pal. Sarcoph. lid top
219.	743.666	[*]	Pal. Creation Tab. D1
170, 171.	1000:666	[*]:142	Yax. L. 25, H5; L. 24, D'3
303.	687:	*	M. 100d
113.	1000.	*[95]	Nar. 29, G14
70.	1000.	*:178	Yax. L. 25, R2
3.	IV.	*:?	Cop. U, F2
217.	VIII.	*.25:23	P.N., L. 2, L1
147.	XIV?.V?:	*?	Bonam. Rm. 2
218.	XIV.?:	*:116	Beyer 269
26, 30.	?:	*	Cop. Rev. Stand, X; H.S. Step D
5.	?.	*[95]	Cop. A, D2
603.	?:	*	Dos Pilas, H.S. 4, C1
69.	?:	*	Yax. L. 25, H3
51, 56, 65, 77, 127.	?:	*	Pal. Inscr. W. N8; Ruz 1, R19; Tower, Sub.; T. 18 Stucco; jade earplug
609.	?.	*	Tamar. H.S. 1, J1
132.	?:	*	Carac. 6, F19
188.	?.	*	Beyer 177
52.	?:?.	*	Pal. Inscr. W. N10
128.	?.?:	*	Mor. 2, A11
131.	?:?:	*	Pal. Pal. Sub. Alt.
20.	?.	*:34	Cop. M, A5
28.	?:	*[95]:34	Cop. H.S., Frag.
117.	?:	*:125?	Nar. 22, E16
6.	?.	*:142	Cop. A, D10
248.	?.	*:142v	D. 34c
133.	?:?:	*:97	Calak. 51, D2
75.	?:	*:?	Yax. L. 14, A4
590.	?.	*:?	Xlabpak 4, C2
115.	?.	*:?	Nar. 23, E10
596.		*.1? or 25?	Chajcar vase. Dieseldorff, 1:171
593.		*:23	Kabah Sq. Alt.
31.		*:23	Cop. T. 11 Step 5

592.	*.23?	Kabah sculpt. jamb
88.	*:23:25	Yax. L. 10, E8
135.	*:23?	Xcalum. S. build. W. pan.
208.	*:24?	Beyer 271
10.	*:25	Cop. J, D7
67.	*.25	Quir. F, A10
32.	*:34	Cop. T. 11, Step 20
54.	*:34	Pal. Ruz 1, D6
81.	*:34	Yax. L. 26, Y'1
83.	*:87	Yax. 20, B2
179–187.	*:87	Beyer 74–76; 78–83
209.	*:87	Beyer 272
273, 274.	*:97:1	M. 34b3; 36
4.	*:102	Cop. A, E7
87.	*:102	Yax. 15, C3
109.	*.102:116	Pab. 1, B6
146.	*.102	Bonam. Rm. 2
301, 302.	*:104.104:8	M. 100d (twice)
599.	*.110	Uaxac. sherd
35.	*P.116	Cop. 13, F2
105.	*.125:92v	Tuxtla Mus. shell
246, 326, 327.	*.136	D. 36b; 39c; 39c
255–262.	*:140	D. 52b; 52b; 55b; 55b; 55b; 56b; 57b; 62
320.	*:140	D. 65a
8, 53.	*:142	Pal. Inscr. W. O9; Fol. Stucco
149.	*:142	Chajcar box frag.
610.	*:142	Tik. jade A5
189.	*:148	Beyer 178
154.	*[95]:150. 528:116	Quir. C, A13
611.	*.181:142?	Dos Pilas 3, A3
111.	*.181	Nar. 24, D11
600.	*.181:?	Dos Pilas H.S. 2, F7
82.	*:188	Yax. L. 26, L'1
374.	*.?:216	Acanceh tomb mural
587.	*[95].248	Hondo, Guat. Seler
297.	*:512.116	M. 36c
156.	*:528	Yax. L. 18, B5
160.	*:528.116	Xcalum. S. build. A4
158.	*[95]P.528. 116	P.N., L. 2, U1

91.	*.552	Yax. L. 18, D2
207.	*:552:?	Beyer 270
19.	*.582[644].	Cop. T. 11 S. door W. pan.
	1:12	C1
606.	*:624[533]	Dos Pilas, 2, C4
148.	*.XVI	Holmul cyl. vase
24, 25.	*:?	Cop. H.S., Frag.
33.	*P.?	Cop. T. 22, Step 5
66.	*:?	Quir. J, D18
177.	*:?	Pusil. D, E8
21.	*.?:?	Cop. M, B9

[1] Occur at the end of a section of text, panel, or side of a stela.

[2] Occur immediately before a D.N., and presumably close the preceding section of text.

[3] Appear before Glyph 1030m, the long-nosed god with upraised axe, which is the last glyph in a panel or side of a stela.

[4] Appear before a kin sign which is followed by the long-nosed god with upraised axe (1030 l–n) which is the last glyph in a panel or side of a stela.

[5] Inverted.

Numerically the most important Maya hieroglyph. Its importance seems best explained by ritualistic rather than phonetic usage. The compound 153–501 seems to have special associations with 13.0.0.0.0 4 Ahau 8 Cumku. The compound 501–25–501 appears to mark the end of a sentence, and may correspond to our "Amen" or the Spanish *"He dicho."*

For further examples of Glyph 501, see under Glyphs 502, 507?, 526, 530, 533?, 552, 558, 585, 586, 591, 594, 602, 625, 652, 686, 715, 733, 747, 760, 761, 765, 830.

GLYPH 502 (Imix-Ahau)
(49 Examples; Sheets 21–23)

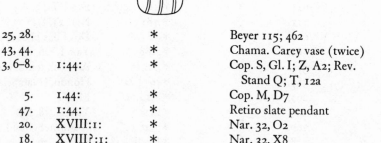

25, 28.		*	Beyer 115; 462
43, 44.		*	Chama. Carey vase (twice)
3, 6–8.	1:44:	*	Cop. S, Gl. I; Z, A2; Rev. Stand Q; T, 12a
5.	1.44:	*	Cop. M, D7
47.	1:44:	*	Retiro slate pendant
20.	XVIII:1:	*	Nar. 32, O2
18.	XVIII?:1:	*	Nar. 32, X8

19.	XVIII:1?:	*	Nar. 32, X2
31.	1.	*.126:23	Beyer 276
22.	13.44:	*	Nar. 35, F8
41.	25.	*.230	Beyer 286
23.	44?:	*:?	Carac. Alt. 12, F1
21.	59.	*:195	Nar. 32, Y3
45.	61.	*	Bonam. Rm. 1.
26.	87:501.533		Beyer 273
49.	103:	*	Sacchana, 2, C2
11.	110.110:	*:142	Cop. H'', C3
14.	IV.117:	*:110:126	Quir., Cart. 4
9.	121:	*	Cop. T. 11, Step 10
32.	126:	*	Beyer 277
33.	133:	*	Beyer 278
1.	168:	*.130	Cop. A, D6
12.	168?:	*.181:142	Cop. 3, A8
36.	188?.	*	Beyer 281
13.	195.	*P	Pal. Creation, A1
48.	220	[*]:178	Pal. T. 18, D17
29, 30.	229.	*:558	Beyer 274; 275
49.	229.	*:?	Ikil L. 1, A
24.	231.	*:565	Pal. T. 18, stucco
42.	533.	*	Beyer 287
34.	679af:	*	Beyer 279
15.	1000.	*:126	P.N. Alt. 1, B
35.	?:	*	Beyer 280
40.		*?:1	Beyer 285
10.		*:13	Cop. T. 11, Step 25
2.		*.25:142	Cop. A, G11
27.		*:110:?	Beyer 448
4.		*.114:25	Cop. J, D4
50.		*.130?	Ikil L. 2, G
37.		*:133	Beyer 282
38.		*:178?	Beyer 283
16.		*.181:25	P.N. shell E3
17.		*.181:?	P.N. 1, F2
39.		*:567.74	Beyer 284
46.		*:?	Chajcar box frag.

GLYPH 503 (Ik)
(50 Examples; Sheets 24, 25; Gates' Glyph 2; Zimmermann's Glyph 1322)

28.		*	Beyer 288
7¹.	1:179.	*:82	Pal. Ruz 1, I11
48.	1:179.	*:82	Tort. 6, D7
13¹.	1.179.	*	Yax. L. 27, F2
12¹, 14¹.	1.179:	*:24	Yax. L. 27, B2; 12, B2
40¹.	1:179.	*?:24	Yax. L. 59, M1
41¹.	1.179.?:	*:24	Yax. L. 28, T1
43.	1.533:103/58.	*:24	Tonina 31, Gl. 8, 9
44¹.	1.533.103:57?/ 1.58	[*]:24?	S. Ton, 2, Gl. 5, 6
30–34.	4v.?.	*:136	D. 69; 71c; 72b; 72c; 73a
37.	4v.?.	*:512	D. 34c
5¹.	11:179.23:	*:24	Pal. Inscr. W, Q10
49.	13.	*.501P:12	Pal. 96 Glyphs, G6. D.N. intro. gl.
35.	23.	*:136	D. 73c
50.	25:	*.151?	Aguatec. 1, A7
23.	40.168:	*	Seib. 10, B10
25.	40.168:	*	Motul 2, F1
38.	52.	*	M. 28d
15, 59.	52.	*:104	M. 28d (twice)
29.	58.	*	D. 73c
46.	86:	*:178	Pal. Sarcoph. edge, W
2.	1000.86:	*	Pal. Inscr. E. L8
3, 45.	1000.86:	*:178	Pal. Inscr. E. L4; Sarcoph. edge, E
19.	86?:	*	Yax. L. 49, N6
36.	122.	*:136	D 73c
27.	1044?.125:	*	Pal. Pal. Sub. Alt. 1
17.	1000.168:	*	Yax. L. 15, C3
16.	?.168?:	*:130	Yax. L. 41, C3
42.	179:	*	Beyer 289
10¹.	179:	*	Quir. E, D10
6.	1000.179:	*:82	Pal. Ruz 1, D9
8.	179.23:	*	Pal. House C, eaves
47¹.	179.23:	*	Tort. 6, G6

1.	179.23:	*	Cop. G, D4
9.	179?.	*?	R. Amarillo Alt. 2, A1
11.	204.179?:	*?:106?	Quir. G, L'2
4.	228.	*:142	Pal. Inscr. W. D10
18.	229.23?:	*:12	Yax. 21, H9
24.	513af:59.126:	*:12	Motul 2, B5
26.	?:	*	Pal. Sarcoph., Gl. 31
22.		*:?	P.N. 12, Capt. 17
20.		*v.255	P.N. Thr. 1, B
21.		*.?	P.N. 12, Capt. 11

1 These compounds follow a spiral (575) glyph often with a dragon-like head above it. In some cases this is Glyph 1021.

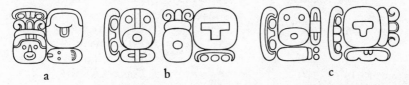

a   b   c

Latitude in Glyphic Writing. Three ways of expressing the same thing: *a*, Entry 7: 1:179.503:82; *b*, Entry 43: 1.533:103/ 58.503:24. In the published photograph Affix 24 looks like Affix 11, as here drawn, the result of a combination of shadow and weathering. In fact, Affix 11 never appears as a postfix. It is surely meant for Affix 24. *c*, Entry 44: 1.533.103:57?/ 1.58[503]:24.

Note that Affix 179 is really Affix 58 with Ahau (533) infixed. This is demonstrated by Nos. 43 and 44, in which Ahau is a separate glyph. In No. 43, Affix 58 is joined to 503; in No. 44, 503 is infixed in Affix 58. This series presents an interesting evidence on methods of glyphic construction. The divisions between the glyph blocks are shown by /. Tonina 31 is the circular altar now in the museum in Mexico City.

For further examples of Glyph 503, see under Glyphs 501, 534, and 559.

GLYPH 504 (Akbal)
(75 Examples; Sheets 27–29, 27a, 27b; Gates' Glyph 3; Zimmermann's Glyph 1323)

70.	107:	*?.178	P.N., L. 2, E2
75.	58.109:	*	Yalloch cyl. jar
14.	13.110:	*?	Nar. 35, D7
64.	122.	*?:178	Nar. 35, E11

6.	125:	*	Pal. Inscr. W, K2
16.	125.	*?:178	Nar. 35, E4
67.	125.	*:236	Xcalum. N. build. Serp. Gl. 13
63.	125:	*:125:544	Cop. Alt. St. 1, K
28.	125:	*.125:544	Ixkun 2, C12
17.	125:	*.125:544	Cop. 6, B7–A8
25.	125:	*.23.125:544. 59	Nar. 23, H21
24.	125:	*:23.125:544: 23	Cop. 16, A4–B4
76.	1.48:125:	*.59:125:544	Cop. 2, C1–C2
23.	40.125:	*?:23.125: 544.59	Carac. 19, Frag. 5
5.	168:?.	*:12	Cop. T. 11, S. door E. pan.
7.	228.	*	Pal. House A
13.	228?.	*	Nar. 22, B3
19.	544:	*	Cop. 2, C9
22.	544?:	*?	Cop. 15, C3
70.	544.	*?	M. 26b
30–50.	544.	*:241	21 examples in Dresden. (Gates' 45.9.1)
51.	544.	*:137	D. 37b
52.	544:116.	*:241	D. 68b
21.	1.544.	*:12	Cop. H.S., Frag. G.
29.	I:544.I:	*	Xcalum. S. build., W. panel
26, 27.	125:544:125	*	Nar. 13, A6–A7; 19, A9–A10
74.	204.544.	*:12	Pal. Pal. Sculpt. frag. D.N. intro. gl. ?
20.	?.?:544:	*:12	Cop. 2, G1
58.	1:	712[*]	Yax. 7, C6
73.	712.125?:	*?	Cop. 10, F3
1.	1.712.125.	*:24	Cop. 7, A11
72.	1.712:125?.	*:4?	Cop. 12, A12
54.	11.	712[*]:81:24	Pal. Cross. E3
56.	12.	712[*]:81:24	Pal. Inscr. W. K3
59.	12?.	712[*]	P.N. 25, F1
4.	13.712:81.125?.	*.82	Cop. 6, D9
3.	13.712.125:	*:24?	Cop. I, C5
10.	74:	712[*].82	Yax. 18, B5
11.	74:	712[*]:178	Pusil. D, D14
53.	89.	712[*]:24	Cop. 6, C2

55.	89.11:	712[*]	Pal. Fol. L2
2.	89:712:81.59:	* :24	Cop. P, A10–B10
9.	89.712.59.122:	* :82	Yax. 18, A10–A11
60.	122:	712[*]	P.N., L. 2, B'1
61.	122.	712[*]	P.N., L. 2, I2
62.	89.712.59.126:	* :24	Tik. L. 4, D3–C4
57.	228.	712[*]:24	Pal. Tower Scribe 1, C1
8.	228:712?.228:	* :24	Pal. Tower Scribe 2, B1
15.	228?.	712[*]	Nar. 35, D11
69.		* .23:60	Xcocha frag.
68.		* .122:102	Xcalum. N. build. Serp. Gl. 17
65.		* .148	Xcalum. N. build. W. col.
66.		* :561	Beyer 290

The 504–544 compound is the well-known light-darkness symbol common on the monuments and in the divinatory almanacs of Codex Dresden. The widely distributed 712–504 compound may occur as two glyphs or as 712 with 504 infixed.

For further examples of Glyph 504, see under Glyphs 501, 670, 712, 756, and 757.

GLYPH 505 (Akbal on side)
(3 Examples; Sheet 30)

3.	172?.	*	Acanceh tomb mural
1.	1000:23.168?:	*	P.N. 3, E4
2.	1000:?.168?:	*	P.N. 3, D3

The glyph before number 1 is 1000. katun; before number 2, 1000.168: katun. See also under Glyphs 501 and 526.

GLYPH 506 Kan (Maize)
(161 Examples; Sheets 31–34; Gates' Glyph 4; Zimmermann's Glyph 1324)

9.		*	Cop. Alt. of E
10.		*P	R. Amarillo Alt. 1, E2
31.		*	R. Amarillo Alt. 1, E1

71, 72, 81, 119.		*	M. 7b; 28c; 96c; 24c
107.		*	D. 43a
114.		* dot circled	D. 7c
125–29.		*:*	M. 93d; 94d; 104b (pictures)
130.		*.*	M. 104b
131.		*.*	P. 18a
138–45.		*:*.*	M. 57b; 68b; 69b; 104b; P. 2b; 4b; 17b; D. 34a
158.	1.	*	Pal. T. 21, Scribe, D3
46.	1.	*:24	Beyer 58
45.	1.	*:24?	Beyer 57
67.	1.	*:8	Beyer 292
68.	1:211?:	*	Beyer 293
77.	10.126.	*:130	D. 67b
44.	11?.	*:24?	Beyer 56
76.	17:	*.130	D. 31b
101.	17:	*.116	D. 27a
102.	17:	*.181	M. 11b
103.	17:	*.*	D. 26c
104.	17:	*.*:104	M. 8
148.	27.86?:	*[178]:2	Holmul tripod, Gl. 15
113.	IX.33:	*.87:104	M. 103b
115.	33?.136:	*.136	M. 35c
111.	58.33:	*	D. 66b
75.	74.	*:130	D. 68b
40.	77?.	*:130?	Xcalum. I.S. build., **rt. col.**
155.	78:	*	D. 62c. Rare variant of Cumku
99.	84:	*	M. 7b
136.	87.	*.*:104	M. 107b
137.	IX.87:	*:104	M. 106b
160.	103?.	*	Chama. bat vase. Seler
108.	109:	*	D. 26b
109.	109.	*	D. 32 (seat)
110.	109.	*.*	D. 41c
3.	115:	*.184.74	Quir. C, C8
33.	115:	*:142	Yax. L. 25, U1
6.	115.	*:125	Cop. Rev. Stand, D
21, 23.	115:	*:178	Pal. Inscr. W. O9; Ruz 1, D4
18.	115.	*:178	Pal. Inscr. W. B7

157.	115.	*:178	Tort. 6, H9
94.	115.	*:136	D. 31b
100.	115.	*:140	D. 47c
8.	3.117:	*	Cop. Alt. of 13, A1
149.	117?.	*[178]:142	Holmul tripod, Gl. 29
90.	120.	*.130:136	D. 68b
44.	120?.	*	Quir. P, Cart. 5
70.	122:	*:178	Beyer 295
98.	126.	*	D. 43a
63.	130.	*	Beyer 86
64.	130:	*	Beyer 87
65, 66.	130:	*:136	Beyer 88; 89
79, 80.	130:	*	D. 42c; 69b
83.	130.	*:136	D. 34a
28.	130?:	*:60?	Quir. M, D1
37.	130?.	*:126?	Tonina 1, D1
78.	136.626.	*:130	D. 67b
43.	143:	*	Yula L. 1, C1
35.	148.?:	*	P.N. jade head
154.	155:	*	Month Cumku glyph
152.	155:	*.25	M. 70b
150.	156:	*.181	D. 43b
151.	181.156:	*.181	D. 42b
106.	162:	*	D. 33a
132, 133.	162:	*.*	M. 10b; 11b
134.	162:	*.*:142?	M. 10b
105.	17.162:	*	D. 27a
2.	173.	*P:178	Cop. B, A9
26, 27.	178:	*P	Pal. 96 Gl. H3; J2
29.	178:	*	Pal. Cross W. Pan. I4
11, 12, 30.	178?:	*	Pal. Cross, O1; Sun, E. Pan. D4; Fol. Cross, F4
25.	178:	*:178?	Pal. Ruz 1, L8
57–59.	190.	*:178	Beyer 74; 75; 78
38.	198:	*	Pal. Sarcoph. Gl. 35
15, 16.	12.198:	*:178	Pal. Inscr. E. L11; N4
93.	199.	*	D. 67b
91, 92.	199.	*:136	D. 72a; 72c
159.	228.	*:60	Chama. bat vase. Seler
19.	228.	*:178	Pal. Inscr. W. B12
34.	228.168:	*	Yax. L. 17, I1
47.	228.	*P:126	Beyer 67

48–56.	228.	*:126	Beyer 61–66; 68; 70; 71
156.	271:	*	Cop. 3, A7. Rare form of Cumku
13.	12.507:	*	Pal. Sun, G1
14.	12:507:	*	Pal. Sun, M3
116.	544:	*	M. 25c
117.	544.	*:136	M. 11b
148, 17.	679af.25:	*	Pal. Inscr. M. A7; A8
4, 5.	Head:	*	Cop. H.S. Step O (twice)
32.	1000:	*:142	Yax. L. 25, G1
153.	1000.	*:178	Pal. Sarcoph. edge W
12.	?.	*	Pal. Fol. F4
20.	?:	*:178	Pal. Inscr. W. D8
22.	?:	*:178?	Pal. Inscr. W. Q2
24.	?.	*:57	Pal. Ruz 1, E14
121.	?:	*	M. 35c
1.	?.?:	*	Cop. N, Ped.
506.	161.?.?:	*	Tamar. H.S. 2, C12
69.		*.8:178	Beyer 294
42.		*:59?	Xcalum. I.S. build. lt. lint.
73.		*:87?	M. 24d
112, 123, 124.		*:104	M. 78c; 77c; 78b
135.		*.*:104	M. 105b
146, 147.		*:*.*:104	M. 77b; 77d
74.	IX.	*:130	D. 65b
84–86.		*.130:136	D. 22a; 22b; 22c
87–89.		*.136:130	D. 30b; 30b; 31b
41.		*:130?	Xcalum. I.S. build. rt. lint.
82, 120.		*:136	D. 53b; 66a
95–97.		*.181:136	D. 14b (3 times)
122.		*.178:136	D. 42a
39.		*P:178	Pal. Sarcoph. Gl. 30
60–61.		*[190]:178	Beyer 76; 80
62.		*[190?]:178	Beyer 81
36.		*:184	M. Cow Alt. 2, B3
118.		*.281	D. 36a

Nos. 63–66 follow Glyphs 568 and 228–608. Nos. 11, 12, 25–30, and perhaps 42 follow Glyph 507 (see also Nos. 13 and 14, which include 507). Nos. 47–56 precede a kin, hand and lunar compound (544:217.181:178). No. 53 is personified.

For further examples of Glyph 506, see under Glyphs 501, 532?, 623, 652, 668, 686, 736, 739, 795, 796, 799, and 839.

GLYPH 507 (Spotted Kan)
(102 Examples; Sheets 35–37; Gates' Glyph 50.4.1 and 14.11; Zimmermann's
Glyph 1362)

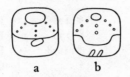

a   b

51.	1.	*P	Xcocha frag.
57.	1.	*?:25	M. 80b
10.	12.	*:126	R. Amarillo Alt. 1, D2
34.	12.1:	*:24	P.N. 12, Capt. Gl. 45
43.	13.	*:24	Beyer 55
83.	59inv.	*	M. 71b
82.	62.	*	M. 29a
58–60.	62.	*:23	M. 40b; 42c; 63b
61–71.	62.	*:24	D. 5a; 8a; 9a; 11c; 14b; 14c; 16b; 22b; 65b 72b; 72c
72–81.	62.	*:24	M. 16a; 19a; 41c; 49c; 50c; (4 times); 101c; 103b
84.		*.62:24	M. 91b
85.	62.	*.24?:25	M. 106c
86, 87.	62.	*:276	M. 17a; 41a
88.	62.	*[573]	M. 103b
99.	62.	*:12	P. 15c
49.	65:	*?	Uaxac. I.S. vase
89, 90.	74.	*:24	D. 4a; 7a
91.	74.	*.24	M. 90a
38.	102:	*	Jonuta 2, B2
55.	109.	*	Carac. conch god vase
92.	109.	*	D. 30b
7, 8.	117:	*	Cop. T. 11 step, 6; 23
39.	117.	*	Pal. T. 18, D18
33.	117?.	*	P.N. jade jaguar head
30.	117?:	*	Yax. L. 43, D3
4.	117.168:	*	Cop. T. 11, W. pan. C3
1, 17.	117?.168:	*	Cop. R, D1; T. 21a, k
9.	150.117.	*	Cop. T. 11, Step 24
44.	head:87.117:	*	Beyer 84
45.	head.87:117:	*	Beyer 85
12.	130:	*	Pal. Fol. C13
13.	12.130:	*	Pal. Fol. F4

47.	177.	*	Nebaj. Fenton vase D6
102.	177.	*	Jade head, Br. Mus.
52–54.	177.	*:1	Holmul tripod vase, Gls. 16; 18; 30
20.	177:	*:178	Pal. Ruz 1, L11
21.	177.	*:178	Pal. Ruz 1, O11
55.	177.	*?:178	Ikil L. 2, D
5.	177?:	*	Cop. 6, C2
2, 3.		*.177	Cop. a, E4; C5
11.	12.177:	*	Pal. Cross O1
19.	12:177:	*	Pal. Ruz 1, L8
25.	177.12:	*	Pal. Cross Shrine
18.	12:177.198:	*:178	Pal. Ruz 1, D12
36.	177?.25:	*	Tuxtla shell B6
93, 94.	181.687a.	*	M. 84b (twice)
95.	181.	*?:687a	M. 84b
6.	200:	*:24?	Cop. W'
22, 23, 26.	12:200:	*	Pal. 96 Gl. H3; J2; Sun E. pan.
29.	12.200:	*	Pal. T. 18 Stucco
14.	200?:130:	*	Pal. Sun N18
24.	?:200.	*	Pal. Ruz 2, G2
41.	228.	*:24	Beyer 53
42.	228.	*.24	Beyer 54
48.	228.	*:142	Huehuetenango vase
50.	228.	*P	R. Hondo blowgun vase
40.	679af.25:	*P	Pal. T. 18 Stucco
28.	513af?:	*	Yax. L. 53, H1
37.	679af.513af:	*	P.N. Thr. 1, B1
96.	1016?.	*?:24	D. 15a
97.		*.1016	D. 15a
46.	1:II:	*:178	Beyer 291
56.	?.	*P	Peten cyl. jar. Thompson 1950
46.	?.	*	Quir. Str. 1 frag.
101.	?.	*:126?	P.N. Sting ray 2.
98.	?.	*:140	D. 41a
37.	?.?:	*	Seib. 7, B5
31.		*.24?	Yax. L. 10, F7
15.		*.178	Holmul. cyl. vase
27.		*.181?	Quir. Str. 1, E'
100.		*:501af?	D. 66b

Some examples of Glyph 507 in the codices are hardly distinguishable from Glyph 558. Glyph 507 appears in association with 506 at Palenque.

GLYPH 508 (Chicchan)
(4 Examples)

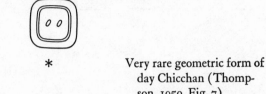

1.		*	Very rare geometric form of day Chicchan (Thompson, 1950, Fig. 7)
2.		*	Rare form of day Chicchan in codices (Bowditch, 1910, Pl. 1, No. 16)
3.	74?:	*:74	Nar. 8, B8
4.		*:23	M. Cow shell disk (Pl. 49, 5)

Glyph 508 also forms Affix 114 and is a constituent of the Yax affix (16) of the Classic period texts, but not in the codices. See also under Glyph 606.

GLYPH 509 (Cimi)
(5 Examples; Gates' Glyph 21 (in part); Zimmermann's Glyph 153)

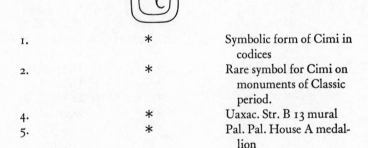

1.		*	Symbolic form of Cimi in codices
2.		*	Rare symbol for Cimi on monuments of Classic period.
4.		*	Uaxac. Str. B 13 mural
5.		*	Pal. Pal. House A medallion
3.	59.	*:669.	M. 40c

See also under Glyph 669.

GLYPH 510 (Lamat-Venus)
(117 Examples; Sheets 38, 39, 39a; Gates' Glyph 326; Zimmermann's Glyph 1328)

a	b	c	d

2.		*	Cop. R, H2
16.		*	Beyer 369
19.		*	Etzna, 18, I2
20–22.		*	D. 24c; 46c; 53a
94^1.		*?	Naachtun 1, A12
91^1.		*?	Quir. Alt. of O, O'2
3.		*^{a}	Cop. C, A4
8, 9.		*^{a}	Quir. E, D18; J, C8
10, 11.		*^{a}	Yax. 10, C5; F3
6.		*^{a}	Pal. House A, corridor
73.		*^{a}	Beyer 390
12.		*^{b}	Yax. L. 10, A4
97.		*^{b}	Nar. H.S. N1
18.		*^{b}	Xcalum. N. build. E. col.
103.	1.	*^{b}:683:12	Pal. 96 Gl. E7. D.N. intro. gl.
92^1.	1.17?:	*	Yax. 12, G3
90^1.	2.	*?:116	Quir. P, Cart. 10
14.	12?.	*	P.N. jade jaguar head
89^1.	16.	*[544]	Cop. 9, B9
81.	35?.	*^{b}:?	Nar. H.S. A2
5.	35?.	*^{b}:575.35?	Pal. Inscr. M. G7
13.	89.	*^{b}:35.575	P.N. Thr. 1, E'6
23–59.	109.	*	D. 24; 46–50
60–62.	109:	*	D. 24 (three times)
63–68.	109:	*^{a}	D. 24; 46; 50
69–71.	109.	*^{a}	D. 46; 46; 47
1.	109:	*	Cop. T. 11, S. door, W. pan.
4.	1.109?:	*^{a}	Los Higos 1, D5
95.	115.	*	M. 59c
113.	119.	*^{b}:575	Carac. 3, F3
85^1.	122.	*[544]	Cop. A, D9

86¹.	122.	*[544]:116	Cop. N, B1
96.	168?:	*	Uaxac. 13, B2
104.	236:	*ᵃ	Chichén Monjas
72.	227 inv.	*	P. 4b
74, 75.	227 inv.	*ᵃ	D. 57b; 58b
102.	325.	*ᵇ:526.326:19	Tort. 6, C4
100.	1.16:586.130:	*ᵃ	Yax. L. 34, I7
101.	586:	*ᵃ?	Xultun, 18, A6
108.	679:	*ᵇ	Tort. 6, A11
79, 80.	1000.	*ᵃ	Nar. L. 1, C4; 8, F5
83.	1021:1044.	*ᵃ	Tik. 5, B11
114–117.	aged head.	*ᵃ:23	Carac. 3, C12b; B15b; F10b; A9
105.	Peccary:	*ᵃ	Chichén Monjas
106.	Sky monster:	*ᵃ	Chichén Monjas
109.	?.?:	*d	Dos Pilas 11, B1
17.	?:	*ᵃ	Beyer 370
107.	?.	*ᵇ?:563.?:178	Tik. Alt. 7
7.	IX.	*ᵇ:575?	Pal. carved pot
15.	?.	*:526	P.N. 12, D1
76.		*ᵇ:17	P. 8c
93¹.		*?:23	Seib. 8, A7
88¹.		[528]*:24	Cop. G', A3
78.		*ᵇ:104?	P. 5d
87¹.		[528]*:116	Cop. S, J
82.		*ᵇ:119.575	Tik. L. 3, B4
84.		*ᵇ:119.575. 119v	Tik. L. 2, B8
77.		*ᵇ.192:526	D. 71a
99.		*ᵇ.544:116	Chajcar, pottery box frag.
111.		*ᵇ:35.176:528. 528.35	Dos Pilas 2, C1
98.		*ᵇ:575	Yax. L. 41, A2
110.		*ᵇ:35?.575. 35?:126	Dos Pilas H.S. 2, A2
112.		*ᵇ:575	Aguatec. 2, A2

ᵃ Only the bottom half or right half of the glyph is present.
ᵇ Only the top half or left half of the glyph is present.
¹ Nos. 85–94 inclusive are somewhat aberrant forms and possibly do not belong here.

Note the use of Glyph 510 as the geometric form of the variable element of the I.S. introductory glyph corresponding to the month Yax. The presence of the *chac* affix (109) both on the monuments and in Codex Dresden is of interest since a name for the planet Venus is *chac ek,* "great" or "red" star.

Unidentifiable gods or animals are joined to Glyph 510 over the doorway of the Monjas east wing in addition to the two already noted.

GLYPH 511 (Muluc)
(56 Examples; Sheets 41–49; Gates' Glyph 9; Zimmermann's Glyph 1329)

40.		*	Day Muluc in codices and sometimes on monuments.
1, 5, 7, 104, 13, 25, 32, 26.	32:168:	*	Yax. L. 25, A4; L. 30, G3; L. 31, L2; 7, C5; 11, I3; L. 9, B8; L. 52, I1; 3, A7
37.	32:168:	*:131	Yax. L. 10, B3
34, 29, 39, 43, 4, 12.	36.168:	*	Yax. L. 58, E4; L. 32, A11; L. 3, I3; 11, J3; 12, D5; 11, E4
105.	36:168:	*	Yax. 19, B2
106, 107.	36?.168:	*	Yax. 1, E13; 13, G3
33.	36?:168:	*	Yax. 11, Z7
42.	36.168:	*:130	Yax. L. 2, J3
35.	36.168:	*:136	Yax. L. 39, C4
27, 41, 28.	37.168:	*	Yax. 18, D7; L. 2, O4; L. 33, H8
24.	37:168:	*	Yax. L. 21, D2
36, 39.	37?.168:	*	Yax. 15, E1; L. 1, H1
11.	37?:168:	*	Yax. Str. 44, mid. step
2.	38:168:	*	Yax. L. 56, L2
109.	38?.168:	*	Yax. 23, D14
31.	?.168:	*	Yax. 10, D4
108.	?.168:	*:130	Yax. 23, A15
6, 30.	?:168?:	*	Yax. L. 31, I2; 10, M2
113.	?.168:	*?	Bonam. L. 2, C4
3.	168:	*.130	Yax. L. 27, D2
114.	1000.168:	*	Yax. L. 14, B1
8.	168?:	*:142	Yax. L. 53, H1
57.	220?:	*:116?	Nar. 23, E21
54, 55.	552 [95].	*	M. 2c; 3b

53.	VII.IX:	*	M. 35a
56.	17.115?.VIII.	*:856	Aguatec. 1, D8
41.		*:74 or 60?: 126	Nar. 8, B8
42–49.		*.181:96	D. 10b; 11b (4 times); 12b (thrice)
50, 51.		*.181:96	P. 2b; c
52.		*.96.181	P. 8b

Of the 35–511 compound with "water" affixes, all, except Nos. 1, 2, 34, 36, 37, 42, and 113 precede the 168–562 (Ben-Ich-cleft sky) compound with similar "water" affixes. Nos. 2 and 104 follow instead of preceding this compound, and others form part of the same clause (Thompson, 1950, Fig. 46). This 168–511 compound is confined to Yaxchilán and its dependency, Bonampak.

It is probable that Affix 196 is connected with Glyph 511, and the two may be identical.

For further examples of Glyph 511, see under Glyphs 103, 552, 607, 670, 683, 743, and 804.

GLYPH 512 (Muluc-Burden)
(28 Examples; Sheets 51–56)

a   b

15.	87.	*	Pal. H.S. C3
14.	87.	*.181:25	Pal. H.S. C4
17.	87.	*:25	Yax. L. 16, A2
19.	87?.	*.181.25	Yax. 18, A4
22.	87?.	*.181:25	Yax. 15, A2
24.	87?.	*?:181?.25	Yax. L. 5, B2
30.	87.	*.203.181	Yax. 19, A3
44.	87?.?:	*	Cop. U, T4
7.	87?.	*	Alt. Sac. 4, D12
2.	87?.	*:103?	P.N., L. 3, B'6
16.	1:87.	*	Quir. Alt. O, S2
83.	12:87?.	*.528?:130?	P.N. 12, D15
12.	25.87.	*	Comitán 1, D1
3.	59:58.1.87?.	*:127	P.N. 8, C22
84.	?.87?.	*:?	P.N. 39, B7

4.	?:84:	*?:142	Seib. H.S. L1
18, 55.	87.	*v.181:25	Yax. Str. 44, S.E. up. step: L. 46, F' '3
58.	87?.	*v.116:126	Bonam. Rm. 1
21.	87?.	*v.180:205	Yax. L. 44, L'3
54a.	87.168:	*.130	Kuna L. 1, D4
52–54.	228.168:197.	*v	Yax. L. 37, T3; L. 35, X3; L. 49, P2
57.	197.	*[501?].226	Tamar. H.S. 2, F1–2
56.	110:236?:	*[192]	Tik. 31, L2
1.	228.115?.	*	P.N., L. 3, Y1
33.	?.	*	Rossbach Coll.

Nos. 512 and 515 are probably variants of the same glyph and No. 532 probably differs only in the infix of the Cauac element.

Nos. 15, 18, 19, 21, 22, 24, 32, 55, and 59–61 have moon and comb (181 and 25) postfixes. No. 30 has fish-head (the personified form of comb) and moon postfixes. No. 15 precedes, all the others in this group immediately follow, the month sign of a C.R. date. No. 17 lacks the lunar postfix, but also immediately follows a C.R. No. 16 has only the comb postfix and is separated by two glyphs from the C.R., but one of those intervening glyphs is the moon sign.

It is a fair assumption that these examples represent a parallel to the burden of the year or time period of the codices (Thompson, 1950, 267–68) particularly because the codex glyph (No. 601) usually has the *te* (87) prefix and may have the comb (25) and Lunar (181) postfixes. Some such generalized meaning as "the count of the journey of time" seems to be indicated.

For further examples of Glyph 512, see under Glyphs 501, 503, 521, and 582?.

The very unusual No. 56 seems to depict a mat seat.

GLYPH 513 (Muluc)
(92 Examples; Sheets 41–50, 60; Gates' Glyph 145.6; Zimmermann with 1308a)

49.		*	P.N., L. 3, X7
127.		*	Day sign Muluc
21.		*	Cop. 6, D9
25.	I.	*:59	Cop. 11, B3
116.	IV.	*	Quir. D, A23
23.	IX.	*	Cop. I, C3
131.	12.	*:59	Ikil, L. 2, F

112.	16.168?:	*:142	Moral. 2, E3
76.	25:	*	Pusil. carved bone
130.	59.	*.87?	Peto vase Gl. 7
119.	59.168:	*	Pal. Death Head H2
20.	59:168:	*:130	Cop. K, K1
69.	62.81:	*	Holmul cyl. vase
111.	62?:	*:4	Pal. Sun, N. pil.
92.	74:	*?:89	Carac. 3, A18b
68.	74?:	*	Bonam. Rm. 1
26.	78:	*	Cop. J, B8
117.	IV:78:	*	Quir. F, A8
115.	IV:78?:	*	Quir. D, B18
118.	IX:78:	*?	Quir. F, A16
114.	XIII.78:	*	Tik. 17, H3
115.	XIV.78:	*	Tik. 5, B8
47.	79:	*.180	P.N. Thr. 1, H2
53.	84:	*:?:126	P.N. Alt. Sup. B3
124.	90:	*	M. 35c
22.	129.	*	Cop. I, C5
30.	129?:	*	Cop. H.S. Frag. Gxii
27.	129.	*?	Cop. J, D8
134, 135.	130:	*.48	Tik. 31, F5; E15
54.	130.86?:	*	P.N. 12, Capt. Gl. 10
9.	168:	*:130	Yax. Str. 44, S.E. up. step
125.	115.168?:	*?	P.N. sting ray 2
121.	125.168:	*	Yax. 12, H1
14.	125v:168:	*	Yax. L. 35, V3
15–18, 32.	125v:168:	*:142?	Yax. L. 37, R5; T2; S5; L. 35, X2; V7
19, 20.	125v:168:	*:142?	Yax. L. 37, T7; L. 35, X6
63.	125.168:	*	Pal. H.S., D1
64.	125.168:	*.130	Carac. 6, E21, F8
65.	125.168:	*.?	Carac. 6, D12
126.	125.168:	*	Ojos Agua, 1, A10
132.	1:125.168:	*	Tik. 31, P2
110.	125?.168?:	*	Tonina 7, C5
124.	126.168:	*?	P.N. sting ray 2
38.	126:168:	*:131	Yax. L. 10, F3
29.	168:	*:130	Cop. H.S. frag.
48.	168:	*.?	P.N. jade jaguar head
61.	168?:	*.181	P.N. 13, E6
60.	?.168?:	*:130	Tik. Alt. 5, Gl. 21
123.	1000.168:	*	P.N. shell C1

122.	Grotesque head.168:	*:130	Yax. L. 45, T2
44.	187:	*	Pal. H.S. D6
101, 102.	187:	*	Xcalum. I.S. Build. Rt. Lint. B1; F1
51.	196.12?:	*	P.N., L. 3, B7
55.	196?.	*:?	Cayo L. 1, D11
50.	220:	*	P.N., L3, E'
45.	220.	*:69?	Pal. Madrid Tab. 1
46.	220.74?:	*?	Quir. D, A20
75.	253:	*.56	Uaxac. I.S. vase
133.	281:	*:23	Tik. 31, C17
52.	513af:	*:131?	P.N. Alt. Sup. A3
79.	679af.	*:59	Quir. C, A12
128.	679af.or:	*.or:59	Count forward or posterior indicator
136.		*.35	Tort. 6, A11
59.		*:57v	M. Cow Alt. 2, B2
77.		*:59	Pal. T. 18, D17
66.		*:59	Calak. 53, A3
129.		*.or:59.or:126	Count backward or anterior indicator
72–74.		*.59:126	Xcalum. S. build. E. inner pan.; front cent. lint.; N. build. Frag. X
80–84.		*:59:126	Quir. C, A9; A11; B13; E, C15; C17; P, E9
95, 96.		*:59:126	Nar. 32, X4; 12, G6
97, 98.		*:59:126	Moral. 2, B10; D12
94.		*.59:126	Nar. 22, G4
56.		*.59:126	Pusil. K, B5
78.		*.126:59	Quir. C, C9
70.		*.126:59	Pal. T. 18, D13
71.		*.?	Carac. Alt. 12, X6
91.		*:59:126	Dos Pilas Sculpt. C, B6

Glyph 513, placed in a cartouche, is the commoner form of the day Muluc. The compounds 513–59–126 and 679af–513–59 are the anterior and posterior date indicators, glyphs which inform us whether a time count is forward or backward. Further examples listed above are irregular in that they are not associated with distance numbers (Thompson, 1950, 162–64).

For further examples of Glyph 513, see under Glyphs 17, 507, 515, 526, 528, 546, 559, 564, 568, 580, 585, 607, 620, 632, 666?, 675?, 679, 698, 757, 758.

GLYPH 514 (Muluc Variant)
(22 Examples; Sheet 40)

10–18.	78:	*	Yax. L. 37, S4; T6; L. 35, U3; U5; W5; L. 49, O1; O6; P7; M1
22.	78:	*	Tonina 27, Gl. 5
21.	78:	*.4	Tzend. 1, A6
19.	78:	*.4:126	Tik. T. 4, L. 2, A15
20.	78:	*:188	Pal. Cross K1
3.	78:	*?	Pal. H.S. C6
4, 6.	196.78:	*	Pal. Death Head D2; frag.
5.	220.78:	*	Pal. Tower Scribe 1, A5
7–9.	220.78:	*	Yax. L. 37, Q3; S1; L. 35, W1
2.	220.78:	*:69	Pal. Ruz 1, Q17
1.	IX.78:	*:126?	Pal. Inscr. W. T11

A rare example of a main sign always compounded with the same affix (78). The compound, confined to Chiapas and Tikal, disappears from Yaxchilán texts at an early date, but in modified form survives as the rare Affix 216.

GLYPH 515 (Muluc Burden)
(88 Examples; Sheets 51–56, 65, 65a, 65b; Gates' Glyph 145; Zimmermann's Glyph 1363)

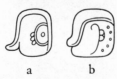

a   b

126.		*	M. 101c
127, 128.		*:*	M. 102c (twice)
86, 87.	1.	*:*	M. 102c
96.	1.	*	M. 101c
136.	1:	*	Pusil. solid-footed flat-based bowl
113.	1.614:	*.181	Pal. frag.
57.	32.	*:126	Xcalum. I.S. build. lt. col.

129.	32[202].	*	P.N. Thr. 1, C′
88.	57.	*.181:25?	D. 3a
25, 26.	87.	*.181:25	Yax. L. 10, B7; L. 41, D1
59, 60.	87.	*.25.181	Bonam. L. 1, A3; L. 2, A3
61.	87.	*.181:25	Bonam. L. 3, A3
20.	87.	*.181:25	Yax. 20, E3
10.	87?.	*.181:25?	Nar. 22, H2
51.	87.	*.181	Chajcar pottery base
31.	87.	*.181	Yax. 5, A2
37.	87?.	*.181	Cop. R, L1
80.	87.	*:528:136	Yax. Str. 44, Mid. Up. Step C9
36.	87.	*:116:125	Cop. 2, C1
34.	87.	*.?	Cop. T. 11, W. door S. pan.
38.	87?.	*?:23	Cop. 2, B7
23.	87.?:	*	Yax. L. 6, B5
8.	87?.	*	Pusil. D, E7
83.	87?.	*?.125:25?	La Mar 3, B11
50.	87.	*?	Bonam. Rm. 1
48.	87.	*:513af	Beyer 624
99–101.	1.87.	*.62	D. 2b; 2b; 2c
102.	1.87.	*.130	D. 2c
103.	1.87.	*.126	D. 2c
137.	12.87?.	*:130?	Tamar. H.S. 1, H1
79.	12.87.	*[?]	La Mar 3, C2
72, 73.	87:197?:	*?	Beyer 176; 177
43.	204.?:87.	*.126:135	Cop. A, B8
39.	92:153.?:	*	Cop. U, Q3
62–65.	197.	*:178	Beyer 412–415
69.	197.	*.118:178	Beyer 410
70.	197.	*.117:178?	Beyer 411
66.	197.	*:254	Beyer 416
71.	1.197.	*?	Beyer 419
68.	IX.197.	*:178	Beyer 418
67.	12:IX.197?.	*:254	Beyer 417
11.	197:?.?:	*	Tik. 5, A11
28.	200.	*.87	Yax. L. 18, D5
42.	217:?:	*	Cop. H′′, C2
136.	221.	*:200?	Tik. 31, C7
135.	221:60:	*:?	Pal. Sun, basement
114.	221:	*?:*	P.N., L. 12, N1
130, 131.	221:	*?:*.48	Pal. House C, eaves F4; Cross Balustr. G1

133.	221:	*?:*.181	Pal. Fol. Balustr. G1
132.	48.221:	*?:*	Pal. House A, Pier C
13.	228.23?:	*	Tonina 8, Side B
84–87.	207.242:	*	M. 106c (4 times)
113.	1.614:	*.181	Pal. frag.
125.	614:115[102]:	*	Poptun Sculpt. Frag. 1
115.	115.614:	*:59	Cop. T. 11 S. door W. pan.
116, 117.	115.614:	*:59	Pal. Ruz 1, R15; House C, eaves
118, 119.	115.614:	*:59	Yax. L. 25, Q1; L. 56, H2
120.	115:614:	*:59	Yax. L. 31, K1
122.	115.614:	*.59	P.N. Thr. 1, K'5
121.	122.115.614:	*	Cop. T. 22, Step 15
123.	151?.614.	*:59	Yax. L. 21, B7
124.	151?.614?.	*?	El Cayo L. 1, C10
134.	565af?.614:	*.59	Pal. 96 Gl. B8
74.	743:197?:	*	Beyer 178
75.	743.197?:	*	Beyer 175
76.	743.?:197?:	*	Beyer 174
109–111.	?:	*	M. 22b; 22b; 23b
112.	?:	*.130	M. 22b
138.	?.	*.181:25	Dos Pilas H.S. 4, B2
29.	?.	*?.181:25	Yax. L. 8, A3
45.		*:25	Pal. 96 Gl. E6
104–108.		*.116	M. 80b; 81b (4 times)

Compare with Glyph 512 as there are difficulties in separating these two glyphs. In that connection I have here included, after considerable hesitation, some examples from Chichén Itzá which Beyer identifies as name glyphs of God K and others which he thought might represent the lower jaw. Probably 512 and 515 are merely variants of the same glyph. In that connection note that both glyphs have postfixes 25 and 181 when they follow immediately after C.R. dates. That is true here of Nos. 20, 29, and 59–61. No. 31 follows a C.R., but lacks the postfixes. With some hesitation I have included all the examples to which Gates assigned the number 145. In a few cases the left edge of the glyph has a marked elongation as has Glyph 601, to which it is undoubtedly related in form and probably in meaning. See also remarks under Glyph 843.

See also under Glyph 614.

GLYPH 516 (jade variant)
(33 Examples; Sheets 58, 59; Gates' Glyphs 144, 145; Zimmermann's Glyph 1308b)

a   b   c

13.	1.59:?:	*c	Beyer 475
30.	12.	*b.?:25	Yax. 9, A2
4, 8.	59.	*b:103	Yax. L. 6, B2; L. 33, D1
22.	59:	*c	D. 55b
23.	59.	*c	D. 56a
24.	59.	*c:23	D. 54a
25.	59.679af?:	*c	D. 53b
6.	103.40?:	*a:181	Yax. L. 7, A2
11.	122?.	*a.181:142	Aguas Cal. 1, C7
10.	126.	*b:130	Cop. Alt. of E, D2
18.	126.16.	*c	Beyer 141
19.	126:16.	*c	Beyer 142
30.	126.168:	*a.130?	Yax. L. 1, C2
20.	187:	*c.130	Beyer 473
21.	187:	*c:?	Beyer 474
32.	230v. 130?:	*c:184?:74?	Aguatec. 7, A5
28, 29.	243:	*c	M. 21c
57.	XIV.78:	*a	Tik. 5, B8
3.	?:	*a.181	Yax. L. 42, C2
26, 27.		*c.126:57	D. 51b
12.		*c:59:126	Seib. H.S., H2
7.		*b:103?:181	Yax. 11, L1
1.		*a.181:103	Yax. L. 9, A4
2, 5.		*b.181:103	Yax. L. 54, A2; L. 6, A3
9.		*b.181:103	P.N., L. 3, F2
33.		*.181:103?	Dos Pilas H.S. 1, G14
14.		*a.181:130?	Aguas Cal. 1, A3
16.		*a.181:82	Tik. Alt. V, Gl. 29
15.		*b.181:4?	Tik. 1.3, G2
17.		*a.181:?	Moral. 1, L3

Nos. 1, 2, 4–9, 11, 14, 16, and 17 follow C.R. dates, with an intervening glyph in the case of No. 4. All, except Nos. 4 and 8, have the lunar postfix (181) and in most cases also postfix 103. Thereby this compound is brought into relationship with Glyphs 512, 515, and 532. In three examples (Nos. 12, 15, and 30) a Cauac

element follows Glyph 516, and this is perhaps additional evidence of the link between Glyphs 516 and 532.

GLYPH 517
(2 Examples; Sheet 220)

1.	19?.86:	*:142	Cop. H.S. Frag. Gxiid
2.		*	Cop. 19, E4

This is an infix of some early glyph. Note Glyphs 772, 840, and 843.

GLYPH 518 (Muluc Variant)
(82 Examples; Sheets 60–64, 292)

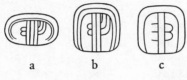

a   b   c

57.	1.		*b:59	Pal. Inscr. jade earplug
2.	1?.168:		*a	R. Amarillo Alt. 1, I2
79, 80.	37.168:		*b:130	Carac. 3, A16a; D12b
54.	38.168:		*a:130	Tik. 5, D10
31.	58:168:		*	Tik. L. 2, B4
32.	59.11:		*b:140v	Tik. 5, B10
27.	59.169:		*b	Holmul cyl. jar.
45.	59:		*b:24	Pal. Sun, J1
34, 42, 36.	III.117:59:		*b	Cop. Q, D5; Rev. Stand Y; T. 11, W. door, S. pan.
43.	III:117?:59:		*b.130	Cop. T. 21a, M
37.	III.117:		*a.153?	Cop. T. 11, S. door E. pan.
35.	III.117?:59?.		*	Cop. 10, D10
39.	III.117?:59:		*?	Cop. N, Ped. 28
44.	III?.117.59:		*b	Cop. 12, C9
40.	III?.117?:		59[*b]	Cop. H.S. Frag. G
41.	III.117?:		59[*b?]	Cop. H.S. Step G
38.	III?.		*b:59	Cop. L, B1
33.	IV.117:59:		*b.585	Cop. G1, C1
27.	122:?:		*b	Beyer 197

62.	125.168:	*.130	Ikil, L. 1, I
78.	125.168:	*a:130?	Tik. 31, L1
1.	168:	*c:130	Cop. T. 11, Step 12
5, 9.	168:	*b.116	Pal. Inscr. W. F12; del Río Tab.
6.	168:	*b.125.116	Pal. Inscr. W. H2
17.	168:	*b.116:125?	Nar. 1, E12
11.	168:	*a.130	R. Amarillo Alt. 1, F2
14.	168:	*a.130	P.N. L. 2, H'3
25.	168?:	*a:130	Xcocha frag.
83.	168:	*b:241?	Tik. jade B5
26.	168?:	*b.?	Holmul tripod bowl
58.	168:	*a	Uxmal Monjas capstone
60.	168:	*b	Uaxac. tripod Tzakol jar
77.	?.168?:	*a:130?	Tik. 31, J2
46, 47.	169:	*a:130?	Yax. L. 37, R2; R8
48.	169?:	*a:130	Yax. L. 35, V2
50–52.	169:	*a	Yax. L. 49, N4; P5; O1
59.	228.168:	*b	Cop. carved bone A3
18.	228.168:	*a:130	Carac. 6, F11
3.	228.168:	*c:130	Pal. Fol. D11
4.	228.168:	*c:103?	Pal. Inscr. E, Q11
10.	228.168:	*c	Pal. Tower Sub., C1
13.	228?.168:	*a	Yax. L. 8, C1
15.	228.168:	*a:130	Alt. Sac. 4, D7
16.	228.168?:	*a:116	Nar. 23, E12
12.	228?.168:	*a:?	Nar. 2, C10
53.	228.168:	*a	Yax. L. 47, G8
55.	228?.168:	*b	Comitán 1, F1
81, 82.	228.16:168:	*b:130	Carac. 3, A9b; B10b
65.	?:228:168:	*a	Cop. 10, H9
63, 70.	IV:87:168:	*c	Cop. 2, C4; T. 21a, H
68, 71, 74.	IV.87.168:	*c	Cop. B', A2; 13, E1; 7, B10
73.	IV:87:168:	*a	Cop. Alt. of E, F2
67.	IV:168:	*c.130?	Cop. 10, G7
66.	IV.87?:168:	*c	Cop. 12, B10
69.	IV.?:168:	*a	Cop. T. 11, W. door, S. pan. A4
64.	IV.87:168:	*?.130?	Cop. R, B2
72.	IV.87?:168?:	*?:?	Cop. O', G3
75.	IV or III.?.?:	*c:?	Pal. T. 18. Shell with glyphs
49.	228.177?:168:	*a	Yax. L. 35, V8

84.	?.?:168:	*b?	Tamar H.S. 2, AB3
76.	59?.248:	*c	Yalloch cyl. vase
61.	?:	*a	Stone Mam in shell
28.	?.?:	*a	Beyer 198
30.	?:	*b	Beyer 139
29.		*b	Beyer 480
19, 21, 22, 24.		*b:59	Xcalum. S. build., S. jamb; E. inner pan.; W. col.; N. build. Frag. I
20, 23.		*b.59	Xcalum. S. build. W. inner pan.; rear lint.

Glyph 518 appears to be merely a variant of Glyph 513, and in some cases it is difficult to tell them apart in design or function; I was tempted to lump them together. Note the compound with number three which occurs eleven times at Copán, and never elsewhere. A twelfth example has a clear coefficient of four. Note the predominance of the Ben-Ich (168) prefix, and the common appearance of Affix 59, both as a prefix and as a postfix. Glyph 514 follows several of the early examples, with 169, at Yaxchilán.

The compound, found only at Copán, with coefficient of 4 is of particular interest because it is usually associated with the glyph of the long-nosed god with coefficient of 9. In examples 64 and 70 the glyph is separated from God 9 Long-nose by an interesting phrase of 5 glyphs, and example 69 may belong in the same group despite some aberrant features.

See also under Glyphs 528 and 592.

GLYPH 519 (Chuen with dots)
(7 Examples; Sheet 69)

7.	3?:	*:130	Cop. K, O1
8.	3?:	*?	Cop. P, E9
9.	86:	*	Cop. 10, F8
55.	11.110:	*	Pal. T. 18, Tab. C15
54.	11.110:	*:130	Pal. 96 Gl. K6
52.	204.110:	*:130	Pal. Fol. G5
53.	III.110:		Pal. Inscr. M. N10

Compare with Glyph 522.

GLYPH 520 (Chuen)
(32 Examples; Sheets 66–70)

29.		*	Day sign Chuen on monuments
42.	4?:	*	Tik. L. 3, E3
28.	6?.	*.181:178	Tort. 1, A3
40.	12.168?:?:	*:130?	Amel. H.S., B3
51.	12?.	*:130?	Nar. 24, D12
30.	25: or .	*:130	Month Zec on monuments
5.	1:187:	*:87	Cop. S, Gl. J
55.	59:187:	*	Nar. 13, H13
65.	59.187:	*	Nar. 19, A8
66.	59.187:	*?:23?	Nar. 35, F6
25.	187.129:	*:178	Yax. L. 35, W2
44.	181.187:	*	Nar. 8, B7
54.	228?.187:	*	Nar. 13, E16
3.	11:XII.187:	*	Cop. 6, A8
12.	111.12?:	*:?	Cop. 3, A9
69.	174:	*Horiz.130:77	Tik. 31, O2
70.	174:	*?.130:77	Tik. 31, K2
7.	130.	*.?:178	Cop. 9, A9
68.	?:220.	*:103	Carac. Alt. 12, Frag. 1, 8
22.	228.?:	*	Quir. H, M2
41.	228.168?:	*:130	Amel. H.S., I3
63.	?.	*:103	Nar. 6, A5
43.	?.	*:130	Moral. 2, C4
45.	?:?:	*	Calak. 51, F6
27.		*.82?:8	Cop. 23, H9
34, 36.		*.126	Yax. Str. 44, S.E. up. step; 18, F2
35.		*:126	Yax. 18, A5
53.		*.134	Nar. 29, F16
33.		*.178	Cop. T. 11 step
38.		*.245?	P.N., L. 3, B'3
8.		*?:*?	Cop. Alt. of E

See also under Glyphs 670 and 846.

GLYPH 521 (Uinal)
(178 Examples; Sheets 66–68, 70; Gates' Glyph 11; Zimmermann's Glyph 1331)

177.		*	P.N. bowl. Coe Fig. 60d
10.		*	Cop. 13, F5
176.		*	Usual form of Uinal on monuments
131–195.		*.* or tripled or quadrupled	See Gates 11.20n–11.22n.
71.	1:207.	*.103	P. 21a
72.	1.	*:103	P. 11d
73.	1.	*:103	M. 13b
75.	4.221V:	*	D. 72a
13.	11.	*:142	Cop. 23, H9
76.	12.	*:103	D. 61
77.	12:	*:103	D. 69
69.	12.58:?.97:	*	Bonam. L. 3, A9
78.	17:	*	P. 7b
79.	VI.24.17:	*	D. 49e
80.	VI:24:17.	*	P. 21a
81.	VI.24.17:	*?	P. 23a
82.	VI?.24?.17:	*	P. 3b
83.	VI.24.17?:	*	P. 24a
61.	59.	*	Nar. 12, G14
62.	59:	*:?	Nar. 12, M1
9.	60?:	*	Cop. 13, E6
84.	74.	*	D. 34c
30.	78:	*:103	Yax. L. 1, G2
74.	4.84:	*	D. 71a
86.	IV.84:219.	*	D. 21b
87.	IV.219:84.	*	D. 13c
15.	86:	*:142?	Pal. Fol. B17
31.	86?:	*	Yax. 11, C'14
199.	16:86:	*:84?	Cop. 1, D1
201.	61?.86:	*:178	Pal. Fol. stone sculpt. A8
88.	III.90:	*	D. 48f
89.	115.	*:?:47	M. 35c
39.	117.	*	P.N. 15, C14

[123]

24.	117.	*:103	Pal. T. 18, stucco
70.	59.117:	*.?	Uaxac. 14 back
17.	122.244:	*	Pal. Ruz 1, D5
16.	122:244:	*	Pal. Inscr. W. P12
90.	122.	*:103	D. 57a
91.	126.126:	*.126:126:1	M. 35a
92.	130.178?:	*.?	Cop. 13, F3
93–112.	161.	*:103	Gates 11.2.5. Twenty occurrences
203.	130 or 122:	*.103	Tamar. H.S. 1, F3
113.	I.161.	*:103	D. 61
121.	I.346.161.	*:103	D. 70
32.	168?:32?:	*	Seib. 7, B6
114–119.	172.	*:103	D. 45b; 46e; 55a; 60a; 60b; 72b
120.	172.?:	*	P. 10c
57, 58.	181.187:	*:103?	Nar. 8, F9; E2
52.	187:	*	Nar. 29, F10
60.	187:	*?:?	Nar. 12, B14
59, 66.	59.187:	*?:103?	Nar. 12, B4; 35, F6
174.	299v:	*:25	Month Zec in D.
122.	207.III:	*	D. 69
23.	228.	*:23?	Yax. 12, E2
53.	228.168?:32?:	*	Seib. 7, A3
19.	230.	*:103	Pal. Ruz 1, D7
21.	237.563af:	*	Pal. Ruz 1, L14
29.		512[*]	Yax. L. 10, F6
202.	1016.?:?:	*:178?	Pal. T. 18 sculpt. stone
123.	II.	*:103	P. 3c
124.	III.	*.24	M. 72b
125.	III.	*.84:136	M. 72a
126.	IV.	*.84:136	M. 72a
127.	X.	*.84	M. 69b
128.	IV.	*:130	P. 17e
46.	V?.	*:23	Calak. 9, G5
129.	VI.548:	*	M. 110b
67.	bird?:	*?:103	Carac. 17, A4
85.	74:558.	*	D. 41b
1.	?:	*	Cop. K, O1
130.	?:	*:613:47	M. 35b
48.	?:	*	Xcalum. S. build. rear L.
44.	?:	*?	Carac. 1, C3
64.	?:	*:103	Nar. 6, B2

196.		*:47	M. 36b
49–51.		*:102	Beyer 146; 296; 297
175.		*:103	Form of Uinal on monuments and D.
197.		*:103	P. 2b
198.		*:103	D. 36b
37.		*:103	Yax. 4, G3
18, 20.		*:103	Pal. Ruz 1, D17; L7
2.		*P:103	Cop. K, L2
47.		*.245	Ixlu Alt. of 2, E3
14.		*:?	Pal. Cross, J1
4.		*:?:?	Cop. 2, A9

Number 122, despite its unusual prefix, functions as a regular uinal sign, and the same is probably true of Nos. 76 and 77. In the codices the details of the day glyph Chuen are indistinguishable from those of the uinal glyph. The piles of uinal signs, usually with numerical coefficients, found in Codices Dresden and Madrid still conceal their function and meaning.

For further examples of Glyph 521 see under Glyphs 526, 548, 558, 613, 663, 666, and 713.

GLYPH 522 (Uinal with added dots)
(15 Examples; Sheet 71; Gates' Glyph 11.19; Zimmermann under 1331)

10, 11.	185:	*v	P. 6b; 8
3.	205.187:	*:217:19	Pal. T. 18, stucco
1.	238:244:	*	Pal. Ruz 2, B5
2.	238.244:	*	Pal. Tower Scribe 1, D2
5, 6.	238?.244?:	*	Pal. Sarcoph. Gl. 17; Gl. 21
13.	244:	*	Yax. 7, C7
7, 8.	244:	*.184.74.142	Tik. L. 3, G1; 16, C2
9.	244:	*.184	Tik. 5, A8
15.	359:	*:360	Tik. 31, G19
12.	?:	*.184.126?:142	Tik. 22, B7
4.	?:59:	*:23	Jonuta, 2, B1
14.	?:	*:125	Yax. Str. 44, mid. up. step

Glyph 522 occurs only in the Chiapas area, at Tikal, and in Codex Paris. It is interesting to find the same unusual prefix No. 244 used in both regions.

See also under Glyph 522, and compare with Glyph 519.

GLYPH 523 (Uinal Semblant)
(16 Examples; Gates' Glyph 11a; Zimmermann under Glyph 1331)

1.	*.47	D. 50b
2–16.	*.116:47	D. 46; 48; 49; 50

This is distinguished from the uinal glyph by the unusual protuberance on the top and by the constant use of Affix 47. It appears only on the Venus pages, between the month signs and the glyphs connected with the directional gods except on Dresden 46, where the glyph follows both.

GLYPH 524 (Ix)
(13 Examples; Gates' Glyph 14 in part; Zimmermann's Glyph 1334)

11.		*	Day sign Ix on monuments
5.		*	Carved shell Tuxtla Mus.
3.	12.	*	Yax. 7, D4
13.	60:	*?	Kuna L. 1, L3
4.	129:	*	P.N., L. 3, K'
12.	279.44:17:	*	Yax. L. 18, C2
1.	1000.	*	Yax. L. 17, H1
2.	1000?.	*:126	Yax. L. 43, D2
7.	IV.	*	Xcalum. N. build. frag.
6.	?.	*	Xcalum. I.S. build. rt. col.
8.	?.	*	M. 79c
10.	?.?:	*	Tonina 52, Gl. 9
9.		*.58:548	D. 26a

For further examples of Glyph 524, see under Glyphs 528 and 548.

GLYPH 525 (Cib)
(3 Examples; Codical form: Gates' Glyph 16; Zimmermann's Glyph 1336)

1.		*	Day sign Cib on monuments
2.		*[578]	Day sign Cib in codices
3.		*P var.	Chama. Carey vase

On the monuments Cib is hardly distinguishable from an inverted Kan. It is not clear whether this resemblance is fortuitous.

GLYPH 526 (Caban)
(355 Examples; Sheets 73–80, 80a; Gates' Glyph 17; Zimmermann's Glyph 1337)

58, 59.		*	Nar. 22, E14; H12
253, 300, 301.		*	D. 40c fig.; M. 28c fig.; 50a
306, 307.		*:*	D. 33a fig.; M. 110c fig.
308.		*.*:*	M. 17b
141.	1.	*	M. 65b
1.	1.	*	Cop. 6, D2
342–345.	1.	*:88	Tik. 31, A19; E19; F13; H16
346.	1.	*.88	Tik. 31, D12
46.	1:	*:126	P.N., L. 3, A'3
33.	1:	*:126	Quir. P, Cart. 2
8, 15.	1:	*:126	Cop. Q, E3; Alt. E, F2
7.	1.	*P:126	Cop. G', B3
140.	1.	*:126	P. 24a
21, 22, 326.	1.	*:246	Pal. Ruz 2, D3; F3; T. 18 stucco gl.
26.	1.	*:246	Quir. E, B16
314.	1.	*?:246	Quir. U, A8
355.	1:	*:246?	Carac. 15, E4
38.	1:	*:246	Yax. L. 10, E4
39.	1.	*:246	Yax. 11, E2

[127]

350.	1.	*:246	Dos Pilas 2, D3
42.	1.	*:246	P.N. Shell Plaque, F2
43.	1.	*:246?	P.N. Shell Plaque, L3
341.	1.	*:246?	Jade head, Br. Mus.
45.	1.	*:246	P.N., L. 3, Y3
51.	1.	*P:246	El Cayo, L. 1, G2
47.	1?:	*?:103?	Seib. 9, D3
69.	1:	*:88:246?	Pal. Sarcoph. Gl. 11
11.	1.	*.181:217	Cop. 7, B7
28.	1.	*:?:126	Quir. F, D18
129.	1.250:	*	M. 27d
130.	1.	*.250	M. 27d
131–180.	1.	*:251	M. Gates 17.1.1.
181.	1.	*?:251	M. 104b–105b
129.	1:	*:23	D. 56a
53, 54.	1:	*:246	Pusil. D, F13; G13
56.	1.	*:246	Nar. 23, F14
57.	1:	*:246	Nar. H.S. C2
61.	1.	*:246	Nar. 25, A9
60.	1.	*:246?	Nar. 22, G16
63.	1.	*:246	Tik. Alt. V, Gl. 19
70.	1:	*:246	Pal. T. 18 Tab. D15
130–139.	1.	*:247	D. 52b; 53b; 54b; 56b; P. 4d; 6d; 7d; 8d; 8d
55.	1.	*:130?	Pusil. D, E6
73.	1:	*:1.598	Yax. L. 56, J2
74.	1.	*:598	Yax. L. 25, V1
77.	1:	*.1:598	Yax. L. 26, C''1
76.	1?:	*.1?:598:23	Yax. 18, C4
	1.	*:?	Uaxac. 26, A8
142, 143.	1.	*:585	M. 110c
144–147.	1.	*:558	M. 103b, 103c
32.	XVIII:1:125:	*	Quir. P, C9
354.	3:	*:246	Carac. 3, C9
37.	11.	*:106?	Yax. L. 39, A3
52.	11:	*:142	Pusil. D, D12
50.	12?:	*	Seib. H.S. A2
44.	13:	*	P.N. 12 Captives Gl. 47
340.	13:	*:246	Pomona frag. Tabasco
324.	13.	*:246	Ikil L. 2, A
49.	13.	*P:246	Seib. 12, A6
62.	13.	*:246	Nar. 35, E2
92.	13.	*:125	Nar. 35, D5

222.	13.194?.168:	*	D. 56b
335.	16:	*:245?	Yax. L. 16, B2
187.	17:	*	M. 24c
188, 189.	17.	*	M. 28c, 60c
314.	21:611:611.	*:251	D. 68a
329.	24 (reversed).	*	Carac. Conch god vase
182–186.	25.	*:252	M. 36b; 62a; 69b; 97d
89.	32:561:	*	Cop. S, F
347, 348.	35.	*P	Tik. 31, B14; F26
91.	35?.117:561. 23:	*	Cop. 7, E8
190.	58.	*:251	D. 67b
191.	58.	*:136	M. 35b
192.	59.	*:251	D. 73c
193.	59.668:	*	M. 8a
194–196.	59.	*:251.663:23	D. 35b; 38b; 38b
86.	62:	*.24	Uaxac. sherd
252.	62?.	*:142	M. 36b
197.	84:head.	*	P. 6c
65.	VI.86:	*:140	Tik. L. 2, A9
325.	86:192:	*.305	Tik. 26, E2
198.	87.	*:252	M. 73b
199.	90.	*:252	D. 48e
200.	90.109?:	*	M. 36d
201.	91.	*:251.663:23	D. 39b
202.	91.	*:663	P. 8c
237.	95:?.	*	D. 30b
203.	95.	*:251	D. 74
204–207.	96.	*:251	M. 78d; 81c; 81c; 90d
208, 209.	96.	*:663	D. 34b; 35b
210.	109:	*	P. 2d
211, 212.	110.	*:251	M. 88b; 88b
236.	110:	*.115?	M. 36b
90.	117?.	*:125:561.23	Cop. 7, E11
213.	122.	*:251	M. 72b
214–216.	III.122.	*:252	M. 68b; 68b; 72b
217.	122.	*:1016	D. 37b
75.	122.	*.207?:600:23	Yax. 18, D1
218.	137.14.	*.23	D. 55a
293.	137.192:	*	D. 71b
294, 295.	137.192?:	*	D. 57a; 73a
80, 81.	III.153:	*.23	Pal. Ruz 1, D8, L13
82.	III.153:	*:23	Pal. Ruz 1, R6

339.	III:153:	*:missing	Pal. T. 4 N. stucco
223, 224.	155:	*	M. 27c; 28c
230, 231.	155:	*.181	M. 28c; D. 38b
225.	156:	*	D. 34c
228, 229.	1.156:	*	M. 28b; 28b
232–234.	163.59:	*	M. 112b; 112b; 112b
235.	163.59:	*.1	M. 111c
237.	172.	*:252	D. 49d
238–240.	172.	*:251	D. 54b; 55a; 72a
244.	172?.	*:251.58[552]	D. 60a
12.	187:	*:23	Cop. 7, A9
245–248.	190.	*	M. 89c; 89c; P. 15f; 16e
34.	1000:190:	*:23	Yax. L. 24, D'2
292.	192:	*?	D. 58b
71.	204.217:	*	Pal. Fol. Bal. A2
351, 352.	204.	*:246?	Carac. 3, C18a; A20b
353.	204.	*:246	Carac. 3, C20b
67.	204.	*:246	Ixkun 2, C6
66.	204.	*:246	Ixkun 2, B12
25.	204.	*P:246	Quir. E, D11
337.	204.	*:314	Pal. T. 4 Sculpt. stone 2, A1
48.	205?:	*:88:246	Seib. 11, G2
3.	205:	*:125	Cop. I, C2
14.	205:	*.125:88	Cop. P, A8
29.	205:	*P	Quir. G, S1
305.	221.521:	*	M. 34c
83.	229.168:247:	*:246	Pal. House C, E2
40.	232?.	*:246	P.N. Thr. 1, A'4
78, 79.	249:	*.181:178	Pal. Inscr. Mid., B4; B5
249, 250.	256:	*	P. 6c; 6c
251.	III.256:	*	D. 6a
313.	IX:283.	*:103	M. 105b
297.	96.IX:283:	*	M. 77f
298.		*.283:?.IX	M. 78d
349.	325.	*	Tort. 6, A11
273.	501:505?.	*	M. 108c
87.	501?.	*	Etzna, 5, A3
4.	513af:	*:126	Cop. I, D4
292.	552.	*	M. 60c
293.	552.	*:251	D. 65b
88.	561:	*	Cop. N, Ped. 19
303.	II:561c.	*	D. 35a
220.	561[544]:	*	P.N. 36, C7

221.	561[544]:	*	Cop. Alt. E, G1
222.	1.561[544]:	*	Used for 1 day
318, 319.	561[544]:	*	Beyer 337; 338
320, 321.	1.561[544]:	*	Beyer 339; 340
322.	1.561[544]:	*.35	Beyer 341
323.	1.*[544]:	*	Beyer 342
334.	12.561a?.	*:12	Cop. T. 11 S. door E. pan. D.N. intro. gl.?
93–95, 98–104.	16.561[544]:	*	Cop. N. ped. 18; U, K3; Q, F3; 8, D2; L, D1; R′′, C1; Z, D1; T, 8; T. 21a
96, 97.	16:561[544]:	*	Cop. R, K2; D′, 7; Rev. Stand, C′1
219.	1003.561[544]:	*	Cop. N, A17
315.	59.561[544]:	*	Beyer 344
316.	125.561[544]:	*	Beyer 343
107–126.	679af.561[544]:	*	P.N., 1, E3; 7, C2; C9; 22, C4; 23, L8; 37, D10; Alt. 1, B2; R2; Alt. 2, D1; K1; L. 2, W11; L. 3, T2; U8; L. 4, E2; I3; Thr. 1, N1, C′2, J′1; Shell Plaque D2; L2
127.	679af.561[544]:	*	El Cayo L. 1, D2
128.	679af.561[544]:	*	Pal. Ruz 1, N14
106.	?.561[544]:	*	Cop. H.S. frag.
317.	?.561[544]?:	*?	Beyer 345
272.	648.	*:251	D. 44b
241–243.	172.	*:251.663:23	D. 57a; 71a; P. 24a
342.	172.	*:663	D. 60b
274.	663.	*	D. 38b, beneath fig.
273.	172.663.	*:23	P. 23a
275, 276.		*.663	D. 42b, beneath fig.; D. 56a
344.	181.	*:23.663:251	M. 90a
277–281.	663:23.	*:251	D. 66a; M. 77e; 77f; P. 3b; 23a
343.	181:663:251.	*:23	P. 5c
311.	682.	*:251	M. 60c
302.	682:	*.?.130	M. 37b
331.	VI.	*P:?	Nar. 30, B9
252.	VI.	*:116	M. 79b
330.	VI?.	*P:126	Nar. 21, A13
332.	VI:	*?	Nar. 13, E13

333.	VI, VII or VIII.	*:260	Xcalum. I.S. Build. lt. col. A6
9.	head:	*:142	Cop. 9, F7
6.	?:	*P:142	Cop. A, H7
10.	?.	*	Cop. 9, E3
16.	?.	*	Cop. 12, C10
17.	?.	*	Cop. 12, B10
72.	?:	*	Beyer 298
20.	?.?:	*	Pal. Inscr. W. M6
24.	?:	*:126	Quir. E, D16
64.	?.	*:88	Tik. 12, F4
336.	?:	*	Yax. L. 15, G3
5.		*.40:178	Cop. B, A12
254, 255.		*:47	M. 51b; 95a
31.		*P:106	Cop. T. 22, Step 9
27.		*P:142	Quir. J, D11
41.		*:142	P.N. Thr. 1, A1
226.		*.155	M. 28c
19.		*.87?:178	Pal. Inscr. W. I11
18.		*P:178	Pal. Inscr. M. B7
309.		*:*.181	D. 37a
36, 338.		*:246	Pal. T. 18, stucco; T. 4 N. stucco
256, 257.		*:251	D. 24b; 73c
258–271.		*:251	M. Gates 17.1
282–285.		*:251.663:23	D. 33b; 40c; 71c; 73a
286.		*:251.663b. 309:308	M. 35d
287, 288.		*:251.?:663b	M. 29c; 29c
328.		*:251.663b:23	M. 37d
289.		*:251.663b: face	M. 34d
327.		*.663b	M. 34d
310.		*:*.528:577	M. 108a
312.		*.544	M. 28c
299.		*:558	M. 104b
85.		*:563a af	Uaxac. sherd
290, 291.		*:585	M. 104a (twice)
296.		*.611.251	M. 78d
304.		*:613?	M. 110c fig.
13.		*.?	Cop. 7, B9

The rarity of this common glyph at Chichén Itzá should be significant.

The combination of 526 and 561—Caban—Caan, sky and earth, or the juxtaposition of the two elements is common both on the monuments and in the codices. The sun at the horizon (561 [544]:526) compound and its use with the number one to record the passage of one day (dawn, *hatzcab?*) has been the subject of comment by more than one writer (Thompson, 1950, p. 172). With the "forward" (141) affix the compound seems to have been confined to Piedras Negras and its assumed dependency, El Cayo, except for a single appearance at Palenque, which presumably represents a borrowing. In combination with the Yax (16) prefix the compound is restricted to Copán. The substitution of the head of God 9 for Yax provides an interesting illustration of the principles of Maya writing. Of great interest is the single occurrence of the compound 1.526[544]:526. The substitution of the Caban (earth) sign for the Caan (sky) sign was one of the reasons which led Beyer to suppose that the Caban sign had the same value as the sky sign. It is more natural to suppose that here we are treating of a sunset glyph in which the sun sinks into the earth, corresponding to the linguistic conception.

The combination of 526 and 663 has received comment (Thompson, 1950, p. 271). The latter glyph is there identified as the sign for seed, and it is natural to find it combined with the sign for earth.

For further examples of Glyph 526, see under Glyphs 510, 528, 558, 585, 604, 613, 648, 663, 668, 671, 682, 686, 713?, 757?, and 758.

GLYPH 527 (Etz'nab)
(8 Examples; Sheets 81, 82; Gates' Glyph 18; Zimmermann's Glyph 1338)

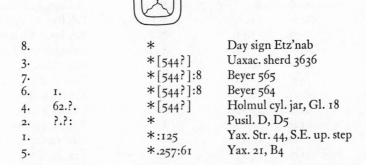

8.		*	Day sign Etz'nab
3.		*[544?]	Uaxac. sherd 3636
7.		*[544?]:8	Beyer 565
6.	1.	*[544?]:8	Beyer 564
4.	62.?.	*[544?]	Holmul cyl. jar, Gl. 18
2.	?.?:	*	Pusil. D, D5
1.		*:125	Yax. Str. 44, S.E. up. step
5.		*.257:61	Yax. 21, B4

The most sterile of all day-sign roots, but the symbol appears sometimes as an infix, for instance with Glyph 759 and Affix 112.

For further examples of Glyph 527 see under Glyphs 561 and 601.

GLYPH 528 (Cauac)
(472 Examples; Sheets 83–105; Gates' Glyph 19; Zimmermann's Glyph 1339)

294, 295.		*	M. 18b; 55b
65.		*	Nebaj. Fenton vase C6
398, 399.		*:*.*	P. 23a; M. 43b
7.	I.	*:116?	Cop. J.W., 6
33.	I.	*.151:24	Pal. Cross, Shrine C1
77.	I.	*:?:?	P.N. 1, J14
266.	I.or:	*.116:217	Completion of haab
299.	I.	*:116	M. 36b
177.	I.4:60:	*P	Pal. T. 18 stucco
II.	I.23:	*.?:82	Cop. 10, G2
274.	I.43:	*.*:60	Pal. Inscr. M., L3
133.	I:92.?:	*.116	R. Amarillo Alt. 1, H2
381.	I.146:	*:219	P. 10d
232.	I.264:	*	Beyer 181
374.	III.2.	*:542	P. 9d
267.	4?.	*.*	Pal. Inscr. M. D10
265.	4.V:	*.or:116	Completion of 5 haab glyph
104.	5:	*	P.N. Thr. 1, F'6
102, 105.	5:	*:116	P.N. Thr. 1, I1; Z6
103.	5:	*.116	P.N. Thr. 1, F'2
106.	5:	*.116	El Cayo, L. 1, C14
51, 52.	11:	*.116:196	Pal. Ruz 2, A3; B2
275.	11.43:	*.*	Pal. Inscr. M. K10
32.	11:74.	*:23	Pal. House C, Plat. D2
76.	11.	*P	P.N. 1, K9
430.	11.262?:	*	Tort. 1, A3
121.	12.1:	*	Yax. L. 9, B6
112.	12:1:	*	Yax. L. 41, D5
124.	12:1:	*	Yax. L. 33, A10
110.	12:1:	*	Yax. 12, C4
116.	12:1:	*P	Yax. 11, E2
238.	12.205:	*.116	P.N. 40, C11
54.	12:	*P:116	Yax. 5, C8
58.	12:	*:23?	P.N. Alt. Sup. A3
50.	12:?:	*P.116	Pal. Ruz 2, A2
195.	12.1:	*	Yax. L. 3, H1

196.	12.1:	*	Yax. L. 1, A8
193.	12.1?:	*	Yax. L. 7, D1
206.	12?.	*.116	Pal. Ruz 2, G1
21.	12.213.	*:116	Cop. 6, C7
123.	12.III:213.	*.116	Yax. 18, D3
108.	12?.61?:	*	Quir. L, Gl. 17
198.	13.219:	*	Yax. L. 13, F2
220.	13.?:	*:116	Quir. M, B4
2.	13?.	*:116	Cop. U, N2
356.	16.or:	*	Month sign Yax
117.	16.3:	*:125?	Yax. L. 37, S2.
276, 280.	16.86:176:	*.*	Cop. 23, H1; 12, D13
277, 278.	16.86:176:	*.*	Pal. Sun, N2; Cross, C7
279.	16.86:176:	*.*	Quir. C, A14
13.	16?:60:	*.*	Cop. K, J2
95.	19:	*	Yax. L. 46, G4
101.	19:	*	Yax. Str. 44, S.E. up. step
352.	19:	*	M. 17a
413.	19.	*	Conch god vase, Carac.
353.	19.84:	*	D. 72c
69–72.	23.	*	P.N., L. 3, V11; 15, B2; Thr. 1, J'3; R
414.	25.	*:13?	Sayil Str. 3B1, Gl. 4
314.	25.217.	*:116	M. 66b
81.	35.32:	*	Pusil. D, A11
82.	35.IX?:32:	*:116	Pusil. D, H11
376.	35?.	*	M. 11
133.	38?.	*	Cop. J, E. 29
393.	39?.	*:*	M. 37c
431.	42:	*.*	Pictun glyph
404.	43:	*.*	Pictun glyph
362–365.	51.	*:281	M. 22c (4 times)
88.	57.60:	*P	Carac. 16, C14
359.	58. or 58:	*	Month sign Zac
37.	58.48:60:	*	Pal. Sun, C3
165–168.	58.58v:	*.4	Pal. 96 Gl. A8; C8; F6; H5
181, 182.	58?.4:60:	*	P.N. 40, A19; C13
87.	59:	*P	Tik. L3, H2
35.	59.23:	*.?	R. Amarillo Alt. 1, K2
185.	59:17v:	*.*.228:116	Yax. L. 35, W6
270.	59:	*.*:60?	Quir. F, D9
421.	48 or 4:60:	*.181	Tort. 6, F6
62.	60.	*	Carac. 16, C14

435.	60?.	*.116?	Sisilhá, lt. jamb 11
229.	60?:	*	P.N., L. 3, X1
408, 410.	61.	*	Pal. Sarcoph. lid top; leg
178.	61:	*:180.526P	Pal. T. 18 Stucco
409.	61:	*	Pal. Sarcoph. lid top
9.	61:	*.2	Cop. Q, C2
25.	61?:?:	*	Cop. F', B2
125.	61:89:	*	Cop. K, K2
367.	62:	*	P. 8d
368.	V.62:	*	M. 85b
369.	62.	*	D. 7c
404.	62.	*:?	D. 60b
343–351.	IV.64:	*	Gates 19.7n. Gl. of god
290.	70:?:	*.*	Carac. 16, C19
223.	74:	*	Quir. P, Cart. 2
31.	74:17:	*	Pal. House C, Plat. A1
152, 157.	74:513.	*:142	Cop. Q, C4; 6, C5
140.	74:513.	*:142	P.N., L. 2, V2
153–155, 163.	74:513.	*:255	Cop. P, C5; D14; Md. 2, reused step; 10, G8
148.	74:513.	*:83	Nakum, D, F1
141.	74:513.	*:83	Pusil. D, D6
135.	74:513.	*	Pal. House C, Plat. F1
156, 158.	74:513.	*	Cop. E, D3; Y, F1
160, 161.	74:	*.513:142	Cop. F', C4; T, Gl. 11
136.	74:	*.513:255	Cop. 13, C10
164.	74:	*.513:255	Pal. House A, Balustr.
145, 440–445.	74:	*.513:255	Tik. 12, F5; 31, D5; D22; H20; O3; L3; E8
159.	74:	*.513:255?	Cop. H.S. Frag. Gxii
429.	74:	*.513.202	Dzibil. 19, A1
143, 144.	74:	*.513	Nar. 24, D10; 29, E19
147, 150.	74:	*.513	Calak. 9, I4; 89, C6
142.	74?:513?.	*:255?	Pusil. M, C3
137.	74:513.	*:7?	Quir. J, D14
139.	?.74:	*.513	Yax. L. 26, X'1
148.	74:513?.	*	Uaxac. I.S. vase
149.	513.	*:83	Carac. 19, Frame 2
146.	74:	*:513:188	Tik. L4, E10
31.	74:17:	*	Pal. House C, Plat. A1
170.	74.184.229:	*P	Pal. 96 Gl. F4
171.	74.184.229:	*P.178	Pal. 96 Gl. I6
172.	74.184.229?:	*:142	Pal. Tower Panel 1, D4

61.	74?.184.229?:	*:178	Pal. T. 18, Tab. C16
467, 468.	74:184:299:	*v	Aguatec. 1, D10; 2, G6
466.	74.184.117?: 299:	*v	Aguatec. 7, F2
109.	74:183?:	*	Yax. L. 25, B1
428.	1.76:	*	Dzibil. bone awl
20.	86:	*	Cop. 6, C6
19.	86:176v?:	*	Cop. E, A11
424.	228.86:	*P	P.N. 3, E6
292.	87.	*:130?	Yax. L. 39, B4
68.	87.	*:142?	Yax. L. 33, A3
200.	87:	*:116	Yax. 11, C'12
202.	87?.	*	Yax. 1, E8
111.	87:	*:?	Yax. 12, C3
333.	87.	*:283	M. 60c
334.	?.87:	*	M. 37b
335.	87:	*.112	M. 38b
261.	87.	*.*	Cop. J. C3
127.	89.85:	*	Cop. P, C14
128.	89.	*.90v?	Cop. T. 11, W. door, S. pan.
126.	89:	*	Cop. U, M4
129.	89.	*.592	Cop. R, E1
132.	89.	*:592	Cop. T. 11, Step, 23
131.	89?:	*:592	Cop. T. 21a, K
130.	89.IV:92:	*	Cop. F', A3
134.	89:	*:23?	Calak. 51, D1
6.	89?.	*P:116	Cop. A, B10
300–304.	90.	*:116	M. 99a; 99a; 100a; 100b; 102a
305.	90.	*:116	D. 32b
336.	90:	*	M. 101b
306.	90.	*:?	D. 34b
337.	III.90:	*	M. 69b
307.	91.	*:116	P. 8c
339.	91.	*:116	D. 35b
357.	95. or 95:	*	Month sign Ch'en
406.	106:218:	*.*	Glyph for Kinchiltun
392.	109.	*:*	P. 7d
425.	109.	*P	Pal. Fol. G6
358.	109. or 109:	*	Month sign Ceh
426.	109.151:	*P?	Pal. Inscr. M. M7
372.	115.	*:116?	M. 88a
53.	115.229.86:	*	Pal. Tower Plat. 2, E5

361.	116.	*:585	M. 21d
186.	118.561:228:	*	Yax. L. 35, U8
317.	122.	*	M. 90b
318–320.	122.	*:87	D. 11b; 11c; 12c
321.	122.	*:87	M. 86b
272.	122.11:	*.*	Pal. Sarcoph. earplug
323–329.	122.87:	*	D. 5a; 36a; 37a; 39a?; 31b; 45b; 19c
330–332.	122.87:	*	M. 106c; 111c; 112c
322.	122.?:	*	M. 111b
64.	122.	*	Beyer 299
245, 246.	122.17:	*.*	Cop. N, B5; Ped. 22
247.	122.17:	*.*:683b	Cop. M, A7
249.	122.17:	*.*	Cop. H.S. Step T
250.	122.17:	*.*	Cop. Review Stand, E'
248.	16.122:	*.*	Cop. 2, C7
251.	16.122?:	*.*	Quir. J, B17
256.	16.122:	*.*	Nar. 29, I12
257.	?:16:122:	*.*	Nar. 29, I17
252.	59:16:122:	*.*	Quir. F, C6
244.	16.122:	*.*:142	Tik. L. 4, A2
258.	122.17:	*.*:126	Nar. 20, B1
259, 260.	16?.122?:	*.*	Nar. 30, D8, G14
240.	124:	*.116	Nar. L. 1, F2
396, 397.	126.265:	*	M. 70b; 71b
448.	126:60:	*.358	Tik. 31, C23
18.	130?.	*:?	Cop. P, D7
219.	130?.168?:	*:?	Quir. G, P'1
422.	131?	*:178	Pal. T. 3 N. stucco
74.	524:150.	*:12	Quir. C, B9
75.	1030:150.	*:116	Quir. C, B11
26.	9.158:130.V:	*.116 or :116	Five haab lacking glyph
308.	166:	*:116	D. 32b
379.	II.166:	*.136	M. 35a picture
99.	168:	*:116	P.N. 12, Capt. 7
98.	168:	*.130:116	P.N. Thr. 1, E1
100.	168:	*.116	P.N. 16, D5
96.	168:	*:116	Yax. L. 46, G''4
101.	168:	*:116	Yax. Str. 44, S.E. up. step
470.	168:176:	*.*	Aguatec. 2, A2
282, 285, 287–289, 291.	168:176:	*.*	Seib. 8, A4; 9, E2; H.S., A2; E1; B'1; 12, A8
283, 284.	?:176:	*.*	Seib. 11, B2; E1

469.	229?.168:176:	*.*	Aguatec. 2, F2
281, 286.	35.168:176:	*.*	Seib. 10, A7; H.S. L2
452.	35.168:	*:360	Tik. 31, E11
179.	173.4:60:	*	P.N. Thr. 1, E'3
400, 401.	176?:	*	P. 9b; 11b
420.	177.	*.178?	Tort. 6, H3
395.	177?.?:	*:*	P. 8b
457, 458.	VI.177.	*	P. 4b; 4c
378.	190?.	*	M. 59c
262.	191.	*.*:60	Pal. Inscr. E, I7
338.	202:	*	M. 83a picture
410.	204.16:	*.116:217	Form of completion of haab
226.	204.60:	*:1	Quir. K, B7
39.	204.	*:151:24	Pal. Inscr. M. N8
411.	204.	*:174?:24	Pal. Fol. jamb, B9
34.	204.151:	*.48:229	Pal. Madrid Pan. B2
23.	204.?:	*:116	Cop. F, A7
28.	205:	*	Cop. 13, E4
218.	205:	*?:116	Quir. G, S'1
404.	205.	*.116:217	Form for completion of haab
27.	213?:	*	Cop. 13, E5
79, 80.	213:	*:116	Pusil. D, C12; E13
83.	213?:	*	Nar. 23, H12
42.	216:	*	Pal. Ruz 1, L7
313.	217.	*:116	M. 66a
46.	217.?:	*	Pal. House A, Pier C
407.	218:	*.*	Glyph for Calabtun
268.	228.	*.116:217	form of completion of haab
176, 432.	228.	*	P.N., L. 4, Y1; Sting Ray 4
47.	228.	*	Pal. House C, Plat. L2
48.	228.	*	Pal. H.S. D4
49.	228.?.	*	Pal. H.S. D4
118.	228:	*	Yax. L. 35, U3
38.	228.	*:142	Pal. Inscr. E, A12
231.	228.264:	*	Beyer 180
57.	229.	*	P.N., L. 2, K'2
68.	229.	*:142?	Yax. L. 33, A3
59.	229.	*	Bonam. 2, D7
115.	229.	*P	M. Cow, Alt. 2, D2
183.	229.	*	Cop. C, B5
184.	229.	*:24?	Quir. D, D20
191.	229.13:	*	Yax. L. 42, G3

465.	229.16?:	*.*:87	Aguatec. 7, D1
216.	229.?:	*:24	Quir. G, M'1
194.	229.	*:142	Yax. L. 5, B3
237.	229.204:	*	Yax. 11, A'6
243.	229?.74:	*.116	Xcalum. N. build. E. col.
239.	229?:	*:?	Nar. H.S., Y2
175.	229?.	*:126	P.N. 12, A17
189.	229?.13?:	*:142	Yax. L. 54, C2
78.	229?.	*P	P.N. 40, C16
201.	229?.	*	Yax. 7, D4
204, 205.	229?.	*	Pal. Cross R11; T5
412.	11.236?:	*.24?	Tik. 26, F2
433.	13.236:	*	Uxmal Tzompantli
436.	258:	*.*:126	Beyer 699
253–255.	17v:258:	*.*	Yax. L. 22, A3; L. 47, F5; F8
94.	261:	*	Pal. Sarcoph. Gl. 47
3.	262:	*P.116	Cop. A, F1
4.	262:	*.116	Cop. A, D3
179.	263:	*:1000?	Beyer 179
360.	281:	*	M. 22c
45.		*[281]:116	Pal. 96 Gl. L4
451.	359:	*:360	Tik. 31, D11
453–456.	361:	*	Tik. 31, L4; N3; G21; H28
461, 472.	XIII.370:	*	Dos Pilas 11, A2; 3, C3
462.	XIII.370.	*	Dos Pilas H.S. 2, D6
120.	513af:	*:61	Yax. L. 21, D6
446.	1.	*.513.368	Tik. 31, E13
447.	1?:	*.513	Tik. 31, D25
459.		*.338:513	Tik. 31, F21
438.	1:258:	*[513]	Beyer 698. Count 1 haab
439.	55.1:258:	*.513:57	Beyer 674. Count 1 haab
463.	510:35.176:	*.*.35	Dos Pilas 2, C1
437.	92.number: 258:513.	*:57	Beyer 695–97. Count *n* haab
17.	518:1?:	*.173?	Cop. P, D7
382–387.	526.	*	M. 104a; 104a; 104c; 108c; 111a; 111a
388.	526.	*:1	M. 71a
460.	*:35.or 177?.	*P	Tik. 31, G8
86.	565af:III.287?:	*:260	Nar. H.S. L3
373.	631:	*	M. 34a
264.	644.	*.116	Seating haab gl.

93.	IV.1:	*[644]:116	Pal. Sarcoph. Gl. 6
315.	669:	*.116	D. 50d
316.	669?.	*:116	M. 67b
371.	682?:	*	M. 36c8
366, 367.	?.	*	M. 22c; 24c
296.	?:	*	M. 17a
389-391.	?:	*	P. 2c; 6c; 6c
15.	?:	*.?:?	Cop. P. F13
309.	?:	*.116	P. 3a
1.	?:	*.116:82?	Cop. I, A9
101.	?:	*:24	Calak. 51, D1
12.	?.	*:116	Cop. 10, F3
73.	?.	*	P.N., L3, G2
263.	?.4:	*:60	Pal. Inscr. E, J11
180.	?.60:	*.83	P.N. Thr. 1, E'4
427.	?.	*:140	Pal. T. 21, Scribe C1
227.	?:60:	*	Cop. K, H2
30.	?:	*.181:126	Cop. 23, I6
394.	?:	*.*	M. 36b
174.	?:1000.?:	*	P.N. Alt. 2, D3
24.	?.?:	*	Cop. 1, C6
423.	?.?:	*	Pal. T. 18 stucco, W1
203.	?.?:	*:116?	Yax. 9, B2
431.	?.?:	*.130:142	Pal. Sarcoph. E. side
55.	?.151?:	*.116:136	P.N. 25, D1
56.	?.86:?:	*	P.N. 16, C2
225.	?.129?:	*:130?	Quir. P, Cart. 5
91.	III.130:	*	Carac. 17, C3
293.	IV.	*P	D. 56b
107.	?.IV:	*	Quir. I, D2
122.	VI or VIII:	*:60?	Yax. 3, A5
418.	IX.60:	*:116:125	Tort. 6, H4
419.	IX:60:	*:181:24?	Tort. 6, C7
402.	XIII.	*:252	M. 107a
221.	XIII:	*:4?	Quir. P, C5
89.	XIV.	*:116	Tik. 5, B12
113.	1000.VIII:	*:116	Yax. L. 15, C2
222.	XVIII:1:124:	*	Quir. P, C9
92.	1000.	*P:116	Tik. Alt. V, Gl. 5
416, 417.	1010.	238M.S.[*]: 178	Pal. T. 18, stucco glyphs
415.	1010.200v:	*:178	Pal. T. 18, stucco glyphs
310.	1027.	*:116	D. 74

311, 312.	1027.	*:33?	D. 69g; 70b
354, 355.		*.1:19	M. 109b; 109b
215, 217.		*.2:116	Quir. G, P2; N′1
213.		*P:116:2	Quir. F, C10
169.		*:4	P.N. Thr. 1, K′4
212.		*:19	Quir. F, D9
341.		*.24	D. 41b
342.		*:24	M. 64c
40.		*.?:24	Pal. Inscr. W, J7
10.		*.24?:116	Cop. 9, A10
90.		*.116:24	Tonina 30, A6
210.		*.116:24	Quir. D, A23
207.		*.116:24?	Pal. House C Eaves A1
29.		*.60?:130	Cop. 3, B9
241.		*.116:24	Tik. 12, B3
405.		*.*:60	Glyph for baktun
26.		*.61:24?:142	Cop. T. 11, Step 2
188.		*P:61	Yax. L. 45, T3
370.		*.62	D. 10a
464.		*P:87	Dos Pilas H.S. 2, B3
340.		*.103	M. 81b
14.		*:114	Cop. J, N. B4
434.		*:116	Sisilhá rt. jamb 2
208, 209, 211, 214, 224.		*:116	Quir. C, A8; A10; F, B5; C18; P, Cart. 12
471.		*:116	Tik. jade, B1
5.		*P:116	Cop. A, F8
297, 298.		*.116	P. 15b; M. 64b
66, 67.		*.116	Xcocha frags.
406.		*.116 or:116	Glyph for haab
233–236.		*.126:116	Beyer 39–41
22.		*:121	Cop. Z, D2
43.		*.1044.116:?	Pal. Ruz 1, M7
242.		*:142	Jonuta 2, B3
271.		*.*:142:87	P.N. 15, B12
36.		*.187.116	R. Amarillo Alt. 1, K2
449, 450.		*:217:117	Tik. 31, D9, D18. Completion haab var.?
187.		*:217:524?	Yax. L. 35, X6
380.		*.219:?	D. 33c
44.		*P.232:116	Pal. Ruz 1, O6
85.		*P:260	Nar. H.S. Y2
403.		*:?	M. 18b

No pattern of association for Glyph 528 referable to the whole Maya area is easily discerned, but various deities, notably Glyphs 1000, 1016 (particularly the 187–1016 combination), 1031, and 764, precede or follow Glyph 528 as though to indicate rulers of the years. It is hard to say whether these associations are fortuitous or not. At Yaxchilán, Glyph 528 appears in the long clause which contains the jaguar glyph; 87–528 is associated with Glyph 552; 89–528 is joined to Glyph 592 at Copán; 5–528 goes with 585 at Piedras Negras, and 23–528 with 29–563 at the same site. The count of the year and world-direction combination has received comment (Thompson, 1950, p. 251). It is of interest to note that the same 513–528 combination, but without Affix 74, occurs as a prefix to Glyph 528 at Chichén Itzá (entries 437, 438, 439. See also Beyer, 1937, Figs. 670–75 and 695–97). Figure 670 is of particular interest because Affix 177 replaces the Cauac main sign (528) clearly without affecting the meaning. Conversely, Glyph 528 serving as a prefatory glyph can replace Affix 177 in association with Glyph 507.

In the codices the Cauac element almost surely has the phonetic values *ku* and *kul* in addition to its normal meanings of *Cauac, haab,* and storm.

For further examples of Glyph 528, see under Glyphs 501, 512?, 515, 526, 529, 544, 548, 558, 559, 561, 568?, 592?, 598?, 601, 644, 657, 668, 669, 671, 731, 738, 743, 744, 746, 747, 751, 756, and 758.

GLYPH 529 (Cauac Variant 1)
(14 Examples; Sheet 106)

3.	58:	*	Cop. Md. 2 reused stone
1.	117:	*	Cop. I, C3
11.	122:	*	Tik. 31, F17
2.	24.150:	*	Cop. 1, AB8
7.	12.168:	*	Xultun 19, B1
6.	297.168:	*	Carac. 16, C15
8.	174:	*	Tik. 22, A3
10.	288:	*.746:130?	Cop. J, E. Gl. 22
9.	11.528af.	*.528af:88	Tik. 26, E7
12.	679:	*.362.181	Tik. 31, C26
4.	?.	*	Cop. J, A5
5.		*.528:181	· Quir. C, G1
13.		*:683b	Dos Pilas H.S. 2, D5
14.		*?:548	Dos Pilas H.S. 2, C4

No. 10 is vertical and almost seems to be serving as an affix. See also under Glyph 746.

GLYPH 530 (Cauac Variant 2)
(16 Examples; Sheet 105)

10.	79.	*:?	Yax. L. 37, Q5
12.	1.174:	*:24	Pal. Sarcoph. Gl. 14
15.	1.174:	*:501	Pal. Fol. sculpt. stone, A6
14.	13.43?:174:	*	Beyer 303
2.	87.174:	*	Cop. Q, F6
13.	103.1:174:	*	Beyer 302 (misdrawn)
6–8.	125.174:	*:178	Pal. Inscr. M. E5; I3; W. A4
1.	126.174:	*	Cop. Q, E2
9.	126:174:	*	Quir. P, C6
11.	174:	*?	P.N., L. 3, F'
4, 5.	Seated bearer. 174:	*	Cop. D', 4; W', D1
3.	IX.174:	*	Cop. Z, E1
16.		*?.1?	Uaxac. mural lower part

GLYPH 531
(3 Examples; Sheet 107)

2.	117:	*	Cop. B, back
1.	238:	*	Cop. B, B3
3.	624.	*	P.N., L. 3, U6

The two examples from Copán differ from the Piedras Negras glyph illustrated, and look more like the head of an animal or reptile set vertically. They carry the Cauac marking. Note the rare presence at Copán of the macaw head prefix (238).

GLYPH 532 (Cauac-burden)
(13 Examples; Sheets 53, 57)

11.	1:174:506?.114.	*:121	Cop. R´´, A2–B2
81.	1.87.	*:126	Yax. L. 46, F´´9
82.	1.87.	*:130	P.N. Thr. 1, A´1
79.	87.	*.126:88	Yax. Str. 44, S.E. up. step
85.	87.	*.151:126	Chinik. 1, U1
77.	87?.	*.181:25	Pal. Ruz 2, E2
12.	87?.	*.181	Tort. 6, D6
78.	87?.	*.130	Pal. House D, Pier G
41.	92.87.	*:178	Cop. 13, E5
35.	219:87?.	*	Cop. I, C4
86.	205.?.	*:104	P.N., L. 4, H1
33.	218.	*:116?	Cop. 4, A5
13.	?.	*.181	La Mar 3, C1
40.	?.	*	Cop. T, S. side

Compare the above with 87.515:528 and 200.515:87. These show that here we are dealing with the Muluc-burden glyph with Cauac infix. Moreover, Glyph 532 with Postfixes 25 and 181 once (No. 77) appears after a C.R. date as do Glyphs 512 and 515. In a second case (No. 37) only Postfix 181 is present, but the compound appears to function in the same way, for it follows a C.R. date. The compound is probably the same as the Cauac over burden (Glyph 528:601) of the codices.

GLYPH 533 (Ahau)
(254 Examples; Sheets 108–113; Gates' Glyph 20; Zimmermann's Glyph 1320)

248.		*	M. 22C
10, 11, 17.	1.	*:24	Pal. Sun, L4; Cross, I5; Sarcoph. 53
14.	1.	*:24	Cayo L. 1, B13
16.	1.	*.102:?	Moral. 2, D5
102.	1.	*	M. 64C
103.	1.	*:25	M. 64C

57[1].	1.	*:102	Tonina Alt. 31, Gl. 8
62.	1.	*.102:82	S. Ton. 2, Gl. 5
105.	1.	*.?:?	P. 3d
106.	1.?:	*	P. 8b
254.	1?.?:	*	Nar. 2, B11
8, 9.	11.	*:24	Pal. Fol. H1; Sun, K2
7.	11:	*:24	Pal. Cross, K4
15.	11:	*:24?	Moral. 2, D3
251.	12:	*?:254	Tulum 1, K7
19–22, 24, 26, 27, 29.	13:	*:102	Yax. L. 25, A3; W1; L. 27, H1; L. 32, A7; L. 53, C2; L. 56, L1; 11, I2; Str. 44, mid. step, C5
251.	13.110:	*	Lamb site, L. 1, F2
25.	59.13:	*:102	Yax. Str. 44, mid. step, D3
31–33.	13.	*:102	Yax. 15, B2; C2; L. 46, G''6
37.	13.	*.102	P.N. 8, Y15
107.	15.	*:736	M. 98b
109.	24.	*	M. 64c
110.	24:	*:23	M. 24a
111–215.	24.	*:24	Gates' Glyph 20.1.1. In all codices
101.	1.24.	*.103:24	M. 63c
88.	25.	*	Cop. carved brown jar
216[2].	25.24.	*:24	M. 70a
40.	43?:	*	Cop. 9, F2
234.	58.	*v:103	D. 20c
42.	61.	*:102	Cop. T. 11, W. door, S. pan. A6
4.	61:117:	*	Cop. H.S. Gxiim
217.	62.	*:24	M. 38c
104.	1.62:	*:23	D. 20b
218, 219.	?.62:	*.?	M. 20d; 36d
235.	87.	*	M. 95d
48.	102.4:	*	Xculoc sculpt. col.
237.	122:	*	P.N. 29, D2
44.	124?:	*	Alt. Sac. 9, F6
54.	125:	*:102	Pal. Fol. E13
97.	125:	*:130	Beyer 176
1, 3.	1:125:	*:23:?	Cop. H.S. Gxiie; Gxiio
13.	1.126:	*:24?	Caribe 1, B1
233.	137.	*:130	M. 97b

229–231.	149:	*	M. 104c
232.	149:	*.21	M. 104c
238.	155?:	*	Pal. T. 18 stucco
64, 65, 75, 80, 81, 89, 92, 99.	168:	*:130	Beyer 305; 306; 41; 78; 79; 134; 140; 198
82.	168:	*:130:24	Beyer 80
63, 73, 74, 83.	168:	*.130	Beyer 304; 39; 40; 81
76.	168:	*.head	Beyer 42
66–69.	168:	*:289	Beyer 307–310
221.	168:	*.?:25	M. 34b
50.	168:	*.102?	Cop. R, D2
70.	35.168:	*:130	Beyer 314
77.	126.168:	*.130:501?: 27?	Beyer 319
71.	229.168:	*:268	Beyer 316
78.	229.168:	*:130	Beyer 48
227.	XI.168:	*	P. 4c
228.	XI.168:	*.130.	D. 60c
51.	168?:	*.102	Cop. T. 21a, I
226.	172.	*:103	P. 5c
220.	172.146.?:	*	D. 47c
222–224.	181.	*:25	M. 63c
225.	199?.	*	M. 59b
12.	204.?:	*.24	P.N. 23, K6
18.	205.1:	*.24	Pal. T. 18, A14
5.	210:	*	Carac. 6, E15
95.	213?:	*.213?	Pusil. K, B3
252.	229.	*	Arenal polychrome vase
23, 28, 30, 34.	229.	*:102	Yax. 12, F4; 18, D4; 20, B1; 23, A14
96.	229?.	*:?	Yax. 7, D1
79.	269:	*:130	Beyer 50
238.	270.	*.116	M. 59b
239–244.	270.	*.181	M. 58b; 59b
253.	134.345:136:	*.134:136	Head for 3.D.9b
39.	544?:116.	*:102?	Comal. tomb E2
250.	610.	*:277?	M. 61c
254.	?.	*:23	Yalloch cyl. jar
38.	?.	*.102	Cop. 4, A4
2.	?.	*:178?	Cop. 9, E10
247.	?.	*:103	M. 36d
249.	?.	*:?	M. 98b
250.	?.	*	Uxmal tecali vase, C1

6.	?:?:	*:24	Cop. H.S. Step O
253.	?:?:	*	Aguatec. 1, A5
36.	?.?:	*.?:?	Cop. J, W. Gl. 46
35.		*:202	Cop. 7, F7
100.		*:24	M. 94b
90.		*.24	M. 19b
45.		*:24?	Bonam. 2, G3
91.		*.24:24	M. 87b
72.		*.24:102	Carved brown sherd, Ulua
46.		*:55?	Xcalum. N. build. W. col.
43.		*:102	Quir. I, C9
52.		*:102	Cop. T. 11, Step 7
55.		*:102	Pal. Ruz 1, P1
56, 58, 59.		*:102	Tik. 22, A3; L. 2, A12; L. 4, E3
61.		*:102	Beyer 321
60.	head.	*:102	Beyer 320
236.		*:103	D. 54b
93.		*v:103	P. 8c
53.		*:102?	Cop. T. 22, Step 11
94.		*.116	M. 21d
49.		*:125	Chajcar box frag.
47.		*.130:102?	Xcalum. N. build. Serp. Gl. 17
98.		*.130	Beyer 177
245.		*.181:114	D. 51a
246[1].		*.210v.210v:242	Chichén Itzá N.E. Colonnade Col. 2

[1] A very rare Maya name glyph above a personage at Chichén Itzá. The postfixes look like conchs but might be something else.

[2] Inverted, probably by mistake.

Note that Nos. 227 and 228 correspond to the forms of Ahau used at Chichén Itzá to mark katun endings.

For further examples of Glyph 533, see under Glyphs 502, 503, 544, 550, 582, 610, 624, 670, 686, 713?, 736, and 802.

GLYPH 534 (Inverted Ahau)
(39 Examples; Sheet 114; Gates includes with Gl. 20; Zimmermann includes with Gl. 1320)

19.	1.	*	Holmul tripod vase
11.	12.130?:	*	Cop. T. 11, S. door, E. pan.
23.	15.	*:130	D. 51a
7.	17.	*:88	P.N., L. 3, J1
25.	24.	*	M. 63c
26.	24.	*:23	M. 63b
14.	25?:	*	Cop. H.S. Gxiif
9.	58.	*:25?	P.N., L. 2, D'2
8.	59.25:	*	P.N., L. 3, O2
39.	59. number	*:113	Used in short D.N. for days. Pasión.
31.	74:	*.?	Acanceh tomb mural
29.	76?:178.	*:103	M. 61c
15.	79?:	*.181	Tik. L. 3, H3
18.	113?.	*:8?	Beyer 324
16.	117.	*:?	Tik. Alt. VIII, B2
34.	122.23:	*.?	Uxmal Ball Crt. W. ring
10.	126.	*:181?	P.N. Alt. support, A2
1.	130?:	*	Cop. T. 11 Step Gl. 4
30.	136inv.:	*:23?	Pal. T. 18 Stucco W1
13.	149:	*	Seib. 12, A5
3.	181?:	*	R. Amarillo Alt. 1, K1
12.	204:	*:?	Bonam. 1, N1
27.	219:	*.116	M. 25d
24.	17:219:	*	P. 8b
4.	220:	*	Pal. House C. Basement E1
35.	224?.736:	*	M. 35d
21.	III.	*:24?	M. 66b
22.	V.	*:24	M. 14a
32.	IX.78:	*	Cop. brown ware. Longyear 110b
36.	number: or.	*:103	Used in short D.N. for days
37.	number: or.	* or 178:565	Used in short D.N. for days
2.	?.	*:27	Los Higos 1, D8

38.	?.	*?:178:?	Sisilhá lt. jamb, 10
5.		*:102	Pusil. carved jawbone
28.		*.116	M. 26b
6.		*[503].181	Pal. Madrid slab
33.		*:731	M. 91c
17.		*:?	Comitán 1, D2

No. 27 appears to be the glyph for west substituted for the usual 219:544.116 compound and is confirmatory evidence that Glyph 534 can have the meaning sun or day (see also entries 36 and 37). Note that Affix 178 corresponds to Glyph 534. See also under Glyph 683.

GLYPH 535 (Decorated Ahau A)
(26 Examples; Sheets 115, 116)

25.		*?	M. Cow celt A5
20.	1.	*	Holmul tripod dish
6.	1.	*	Bonam. 2, G3
7.	1:	*	Bonam. 1, K1
9.	1.	*:23	Nar. 24, E10
1, 19.	1.	*:23	Cop. 9, E7; T. 11, reused stone
13.	1.	*:23	Tik. 13, B7
26.	1:	*:23	Tik. 31, K4
12, 14.	1.	*:23?	Tik. 3, D6; 19, B7
18.	1.	*:23?	Ojos de Agua 1, B10
3.	1:	*:82	Pal. T. 18 stucco
2.	1.	*:?	R. Amarillo Alt. 1, D1
5.	1.	*:?	P.N. 1, K8
24.	3.	*:24	Pal. incised yoke frag.
4.	117.	*:23	Yax. L. 22, B1
11.	204.	*:23	Tik. 17, H7
15.	204.	*:23	Pal. Cross E. balustr. I2
21.	204.	*	Tik. 22, B6
10.	204.	*:24	Tik. 5, C11
8.	232?:	*	Alt. Sac. 12, D4
16.	?.	*:23	Honradez 7, B8
17.	?.	*:82	Pal. Fol. Balustr. I2

| 22. | ?. | *?:23 | Cop. I, D5 |
| 23. | | * on side | Beyer 323 |

See also under Glyph 670.

GLYPH 536 (Decorated Ahau 2)
(7 Examples; Sheet 117)

1.	110:	*	Cop. W', D2
3–5.	177.	*:142	Pal. Inscr. M. I6; L4; M1
7.	203?:	*.32:288	Carac. 3, B10b
2.	?.?:	*	Cop. O', B1
6.		*:103	P.N. 15, C12

GLYPH 537 (Xipe)
(23 Examples; Sheets 118, 119, 128; Gates' Glyph 348; Zimmermann's Glyph 1342a)

1.	12:	*	Cop. T. 11, S. door, W. pan.
9.	12:27:	*	Beyer 184
4.	25:	*	P.N., L. 3, G'
17, 18.	27:27:90.	*:178	D. 47f; 50e
14.	59.	*.?	D. 33c
7.	60?:	*	Tonina, 31, Gl. 4.
10.	92.V?:271:	*(inv.)	Cop. H.S. Frag. Gxii
15, 16.	146.	*:23	D. 46b; 46c
19.	186:	*	D. 61d
20.	207.	*:24	M. 16a
21.	207?.	*:23	M. 16a
28.	229.?:	*	Comal. tomb E4
13.	283.	*	M. 82b
22.	552.	*.116?	M. 40c
23.	1.552:	*	M. 41c
24.	1.70.552:	*	M. 40c
25.	74.552:	*	M. 40b.

26.	X. 552:	*	M. 40c
12.		*.552	M. 26b
11.	IX.III?:	*	D. 65a
8.	?:	*?	Cop. T. 11, S. door, W. pan.

For further examples of Glyph 537, see under Glyphs 552 and 624.

GLYPH 538 (Xipe Variant 1)
(4 Examples; Sheet 120)

3.	95:?.86:	*	Quir. A, D4
1, 2.	122.48:	*v:23	Cop. 7, B11; 12, B12
4.		*v	Quir. Str. 2, façade

Nos. 2 and 3 have three adjoining circles to represent eyes and mouth. No. 4 technically is not a glyph, but a decorative motif set at ground level in the façade of a building. The features are naturalistic, and from them radiate the curved spokes, as in the other examples, to the enclosing ring of circlets (photograph in files of School of American Research).

GLYPH 539 (Half-spotted Ahau)
(27 Examples; Sheets 121–122)

1.	1:	*:179[130]?	Cop. T. 11, S. door E. pan. B3
15.	1.	*:114.	Cop. K'', A1
16.	1.	*:125	Yax. L. 15, F1
17.	1:	*.181:?	Yax. L. 14, B4
5.	11:	*:130	Pal. Fol., F4
22.	60?:	*:23	Yax. L. 10, E1
9.	74.184.198:	*	Pal. Sun, D1
4.	95:	*	Pal. Fol. N11
10.	95:	*:179[130]	Pal. Ruz 1, F12
2.	III:	*:179[130]	Pal. Cross, O1

3, 8.	III.	*:179[130]	Pal. Fol., O3; Sun, K1
12–14.	III.	*:179[130]?	Pal. Cross, W. pan.; Sun, E. pan.; Death's head, F1
23, 26, 27.	III.	*:179	Pal. Cross, Balustr. D1; J1; Fol. Balustr. J1
20.	III.	*.130:179	P.N. 25, F2
7.	III?.130:	*.130?	Pal. Sun, Q9
11.	130?:	*:179[130]	Pal. 96 Gl. I2.
19.	130.	*	P.N. 15, C11
21.	198?:	*.130:179?	P.N. 25, I10
6.	204.	*:23	Pal. Sun, O5
28.	758?.	*	El Cayo L. 1, A14
18.	?.	*.181	Covarrubias *sub judice* A1
24.	?.	*:1344	Covarrubias *sub judice* A4

See also under Glyph 751.

GLYPH 540 (Half-hatched Ahau)
(8 Examples; Sheets 122, 123)

24.	1.95:	*	Pal. Sun detached stucco
18.	95:	*	Pal. T. 18 stucco
25.	203.95:	*	Pal. Sun detached stucco
1.	VI.	*:88:126	Yax. L. 29, C4
2, 3.	VI.	*:88?:126	Yax. 1, C8; 11, B'15
4.	VI.	*?:?	Moral. 2, C4
5.	1017.	*:200	Cop. Frag. V'10

GLYPH 541 (Hatched Ahau)
(3 Examples; Sheet 124)

3.		*	P.N., L. 3, F''2
1.	226.	*:125	Cop. E, B8
2.	XVII.	*:125	Cop. 10, H2

No. 3 lacks the cartouche.

GLYPH 542 (Ahau semblant)
(43 Examples; Sheets 118, 125–27; Gates' Glyph 347; Zimmermann's Glyph 1342b)

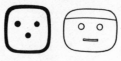

a   b

40.		*	Form of day sign Ahau
1, 2.	12:	*	Cop. V, F1; T. 11, S. door
			W. pan.
3.	12.74?:	*	Pal. House C Plat. K2
37.	60:	*.25	Beyer 136
38.	60.27:	*	Beyer 134
6.	65?:	*	P.N. 29, C4
23[1], 24, 25.	87.	*	M. 97b; 98b; 98b
32.	87:	*.130	P. 3d
26.	1.87:	*	M. 42c
27–30.	59.87:	*	M. 102b; 102b; 102d; 102d
31.	109.	*:87	D. 30c
16–21.		*:87	M. 42c (thrice); 98b; 98b;
			P. 10
22.		*.87	M. 97b
41.	144:	*	Tohcok painted jamb
4.	1.145:	*	M. 42c
12.	146:	*	M. 102c
14, 15.	146:	*.181	M. 102c; 102c
13.	1.146:	*	M. 102c
10.	181.43?:	*	Pal. Ruz 2, H1
42.	217.48:	*	Uaxac. red bowl, A1
43.	217.48?:	*	Tik. 31, A24
34, 35.	227inv.	*:163	D. 20b; 20b
8.	?.11:	*:130:136	Pal. Inscr. E. O10
36.	1.612:	*	M. 91a
4.	?.?:	*:142	Ixlu Alt. St. 2, E5
11[1].	?.	*	Carac. 6, D15
39.	?.	*?:?	Yax. L. 33, A2
9[2].		*.24	D. 66a
7.		*.181:53	Quir. L. Gl. 21
33.		*.?	M. 97b

[1] On side.

[2] Dotted outline.

On M. 97b–98b, Glyph 542 with Affix 87 almost certainly means wooden mask or idol; on M. 102, with variable affixes, it appears to stand for spindlewhorl and loom or weaving stick.

For further examples of Glyph 542, see under Glyphs 236, 528, 582, 612, and 758.

GLYPH 543 (Xipe variant 2)
(6 Examples; Sheet 129)

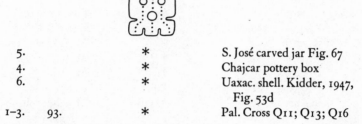

5.		*	S. José carved jar Fig. 67
4.		*	Chajcar pottery box
6.		*	Uaxac. shell. Kidder, 1947, Fig. 53d
1–3.	93.	*	Pal. Cross Q11; Q13; Q16

Nos. 4 and 5 lack the lines of dots. The resemblance of this glyph to Glyphs 628 and 629 may be significant.

GLYPH 544 (Kin)
(425 Examples; Sheets 130–42; Gates' Glyph 45; Zimmermann's Glyph 1341)

417.		*	Xkichmook Pal. Rm. 11 painting
29.		*	Pusil. P, H5
415.		*	P.N. bowl. Coe Fig. 60d
416.		*	S. José carved jar, Fig. 67
86.		*	M. 90b
319[1].		*	P. 6d
102.	1.	*	M. 90b
91.	1.	*.116	M. 34d
21[2].	1:	*:116?	Yax. L. 56, J2
48.	1.	*:116	Beyer 347
408.	12.	*:23	Site Pal. X, 1, C1
36.	12:	*:130?	Xcalum. S. build. W. pan. A1
37.	12.?:	*.228:116	Xcalum. S. build. E. pan. B3

409.	12.	*:?	Xcalum. N. build. Serp. Gl. 23
65.	12:	*.?:60	P.N. 12, A15
354, 355.	12.I:	*:116	Seib. 9, D1; 10, A4
305.	16: or .	*: or.116	Month Yaxkin
103, 104.	23.	*	M. 37b?; 91c
307.	24.	*:136	M. 62a
281.	47:?:	*	M. 35b
93.	58.	*:116	D. 67a
63.	58:?:	*	P.N. 12, A15
49.	59.	*:116	Beyer 348
276–278.	64:	*	M. 34b; 36b; 37b
280.	64:	*.?	M. 35b
282.	70:	*	M. 36d
355.	84:	*.611	D. 65a
94–98.	90.	*:116	M. 99b; 100b; 100b; 101a; 102a
327.	92.	*:116	Beyer 346
279.	95:	*	M. 99d
309.	109.	*	D. 25c
71.	109?.135:	*	Shell. Tuxtla Mus.
358.	44:115?.	*	Carac. Conch god vase
274.	122:	*	P. 24a
35.	122.11:	*:24?	Pal. jade earplug
3.	125:?:	*:181	Cop. M, D5
351.	136.	*:23	D. 54b
2.	142?:	*.181:23	Cop. P, D4
317.	143?.	*:186	M. 90d
19.	153:	*.116:179?	Pal. Ruz 2, D3
310.	163?:	*:103	M. 8c
100.	13.163:	*:116	D. 61
286.	168:	*	M. 89d
66, 68.	168:	*.116	P.N. 25, B2; L. 2, R2
69.	168:	*.116	Xcalum. N. build. frag.
70.	168:	*.116	Calak. 89, D8
61, 67.	168:	*.116	P.N. 25, I7; Shell, L5
62.	1002.168:	*.116	P.N. 3, D7
4.	168:	*.116:130	Cop. Alt. St. 13
287–299.	168:	*.130	All codices. Gates 45.18.1
345.	168:	219[*].130: 116	Bonam. Mur. Rm. 2
336.	16.168:	219[*]:116	Yax. L. 58, D3
335.	17?.168:	219[*]:116	Yax. L. 58, C1

302, 303.	25.168:	*.130	M. 97d; 99c
301.	130.168:	*.	M. 26a
304.	172.130.168:	*	P. 23a
300³.	168.:	*.130	M. 85b
31.	168?:	*:130?	Nar. 32, S2
312.	171.33:	*	D. 71a
352.	172.	*:23	D. 53a
353.	172?.	*:23	M. 35d
186.	178:	*.273	M. 34d
183.	178:	*.1:116	M. 86e
184.	59.178:	*.116	D. 30c
185.	59?.178:	*	D. 42a
182.	VI?.178:	*.116	M. 86c
418.	183:	*	M. Cow shell disk
1.	183:	*:116	Cop. A, G8
12.	183:	*:116	Uaxac. 13, A7
5.	183:	*.116	Cop. Alt. St. 13
6, 7, 18.	183:	*.116	Pal. Inscr. M, H7; carved pot; Ruz 1, O14
22.	183:	*.116	Yax. L. 30, F3
33.	183?:	*.116	Nar. 21, B11
11.	183:	*.12?	Nar. 13, E15
411.	187.	*.187:142	Poco Uinic 3, B23
357.	202:	*	M. 99d
99.	I.207.	*:116	D. 69 (Kin variant)
420.	218:	*.363:23	Tik. 31, D21
332, 347.	24:	217[*].116	Nar. 23, G9; 30, G13
356.	184.217		Cop. carved brown pot
357.	74.184.24:217		Jonuta, 1, A3
187–190.	219:	*	D. 43a; M. 31a; 76; 84a
410.	219:	*	Kabah mural (Brinton)
328.	219.	*	P. 16a
191–237.	219:	*.116	West. D. and M. Gates 45.5.1, 2
238–246.		219[*].116	West. D. 29c; 46b; c; 47b; c; 48b; c; 49b; 50b
338, 340–343.		219[*]:116	Beyer 352; 354–57
57.	219[*]:	*	Quir. U, A8
348.		220[*]:116	Pal. Sun, N9
329.		220[*]:116	Yax. L. 10, C2
331.		220[*]:116	Pusil. D, D4
339.		220[*]:116	Beyer 353
330.		220[*].116	Shell. Tuxtla Mus.

29.		220[*].116: 82.	Xultun 18, A8
349.		220[*]:116: 125	Quir. F, D17
352.		220[*]?:116	Cop. U, M2
353.		220[*]?.116: 130?	Cop. T, front
358, 359.		220[*]:?	Nar. 22, E14, H12
355.	11.	220[*]?.6:59: 116	Pal. Fol. O8
350.	62:	220[*].116	Cop. 11, A6
351.	68.	220[*].116	Cop. 10, G9
354.	204.	220[*]?.6:59: 116	Pal. Fol. M2
53.	221[*]:	* :116	Cop. A, H8
30, 32.	221[*]?:	* :116	Nar. 24, A2; 32, V4
54.	221[*]:	* .116	Cop. Q, D3
55, 56.	221[*]:	* .116	Pal. Fol. B15; Inscr. M. H8
26.	221[*]:	* .116	Yax. L. 33, H10
58.	221[*]:	* .116	Nar. 13, H6
275.	122.221:	*	P. 24a
101.	228.	* .116	M. 70a
283.	267:	*	D. 50d
284.	267:	* .116	D. 24a
265.	268:	* .612af	D. 55b
357–409.	326.	* .326	Cloudy day? Black areas perhaps to indicate rain clouds. Gates Gl. 451
248–251.	528:	* .116	M. 21d; 22d; 22d; 91a
252–261.	528:	* .548.24	Drought. D. 27c; 31b; 33b; 37a; 42c; 45b; 45c; 71b; 72a; 72c
262.	528:	* .548	Drought. D. 40b
412.		* :528:24.?	Damaged; drought. P. 11c
413.		* :528.548?:24	Damaged; drought. P. 6c
263.		* :528.548:142	Drought. D. 26a
264.		* .528:548	Drought. D. 25c
247.	548:24	* .528:116	Drought (2 glyphs). D. 72c
421–424.	267:	* .548	D. 36b; 39b; 58e; 60a
106–173.	533:	* .116	East D. and M. Gates 45.4.1
174–181.		* :178.116	East M. Gates 45.4.1a
72.		* .116:178	Holmul tripod bowl
268–270.	662:	*	M. 85b (thrice)

271–273.	662:	*.116	M. 85b (thrice)
74.	?:	*.*:116	Nar. 30, C12
28.	?:	*:116	Bonam. 3, A2
34.	?:	*:1	Beyer 359
13.	I.?:	*.116	Pal. T. 18 Tab. A12
410.	?.11?:	*:82	Tort. 6, E6
285.	?:	*	M. 37b
311.	?:	*:103	M. 96a
314.	?:	*:130	M. 95a
318.	?.?:	*:24	M. 34b
316.	?.155?:	*	M. 81b
40, 42, 43.		*:8.116	Beyer 123; 125; 126
38, 41.		*:116:8	Beyer 121; 124
39.		*.116:8	Beyer 122
315.		*.*:60?	M. 34a
320–323[1].		*:87	D. 12c (thrice); M. 69a
324–326[1].		*.116:87	D. 15c (twice); P. 18c
45.		*:92.116	Beyer 128
46, 47.		*:116:92	Beyer 129; 130
306.		*.96	M. 100c
414.		*. or :116	Normal form of kin .116 may be omitted
17.		*:116	Pal. Sun, C2
10.		*:116	P.N. Thr. 1, A2
24, 25.		*:116	Yax. 18, C1; L. 26, X1.
50–52.		*:116	Beyer 349–51
419.		*:116	Sisilhá L. 2
20.		*.116	Quir. E, A16
14.		*.116	Cop. 7, D12
87–90.		*.116	D. 57b; M. 32b; 37c; 100c
105.		*.116:136	D. 73b
92.		*.116:140	D. 72b
75–79, 82–85.		*:217.181:179	Beyer 61–65; 68–71
80.		*:217:181.179	Beyer 66
81.		*:217?.?:179?	Beyer 67
308.		*.281:136	M. 10b
313.		*.632	M. 35d
425.		*.186?:712 [504]	Tik. 31, B9. Aberrant form of Gl. G9
267.		*:783.612af	D. 51b

[1] Dotted outline.
[2] Probably the prefatory part of Glyph 1001 set above the god's head, instead of to the left.
[3] Set at an angle of 45°.

Glyph 544 usually with 116 postfixed is the glyph kin, "sun," "day," "time," and (only in post-Columbian times?) "festival." It appears in the glyphic compounds for east and west, *likin* and *chikin* in Yucatec, and in the month sign Yaxkin. Note the straight lines in examples from Yucatán and in the codices. Glyph 544 is prefixed to the portrait glyph 1001; prefixed to the macaw glyph (744), it reminds one of the deity Kinich Kakmo, "Sun-eye fire macaw," worshiped at Izamal.

For further examples of Glyph 544, see under Glyphs 17, 233, 504, 506, 510, 526, 548, 552, 568, 611, 619, 624, 662, 670, 671, 712, 738, 743, 744, 751, 754, 756, 760, 762, 765, 783, 798, and 804.

GLYPH 545 (Half-cross-hatched Kin)
(7 Examples; Sheet 143)

2.	51.19?:	*:116	Yax. 18, A1
5.	59.	*:116	P.N., L. 3, O1
3.	103.	*:116	P.N. Thr. 1, Z1
4.	103:	*.116	P.N. Thr. 1, F'3
1.	113.	*:116	Pal. Fol. L5
6.	86: or 135	*	Name glyph of sun in underworld as lord of night, Glyph G9
7	116:	*v	Cop. 3, Ped. on two-headed monster

Glyph 545 probably stands in all cases for the sun or sun god in his underworld aspect. Indeed, the example from Palenque, standing between two consecutive days, probably serves as a sort of distance number to mark the passage of one night. I know of only one portrait glyph of the night sun unassociated with the night over which the god ruled. This is at Caracol 6, E23, dedicated at 9.8.10.0.0.

GLYPH 546 (Kin variant)
(17 Examples; Sheet 134; Gates under Glyph 45; Zimmermann under Glyph 1341)

1, 2.	84:	*.181	D. 72a; 72b
266.	84:	*:612af	D. 73b
3.	III.84.122:	*	D. 73b

4.	III.122.84:	*	D. 72c
64.	95?.122:	[III?]*.48	P.N., L. 12, L1
59.	272:	*:178	Pal. Inscr. M., D5
441–444.	272:	*.178	Cop. Ball Court markers N.; M.; S.
60.	513af:272:	*	Pal. Inscr. M. J8
8.		*.4	P.N. Thr. 1, K'3
5.		*?.116	M. 20d
6.		*.116:24?	Yax. L. 40, C4
445.		*.173?	Jade head Br. Mus.
7.		*:733af?	Yax. L. 21, A7

Glyph 546 sometimes serves as prefix of Glyph 1001. See also Glyphs 183, 713, and 738.

GLYPH 547 (Kin compound)
(6 Examples; Sheet 144)

5.	136.	*?:27?	Quir. U, A7
1, 2.	12:168:	*:?	Quir. E, D20; Alt. O, C'1
3.	12.168:	*:130?	Cop. F, B10
4.	229.168:	*:102?	Quir. Str. 1, J'
6.		*:102	Pal. T. 18, shell with glyphs

No. 6 has the kin sign on the left side. Perhaps Glyph B' of the Review Stand, Temple 11, Copán, belongs with the above.

GLYPH 548 (Tun)
(156 Examples; Sheet 145; Gates' Glyph 50; Zimmermann's Glyph 1340)

1.		*:23	Tun sign
121.	11:	*:87	Cop. 7, B10
131.	12:	*:87:178	Beyer 510
130.	12:	*:87:254	Beyer 509
137.	12.VI:	*:178	Beyer 507
138.	12.VI:	*	Beyer 508

[161]

134.	13.	*.126:142?	Beyer 513
133.	13.	*.8:585?	Beyer 512
123.	13.124?:	*.82:130?	Cop. 6, C9
43–45.	17.	*:24	D. 27c; 28c; 41b
50.	24.	*:24	P. 2c
71.	24.	*:136	D. 28a
105.	28:	*	Katun sign
118.	168:28:	*	"Ben-Ich katun"
106–108.	207.28:	*	D. 70c; 73a; 31a
145.	58.	*	D. 31c. Name of tree. Zactun?
46.	58.	*:24	P. 4b
126.	58?:	*:142	Pal. Inscr. W. K2
47, 48.	59.	*:24	D. 50d; 75a
128.	59.87?:	*	Nar. 30, A4
49.	62.	*:24	P. 7c
97–99.	V.63:	*	D. 37a; P. 4b; M. 63c
100.	IV.63:	*:?	P. 3b
147.	64:	*	M. 94a
103.	IV.64:	*	D. 47b
101, 102.	V.64:	*	M. 104b; 106b
135.	68:	*	Xcalum. N. build. E. col. A5
150.	68:	*.59	Xcalum. N. build. jamb frag.
122.	68:	*.59	Holmul tripod bowl
148.	71:	*.116:612	M. 104b
129.	86:	*:142	Tik. L. 3, G4
52–63.	number.90.	*:24	M. 65–73; Gates 50.1.7n
96.	III.90:	*	M. 71b
93, 94.	III.	*.90	M. 68a; 71a
95.	X.	*.90	M. 69a
51.	112?.	*:24	D. 26a
119.	124:25. variable:	*.25	I.S. intro. gl. normal form
154.	124:203. variable:	*.203	I.S. intro. gl. rarer form
120.	127 or 128:	*	Indicates 20th day of uinal
144.	157:	*	Uayeb glyph
87.	168.	*	D. 37c. Only case of Affix 168 to left.
153.	168?:	*:131	Itsimte Alt. 1, B1
24.	228.168:	*.125:60	Pal. Inscr. E. S4

88.	238.168:	*.130	M. 65b
65–67.	172.	*:24	P. 4d; 11e; 24a
125.	head.178:	*:142	Pal. Inscr. M. H5
68.	181.	*:24	P. 4d
139.	194?.VIII:	*	Chama. Carey vase
104.	207:	*:142	D. 70c
90.	236:	*	P. 3c
109–112.	267:	*	D. 24a; 50d; P. 23a; M. 35c
113–116.	267:544.	*	D. 36b; 39b; 58c; 60c?
127.	1.268:	*	Yax. L. 42, E1
69.	290:	*:24	M. 37c
156.	?.	512[*]	Tik. 31, F22
83.	524?.	*	D. 26a
84.	528.	*	M. 26b
85.		*.528	M. 26a
117.	528.528:	*	Rare Baktun variant
91.	236:528:	*	P. 3c
136.	528.116:	*:142	Iturbide Stone, A3
86.	528.687:	*	P. 16f
92.	626:	*.?	P. 3c
146.	136.626.	*:142	D. 73b
36.	648:	*	P. 5c
37.	648:140.	*:24	P. 5c
38.	648:25.	*:24	D. 72c
39–43.	736:140.	*:24	P. 5d; 9c; 9c; 11b; D. 72a
72.	747?.	*	P. 11d
73–79.	1052.	*:24	P. 5c; 5d; 9c; 23a (thrice); 24a
80–82.	1052.	*?:24?	P. 8c, 24a (twice)
152.	bird?head.	*:142	D. 73a. Zimmermann's Gl. 728
64.	III.	*.122:24	M. 65a
89.	VI.	*:521	M. 110b
2.	VIII.1006	[*]	D. 61a
3–35.	With or without number	*:24	Gates 50.1; 1n; 15–19; 25; 29; 30
70.		*.24:136	D. 27a
143.		*:103 or 126	Tun used as anniversary
142.		*:142	Tun used in I.S. or P.E.
132.		*:142:8	Beyer 511
155.		*:54	Tun form used rarely in D.N.
149.		*:575.125	Pal. Ruz 1, C2

Entries 97–103 are name glyphs of Schellhas' God N, the Mam or old god of the end of the year and of the interior of the earth. Note the use of the tun glyph with Affixes 127 or 128 to indicate "end" when joined to month glyphs, an example of rebus writing (Thompson, 1950, p. 121), and again the tun has a phonetic value in the *ḳintunyabil* (544:528.548.24) compound listed under 544.

The tun glyph is also used with the meaning of bedrock in the codices. In the divinatory almanac of Madrid 25d which treats of the fate of the young maize plant, two of the scenes rest on the Caban (earth) sign, whereas the other two rest on the tun sign. Surely, here we have a parallel to the biblical parable of the corn, some of which fell on rock and some on good soil. The figures at the bottom left corner of Dresden 25 to 28 which deal with the new year rest on tun glyphs. Here it is reasonable to suppose the signs refer to the piles of rock at the exits of the towns, which played an important part in the new year ceremonies. See also Madrid, pp. 34–37 and Paris, pp. 19 and 20.

It is tempting to read 236:548, a combination of *chich*, "bird," and tun, or 236:528.548 as the *chich* or tidings of the tun or katun, particularly in view of the occurrence of those compounds on the pages of tun or katun prophecies in Codex Paris. Similarly, the 648–548 compounds would indicate a year of misfortune, and the 736–548 compounds a year of death. Possibly in some of these cases Glyph 548 has the more general meaning of period.

For further examples of Glyph 548 see under Glyphs 521, 524, 544, 575, 612, 624, 648, 668, 671, 672, 713, 736, 769, and 802.

GLYPH 549 (Pax)
(1 Example; Gates' Glyph 41; Zimmermann's Glyph 1340a)

1.   *   Month sign Pax. Symbolic
                                                          form

Affix 142 is often postfixed. The glyph is really 548 with 299 as superfix.

GLYPH 550 (Tun variant)
(3 Examples; Sheet 146)

3.	679af.	*	Tik. 5, A10
2.		*.181	P.N. Thr. 1, F′4
1.		*[533].181	P.N. Thr. 1, H1

An unusual glyph found at Tikal at 9.15.5.0.0 and at Piedras Negras some fifty years later. It is not completely certain that the Tikal example has the appendage.

GLYPH 551 (Pop)
(3 Examples; Gates' Glyph 26; Zimmermann's Glyph 1349)

1.	*. or :130	Month Pop normal forms
2.	*:21	Month Pop rare form
3.	*:?	Quir. Alt. O, D′2

No. 3 by context cannot be the month sign Pop. Furthermore, it lacks a numerical coefficient. The 281 infix is not clear, but there is an infix of the required shape in the bottom right corner.

See also under Glyph 663.

GLYPH 552 (Crossed Bands)
(154 Examples; Sheets 147–49; Gates' Glyph 302; Zimmermann's Glyph 1350)

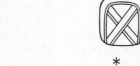

31, 137.		*	M. 27b; 52a
37, 38.		*[95]	M. 13b; P. 17c
105.	1.	*	M. 19b
9.	1.	*:103	Xcalum. N. build. Serp. Gl. 18
124.	1.	*:70	M. 41b

[165]

101.	1.70	* :537	M. 40c
100.	1.	* :537	M. 41c
151.	13?.	*	Sayil, Str. 3B1, Gl. 2
113.	16.	*	M. 61c
114.	16.	* [95]	M. 61c
108–111.	17.	*	M. 59c; 62c (thrice)
112.	17:	* [95]	P. 6b
67.	25.	* :24	M. 66b
147.	39.168:	* .130:60	Holmul tripod bowl 23
40–48.	47.	* :23	D. 2a (thrice); 2b; 2c (twice); 19b; 21c (thrice)
62, 63.	47:	* :23	D. 21a; 22a
64.	47:	* [95]:23	D. 22a
68–80.	47.	* :24	D. Gates 302.2.2
83, 84.	47.	* [95]:24	D. 19b (twice)
107.	58.	* [95].74	D. 58e
140.	58.	* [95]:501	D. 50f
115–117.	60.	*	M. 23a (thrice)
118.	60?.	*	M. 23a
120.	62:	* [95]	D. 25c
144.	65.	* :23	Nar. 23, F13
16.	65?.	* :145	P.N., L. 2, R1
123.	70.	* :103	M. 41c
106.	74.	*	M. 40c
50–59.	74.	* :23	Gates 302.1.2
60.	74.	* :537	M. 40b
128.	90.	* :276	M. 67b
127.	91.91:	* [95]	P. 2b
4.	92.?:	* .103	Yax. L. 6, B6
25.	95: or 95.	*	Glyph of month Uo
29.	95: or 95.	* :103 or 142	Rarer forms of Uo
24.	102:	*	Beyer 599
23.	12.102:	*	Beyer 598
28.	109: or 109.	*	Glyph of month Zip
30.	109: or 109.	* :103 or 142	Rarer forms of Zip
119.	109.	* [95]v:116	D. 25c
122.	110.68:	*	D. 53b
1.	115.	* :103	Cop. T. 11, Step Gl. 13
146.	115.?:	* :103	Cop. T. 11, cornice
18.	122:	* :293	Uxmal 1, A2
148.	122.	* :?:178?	Uxmal Col. Alt. B1
155.	IX.122	[*]?	Pal. Sun, Balustr. G1

7.	1.IV?:125:	*:103?	Xcalum. S. build. E. pan.
2.	VIII?:125:	*	Quir. P, P2
26.	59.?:125:	*	Xcalum. S. build. inner S. jamb
49.	126.	*:23	D. 2c
143.	126:23 Inv.	*	Beyer 629
149.	129.	*	Sayil Str. 3B1, Gl. 13
150.		*.129	Sayil Str. 3B1, Gl. 19
136.	146.?:	*	P. 10b
125.	155:	*	M. 43c
104.	181.	*[95]	M. 89a
135.	199v?.	*	M. 15b
19.	228.	*:178	Beyer 195a
85–87.	238.	*	M. 94b (thrice)
89.	238.	*[95]:8:25	M. 94b
88.	238.	*[95]:?	M. 94b
90.	12.238.	*[95]:23	D. 68b
103.	274.	*	M. 36c
134.	274.	*:62?	M. 36a
113.	275.	*	M. 61c
114.	275.	*[95]	M. 61c
131.	283inv.	*:277	M. 68a
10, 12, 13.	291:	*:292?	Yax. 12, C3; L. 21, D6; L. 39, C1
11, 15.	291.	*:292	Yax. L. 33; A4; 1, F8
5.	59:291:	*:292	Yax. 11, C'8
6.	59.291?:	*:?	Yax. 1, E5
96.	296.	*	M. 100c
138.	537.	*	M. 26b
129.	596?.	*[95]	M. 61c
21.	679af:	*:139	Beyer 196a
22.	679af?:	*:145	Beyer 196b
152–154.	I.	*[544]:?	Beyer 716–18. One sunrise?
65.	V.	*[95]:24	D. 69F
142.	IX.	*:24	M. 41c
91.	VI.	*:116	M. 86c
92.	VI.	*:669	M. 86c
93, 94.	IX.	*:295	D. 33a; 35a
95.	V.	*:?	M. 37c
3.	VIII?.XII:	*	Quir. P, P4
99.	X.	*:537	M. 40c
98.	V or VI?.	*?:178	D. 5a

8.	?.	*:?	Xcalum. N. build. Frag. F′
139.	?.?:	*	M. 90a
32–36.		*:23	D. 22a; M. 10b; 11b; 42c; 89d
39.		*[95]:23	P. 16e
61.		*:24	M. 10b
66.		*.24?	M. 61c
81.		*.47:24	D. 28a
82.	III.	*.47:24	M. 67a
97.		*[95].96	M. 100c
102.		*.116:537	M. 40c
20.		*.145:126	Beyer 195b
141.		*.227	D. 66b
17.		*:292	Calak. 9, H5
132, 133.		*[95].511	M. 2b; 3b
130.		*.596?	M. 19b
121.		*?:60	M. 95c

The crossed-band element can be an infix of several main signs, notably Glyph 553, the sky glyph (561), the serpent segment (565), the half completion (173), and the hand with palm to front (673).

This glyphic element is particularly frequent in celestial bands, in addition to being infixed in the sky sign, but it also appears under conditions which would indicate association with the underworld.

For further examples of Glyph 552, see under Glyphs 501, 511, 526, 537, 558, 580, 596, 613, 626, 671, 673, 696, 736, 738, 768, 769.

GLYPH 553 (Crossed bands-Sky Variant)
(34 Examples; Sheets 150, 151)

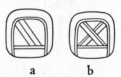

a   b

5.	168:278:	*.60?	Nar. 23, G13
22.	32:168:278:	*	Nar. 32, X9
24, 25.	32?:168:278:	*	Nar. 12, G9; G14
2.	35.168:278:	*	Nar. 24, C17
1, 6, 8, 18.	36.168:278:	*	Nar. 24, C14; 23, F13; 13, E12; 30, B8
3, 9, 16, 17.	36?.168:278:	*	Nar. 21, A12; 13, A12; 20, B3; 8, F2

23.	36?:168:278:	*	Nar. 32, V3
4, 28, 29.	38?.168:278:	*	Nar. 23, H20; 35, E6; 21, FII
27.	38?.168?:278:	*	Nar. 2, A5
12–14.	41.168:278:	*	Nar. 22, E8; FII; H17
15, 19.	?.168:278:	*	Nar. 22, A6; 30, DII
7, 30.	269.168:278:	*	Nar. 31, J9; G15
10.	291.510:278:	*.269:23?	Nar. H.S. NI
11.	278:	[*]219:177	Nar. H.S. K3
33.	58:278?:	*.145:671	Cop. K, N2
32.	278:	*:24?	Carac. 3, F3
34.	?.?:	*	Uaxac. mural B2
20, 21, 26.	?:?:?:	*	Nar. 30, F6; H15; 12, MI
31.		*?:23?	Uaxac. sherd 3124

Glyph 553 seems to be a variant of the normal sky glyph (561) as used with Ben-Ich (Affix 168) and certain water affixes. In sixteen examples (Nos. 1, 4, 6, 9, 12, 13, 15, 16, 18–21, 25, 27, 29, 31) the compound follows the glyph of the long-nosed god (1300) with sky prefix (561); in example 17 it precedes this same glyph. One is tempted to see in the pair some such meaning as Chac in the sky is the aspect of the rainy heavens. The geographical distribution of this glyph is of interest. Other glyphs seem to have passed from Copán to the eastern Petén; here the movement may have been in the opposite direction.

GLYPH 554
(2 Examples; Sheet 219)

1.	134.	*.134.?	Yax. 18, B4
2.		*:23	Yax. 18, B3

GLYPH 555
(1 Example; Sheet 218)

1.	1:	*:23	Pal. 96 Gl. J5

At first sight this seems to be Glyph 630 on its side, but the two signs are distinct.

GLYPH 556
(9 Examples; Sheet 224)

1.		*	Cop. T. 22, Step 3c
5.	13.	*	Los Higos, 1, C5
6.	74:	*:125?:178	Cop. P, C9
7.	74:	*.228?:178	Cop. 13, E2
8.	1:74:	*	Pal. Sarcoph, Gl. 11
4.	115.44:	*:59	Yax. L. 26, X'2
9.	676af.v.	*:116	Glyph X var. Cop. J
2.	?.	*:?	Bone figure (Caso)
3.		*:87	Yax. 18, D2

The element infixed in the circle is variable. In some cases the dots beneath the circle are absent, which further differentiates this glyph from 501 (Imix).

GLYPH 557
(11 Examples; Gates' Glyph 38; Zimmermann's Glyph 1361)

1.		*	D. 14c
2.	59.	*	P. 2d
3.	62.	*	P. 7d
4.	1.74:	*?	D. 26a
5.	21:115.	*:17	P. 9d
6.	141.593:	*	D. 46f
9, 10.	181.687.	*	M. 84b (twice)
11.	181.	*?:687	M. 84b
7.		*:25 or .25	Month Mac in D.
8.		*.181	P. 4c

A rare sign easily confused with Glyph 558 and, when weathering has occurred, hard to distinguish from the Imix (501) Glyph.

See also under Glyphs 502, 593, and 648.

GLYPH 558

(72 Examples; Sheet 221; Gates' Glyph 336; Zimmermann's Glyph 1360)

1, 2.	20:	*	D. 71a; 72c
62.	62.	*[573]:24	M. 103b
3.	74:	*.521	D. 416
4.	74.62.	*:24	M. 94a
5.	90:	*	D. 60a
63.	92.669:	*	Beyer 234
6.	112.	*:87	M. 40a
65.	211.669:	*.35	Beyer 232
66.	211.669:	*.24	Beyer 233
7–10.	234.	*:178	D. 10c; 13a; 17a; 18a
11, 12.	234.	*:186	D. 10c; 21c
13.	521:234.	*:186	D. 22a
14–15, 54.	207.91.528:	*	D. 11a (twice); 12a
16.	217:217.25:	*	D. 42a
17.	219:	*	D. 61d
18.	251.	*	M. 82b
19.	251.	*.1	M. 82b
35–49.	283:	*	M. 42c (thrice); 43a; 43b (6 times); 43c (5 times)
50–53.	283.	*	M. 61a (4 times)
33.	283.	*:25	D. 29b
34.	283.	*:103	D. 30b
68–72.	1.283:	*	M. 42c (twice); 43b (twice); 43c(?)
55.	283?:	*	D. 41b
20.	501.	*:192	M. 93d
21.		*.501:103	M. 95c
22.		*.501:612	M. 92d
23.	526:	*	M. 104b
24.	526:	*	D. 33b
25.	1.526.	*	M. 103c
26, 27.	1.526:	*	M. 103b (twice)
28.	1.	*.526	M. 103c
29.	526:	*.663:23	D. 33b
30.	58.552:	*	D. 50f
31.	563af.	*:192	M. 91d

32.	568.	*	D. 37a
64.	669.	*:35	Beyer 236
67.	679af.	*:669.	D. 21b
56.	III.	*:103	M. 104b
57.		*:521	D. 67a
58.	521:17.	*:241	D. 66a
59.		*v on side	Uaxac. sherd 1993
60.	?	*v on side	Uaxac. sherd 1993

Except for two variant examples on a pottery vessel this glyph occurs only at Chichén Itzá and in Codices Dresden and Madrid unless examples on stone have weathered to an Imix appearance.

The two variant forms which are placed horizontally have the two larger dots in the middle with the smaller dots continuing on each side to the edge of the frame.

It is probable that Affix 1 has been suppressed before Nos. 35–49 to save space, as the glyphs at start and finish of each line have that affix. See Glyph 667 footnote.

For further examples of Glyph 558, see under Glyphs 501, 526, 568?, 573, 668, 669, and 679.

GLYPH 559 (Kankin)
(35 Examples; Sheets 216–17; Gates' Glyphs 39 and 349; Zimmermann's Glyph 1355)

23.		*	Kankin. Cop. X, BI
57.		*[95]	Cop. Frag. V′1
53.	84:503.	*	P. 10
26.	758:110.	*	Pal. Sun, I2
30.	II.202:110.	*	Pal. carved pot, G2
28, 29.	168:	*	Pal. Inscr. Mid. G8; G9
27.	168:	*.130	Pal. Inscr. E, O11
34, 35.	168:	*.130	M. 34d; 37d
1.	168:	*:130	Quir. A, D9
36–38.	12.168:	*	D. 24a; 53a; 58b
39.	12.168:	*	P. 6b; 6d
40.	172.168:	*	D. 47f
19.	513af.	*:125	Aguas Cal. 1, D2
41, 42.	528af.	*	D. 17c; 30b
43.	528af.	*	M. 91a

44.	528af:	*(horizontal)	D. 44c
45.	21:528af?.	*	D. 66b
52.	568.	*	D. 39a
46–50.		*.568	D. 7a; 13c; 17b; 21b; 40b
51.		*.568	M. 94c
54.	IV:	*:568	Beyer 444
55.		*:116	Beyer 443
33.		*:116:130	Kankin. Seib. H.S., K1
31.		*:130	Normal form of Kankin of monuments.
32.		*.130 or :130	Kankin in Dresden Codex
56.		*.181	P.N., L. 3, F2

The 559–568 compounds form the glyph of the dog in the codices. Note that, as in a number of other compounds of main signs, the order can be reversed. This would perhaps argue against a phonetic system of reading. The 528–559 compound forms the glyph for the turkey. The rare winged variant of Kankin is of interest. Note that in the codices the curvilinear treatment of the monuments gives place to rigid lines. The right half of No. 35 is cross-hatched.

See also under Glyph 568.

GLYPH 560 (Kankin Horizontal)
(24 Examples; Sheets 216–17)

18.	44:	*:142	Tuxtla Mus. shell. C6
10.	168:	*:130	Quir. P, Cart. 2
13.	35.168:	*	Quir. I, D4
12.	35.168?:	*	Quir. K, D7
15.	36?.168:	*:130.	Quir. Str. I, F'
3, 6, 14.	38.168:	*:130.	Quir. J, F8; F, A10; Alt. O, O1
4, 8.	38?.168:	*:130	Quir. D, A24; H, R1
5, 11.	39.168:	*:130?	Quir. D, D19; P, Cart. 12
2.	40.168:	*:130	Quir. C, D8
7, 9, 23.	?.168:	*:130	Quir. M, D5; P, F1; G, B'2
16.	?:168:	*:130	Quir. Str. 1, Frags.
17.	?:168:	*:178	Cop. H.S., Gxiig
22.	IV:287:	*	Cop. 7, D10
20.	IV.287:110.	*(Vert.)	Cop. 6, B8

24.	IV:87:287:110. 168?:	*(Vert.):?	Cop. H, CD4
21.	IV.87.758 [110]:	*	Cop. I, D2
26.	IV?:	*130	Quir. Str. 1, Miscel. Gl. 5
25.	IV?:287:110.	*(Vert.)	Cop. 12, C4

Glyph 560 differs from Glyph 559 only in that it is horizontal. The many examples from Quiriguá of the compound 168–560 with water affix leads one to conclude that the horizontal position was deliberate, and may affect the meaning of the glyph. In the case of the IV–287–110–560 compound, a vertical or horizontal position for 560 depends on the space available. It may well be that 559 and 560 are identical in meaning, but until that is established it is as well to keep them apart.

GLYPH 561 (Sky)
(354 Examples; Sheets 172–84; Gates' Glyphs 125.6–8, 143, 307, 329, 330, 427.7; Zimmermann's Glyphs 1345–1347)

| a | b | c | d | e | f | g |

	68.		*a		Quir. A, C11	
	21.		*b		Cop. T. 11, E. door S. pan.	
	170.		*c		Beyer 189	
249, 267, 311.			*c		D. 14b; 35c; 65a	
	331.		*c		Uaxac. mural O12	
	114.		*g		Tik. L. 3, H4	
	350.		*g		Leyden plate A9	
	244.		*g		P. 17f	
	143.		*		Uaxac. sherd 3122	
	126.	1.	*g		Nebaj. Fenton Vase C1	
	147.	1.	*g:23		Tonina, 20, E8	
	262.	1.	*c:23		D. 56a	
	128.	1?.206?:	*		Tik. 5, D6	
	149.	1?.?:	*		Nar. 35, C5	
	70.	4:?:	*		Quir. C, A9	
	139.	4.V:	*a:23		Ixlu Alt. St. 2, D6	
	218.	X:4?:	*		Quir. P, P4	
	138.	7.48:	*a:23		Carac. 6, D19	
	173.	12.	*c:23:178		Beyer 191	

141.	12.136:	*	Xcalum. N. build. Serp. Gl. 25
186.	13.	*ginv.:568	Beyer 336
285.	15.	*c:23	D. 39a
314, 315.	16.	*a:23	Pal. Sarcoph. lid top; support
25.	16.218:	*[128?]:23	Cop. F, A6
30.	19:	*a	Carac. 16, C13
245.	23.	*	P. 24a
297.	23:	*c	D. 67a
123.	23 inv.?.?:	*g	Nar. 13, E14
51.	24?:	*?:23	Pal. Inscr. M. A4
263.	25.	*c:23	M. 72a
246.	25.97.	*g:23	M. 99c
119.	35:	*	Pusil. D, G14
337, 338.	35.	*P	Tik. 31, A14; F25
183.	35.	*:23	Beyer 333
142.	35.	*:?	Uaxac. sherd 1202
73.	40?.	*:23	Quir. M, C3
22.	44:	*f.?	Cop. T. 11, S. door, W. pan.
282, 283.	48.	*c:23	D. 52b; 58a
316.	48:V?:284:	*a:23	Pal. Fol. jamb, B9
284.	51.	*c:23	D. 66b
112.	59:	*c	Tik. L. 3, F3
273.	59.	*c	D. 40c
269–272.	59.	*c:23	D. 32c; 36a; 36b; 40b
175.	59.	*d:23	Beyer 325
247.	59.	*g:23	M. 34d
146.	59.19:	*	Cop. carved brown Longyear, Fig. 110b
237, 238.	59.	[*c]755	P. 5b; 6b
64.	59.133?:	*f:23	Pal. Ruz 2, C4
144.	60?:	*	Uaxac. sherd 3506
276.	84.	*c:23	P. 8b
293, 294.	XIII.84:	*c	D. 10a; 12a (Moan bird)
301, 302.	XIII.85:	*[648]	D. 47b; 47c (Moan bird)
300.	XIII.	*[731]	D. 7c (Moan bird)
109.	86:	*a	P.N., L. 2, Y1
332.	86:	*e:23	Pomona frag.
6.	86:	*e.40:23	Cop. B, A10
131.	86:	*c:140	Tik. L. 4, F1
84.	86:	*a:142	Yax. L. 14, B3
111.	86:	*:125?	P.N. L. 7, X9

325.	86:	*.?	P.N. 6, J2
52.	?.86:	*b:?:23	Pal. Inscr. M. B6
7.	IV:87:	*b:23	Cop. A, H2
127.	89.	*b:23	Nar. H.S., X1
97.	89:	*:23	Yax. 10, K1
20.	89?.95?:	*f.74:117	Cop. T. 11, E. door N. pan. B5
320.	92.16:	*a:23	Tort. 6, C8
140.	95.	*:23	Ixlu, Alt. St. 2, F5
274.	95.	*c:23	D. 74
275.	95:595.	*c:23	D. 67a
264–266.	96.	*c:23	D. 46b; P. 9c; 9d
312, 313.	109.	*a:23	Pal. Sarcoph. lid top; support
65.	1:113.	*a:23	Pal. House C, eaves, B2
43.	758.113:	*a:23	Pal. Cross, D7
121.	113.24:	*e	Nar. 24, D5
133.	115P.	*a:23	Pal. T. 18, B14
8.	IV:116:	*e:23	Cop. A, H3
27.	IV.118.	*g:23	Cop. B, back.
81.	122.	*P:23	Quir. Str. 1, Q'
152, 163.	122:175:	*a	Quir. E, C19; P, C6
151.	122.175:	*a	Quir. C, D13
154, 160.	122:175:	*e	Quir. E, B19; F, C12
155, 161, 164.	122.175:	*c	Quir. D, A18; G, Y2; P, Cart. 8
153.	122:175:	*g	Quir. E, A9
157.	122.175:	*g	Quir. D, D22
158, 165.	122.175:	*	Quir. F, A7; Alt. O, Z2
321.	122.175:	*?	Quir. D, B23
156.	122:175:	*g:23	Quir. D, C19
150.	122.175:	*f:117	Quir. A, D6
159.	122.175?:	*:117	Quir. F, B13
204.	168:175:122?:	*?	Quir. G, T'1
12.	122:?:	*	Cop. G', D6
36.	122.128:	*f.23	Cop. T. 11, Step 24
38.	122.168?:	*a.	Cop. C'
76.	126:	*	Quir. P, Cart. 2
77.	1010.126:	*:23	Quir. K, C7
42.	128.	*a:23	Pal. Cross, D6
69.	128.	*a:23	Quir. C, B13
125.	128?:	*	Nar. 13, A8
105.	129?.	*	Yax. 11, L2

288–290.	137.	*c (on side)	D. 71c; 72b; 72c
291, 292.	137.192:	*c	D. 73c; 74
226.	137.33.	*d:285	D. 53b
229.	137.14.	*a:23	D. 55a
329.	137.?:	*c	D. 72a
303.	IV.145.	*c?:103	M. 62c
118.	145.135:	*a?	Pusil. D, H12
45.	151.168:	*a:23	Pal. Cross, O10
46.	151.125:168:	*b	Pal. Fol. L11
202.	151.168?	*	Tik. 19, B8
136.	151.35.245:	*a:23	Pal. sub. altar
59.	51?.151?:	*	Pal. Ruz 1, P7
318.	160.	*	Carac. conch god vase
279–281.	166.	*c:23	D. 51b; 55b; 57a
287.	166.219:	*.24	P. 11d
205.	168:	*	Uaxac. 2, B9
191.	126.168:	*c	Bonam. 2, G1
192.	126.168:	*f	Bonam. 3, A5
190.	126.168:	*P	Bonam. 2, D1
194.	32.168:	*?	Nar. 24, D13
188.	181.168	*	Yax. L. 41, C2
213.	VI.170 or 168:	*	Calak. 89, C4
216.	VI.170 or 168:	*g:130	Quir. B, C15
189.	?.168?:	*?	Yax. L. 13. F4
206.	VI.170:	*a:23	Pal. Cross, D10
212.	VI.170:	*b:23	Pal. Inscr. M. M8
214.	VI.170:	*e:23	Pal. Cross W. shrine pan.
215.	VI.170?:	*g:23	Pal. Blom Tablet
228.	172.	*[?]:138	D. 55a
268.	172.	*c:23	D. 41b
224.	172.	*d:23	D. 54b
234.	172.	*a:?	D. 55a
286.	181.	*c:23	P. 23a
10.	189?.	*b:23	Cop. A, G7
227.	192:	*d	D. 58b
2.	205?.	*:23?	Cop. U, P5
62.	220?.	*g:23	Pal. H.S. D1
63.	222.	*a:181	Pal. H.S. D2
82.	16:222:	*a	Quir. Str. 1, V'
23.	16:222:	*c	Cop. T. 11, S. door W. pan.
35.	16.222:	*f	Cop. T. 11, Step Gl. 16
33, 145.	16.222:	*e	Cop. F', B4; bone ornament
310.	227.	*a	D. 58a

305.	227.	*c	D. 35c. Seat of god.
306–309.	227.	*c:23	D. 51b; 54a; 56a; 68a
225.	227.	*d:23	D. 65a
248.	234.	*g:62	M. 95c
344, 345.	236.	*:23	Dos Pilas H.S. 2, A6;
			Sculpt. C, A5
346.	236?.	*:23	Dos Pilas H.S. 2, C8
347, 348.	238?.	*:23	Dos Pilas H.S. A6; B7
349.	238?.	*	Dos Pilas 11, B3
37.	282.128:168:	*b	Cop. T South A1
13.	282.128[168]:	*	Cop. G1, D1
193, 195, 196.	284:	*a.23 or 245	Nar. 24, A7; E6; E17
197, 201.	284:	*.23 or 245	Nar. 24, C9; 31, F15
198, 199.	284:	*.232	Nar. 29, F11; I13
200.	284?:	*.232	Nar. 29, J18
203.	1.V?:284?:	*	Tonina 42
239–242.	286.	*c	D. 24a; 53a; 56b; 58b
243.	286.	*b:140	D. 54b
296.	287:526.	*c	D. 66a
322.	219.?:	*?:135	Yax. L. 49, P1
9.	IV:294:	*e:23	Cop. A, G4
319.	313:	*a:23	P.N. L. 12, P4
328.	355.	*g	P. 17c
335.	367.	*g:23	Tik. 31, C13
44.	367:	*a:102	Pal. Cross, D15
50.	367.	*a:102	Pal. Sun, D9
129.	554.	*c	P. 18c
336.	528.	*g:526	Tik. 31, E27
171.	528:528:	*cinv.	Beyer 190
169.	528.528.	*ainv.	Beyer 189
318.	589.	*c	D. 66a
86.	632af.	*a:23	Yax. 21, G3
102.	632af.	*:23	Yax. L. 2, I1
343.	155:670:	*g.365.74	Tik. 31, M2
342.	740:	*g.365.74	Tik. 31, F23
61.	1021:	*a:23	Pal. House C, Plat. G1
48.	1073?.	*a:23	Pal. Sun O1
304.	III.	*c.122:24	M. 67a
75.	III.	*.*?:126	Quir. P, I7
333.	IV.1:?.	*a	Cop. Frag. V'6
108.	V.	*a:130?	P.N. 15 incised D2
116.	V.	*a:130?	Yax. 16, back
220.	V.V:168	*b:23	Carac. 16, B16

207.	VI.	*a:23?	Pal. Fol., L16
261.	VI.	*c:23	D. 56a
208.	IX.	*a:23	Pal. Inscr. E, P12
211.	IX.	*b:23	Pal. Inscr. M. G10
209.	IX.	*f.23?	Pal. Inscr. E, S6
210.	IX.	*g:23	Pal. Inscr. M. B9
217.	IX.	*g:23	Beyer 193
221.	IX.	*:23	Xcalum. N. build. frag.
324.	IX.	*:23	Nar. 13, D5
57.	IX.	*:23?	Comitán 1, E2
219.	IX.	*g:23?	Uaxac. I.S. vase
298, 299.	X.	*c:293	D. 24c; 47e (Lahun Chan name glyph)
351.	?:	*	Dos Pilas H.S. 2, F5
11.	?:	*	Cop. J, East 28
339.	?:	*g	Tik. 31, A22
28.	?:	*b:181	Cop. H.S. Frag. Gxii
187.	?:	*.?:181	Chajcar box
353.	?:	*:23	Carac. 3, D9
354.	?:	*	Carac. 3, A13
32.	?:	*a:23	Cop. H.S. Step M
74.	?:	*:23	Quir. H, L1
89.	?:	*:23	Pal. stone frag.
132.	?.	*:23?	Nakum, C, A9
334.	?.?:	*:23	La Milpa 7, front, E1
137.	?.?:	*a:23?	Carac. 16, C11
16.		*a:23	Cop. 10, D9
41, 47, 58, 66, 323.		*a:23	Pal. Cross, B15; Fol., L15; Ruz 1, D3; House D Pier d; T. 18 stucco
80, 83.		*a:23	Quir. Str. 1, E'; W'
94, 98.		*a:23	Yax. 18, C3; 11, V3
122.		*a:23	Nar. 23, F15
174.		*a:23	Uaxac. I.S. vase
176.		*a:23	Beyer 326
230–233.		*a:23	D. 51b; 53a; 54a; 54b
15, 19.		*a.23	Cop. 9, C5; P, D5
352.		*a:23	Aguatec. 1, A4
95.		*a.23	Yax. L. 33, F1
88.		*a.23?:23	Yax. L. 12, G2
91.		*aP:23	Yax. L. 22, C2
107.		*b:23	P.N., L3, W'1
29.		*b.23	Cop. H.S. Frag. Gxiim

327.	*b.23	Dzibil. 19, A3
1, 14.	*c.23	Cop. U, S4; Q, E4
260.	*c.23	P. 18f
3, 4.	*c:23	Cop. U, L3; C2
71, 72.	*c:23	Quir. E, A19; J, F7
250–258, 277, 278.	*c:23	D. 52b; 52b; 53b; 54a; 54b; 55b; 55b; 56b; 56b; 66a; P24a
222.	*d:23	D. 57b
223.	*d.23	D. 54b
18.	*e:23	Cop. 4, A10
49, 55.	*e:23	Pal. Sun, N15; Inscr. W. J8
60.	*f:23	Pal. Pal. A, E pier
79.	*f:23	Quir. I, C4
39.	*g:23	Cop. Alt. St. 19
110.	*g:23	P.N., L. 2, H'1
117.	*g:23	Pusil. D, B14
124.	*g:23	Nar. 13, G10
104.	*g:23	Yax. L. 28, U1
177.	*g:23	Beyer 327
26.	*g.23	Cop. 1, D2
5, 17, 24, 148.	*:23	Cop. B, B2; 10, F9; M, A3; R, K2
90, 92, 93.	*:23	Yax. L. 47, H7; L. 21, A8; C7
67, 134, 135.	*:23	Pal. Peñafiel Tab. B3; Fol. Balustr. L2; Cross, Balustr. L2
34.	*:23?	Cop. T. 21a, G
172.	*c:23:24	Beyer 190
85.	*.24:23	Yax. L. 53, F1
96.	*.24?:23	Yax. 32, J3
182.	*.23:25	Beyer 332
56.	*a.36:23	Pal. Inscr. W. J10
326.	*a.112:23	Ikil, L. 2, E
78.	*f:23:116	Quir. I, A8
331.	*.?:23	Uxmal Ball Crt. E. ring
181.	*g:35	Beyer 331
180.	*g.35	Beyer 330
178, 179.	*b:40	Beyer 328; 329
130.	*P:102	Tik. L. 2, A14
115.	*aP:140	Tik. L3, H8
166–168.	*(inv.):145	Beyer 112; 113; 114

204.	*:175?	Quir. G, F′4
101.	*.184:23	Yax. L. 2, J2
106.	*a:184:74	Yax. 7, D3
87, 100.	*a.184.74:23	Yax. 21, H4; L. 58, E2
99.	*.184.74:23	Yax. L. 52, H5
103.	*e.184?.74?: 23	Yax. L. 13, B1
53, 54.	*e.245:23	Pal. Inscr. M. L6; N7
295.	*:285	D. 61a
185.	*c inv.:568	Beyer 335
341.	*g:571	Tik. 31, C17
340.	*g.571:23	Tik. 31, H23
184.	*c:670.?	Beyer 334
236.	*c:670	P. 7b
259.	*c:?	P. 5b
120, 126.	*:?	Nar. 24, E11; 13, A11
113.	*c:?	Tik. L. 3, E3
31.	*.?	Cop. H.S. Step M
40.	*g.?	Cop. K′′, B2

Asterisk without following letter indicates that variable infix is uncertain.

Variation in the infix probably does not affect the general meaning of the sign as "sky," although, conceivably, the variant 561c with crossed bands qualifies the sky as outstretched or extending from horizon to horizon (the root *kat*).

The rarity of Glyph 561 in Codex Madrid and in Codex Paris is of interest.

The sky sign, sometimes prefixed to the head of the long-nosed god (1030), probably reflects one of the titles of the rain god Chac which associates him with the sky. Such titles survive among the present-day Yucatec Maya.

At Quiriguá the compound 122–175–561 usually precedes the glyph of the long-nosed god carrying the Cauac symbol (Glyph 1030h) in clauses which show some variability.

Quite frequently and in widely scattered cities the sky sign precedes Glyph 758 with prefix 115. It is also associated with Glyph 598. At Naranjo the glyph with Prefix 284 appears in a long clause (Thompson, 1950, Fig. 3, 3–9, but prefix there is 168).

Glyph 561 with coefficient of nine precedes a kin glyph at Palenque, Comitán, Chichén Itzá, Xcalumkin, and on the I.S. vase at Uaxactún; at Palenque and Chichén Itzá there follows a record of sixteen kins. This is a rare case of the appearance of a noncalendrical clause in more than one city. At Yaxchilán there is a common clause in which the sky symbol follows 145–568, and usually precedes 168–511.

In addition to the examples listed under Glyph 526, there are other cases in which the sky and Caban (526) signs are juxtaposed.

For further examples of Glyph 561 see under Glyphs 504, 526, 528, 565, 589, 595, 670, and 684.

GLYPH 562 (Cleft Sky)
(71 Examples; Sheets 185–188)

6, 7, 65.		*	Yax. L. 25, M2; U2; L. 10, E2
67.	122:	*.24	Obsidian blade, Pal.
11, 12, 13, 16, 19, 20, 25, 34, 35.	32:168:	*	Yax. L. 30, G3; L. 31, I2; K2; 11, I3; L. 9, B7; 3, A7; 10, M2; L. 10, A7; E4
59.	32.168:299:	*	P.N., L. 3, K'1
36.	32?.168:	*	Yax. L. 10, F8
22.	36:168:	*	Yax. L. 26, C2
52, 57, 58.	36.168:	*	Yax. 1, F13; 23, D15; 6, C9
15, 23, 27, 42, 56.	36.168:	*:23	Yax. Str. 44 mid. step, C8; L. 33, H9; 11, A'7; J4; 23, C16
4, 49.	36:168:	*:130	Yax. L. 56, K2; 19, B2
5, 26, 37.	36:168:	*:130	Yax. L. 25, W2; 10, D5; L. I, I1
21.	36:168:	*:130?	Yax. 18, E6
41, 53, 54.	36?.168:	*	Yax. L. 8, E3; 9, DI; 13, H3
18.	36?:168:	*	Yax. L. 21, D2
31.	36?.168:	*.130	Yax. L. 42, G4
17.	37.168:	*	Yax. 11, F4
9, 10.	37.168:	*:23	Yax. 12, C6; L. 16, F5
38.	37.168 or 170:	*:23	Yax. L. 2, N4
55.	37?.168:	*	Yax. 16, D3
8.	37?:168:	*	Yax. L. 27, G2
30.	38.168:	*	Yax. L. 43, C2
32, 48.	38.168:	*:23	Yax. L. 39, D4; L. 3, J3
3, 40.	38.168:	*:130	Yax. L. 24, C'3; L. 46, F'7
45.	38:168:	*	Yax. 7, C5

24, 51.	38?.168:	*	Yax. L. 32, A12; 27, front
14.	41.168:	*:23	Yax. Str. 44, up. step, X4
29, 43, 44.	?:168:	*	Yax. L. 52, J1; 11, L3; C'16
33.	?.168:	*	Yax. 15, B5
46.	?.168:	*	Bonam. L. 2, D3
28.	?:168:	*.130?	Yax. 11, A'4
50.	?.168?:	*.	Yax. 29, A4
47.	1000:168	*	Bonam. Mur. Rm. 2
61.	168:	*	Bonam. 2, I3
62.	168:	*.23	Bonam. 1, H4
1.	168:299:	*	Pal. H.S., C3
60.	168:299:	*.130	P.N. L. 3 person gl.
71.	168:299:	*.130	Dos Pilas H.S. 4, C2
39.	59.	*:23:82	Yax. L. 1, F1
66, 68.	233:	*	Tik. 26, E4; 31, G9
69, 70.	233:	*:23	Tik. 31, B20; G17
64.	299:	*.181:23	D. 68a
63.	299:	*:291?	P.N. L. 2, A'2
2.		*:23	Yax. L. 25, 2

Glyph 562 almost invariably appears with Prefix 168 and one of the group of water affixes, Nos. 32, 36, 37, and 38, and in such compounds is confined to Yaxchilán and the closely related Bonampak, where it is the emblem glyph. Several examples of this glyph from other cities (Piedras Negras, 2; Palenque, 1; Dos Pilas, 1; Codex Dresden, 1) have also the prefix 299. Possibly the Yaxchilán version of the glyph implies the presence of Affix 299.

GLYPH 563 (Fire)
(90 Examples; Sheets 189–192; Gates' Glyphs 306, 320; Zimmermann's Glyphs 1348, 1357)

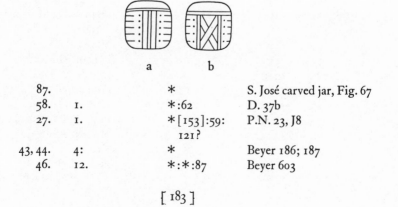

a   b

87.		*	S. José carved jar, Fig. 67
58.	1.	*:62	D. 37b
27.	1.	*[153]:59: 121?	P.N. 23, J8
43, 44.	4:	*	Beyer 186; 187
46.	12.	*:*:87	Beyer 603

57.	2.13.	*?:?	Uxmal Capstone
35.	18.	*:23	Carac. 6, F22
81¹, 82¹.	12.I:29:	*[153]	P.N. L. 3, U11; Thr. 1, I'3
79¹.	12.I:29:	*[153]	P.N. Thr. 1, R1
80.	12.I:29:	*?	P.N. Thr. 1, C'4
83.	12.I:29:	*?	P.N. 15, B2
84.	59?.I:29?:	*	P.N. 1, K17
78.	229.I:29:	*[153]:110	Yax. 18, E2
19.	12:29:	*[153]	Yax. Str. 44, Mid. Step C7
39.	44:	*[153].82:122	Ixlu Alt. 2, B5
73¹.	44:	*[153]:181	D. 72b
47¹.	1:44:	*[153]:142	Pal. Fol. Tab. A11
90.	1.44:	*[153]	Tort. 7, C4
53.	1:44:	*[153]	P.N. jade, cenote
15.	1.44?:	*[153?]	Quir. G, F'2
8.	1?.44:	*[153]	Pal. Inscr. W. G6
28.	3.44:	*[153]:142	Tzend. 1, A15
14.	11.44:	*[153?]:122?	Quir. G, C'1
85.	11.44:	*[153]	Pal. T. 18 Sculpt. Stone A2
33.	11.44:	*[153]	Nar. 23, H16
2.	11.44:	*[153]:142	Pal. Fol. O14
11.	11:44?:	*[153]:122?	Pal. Ruz 2, H2
3.	115?.44:	*[153]:59	Pal. Fol. F2
7.	679af.44:	*[153]:142	Pal. Inscr. W. G10
6.	191?.44:	*[153]:142	Pal. Inscr. W. D12
1.	204:44:	*[153]	Cop. A, E11
26.	210:44:	*[153]	P.N. 12. Captives
40.	?.44?:	*[153]	Oxpemul 7, B7
34.	?.44:	*[153]:?	Pal. Pal. Sub. Alt. G
77¹.	96.	*:*	D. 68b
48.	122:	*P	Bonam. Mur. I.S., H2
20.	122:	*	Yax. Str. 44, Mid. Step D12
66–70.	122:	*	D. 19c; 58e; M. 11b; 15b; 16b
71.	122.	*:23	M. 38a
49.	122:	*.130:?	Bonam. Mur. Rm. 2
75¹.	122:	*.181	D. 72b
51.	122.	*:?	Ikil L. 2, H
37.	122.	*?:130?	Nar. 12, G3
30.	1.122:	*	Pusil. E, B7
52.	1.122:	*	M. Cow Alt. 2, C2
25.	1.122:	*	Yax. 1, C9
31.	1.122:	*P	Pusil. U, B9

59–65.	1.122:	*	D. 40b; M. 13b; 38b (four times); P. 2c
23.	12:122:	*	Yax. L. 10, E1
56.	12.122:	*	Yax. L. 42, E2
38.	17?.122:	* :25?	Pal. jade earplug
13.	17?.	*:23?	Pal. death head A3
16.	59.122:	*:178	Yax. L. 24, A'1
12.	115?:122:	*	Pal. death head B2
9.	118:122:	*P	Yax. L. 25, C1
24.	125.122:	*P	Cop. Md. 2 reused
5.	125.168:122:	*	Pal. Inscr. Mid. N4
10.	125:168:	*:122?	Pal. Ruz 2, E1
18.	204.122:	*:23?	Yax. L. 29, C5
17.	207:219.122:	*	Yax. L. 31, J4
4.	?:122:	*	Pal. Inscr. Mid. J7
32.	?.122:	*	Nar. 29, F15
22.	?:122:	*	Yax. L. 26, W'
54.	?:122:	*:?	Tik. T. 6, I'3
55.	122?:	*[153]:126 inv.	Cop. I, C5
21.	12.210:	*[153]	Yax. L. 35, U6
36.	210:	*	Nebaj Fenton vase
76[1].	283:	*	D. 68b
89.	357.	*:713?	S. José carved jar, Fig. 67
86.	?.510b?:	*.?:178	Tik. Alt. 7
29.	669:	*:122?	Pusil. D, F12
88.	IX.2?	*	S. José carved jar, Fig. 67
74[1].		*:*:47	M. 36c
72.		*.87	D. 33c
42.		*.*.87	Beyer 185
41.		*.*:87	Beyer 184
50[2].		*:?	Uxmal 1, A4

[1] The right third of the glyph is not shown, as in the variant drawing.

[2] It is likely that in these two compounds from Uxmal the fire glyph is not the main element 563, but the affix form of the same sign, Affix 248.

The two forms here brought together under the number 563 are treated as separate glyphs by Gates and Zimmermann. However, the only essential difference is the infixing of the cross bands, Affix 153. The absence of the right third of the glyph in the examples in the codices does not justify setting apart these variants as a separate glyph, for we find the same truncating occurs in Nos. 47, 81 and 82, and of these the elimination is due to lack of space only in the case of No. 82.

When the infix is absent, Affix 44 also disappears, but is usually replaced by

Affix 122. Affix 122, however, appears once with Infix 153, which further justifies the grouping of the variant with and without infix as the same glyph.

The form with Prefix 44 and Infix 153 is often present before or after Period Endings or Calendar Round dates; less commonly (Nos. 12, 13, 17, 22), the form without infix has the same association, which again supports the grouping of the two forms as a single glyph. The form 44:553(153) also serves as the variable element in the I.S. introductory glyph corresponding to the month Ceh.

The glyph is occasionally used as an affix. See Glyphs 501, 521, and 526.

The compound 12.I.29.563 occurs only at Piedras Negras, but seems to have been borrowed in a slightly altered form by neighboring Yaxchilán (Nos. 19 and 39).

The compound involving the rare conch(?) shell affix (210) is of interest. The three examples come from Yaxchilán, Piedras Negras, and the Nebaj (Fenton) vase. Infix 153 is present in two cases, but absent in the third.

It has long been recognized that this is a glyph for fire with the more restricted meanings of sacred fire or bundle of fire wood. There is good reason to believe that the meaning *kak*, "fire," was extended in Codex Dresden to cover *Kak*, eruptive skin diseases (Thompson, 1958), and with Affix 87 it becomes *Kakche*, a Yucatecan hardwood tree (Dresden 33c).

For further examples of Glyph 563, see under Glyphs 501, 521, 526, 558, 585, 586, and 731.

GLYPH 564 (Fire Semblant)
(15 Examples; Sheet 215; Gates' Glyph 332; Zimmermann's Glyph 1358)

2, 3.		*	Beyer 601
14.	74:	*	D. 57b
8.	166.84:	*	D. 72b
5, 6.	126.168:	*	D. 49f; 60b
7.	126.168:	*	P. 21
9.	168:	* :130	D. 60b
4.	513af:	*	Beyer 601
1.	1000.626?:	* ?	Tik. L. 4, F2

Except for the dubious occurrence at Tikal, this glyph is confined to Chichén Itzá and the codices. This is supporting evidence that the Maya codices originated in Yucatán.

GLYPH 565 (Serpent Segment)
(137 Examples; Sheets 165–71; Gates' Glyphs 147, 304, 305; Zimmermann's Glyphs 1351, 1352)

a   b   c

55, 58.		*a	Xcalum. I.S. build. rt. col.; S. build. E. inner pan.
132.		*a	P.N. bowl. Coe Fig. 60d
25.		*a	Uaxac. sherd 1993
133.		*aP	Nebaj painted stucco
94.		*c	Uaxac. I.S. vase, Gl. 2
100.		*c[95]	D. 67b
7.		*a	Cop. H.S. Frag. Gxiim
15.		*a	Pal. Fol. G2
69.	II.16.	*a	Tik. 10, D10
48.	16?:	*a	Yax. Str. 44 Mid. Up. Step C11
71.	17.	*a:88	Pal. T. 18 Tab., C14
45.	18.	*a:18	Quir. Str. 1, S′
134.	18?.	*a:18	La Milpa 7, Gl. on back
75.	18.	*a:88	Carac. 6, E22
123.	18.	*a	Nar. 13, D1
87–89.	18.	*c:69	Beyer 519–521
90–92.	18.	*c:136	Beyer 522–524
118, 119.	18.	*a:136?	Uxmal Columnar Alt., A3; B4
43.	18.	*a:136	Quir. Str. 1, H′
78.	18:	*a:136?	Calak. 51, D2
137.	18?:	*?	Dos Pilas H.S. 2, F5
115.	18 or 19?.	*a:136	Jade head in Br. Mus.
39.	19.	*a:18	Quir. D, A24
122.	19.	*a:136	Stone head (Maudslay 1, Pl. 32)
6.	19:	*a:136	Cop. H.S. Frag. Gxiil
64.	19:	*a:136	P.N. 12, A14
60.	19.	*a:88	Kuna L. 1, I3
120.	19.	*a88	Tort. 6, H6
65, 66.	I.23:	*a:	P.N. 12, Captive 2; 15, C5

31–34.	I.23:	*a:136	Pal. House C, Eaves C1; C2; D1; D2
130.	44.1:	*a	Pusil. tripod bowl. Joyce, 1929
95–98.	47.	*b:24	D. 13c; 13c; 14c; 22c
81.	58.	*a.173	Beyer 612
93.	58.	*c.173	Beyer 613
59.	58.62:	*a	Holmul cyl. jar
54.	1.58?:	*a:?	Yax. 7, A3
99.	59.	*c[95]	D. 35c
117.	59.168:	*a	Bonam 2, C2
2.	59.61:	*a:178	Cop. K, N1
121.	60.61:	*a	Mexicanos carved cyl. vase
56.	56?.67:	*a.24?	Xcalum. S. build. E. inner pan.
57.	67?:	*a	Xcalum. S. build. W. outer pan.
27, 30, 11, 17, 52, 70, 128.	74:	*a	Pal. Ruz 1, E9; Ruz 2, F7; Cross, F14; Inscr. E, K12; T. 18, stucco (twice); Sarcoph. Gl. 36
129.	74:	*a:130?	Pal. T. 18, stucco V2
28.	74:	*a:142	Pal. Ruz 1, R1
9, 10, 13, 16, 37, 72–74.	74:	*a.117:178	Pal. Cross, D17; F2; Fol. D6; Sun. D10; Found. S. side; T. 18 Tab. D12; Fol. Balustr. B2; Cross Balustr. C1
53.	74:	*a.1000:130	Pal. T. 18, stucco
14.	38.74:	*a.117:178	Pal. Fol. C11
24.	51.74:	*a:117	Pal. Inscr. W. D4
63.	head:74:	*a	P.N. shell plaque, K3
38.	74.168:	*a.117	Pal. Tower Scribe, 2, B2
49.	231.561:74:	*a	Pal. T. 18, stucco
77.	231?.?.74:	*a	Pal. T. 18, stucco
50, 51.	231.IV.74:	*a	Pal. T. 18, stucco (twice)
21.	74?.III:	*a:178	Pal. Inscr. M. F9
124, 125.	IV:74:	*a	Pal. T. 18, stucco (twice)
101.	91.	*c	D. 35a
29.	91.	*b:24	D. 11a
23.	1.91.	*c	D. 34a
82.	92.13.1044:	*c.?.24?	Beyer 514
83.	92?.III.	*c:?:24?	Beyer 515

113.	13.102:	*c	Beyer 596
112.	229.102:	*c:178	Beyer 595
76.	125.?	*a:40	Ixlu, Alt. St. 2, C3
62.	126.25:	*a:136	P.N. Thr. 1, Z5
79.	130:	*a	Beyer 99
127.	1000.132?:	*a:130	Pal. Fol. Sculpt. stone, A11
103.	145.	*a:69	Beyer 175
109.	145.	*c:69	Beyer 206
102, 106, 107.	145.	*c:136	Beyer 174; 203; 204
104.	145:	*c (on side) .136	Beyer 176
105.	145:	*a:136	Beyer 177
108.	145.	*a:136	Beyer 205
116.	103:168:	*a:24?	Poco Uinic 3, B20
67, 68.	174:	*a.181	Tik. L. 3, E8; L. 4, C2
61.	181.	*a:122	P.N. Thr. 1, Z2
44.	181.81:	*a	Quir. Str. 1, I′
47.	181.81:	*a:18	Quir. Str. 1, frag.
40.	81?.	*a	Quir. D, B24
18.	191?.58?:	*a:24	Pal. Inscr. E, O12
12.	204.III:	*a:178?	Pal. Fol. A16
20.	205.168:	*a:178	Pal. Inscr. M. A1
19.	228.48:	*a:178	Pal. Inscr. E. S9
126.	228?:	*a.130	Obsidian blade, Pal.
132.	568:	*a	Pal. Sun Pil. stucco
136.	634:	*a	Tik. 31, J4
42.	679af.	*a?:60	Quir. Alt. O, D′
41.	679af.	*a:?	Quir. M, A4
1.	679af:74?.	*a:136	Cop. U, P5
80.	Vomiting? head:	*a	Beyer 103
8.	?:	*a	Cop. H.S. Step R
26.	?.	*a:88	Pal. Inscr. W. N9
5.	?:	*a	Cop. H.S. Frag. Gxiiig
84.	1?:III?.	*c:?:?	Beyer 516
135.		*a:18?	Tulum 1, K6
111.		*c.35?	Beyer 397
131.		*a:47	Pusil. tripod bowl. Joyce, 1929
46.		*b.82:24	D. 14c
35, 36.		*a:88	Pal. H.S. C3; C4
3, 4.		*a:136	Cop. 6, B7; 11, A3
86.		*c:130	Beyer 518

| 85. | | *c:178 | Beyer 517 |
| 22. | | *a.181:102 | Pal. Inscr. M. G6 |

It is significant that the two principal infixes of this glyph (565a and 565c) are also the two principal infixes of the sky glyph (561a and 561c). Glyph 565 has been determined by Beyer (1928) as the under scales of a serpent or celestial two-headed monster, an acceptable identification. Beyer further believed that the cross-hatch markings on the upper part of the sign Akbal represented the black spots on the serpent's skin. I prefer to see in these merely the infix black, and would read the whole as black underside of the serpent. As the underside of the serpent was the sky, the meaning might well be black sky, that is to say, night. The cross-band symbol certainly has a celestial connotation. Note that it is infixed only at Chichén Itzá, in Codex Dresden, and on a painted sherd from Uaxactún.

Glyph 565 does not commonly figure in clauses except at Chichén Itzá. In connection with Nos. 112 and 113, it is interesting to note the parallel 229.518a.565af which is the equivalent save that main sign in one is affix in the other.

For further examples of Glyph 565 see under Glyphs 502, 515, 528, 568, 580, 582, 606, 713, 750, 758, and 765.

GLYPH 566 (Serpent Segment 2)
(15 Examples; Sheet 164)

1, 2.	114:	*:23	Cop. A, G1; H9
3.	114.	*:23	Pal. Cross C13
4.	168:	*.130:116	Yax. L. 45, T4
6.	23.168:	*	P.N. shell plaque, G1
15.	38 or 40:168:	*:130	Yax. L. 44, L'6
12, 13.	110P.168:	*	Tik. 5, A5; D9
11.	110P.168:	*:23	Tik. L. 3, H6
5.	1000:168:	*	P.N. shell plaque, L3
8.	1000?.168:	*:116	P.N. 1, E1
9.	1000?.168:	*:?	P.N. 1, G2
7.	?.168:	*?:130	P.N. 16, C3
10.	?.168?:	*:23?	P.N. 1, J11
14.	175:	*:23	Stone fig. of Mam

Glyph 566 represents a section of the body of a two-headed celestial dragon or snake (cf. Seler, 1915, Figs. 116 and 117) and appears as an element in a celestial

band on Pier E of House A of the Palace, Palenque. Accordingly, the glyph probably is in close relationship to the usual sky glyph (561), and I have wondered
whether it might represent the zenith (note that snake is *can* and sky *caan* in
Yucatec). The bone affix (110) surmounted by a gross manikin head, which presumably personifies it, is of unusual interest.

GLYPH 567 (Good Tidings)
(102 Examples; Sheet 246; Gates' Glyph 24; Zimmermann's Glyph 1330)

3.	15.	*:130	D. 72
4.	15?.	*:130	D. 54a
2.	59.	*:59	Bonam. Rm. 1 bottom
1.	59.	*:?	Bonam. Rm. 1 attiring
5.	172.	*:130	P. 3c
6.	221.	*:130	D. 66b
101.	648:25.	*:130	D. 65a
7–89.	III.	*:130	All codices. 83 examples
90–93.	III.	*.130	M. 103b; 104a; 104b; 105a
100.	III.	*:130.648	D. 69a
94.		*.III:130	M. 65a
95.		*.III.1:130	M. 37d
96–98.		*:130	M. 10a; 12a; 87a
99.		*.1:130	M. 36d
102.		*:130.1006	D. 68a

In the codices this is an augural glyph for which I have offered the interpretation "good tidings." One of the examples from the murals at Bonampak definitely
lacks the Postfix 130, and the other probably is also without it.

For further examples of Glyph 567, see under Glyphs 502 and 648.

GLYPH 568 (Sacrifice)
(136 Examples; Sheets 266–71; Gates' Glyph 344; Zimmermann's Glyph 1354)

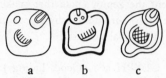

a   b   c

2, 6, 7.		*	Cop. R, G1; T. 11, Step 26; T, S. B3
21.		*	Yax. L. 37, S7
30.		*	Comitán 1, C2
41.		*	Holmul cyl. jar, Gl. 16
34.		*	Carac. Alt. 12, 1–4
62.		*	Beyer 445
78–87.		*	M. 20b (thrice); 21b (thrice); 25b (4 times)
3.		*?.*	Cop. R, J1
20.	1:	*:604	Pal. T. 18, stucco
88–93.	1.	*	D. 34a; 46e; 47e; 48e; 49e; 50e
94, 95.	1.	*:19	D. 46b; 47c
96–99.	19:	*	M. 24b (4 times)
23.	12:	*	Yax. L. 10, F8
33.	303:32:	*	Carac. 17, A1
42.	35:	*	Kuna L. 1, L2
123.	35.	*.77?	Tik. 5, B4
43, 44, 53–55.	35.	*	Beyer 86; 87; 164–66
46, 50, 51, 56, 58, 61, 127, 128.	35:	*	Beyer 89; 115; 116; 169; 179; 221; 239; 317
118, 119.	35.	*:87	Beyer 93; 94
48.	35?.	*	Beyer 91
47.	35?:	*	Beyer 90
45.	1.35:	*	Beyer 88
49, 52, 57, 59, 60.	35.513af:	*	Beyer 92; 163; 170; 186; 187
129.	35.12.	*.669	Beyer 222
65.	513af.:	*:35	Beyer 610
1.	38.	*	Cop. U, G3
24.	38.	*	P.N. 12, A18
5.	41?:	*	Cop. H, D1
19.	44:110?:	*:102	Yax. Str. 44, S.E. up. step, V3

132.	58.	*	Cop. Q. Beneath person
36.	52.	*	Chinkul. Marker Gl. 17
131.	125:60:	*.756	Seib. H.S., R1
8.	61.	*	R. Amarillo 1, H1
134.	1.62.	*?	Chajcar carved vase. Dieseldorff, 1926–33
26.	152?.	*	P.N. 23, I8
27.	204?.	*	Cop. 7, A14
15, 130.	12.216:	*	Pal. T. 4 Sculpt. Stone 1, D1; Madrid Tab. 1, B6
28.	229.	*	Bonam. 1, I1
102.	259.	*	M. 15a
10, 12.	266.	*:19	Pal. Fol. L2; Sun, N5
16, 17.	266.	*	Yax. L. 24, A'1; L. 25, B1
9, 11.	565aaf:266.	*:19	Pal. Cross, O5; Fol. N8
31.	565aaf.	*	Pal. Sun Tablero
40.	565aaf?.?.	*:19?	Uaxac. sherd 3572
18.	12:59:565a?.	*:	Yax. L. 14, O3
104.	304.	*	M. 109b
105–107.	304[95].	*	M. 107b; 108b; 109b
64.	IIIP.19:	*	Beyer 608
100.	III.33.	*	D. 47e
101.	III.59:	*	D. 69f2
126.	III?:	*?.35:59	Nar. H.S., C2
135.	VI:19.	*:501.181:88?	Tort. 6, F12
121.	544.	*	D. 55b
122.		*.544	D. 54b
115.	IV.559:	*	Beyer 444
108–112.	559.	*	D. 7a; 13c; 17b; 21b; 40b
113.	559.	*	M. 94c
114.		*.559	D. 39a
103.	608af.	*	D. 50f
29.	1000.?.	*	Nar. 8, C10'
22, 66, 67.	1.756:	*	Beyer 150; 151; 162
68–73.	1.756.	*:23	Beyer 152–57
37.	61:756.	*	Xcalum. I.S. build. Rt. Lint. C1
74.	61.756:	*	Beyer 158
75.	228.756:	*	Beyer 159
76.	?.756.	*	Beyer 160
77.	?.756?:	*	Beyer 161
4, 124.	?:	*	Cop. 7, E7; T. 11, W. door S. pan. B3

14.	?:	*	Pal. House C, Found. B1
13.	?.	*:87	Pal. H.S., C1
25.	?:	*:142	P.N. 12, D5
116.	?.	*:528?	D. 19a
136.	?:?:	*	Dos Pilas 2, C4
35.	?.	*?	Carac. 1, G2
125.	?.	*?	Nar. 24, D9
125, 126.		*?.24	Xculoc Center Lint. B; G
38.		*:27?	Xcalum. I.S. build. Lt. Col. A2
32.		*:82?	Ixkun, 2, A12
63.		*:102	Beyer 446
39.		*.?:86?	Xcalum. N. build., Frag. F
117.		*.558?	D. 37c
133.		*:565a	Pal. Sun Pil. stucco

This glyph has been discussed by Beyer, Lizardi, and Barthel, who accept it as the symbol of sacrifice. The two examples from Xculoc are unusual, but the bat glyph which precedes both of them, as at Chichén Itzá, helps to authenticate this assignment. Example 129 is of interest, because on being joined to Glyph 671, it has the latter's affix prefixed to it. See Glyph 756 (Bat) for many examples of Glyph 568 used as infix. Most of the 568–756 compounds at Chichén Itzá form a clause with the moon glyph as Beyer demonstrated. Glyph 568 is essentially Affix 82 placed diagonally.

For further examples of Glyph 568, see under Glyphs 558, 559, 561, 565, 608, and 669.

GLYPH 569 (Tied Pouch)
(44 Examples; Sheets 205, 206)

18.		*	Tik. L. 4, F11
33.	12.	*	Silán, 1, A
13.	16?:	*:140?	Tik. L. 3, H4
34.	35.	*	Tik. 1, A8
26.	168:	*	Yax. L. 37, T8
1, 3, 5, 6, 7, 8.	36.168:	*	Nar. 24, A8; D18; 29, G11; E17; H14; I18
20, 23.	36.168:	*	Tik. L. 4, D6; Temp. VI, K4

[194]

16, 17, 28.	38.168:	*	Tik. L. 4, D5; D6; 19, B8
27.	38.168:	*	Seib. 10, B8
24.	38.168:	*:130?	Cop. A, G5
14.	38?.168:	*	Tik. 5, B7
39–41.	38?.168:	*	Dos Pilas H.S. 2, B6; D7; Sculpt. C, D5
31.	40.168:	*	Ixlu, Alt. of 2, C2
2, 9, 11.	1000.168:	*	Nar. 24, D18; 23, E14; 31, G1
10.	231?.168:	*	Nar. 31, J15
29.	1000.168?:98:	*	Tik. 23, C4
25.	1000.168:	*:92	Yax. L. 17, FI
44.	1016?.168:	*	Dos Pilas H.S. 2, H8
4.	?.168:	*	Nar. 24, C10
42, 43.	?.168:	*	Dos Pilas H.S. 2, F6; F8
19, 21, 22, 30.	?.168:	*	Tik. L. 4, E7; 22, A4; T. VI, I3; L. 5, A19
35, 36.	168?:	*	Tik. 31, A21; I4
15.	?.168?:	*	Tik. 9, B7
37.	364:	*	Tik. 31, P3
32.	1000.	*	Tik. 26, F9
38.		*	Tik. 31, G24
12.		*:140?	Tik. L. 3, E1

A glyph somewhat resembling Glyph 569 appears at Monte Albán, and has been assigned the letter Z by Caso (1947, Fig. 67), who identifies it as a day sign. I am inclined to believe that the resemblance, which is not marked, is fortuitous.

The distribution of the glyph is interesting. Except for one occurrence on Stela A, Copán, a monument which carries other intrusions, and on the Petén-inspired sculpture of Silán, Glyph 569 is found only in the Petén and in adjacent sites on the middle Usumacinta. It does not appear in any of the three codices. It is found in quite early texts at Tikal (Stelae 9, 23, and 31) and at Yaxchilán (Lintel 37). With few exceptions the glyph carries the Ben-Ich (168) superfix, and usually one of the group of water prefixes. At Naranjo, Glyph 569 follows the Ben-Ich cleft sky compound (168:562) with water prefix; at Tikal it may follow the glyph of the long-nosed god with sky prefix (561–1030). Fairly often the glyph is at the end of a section of text, or it is immediately followed by a distance number.

GLYPH 570 (Wavy Bone)
(66 Examples; Sheets 202–204; Gates' Glyph 401 in part; Zimmermann's Glyph 1374 in part)

49, 50.	168:	*	Pal. Sarcoph. edge, E.; W
27.	32.168:	*:140	Tuxtla Mus. shell, C4
42.	35.168:	*	Pal. Pal. Sub. Alt. K
3¹.	35:168:	*:130	Pal. Fol. O17
18.	35:168:	*:178	Pal. Inscr. W. T12
45.	35?.168:	*:142	Retiro slate pendant
10, 53.	36.168:	*	Pal. Inscr. E, L12; Sarcoph. edge, E
22.	36.168:	*:140?	Pal. House A, Balustr. A4
23.	36.168:	*:178	Pal. House C, eaves, E2
2.	36.168:	*:140?	Pal. Fol. L17
26.	36.168:	*:254	Pal. Madrid Tab.
44.	36.168:	*.130:178	Miraflores Tab.
9.	36?.168:	*.130:178	Pal. Inscr. E. L1
37.	36.168:	*:178	Jonuta 1, A4
24.	36.168:	*:142	Pal. Pal. House E slab
14, 15, 38–40.	38.168:	*	Pal. Inscr. M. E9; W. H3; Sarcoph. Gls. 37; 42; 52
12.	38.168:	*.130	Pal. Inscr. E. Q12
19.	38.168:	*:130	Pal. Ruz, Tab. 1, Q1
7, 11.	38.168:	*.130:178	Pal. Inscr. E. J1; Q9
25.	38.168:	*.130:140	Pal. Cross, E. pan. shrine
41.	38.168:	*:140	Pal. T. 18, Tab. C17
1.	38.168:	*:125?	Pal. Cross, Q3
61.	38.168:	*:178	Tort. 1, C1
21.	38.168:	*:?	Pal. Ruz 1, Q18
46.	38.168:	*:?	Br. Mus. jade head
20.	38?.168:	*:140	Pal. Ruz Tab. 1, Q8
17.	38?.168:	*.130:178	Pal. Inscr. W. T10
34.	38?.168:	*:130?	Cop. A, G6
56.	38?.168:	*:178	Pal. Fol. Sculpt. stone
4, 51, 52.	40.168:	*:140	Pal. Sun, K3; Sarcoph. edge, N. E.
5.	?.168:	*:140	Pal. Sun, M6
8.	?.168	*:178	Pal. Inscr. E. J4

13.	?.168:	*	Pal. Inscr. E. T12
16.	?.168:	*?130:140	Pal. Inscr. W. P2
59.	110.	*[109]:595?	D. 67b
6.	59.	*:48	Pal. Sun, D3
54.	1003.?:	*:178?	Tort. 6, G1
31.	I:	*[109]	Yax. L. 10, F7
35.	I.	*[109]:7?	Nar. 23, E19
33.	12.I:	*[109]:?	Caribe 1, B5
57.	12.I:	*[109]	La Mar, 2, G3
28.	12.II:	*[109]:?	Seibal 5, C1
63–65.	12:II:	*[109]:102	Aguatec. 1, A10; A14; D5
62.	12.III:	*[109]:102	Aguatec. 7, C1
66.	12:III:	*[109]	Tamar. H.S. 2, F7
30.	12.VII:	*[109]	Yax. L. 9, C4
29.	12.X:	*[109]	P.N. 12. Captives
47.	12:XVI:	*[109?]	Yax. L. 10, A7
32.	59:	*[109]	Yax. L. 10, F2
58.	?.	*[109]:8	Xlabpak 4, B1
36.		*:23	Tik. L. 4, A6
60.		*[109]:130	D. 34a
43.		*[109].?	Ixlu Alt. St. 2, A5
48.		*?:24	M. 107b
55.	Missing	*:178	Pal. Fol. stucco

[1] I have previously published this as having a Yax(16) prefix, but a fresh examination leads me to believe that the prefix is 35.

The compound 168:570 with water-symbol prefix is confined to Palenque and sites in the vicinity with the exception of one record on Stela A, Copán, which carries other non-local glyphs, notably the tied pouch glyph (569). The use of Glyph 570 apparently with 109 infixed is interesting, for it is not uncommon in the middle Usumacinta and Pasión drainage, and carries numbers (at Aguateca it appears in phrases). Beyer (1938) lists also an occurrence with coefficient of nine on Stela 20, Tonina, but the glyph is badly eroded and one is reluctant to extend the distribution by including this example. Note the combination of the 570 [109] compound with the moon sign (p. 283), which Beyer has also discussed in the paper just cited.

Our so-called wavy bone glyph may not be derived at all from a bone; without the wavy line it closely resembles the simpler forms of Affix 109, the *chac*, "red" or "great" sign.

Many (Nos. 1–5, 9, 11–13, 15, 16, 18, 20, 22, 24, and 25) of the 168:570 and water-affix compounds at Palenque appear where there is a break in the text or at the end of a text. This may be fortuitous.

The glyph is unknown in the codices except for the one dubious example listed. See also under Glyph 501.

GLYPH 571 (Upright Bone)
(5 Examples; Sheet 226)

5.	561g:	*	Tik. 31, C17
4.	561g:	*:23	Tik. 31, H23
3.	aged head	*:23	Carac. 16, C18
1.		*:23	Carac. 16, C14
2.		*:23	Tik. 31, F27

This rare glyph, confined to the Petén area, confirms the correctness of Beyer's identification of Glyph 570 as a bone.

GLYPH 572
(5 Examples; Gates' Glyph 351; Zimmermann's Glyph 1307)

3.	58?.130?:	*:126	D. 27a
1.	95.130:	*:126	D. 28a
2.	109.130:	*:126	D. 26a
4.	245? or 114?.	*:87	Cop. J, W. 16
5.		*.181:113?	Xcalum. I.S. build., lt. lint.

Another example with yellow (281) affix was almost certainly once visible on Dresden p.25a.

GLYPH 573 (Hel)
(159 Examples; Sheets 227–29, 184; Gates' Glyph 331; Zimmermann's Glyph 1319)

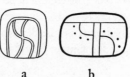

a   b

129.	1. or 1:	*:12	Form of D.N. intro. gl.
153.	1.	*:12	Tik. 31, F15 (not D.N. intro. gl.)

7.	1:	*.21:24	Cop. P, D10
43.	1:	*:21:136	Quir. P, Cart. 10
133.	1:	*:25:12	Form of D.N. intro. gl.
149.	1.	*.181:25:12	Form of D.N. intro. gl., Yax.
111.	1:	*:27	M. 34a
49.	1?:100:	*:24?	Carac., 16, D15
139.	3:	*:25:12	Form of D.N. intro. gl.
42.	11.	*:12	Pal. Sun, N7. Also form of D.N. intro. gl.
48.	11.	*.21:88?	Pal. Sarcoph., Gl. 10
40.	12.	*:21	Xkal N. build. Serp.
37.	12.	*.21:23?	Yax. L. 21, C1
19.	12.48:	*:178?	Pal. Sun, Q7
152.	13.	*.21:?	Pomona frag.
5.	13?.	*.25	Cop. 6, D1
128.	62.	[*]558:24	M. 103b
148.	21?:	*:?	Alt. Sac. 9, F7
122.	85:	*	M. 37b
123–126.	168:	*	D. 10b; 28b; M. 37c; 101d
32.	168:	*	Pal. T. 18, stucco
134–138.	168:	*.116	D. 25b; 27b; M. 68b; 68b; 72b
50–106.	168:	*.130	57 examples in all codices
142.	168:	*.130 (defective)	M. 28c
115.	25.168:	*	M. 70a
114.	25.168:	*.130	M. 91c
116.	58.168:	*.130	D. 3a
112, 113.	59.168:	*	M. 65a; 66b
107–109.	115.168:	*.130	M. 66b; 70b; 71b
110.	115.168:	*.130 (defective)	M. 72a
127.	172.168:	*	P. 24a
121.	238.168:	*	M. 68a
15, 22, 23.	1000.168:	*	Pal. Cross, K6; Inscr. W. R5; R10
24, 30, 31.	1000.168:	*:130	Pal. Ruz 1, D16; Cross balustr., L1; Fol. Cross balustr., L1
131.	204. or:	*:12	Form of D.N. intro. gl.
8.	204.?:	*.21?	Cop. H.S., Gxiiq
130.	205. or:	*:12	Form of D.N. intro. gl.

150.	205.	*.181:12	Form of D.N. intro. gl. Yax.
47.	228?.	*.12	Cop .6, D1
35.	228.	*:21:136	Pal. T. 18, stucco
38.	228.	*:21:136	Yax. L. 45, T5
132.	230.	*:12	Form of D.N. intro. gl.
10.	238?.	*.?	Cop. H.S., Step E10
141.	300.	*	M. 25a
45.	679af?.	*:24	Tik. 17, H1
118.	III.	*:103	M. 65b
34.	III.	*.?:?	Calak. 89, I5
17.	11.III:	*:178?	Pal. Fol. L10
18.	204.III:	*:178?	Pal. Cross, O8
16.	204.III:	*:?	Pal. Sun, N13
151.	204.III:	*:178	Pal. Ruz 1, O13
11.	135?.III:	*:25:246	Cop. W', I1
147.	IX.	*.?.21?:683 [178]	Cop. A, E6
158.	IX:21.	*	Tik. 31, G22
33.	IX.31.	*	Uaxac. tripod cyl. vase
20.	IX.168:	*	Pal. Inscr. W. L3
159.	IX:168:21.	*	Tik. 31, B18
211.	IX.168:	*.21	Pal. Inscr. Mid. J1
25.	IX.168:	*.21:?	Pal. Ruz 1, Y1
208.	IX.168?:	*.21?	Pal. Inscr. Mid. Q2
209.	IXP.168:	*:130	Pal. Inscr. E. S7
21.	IX.168:	*:130?	Pal. Inscr. W. K7
210.	IX.168?:	*?	Pal. Inscr. Mid. C1
13.	X:	*:21?	Cop. T. 11, Stand E'
6.	1.X?:	*:25:200?	Cop. 10, H8
4.	XII:	*.21:23	Cop. 7, E13
119.	XII.49:	*	M. 38a
2.	XIII:	*:21:82	Cop. B, B11
117.	XIII.168:	*	M. 73b
3.	1:XIV:	*.24	Cop. 9, F5
27.	1:XIV:	*?:?	Quir. F, B7
1.	12?.XIV:	*:22	Cop. N. Ped., Gl. 14
29.	21.XIV or IX?:?:	*	Tik. 3, A8
26.	?.XIV:	*.21:24?	Quir. J, C16
14.	XVI.	*:25	Cop. T. 11, Step 17
28.	XVI:	*.?:?	Quir. I, B9
12.	13:XVI:	*.25?:21	Cop. T. 11, Stand D'

155, 156.	1.21.	*:88	Tik. 31, C12; E23
154.	1:21.	*:88	Tik. 31, D7
157.	1:21.	*: missing	Tik. 31, A26
9.	?	*:21:23	Cop. H.S., gxiil
46.		*.21:23	Xultun 18, A5
41.		*.21:25?	Tik. 22, B5
39.		*.21:82?	Tik. 5, B6
44.		*.21:?.82	Nar. 24, C15
140.		*:103:25	M. 35a
36.		*.181:21	Pal. T. 18, stucco

In connection with the examples with numerical coefficients, one should note a few cases in which Glyph 683 (moon) sign with coefficient precedes Glyph 573. In these cases the moon sign presumably has a numerical value of 20. The highest certain coefficient is 29 with a possible example of 36 at Altar de Sacrificios. Glyph 573 has received comment by Thompson (1950, pp. 161–62), where the meaning *hel*, "change" or "rotation" is suggested.

For further examples of the use of Glyph 573, see under Glyphs 558 and 633.

GLYPH 574 (Shell)
(1 Example)

1.		* or *:130	Form of kin used in D.N., but never in I.S.

The central element of Glyph 739 is almost certainly Glyph 574. Glyph 574 placed upside down becomes Glyph 575.

GLYPH 575
(53 Examples; Sheets 254–56, 378)

40.	17.?:	*	Nar. 22, H1
41.	?.21:	*	Pal. Sun, P16
42.	110.21?:	*	Pal. Sun, I1
43.	45.	*	Cop. Q, F1

44.	45.74:	*	Cop. G2, B2
45.	679af.45:	*	Cop. Z, B3
20.	74:	*	Pal. Conde T.
11.	134.74:	*	Quir. H, S1. South
6, 39.	134.74:	*.134	Cop. T. 21a, F; T, Gl. O. South
48.	134.74:	*.134	Uaxac. mur. B6
1–3, 7.	134.74:	*.134:178	Cop. A, G9; T. 11, S. door A4; 6, C5; C′, F2
10.	134.74:	*.134:178	Quir. M, D4
9.	134.74?:	*	Quir. A, C11
13.	134?.74:	*	Pal. Inscr. bur. jade
4.	59.134.74:	*.134	Cop. M, D9
5.	209.134.74:	*.134:178	Cop. J, E. Gl. 15
8.	151.74:	*:178	Pal. Cross, A5
12.	134.	*.134:116?	P.N., L. 2, Y2
15.	76:	*.125	Pal. Ruz 1, J10
30.	679P.76:	*	Pal. T. 18, stucco
35.	679.76:	*	S. Ton Alt. 2, Gl. 4
31.	77:	*	P.N., L. 3, U2
40.	679.77:	*	Cop. H.S., Frag. Gxiie
24.	168:	*	Quir. Alt. P, S2
33.	204.168:	*?	Jonuta 1, B2
38.	679.217?:	*	Pal. Inscr. W. R9
46.	218:	*.165	Alt. Sac. 4, B8
47.	331?.	*	Hondo bowl, Guat. Seler
52.	359:	*:713	Tik. 31, C20
28.	510:	*	Yax. L. 41, A2
36.	35?.510:	*.35	Pal. Inscr. M. G7
49.	510:35?.	*?:126	Dos Pilas H.S. 2, A2
34.	89.510:35.	*	P.N. Thr. 1, E′6
51.	119.510:	*	Carac. 3, F3
16.	548:	*.125	Pal. Ruz 1, C2
21, 23, 25, 26, 27.	793:	*	Yax. L. 28, S1; L. 59, M1; L. 27, A2; F2; 12, A2
37.	793?:	*	Tonina 31, Gl. 4
14.	1000.4:	*	Pal. Ruz 1, J10
17.	1003?:	*	Cop. K, I2
19.	1006:	*	Cop. H.S., Step G
29.	59:IX:	*	Yax. Str. 44, M. Up. Step D4
48.	?.	*	Acasaguastlán carved brown vessel

50.	?.	*	Dos Pilas H.S. 2, A3
32.		*.59	Carved shell, Tuxtla Mus.
39.		*:130:671	Cop. F', A4

Glyph 575 appears to be the same as some variants of Affix 17. They may be the same, but I suspect there may be convergence, for Affix 17 often functions as the symbol for Yax and has its peculiar irregular outline, whereas Glyph 575 appears in contexts which in some cases seem to have no connection with Yax ("green" or "new") and is not irregular in shape. Other examples of this sign are listed with hand signs (Affixes 217–220).

Glyph 575 several times is joined to the Venus glyph (510) or to Glyph 793, a head of a monster with upturned snout which may represent the Venus monster. With Affixes 74 and 134, it is the glyph for "south" on the monuments, a glyph somewhat different from the codex form which has as its main element the Yax sign. This does show a connection between Glyph 575 and Yax.

Spinden (1924, Figs. 8, 9) recognizes our Glyph 575 as a shell, an identification which, I think, one must accept. Note that in inverted position this becomes Glyph 574. The old god, Mam (Glyph 1014), wears Glyph 575 on his cheek as one of his symbols.

For further examples of Glyph 575 see under Glyphs 510, 548, 627, 683, and 713.

GLYPH 576 (Spiral hatched background)
(2 Examples; Sheet 367)

| 1. | 1. | * | Nar. 13, H4 |
| 2. | 755?. | * | Nar. 8, B1 |

Possibly this is a variant of Glyph 856.

GLYPH 577 (Spiral)
(11 Examples; Gates' Glyph 353; Zimmermann's Glyph 1311)

3.	17:281:	*	D. 29c, picture
4.	17.281.	*	D. 30c, picture
1.	60:	*	D. 29c, picture

2.	93.	*?:24?	M. 60a
8.	I.	*?:24	M. 95a
5-7.	IX.	*:24	D. 33b; 34b; 35b
9.		*:686	D. 36c
10.		*:686	M. 86c
11.		*?:686	M. 86c (drum)

The pictorial and glyphic associations are with water and with pottery vessels, including a drum.

See also under Glyph 526.

GLYPH 578 (Spiral)
(12 Examples; Sheets 361, 367)

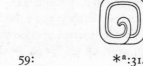

2.	59:	*ᵃ:314	Seib. H.S. H2
9.	109.86:	*ᵃ:142	Tik. Alt. V, Gl. 7
5.	126.59:49:	*ᵃ.89?	Xcalum. I.S. build., Lt. Col. B2
12.	17?.129?:	*ᵇ	P.N. Lint. 2, S1
6.	145.?:	*ᶜ	Xcalum. N. build., Serp. Gl. 15
8.	181?.	*ᵃ?	Uaxac. stucco tripod vase
7.	222.	*ᶜ:126	Chajcar pottery box supports
3.	204?.?:	*ᵇ	Alt. Sac. 5, B12
4.	329.?:	*.9:288	P.N. 12, Capt. 26
1.		*ᵃ:?:12	Cop. H.S. Gxiih
10.		*ᵃ?.59	Nar. 23, G15
11.		*ᵇ:?	Pusil. D, F3

ᵃ Spiral anticlockwise.
ᵇ Spiral clockwise.
ᶜ Spiral depends from top of glyph.

In Glyph 578, the spiral springs from the edge of the glyph, whereas in Glyph 19 M.S., the hook or hooklike spiral has the appearance of being independent of the cartouche or enclosing line of the glyph. Nos. 9, 11, and 12 have a scalloped outline. No. 10 might be something quite different, perhaps Glyph 1016. No. 2 is perhaps Glyph 856.

See also under Glyph 585.

GLYPH 579
(4 Examples; Sheet 241)

1.	65:	*	Cop. N, Ped. 25
2.	128:	*:89?	Cop. T. 11, S. door, E. pan.
3.	188.	*	Slate mirror-back
4.		*:136	Beyer 609

No. 3 is in vertical position. In No. 4 the hook is entirely within the cartouche, and perhaps this may indicate a different glyph.

GLYPH 580 (Jade)
(61 Examples; Sheets 251–52; Gates' Glyph 356; Zimmermann's Glyph 1308a)

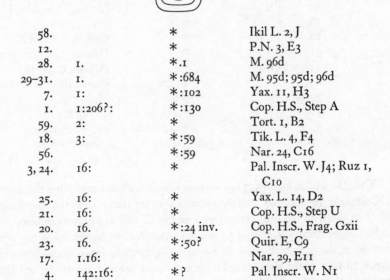

58.		*	Ikil L. 2, J
12.		*	P.N. 3, E3
28.	1.	*.1	M. 96d
29–31.	1.	*:684	M. 95d; 95d; 96d
7.	1:	*:102	Yax. 11, H3
1.	1:206?:	*:130	Cop. H.S., Step A
59.	2:	*	Tort. 1, B2
18.	3:	*:59	Tik. L. 4, F4
56.		*:59	Nar. 24, C16
3, 24.	16:	*	Pal. Inscr. W. J4; Ruz 1, C10
25.	16:	*	Yax. L. 14, D2
21.	16:	*	Cop. H.S., Step U
20.	16.	*:24 inv.	Cop. H.S., Frag. Gxii
23.	16.	*:50?	Quir. E, C9
17.	1.16:	*	Nar. 29, E11
4.	142:16:	*?	Pal. Inscr. W. N1
26.	1000.16:	*:?	Calak. 9, H2
27.	17:	*	Pal. House C, Eaves C2
36.	21:	*.217:301	D. 38a
37.	21:	*.217?:765?	D. 36c

50.	44.	*	Bonam. Rm. 2, judgment
14.	110.44:	*	P.N. 13, E2 (incised)
5.	12.58:	*	Kuna L. 1, D1
42–46.	90.	*	M. 97c; 97c; 97d; 98c; 100c
8.	126:	*	Pal. T. 18, stucco frag.
10.	229.565af?:	*	Yax. 18, F1
15.	230.	*:188	Seib. 10, B6
61.	265?.	*:582.582	B. Viejo Cambridge Expedtn.
32–34.	589.	*	D. 8b; 8b; 9b
47.	589.	*	Beyer 587
35.	13.589.	*	D. 9b
49.	607:	*	Beyer 586
48.	1.607:	*	Beyer 583
50.	513:607:	*	Beyer 584
6.	622.	*	Yax. Str. 44, Y6
9.	12.622:	*	Yax. 18, A5
54.	673[552]:	*	Beyer 458
55.	673[552].	*	Beyer 459
52.	VII	*	Xculoc, N. lint., B
53.	VII	*:12?	Xculoc, Cent. lint., I
16.	?	*	Seib. 12, A3
22.	?	*	Cop. Rev. Stand X
51.	?	*	Bonam. Rm. 1, attiring
13.	?.?:	*	P.N. 12, Capt. 36
60.		*:67inv.	Uxmal Ball Crt. E. ring
38, 39.		*.96	M. 99c; 99c
11.		*.113:40	Yax. 4, G3
57.		*:148:188	Pal. T. 18, stucco
40, 41.		*:687	M. 96d; 96d
2.		*.?	Cop. 12, A14

This, the Muluc sign (513) in vertical position, almost surely has the value jade (Thompson, 1950, p. 78). It is the same as 581 save that it lacks the encircling dots. Note its use with the drill glyph (589) and with 607, probably to indicate drilling jade. Conceivably Nos. 52 and 53 are tun signs. No. 50 stands beside the unhappy captive in the judgment scene in Room 2, Bonampak, from whose fingers blood drops. In view of the association between jade, the precious substance, and blood in ancient Mexico, one wonders whether this glyph in this passage refers to the blood from the captive's fingers.

For further examples of Glyph 580, see under Glyphs 589, 607, 662, 673, 683, 758, and 769.

GLYPH 581 (Mol)
(12 Examples; Gates' Glyph 33; Zimmermann's Glyph 1308)

1.		*	Month sign Mol.
12.		*	Acanceh mur.
2.		*	D. 10c
3–6.	1.	*	D. 10c; 11c (thrice)
7.	13.	*	D. 10c
8.	112.	*	D. 6c
9.		*.34?	Xcocha Capital
10.		*.577?	Chama. Carey vase F2
11.		*?	Cop. Alt. G'

GLYPH 582 (Mol semblant)
(61 Examples; Sheets 152, 153; Gates' Glyph 357; Zimmermann's Glyph 1301)

30.		*	Uaxac. 13, A5
32–34.		*	M. 108a (thrice)
19.		*[533]	Yax. 7, D2
61.		*[542]	Uaxac. red bowl A2
10, 14.		*[1044]	Yax. L. 41, D2; L. 33, A12
16.	1.	*[1044]	Yax. L. 3, H2
39–42.	25.25:	*.25:25	Affixes in corners. M. 15a (4 times)
43–48.	47.	*.47	M. 20b (thrice); 21b (thrice)
3.	57?:	*	Cop. H.S. Gxii
8.	57?:	*	R. Amarillo Alt. 1, C1
9.	109.118:	*	Pal. carved pot, F3
20.	145?:	*:279	Yax. L. 7, C4
15.	145?:	*[758?]	Yax. L. 32, F1
22.	145?.?:	*[1044]	Yax. 1, F12
49, 50.	159:	*	M. 93a; 96c
51–53.	159	[*]	M. 61b; 70a; 94b
54–58.	VII.159:	*	D. 19b; 50b; 50c; M. 41b; 91a

59.	122.159:	*	D. 45b
31.	181.	*	Tonina 31, Gl. 12
17.	204.	*[1044]	Yax. L. 1, B9
23.	204?:	*	Cop. H.S., Step D
24.	279?.	*:136	P.N. 12, Capt. 3
2.	126.279:	*	Cop. R, H1
26.	280.	*:136	P.N. 15, C6
28.	565af.	*[1044]	P.N., L. 2, T1
59.	512?.	*:17	Cop. 11, B1
25.	?.	*?	P.N. 14, A12
29.	?.?:	*	Pusil. E, D8
18.		*.99	D. 46c
35–38.		*.116	M. 109c (thrice); 110c
12.		*.178	Yax. Str. 44, E. Up. Step X7
13.		*.178:279	Yax. 18, A7
11.		*[1044].181 :126	Yax. L. 17, A3
1.		*:279	Cop. R, C2
21.		*:279	Yax. 19, A6
6.		*:279?	Cop. T. 11, Step 22
4, 60.		*:?	Cop. T. 21a, J; Frag. V'9

Nos. 1, 4, 5, and 6, all from Copán, appear in a clause with Glyphs 604, 533, 507, and others, in all cases with the important date 9.16.12.5.17 6 Caban 10 Mol. There is also a certain relationship in several texts at Yaxchilán containing Glyph 582.

For further examples of Glyph 582, see under Glyphs 501, 580, 583, and 687.

GLYPH 583 (Mol with propeller infix)
(8 Examples; Sheet 157)

1.		*	Gl. G3 (Thompson, 1950, Fig. 34, *16*, and *17*)
5.		*	Seib. H.S. Q2
6.		*	Pal. Sarcoph., Gl. 41
8.	59.	*:?	Yax. L. 3, C3
3.	281.	*:87?	P.N., L. 3, J'
2.	1000.122.	* or 582.122 :19	Yax. 7, D6
7.	1010.25?:	*:142	Pal. Pal. Sub. Alt. I
4.		*?:60:23	P.N. Alt. 1, N'3

This propeller element is usually infixed in Glyph 624, the shield glyph. In one example, listed under 624, the two are juxtaposed.

GLYPH 584 (Ben)
(2 Examples; Gates' Glyph 13; Zimmermann's Glyph 1333)

1.	*	The day sign Ben
2.	*:682.1016	P. 17c

Ben is a completely sterile root except in the formation of a few affixes (Nos. 168, 169, 170, and 284). It also appears resting on an outstretched hand (Glyph 670). See also under Glyphs 671 and 803.

GLYPH 585 (Quincunx)
(169 Examples; Sheets 195–201; Gates' Glyph 311; Zimmermann's Glyph 1343)

a   b   c

	a	b	c
62.		*	Beyer 480
71.		*	Chama. Carey vase
72.		*	Uaxac. I.S. vase
73.		*	Uaxac. sherd 4977
110, 111.	1.	*:23	M. 105a
143.	1.	*:?	D. 52b
61.	23:	*	Beyer 479
81.	12.23:	*:142	Bonam. Mur., Rm. 1, lower
107.	23:	*.?	Stone figure of Mam, Br. Hond.
28, 64.	12.	*:?	P.N. 12, Capt.
23.	1000.12:	*.?:?	P.N. shell plaque, J2
150.	12.	*:?:?	P.N. 12, Capt.
93.	13.	*?:126	Cancuen Alt. 1, B1
108.	13.324?:126:	*.202	Ikil L. 1, C
140.	17.	*	P. 16b
141.	17:	*	P. 16b
142.	59.	*.17	P. 17a

121.	25.	*	M. 101b
144.	25:	*	D. 74a
143.	25:	*:23	D. 69b
98.	27.	*	Nebaj. Fenton vase
67.	32:	*	Nar. 13, F16
160.	61.	*	Cyl. jar, Petén. Thompson, 1954.
70.	62.73:	*	Huehuetenango vase
146.	74:	*:24	D. 42c
169.	12:?:74?:	*	Tamar. H.S. 2, D12
102.	74.61.	*	Uaxac. Tzakol stuccoed vessel
32, 89.	12.	*:77	P.N. Thr. 1, A4; 15, C7
21, 90–92.	12.	*:77?	P.N., L. 3, E'; B'2; 12, Capt.; 12, 18
76.	145.77:	*	Uaxac. sherd 3506
77.	60.77:	*:?	Uaxac. sherd 1202
159.	60.77:	*	Hondo bowl, Guat. Seler
156.	61.77:	*	Carac. conch god vase
162.	61.77:	*	Peto jaguar vase
78, 79.	61.77:	*	Cop. tripod jar
109.	61.77:	*	Nebaj. Fenton vase
85.	61.77?:	*	Holmul cyl. jar
163.	61.77:	*	Pusil. slab-footed flat-based bowl
155.	61.77	*	Bliss conch god vase
95.	77?:78:	*:246	Jonuta, 2, B1
96.	?.77?:	*	Tonina 27, Gl. 4
5.	78:	*246	Pal. Inscr. W. Q12
99.	89.291?.18?:	*	Xcalum. I.S. build., Rt. Col. B6
7.	92.168:	*.48:24	Pal. Death, C2
124–128.	96	*:186	D. 41c; 65b; M. 11c; 108c; 97d
129.	1.96.	*:186	M. 97d
44, 45.	100.	*	Pal. Sarcoph., Gl. 34; 40
46–52.	100:	*	Pal. Sarcoph., Gl. 17; 19; 21; 27; 29; 48; 51
34.	100.	*:125	P.N., L. 4, M2
43.	679af.100:	*	Pal. Sarcoph., Gl. 7
6.	679af.100:	*.181	Pal. Ruz 1, N7
3.	100?.	*:292?	Pal. Fol. F1
86.	100?:	*:142	Cop. A. C8

1, 2.	100?:23?	*	Pal. Cross, T5; Fol. F1
35–38.	101.100:	*	P.N., L. 2, M2; W7; Y3; K'4
31.	101?.100?:168:	*	P.N. 12, D6
22.	101?.168:100?	*	P.N. shell plaque, G3
11.	101.168:100:	*	Yax. L. 49, O7
12–18, 24, 29, 94.	101.168:	*[100]	P.N. Thr. 1, Z4; E'1; I'4; L. 3, I1; N2; V3; V12; Alt. 2, F2; 23, K7; 6, B14
161.	100?.168:	*[100]	P.N. sting ray 2
26.	101.168?:	*[100]?	P.N. Alt. 2, L2
25, 33.	101.168:	*[100]:130	P.N. 8, X2; Alt. 2, I1
19.	115.168:	*[100]	P.N., L. 3, T'2
39.	205?.101.168:	*[100]:130	P.N. 23, G8
153.	1000:23.?:	*[100]	P.N. 3, A10
147, 148.	116.578:	*	Pusil. D, C13; E14
27.	116.87:	*:130?	P.N. 12, A17
40.	126.87?:	*:24?	Bonam. 1, H3
97.	1000:?.513af:	*	Pal. T. 18, stucco
87.	176:	*	Cop. T. 11, E. door, N. pan.
167.	1:177:	*.4	Tort. 7, A4
9, 154.	181.23:	*	Pal. carved I.S. pot; Sarcoph. edge, W
8.	23:	*.181	Pal. Madrid Slab 2, B3
69.	184.61:	*:24?	Carac. Alt. 12, H4
112–120.	186.	*	M. 97c; 98d; 99b; 99d (4 times); 100c
122.	186	*:23	M. 100d
123.	25.186	*	M. 98d
166.	218:	*.181	Tik. 31, G28
54.	229:	*	Beyer 99
55, 57.	229.	*	Beyer 100, 101
168.	229.	*	Kabah jamb. Amer. Mus. Nat. Hist.
20.	229.23:	*	P.N., L. 3, R'
104–106.	229.23:	*	Kuna L. 1, D2; G1; L5
82.	229.23:	*:142	Bonam. mur. Rm. 1, attiring
83.	229.	*:23?	Bonam. mur. Rm. 1, attiring
58.	230?:	*	Beyer 103
4, 53, 157.	238.23:	*	Pal. Inscr. E. B12; T. 18, Tab. D16; Scribe C2

139.	296.	*	M. 102a
101, 151.	526:	*	M. 104a (twice)
130, 131.	1:526:	*	M. 110c (twice)
138.	1.563af:	*	Holmul tripod bowl
84.	1.563af:	*	M. 23c
41.	1000.769?:	*	Cayo L. 1, A13
149.	1048:	*	D. 22c
132.	1048.	*	D. 22c
133–136.	1048:	*.145	M. 89a (twice); 90a (twice)
10.	animal head:	[*]16?	Yax. L. 37, T4
137.	X.	*.1050	M. 52a
80.	?.	*:?	Xcocha, milpa frag.
88.	?:	*	Cop. C'
165.	?.4:	*	B. Viejo Cambridge Expedtn.
100.	?:	*	Xcalum. I.S. build., rt. col.
74.	?:	*	Uaxac. sherd 3917
72.	?:	*.?	Pusil. D, A13
75.	?.?:	*	Uaxac. sherd 3917
56.	?.229?:	*	Beyer 101
64.	?.?:	*.?	Nar. 29, G15
59.		*:23	Chichén, Carac. Band 8
68.		*:23:?	Nar. 14, H1
103.		*.117:23?:125	Uaxac. Tzakol stuccoed vessel
145.		*.25:24	D. 30b
30.		*:136	P.N., L. 3, X3
63.		*:219	Beyer 482
66.		*:?	Nar. 13, G16
152.		*?.181:?	Xcocha, milpa frag.
164.		*:501?	Br. Mus. Fenton tripod bowl

The rarity of this glyph in the eastern part of the Maya area is worth noting when it is remembered that Glyph 585 is found in the hieroglyphic writing or the symbolism of other cultures (e.g., the Zapotec Glyph E in the Caso enumeration). It seems to be distinct in its functions and affixes from the Kan cross (Glyph 586), which it closely resembles. It has no connection with Glyph 510 (Venus Lamat.). See discussion in Thompson, 1951.

The compound with Ben Ich and water (168 and 301) prefixes and the unusual 300 infix frequently follows the glyph of the god of number seven. The Palenque compounds usually follow a C.R. or appear to be connected with Cauac. At Piedras Negras, too, there may be a Cauac association. No pattern in the usages of the glyph in the codices is immediately apparent. The Piedras Negras 585[100] form is Fig. 585c.

For further examples of Glyph 585, see under Glyphs 518, 526, 528, 673, and 757.

GLYPH 586 (Hatched dot)
(123 Examples; Sheets 275–80; Gates' Glyph 319; Zimmermann's Glyph 1303)

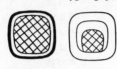

a   b

56.	1:	*	Beyer 188
90.	1.	*:59	R. Amarillo Alt. 1, J2
37.	1.	*.102:155:18	Cop. R'', B3
45.	1.	*:102 or 103	Carac. 17, B2
87.	1.	*.102 or 103 :18:65?	Cop. Z, C3
106, 107.	1.	*:25.501	Beyer 32; 38
108, 109.	12.	*:25.501	Beyer 35; 36
110.	12.	*:25:501	Beyer 252
104.	13.	*:25:501	Beyer 34
105.	13.	*.205:501	Beyer 37
112–115.	228.	*.25:501	Beyer 33; 39; 41; 42
116.	228.	*:25?:501	Beyer 40
111.	III?.	*.25:501	Beyer 253
71.	228.	*:8	Beyer 538
72.	228.	*:8?	Beyer 539
26.	12.	*:59	P.N., L. 2, J'1
38.	1.16:	*.130:510	Yax. L. 34, I7
53.	18.	*:130	Beyer 53
54.	18.	*130?	Beyer 54
55.	18:	*.?	Beyer 55
121.	21.	*	Chama vase. Gordon, Pl. 7
89.	25.126:	*:?	Los Higos, 1, C6
17.		*.126	Yax. L. 16, C1
18.	229.	*.126	Yax. Str. 44, S.E. Up. Step X7
20.	229.	*:126:126	Yax. 18, A6
73.	53:	*.92:102	Beyer 540

51.	59.?:	*	Bonam. Rm. 1 bottom, attiring scene
46.	59.60?:	*	Carac. 6, F13
24.	60:	*	P.N., L. 3, E'1
30.	60?:	*.181	Carac. 1, C2
100–102.	1.61:	*	M. 74b (thrice)
52.	1?.61?:	*	Cop. carved brown ware
95, 96.	68:	*	M. 60b (twice)
31.	68:	*:12?	Iturbide, A3
94.	68:	*.122	M. 60b
16.	68:	*.126	Quir. I, C3
36.	68:	*.130	Etzná, 5, B1
10.	1.68:	*:130	Quir. C, B7
9.	11.68:	*.130	Quir. C, C7
11.	11:68:	*:130	Quir. C, A10
13.	204?.68:	*.130:121?	Quir. J, A17
4.	68:	*.181	Cop. 1, C3
12, 15.	68:	*.181	Quir. E, D9; H, N1
14.	68:	*:181P.	Quir. D, D17
3.	68:	*:181	Cop. M, D4
8.	68:	*.181:121?	Quir. A, A10
42.	1.68:	*.181	Nar. 36, C1
2.	679af.68:	*.181	Cop. 4, A8
1.	679af.68?:	*.181	Cop. 6, C6
6.	679af.68:	*.202.181: 121?	Cop. B, B1
43.	68?:	*	Nar. L. 1, D2
5.	68.	*?:19:116:181	Cop. C, A10
119.	68?:	*.21:25	La Mar 3, B16
85.	IX?:74:	*.25?:?	Cop. 15, C6
35.	115.	*.116.24	Nebaj. vase (42–9–626)
40.	128:	*:202	Nar. 10, B4
91–93.	136:	*	M. 27b; 56b? (twice)
97–99.	1.136:	*	M. 28b (thrice)
28.	151:	*.181	Bonam. 2, D5
80.	1.187:	*	Cop. M, B5
47.	196.	*:131	Ixlu Alt. St. 2, B6
23.	202.	*	P.N. 12, Capt. 49
81.	202.	*	Cop. M, C9
83.	202:	*:25	Cop. H.S., Frag. Gxiie
29.	202:513af.	*:59	Pal. Pal. Sub, Alt. I
41.	202?:	*:?	Nar. 32, X3
84.		*:202?:59?	Cop. Rev. Stand, A'1

88.	204?:	*	Cop. 3, B8
32.	269.	*	Chajcar box (52–1–45)
34.	181:269:	*.23	Chajcar box (52–1–45)
86.	283.	*	D. 53b
120.	357.142?:	*	S. José carved jar, Fig. 67
118.	1.44:669.	*:25:178	Yax. L. 46, F′ ′8
39.	IV?	*.25:23	El Cayo, L. 1, D14
82.	?.	*	Cop. M, C10
78.	?:	*.87	Cop. 7, E4
77.	?:	*.?:23	Cop. 7, E7
58.		*:25:178	Beyer 2
74.		*:25.178	Beyer 541
61, 68.		*.25.178	Beyer 5; 12
62, 66, 76.		*:25.178	Beyer 6; 10; 543
21.	?:	*:25:178	P.N. Support, B2
25.		*:25:178?	P.N. 12, D13
22.	?:	*:25?:178	P.N. 12, D20
117.	1.	*:25.178?	Jade head in Br. Mus.
57.		*:27.178	Beyer 1
60.		*.27:178	Beyer 4
75.		*.203:178	Beyer 542
63, 64.		*.205:178	Beyer 7; 8
69.		*:205.178	Beyer 13
65.		*:25:254	Beyer 9
70.		*:205:254	Beyer 14
122.		*:59	Dos Pilas 2, C3
123.		*:59	Aguatec. 2, C2
59, 67.		*?.?:178	Beyer 3; 11
19.		*:103	Bonam. Rm. 1, Lint. B3
33.		*:103	Uaxac. sherd 1844
50.		*.116:126	Bonam. Rm. 1, 1st attendant
103.		*.181:96?	P. 9b
48.		*.173?	Xcalum. N. build., Frag. A
49.		*:173?	Xcalum. S. build., E. jamb A4
117.		*.501.563	Cop. Quetzal vase
44.		*:510?	Xultun 18, A6

It is probable that Glyph 602 is only a local variant, confined to Palenque and the adjacent area, of Glyph 586. At least both appear with the 25 and 178 group of postfixes. In some cases the distinguishing characteristic of Glyph 602, the line of circlets beneath the hatched area, may have been eroded. It is interesting to note the use of Affix 12 and its personified form, Affix 228, at Chichén Itzá, and likewise Affix 25 (and its reversed form 27) and its personified forms, Affixes 203 and 205. The dubious No. 5 is in horizontal position.

For further examples of Glyph 586, see under Glyphs 501, 510, 519, and 669.

GLYPH 587
(2 Examples; Sheet 367)

| 2. | 60: | * | Moxviquil incised sherd |
| 1. | 220. | *.87 | Yax. Str. 44, S.E. Step Y2 |

GLYPH 588
(59 Examples; Sheet 354; Gates' Glyph 92; Zimmermann's Glyph 702)

a   b

14–16.		*	M. 10b?; 17b; 19b
55.	227.	*	D. 35c
54.	130.	*.181:140	D. 32a
3.	130:	*:?	Pal. T. 18, A11
10.	130.	*:136?	Yax. 1, E3
13.	?.	*	Pal. T. 4, N. stucco
5.		*.88:47	Pal. carved I.S. pot
2.		*.125:314	Pal. Cross, A14
11.		*:126	Yax. 1, D8
7.		*.181:178	Quir. K, D4
9.		*.181:178	Yax. 11, C'6
6.		*[181]:178 [126]	Quir. K, A7
8.		*.181:178 [126]	Yax. L. 30, E3
4.		*.181.130	Pal. Conde, stucco
1.		*:?:130	Cop. T. 11, S. door, E. pan., A2
56–59.		*.181	D. 38c; 44c; M. 108c; P. 6

17–51.		*.181:140	Gates 92.1.1. All codices
52.	181.	*:140	M. 107c
53.		*.59:140	D. 34c
12.		*?:?	Xcalum. N. build., E. col., B5

Except for the dubious No. 12, those on the monuments are with the 819-day count (Thompson, 1950, pp. 212–17). No. 13 is a detached stucco glyph, but in the scant group of stucco glyphs from that temple is another belonging to the 819-day clause.

See also under Glyph 82.

GLYPH 589 (Drill)
(20 Examples; Sheet 253; Gates' Glyph 314; Zimmermann's Glyph 1369)

19.	13.	*.580	D. 9b
2.	93:	*:141?	Beyer 591
1.	136:626:	*	Beyer 168
4–11.		*.93	M. 38b; 38c (each 4 times)
12.		*.93:25	M. 101b
20.		*.561c:23	D. 66a
16–18.		*.580	D. 8b; 8b; 9b
3.		*.580	Beyer 587
13–15.		*.765	D. 5b; 5b; 6b

The drill (*hax*) glyph. With Affix 93 it is the symbol for drilling for fire; with Glyph 580 it probably indicates drilling jade. See under Glyph 60. Glyph 765 postfixed probably is a reference to fire, for the dog is a symbol of drought and in that connection he bears a firebrand. Legend also recounts that he brought fire to man (Thompson, 1930, p. 151).

For further examples of Glyph 589, see under Glyphs 561, 580, 626, 758, and 765.

GLYPH 590 (Jawbone)
(26 Examples; Sheet 259)

a   b

	a	b	
26.	1:	*	Yax. L. 10, F5
8.	59.	*?:?	P.N. Support A4
6.	59.	*:683	Yax. 7, A3
5.		*:27:683P	Quir. F, C9
3.	120?.	*	Cop. B, B10
17.	165v.	*:627.627	Beyer 108
19.	165v.	*:25:?	Beyer 109
18.		*.627.627	Beyer 110
24.	168:	*.181	Pal. Sarcoph. N.
25.	168:	*.181:?	Pal. Sarcoph. S.
4.		*[?]	Cop. J, D7
16.	?	*:103	Beyer 106
21.		*:*	Beyer 112
23.		*.*	Beyer 114
22.	1?.	*:*	Beyer 113
10.	211.	*:110	Beyer 99
1.		*.110	Bonam. Rm. 1, attiring
2.		*:110	Bonam. Rm. 1, attiring
12, 13, 15.		*:110	Beyer 101; 102; 105
7.		*:110	P.N. 12, Capt. 30
9.		*:110	Sacchaná 2, D2
14.	1.	*.130:110	Beyer 100
11.	1 (detached).	*.130:110	Beyer 104
20.		*.35?.35?	Beyer 111

Usually two incisors are shown. The earliest occurrence of the glyph is at 9.13.10.0.0, on Stela J, Copán, where, however, it may have served as an affix to the Imix glyph beneath.

For further examples of Glyph 590 see under Glyphs 110, 627, and 748.

GLYPH 591 (Cenote)
(3 Examples; Gates' Glyph 313; Zimmermann's Glyph 1371)

1.		*	P. 16a
2.	96.	*	D. 43a
3.	501:136.	*	D. 39c

This glyph, which appears only in the codices, is rare in texts, but it appears often in pictures (e.g., D. 29c, 33a, 36c, 39c, 43a; M. 91a, 92a; P. 16b). Amending a suggestion of José Franco, one can suppose it is the sign for a cenote, usually, but not invariably, containing water.

GLYPH 592
(19 Examples; Sheet 211; Gates' Glyph 310 [in part]; Zimmermann's Glyph 1305 [in part])

1.		*	Cop. R, E1
5.		*	Nakum C, A6
3.	12:	*	Yax. 8, A1
7.	25?:	*	Cop. H.S., Step M
10.	518af:	*:130	Pal. T. 18, Tab. C13
11.	1000.518af:	*:117	Pal. T. 18, stucco glyphs
19.	1000.518af:	*:117?	Pal. Ruz 2, F6
8.	528?:	*	Cop. T. 11, 23
12.	68:	*.1	M. 112c
15, 16.	1.68:	*	M. 112c (twice)
13, 14.	68:	*.181	D. 25c; 26c
18.	129:	*	Acasaguastlán, carved sherd
2.	203.	*	Quir. C, C10
4.	203.	*:87?	P.N., L. 3, I'1
6.	228.	*	Nar. 24, D4
9.	IV:	*	Chajcar pottery box frag.
17.		*:186?	P. 8b

Nos. 2, 4, 6, and 9 have small circles in each corner, like those of Glyph 624. Nos.

1, 2, 8, and 9 follow or are joined to a cauac (528) glyph, on three occasions with No. 89 prefixed.

It is not easy to separate Glyphs 592 and 593. Gates and Zimmermann treat them as a single glyph, but the rare examples of Glyph 593 on the monuments differ so markedly from Glyph 592 that it seems advisable to keep them apart until evidence that they are the same is forthcoming. On the monuments the unhachured segments are decorated with two or three small circles, but these are absent in examples in the codices, except in Codex Madrid, p. 52c. Gates (1931, p. 141) suggests that the two glyphs probably denote the four world quarters.

See also under Glyph 528.

GLYPH 593
(11 Examples; Sheet 212; Gates' Glyph 310 [in part]; Zimmermann's Glyph 1305 [in part])

4.		*	M. 52c
5, 6.	68:	*.181	D. 27c; 28c
7.	141.	*:557	D. 46f
8.	115.168:	*.116[130?]	M. 67a
9.	IX.168:	*	D. 4a
10.	IX reversed.	*?	M. 19b
2.		*:125?	Quir. P, O2
11.		*.130:?	M. 8a
1, 3.		*:136?	Quir. P, D9; O2

As noted under No. 592, that glyph and No. 593 may well be variants of the same sign. Glyph 593 appears on the vessels from which long-nosed gods are pouring liquid in the design on Quiriguá P (Maudslay, 1889–1902, II, Pl. 60). Presumably these vessels represent the jars or gourds in which the rain gods, both Maya and Mexican, stored rain.

See also under Glyph 557.

GLYPH 594 (Checkerboard)
(17 Examples; Sheets 214 and 158)

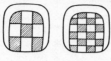

a   b

	a	b	
1, 10, 11.	74:184:239.	*:130	Pal. Fol. O10; Ruz Tab. 1, E12; I7
2, 4–9.	74.184.239:	*	Pal. Sun, O6; Inscr. E. B9; D12; F10; M. E7; M5; W. A6
3, 13.	239.	*:130	Pal. Sun, D6; T. 18, stucco
12.	239.	*:130?	Pal. H.S., C2
14.	Face.	*.184:130?	Carac. Alt. 12, 1:12
15.	?	*?	Yax. 4, G2
17.	122?:?:	*.178	Beyer 616
16.	501:	*:178	Beyer 615

Glyph 594, a simple checker pattern, is twice infixed in Glyph 624, the shield glyph, and shares with that glyph the use of the rather unusual combination of Affixes 74 and 184. Affix 239 is very unusual.

With the exception of one record on a late stela at Caracol (the face prefixed to this may well correspond to Affix 239) and a quite dubious example on a Yaxchilán stela, this glyph is confined to Palenque and Chichén Itzá.

GLYPH 595 (Cotton)
(14 Examples; Sheet 213; Gates' Glyph 401 [in part]; Zimmermann's Glyph 1312)

10.	2.	*:23	Xculoc, N. lint., D
11.	95:	*.561c:23	D. 67a
12.	110.109?:	*	D. 67b
3.	134.110:	*.110	Cop. T. 11, W. door, S. pan.
4.	136.110:	*.110:142	Cop. T. 11, S. door, E. pan.
7.	136.110:110	*:142	Cop. T. 21a, M
6.	134.122:	*	Chinikiha Thr., B'2

1.	134.	*.74	Cop. A, G11
2.	134.	*:74	Cop. A, H11
13.	163.122:669a. 155:	*	D. 67a
5.	228.669b:	*:142	Pal. Inscr. W. C6
14.	743:	*?	Poptun, Frag. 2
8.		*.1	Beyer 617
9.		*:23?	Beyer 618

The term cotton is applied to this glyph purely for convenience. The series of little *u*'s are reminiscent of the Nahuatl symbol for cotton, but there is no evidence that the Maya glyph had that meaning. The two examples of Affix 136 almost surely represent examples of Affix 134 with the right half of the affix eliminated to save space, for Affix 134 is merely Affix 136 doubled to serve as prefix and postfix. Affix 134 is of limited use. No. 14 may be an unrelated glyph.

For further examples of Glyph 595, see under Glyphs 561, 570, 669, and 756.

GLYPH 596 (Cotton semblant)
(4 Examples)

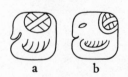

2.	16?:129:	*:142	Pal. Pal. Sub. Alt. H
1.	341.	*	P.N. 12, Capt. 44
3.	552.	*?	M. 19b
4.		*?.552[95]	M. 61c

A rare glyph.

GLYPH 597
(15 Examples; Sheet 231)

a   b

1, 2, 8.	III.	*.35:59	Pal. Cross, O7; Fol. L3; Inscr. W. N11
3, 5–7.	III.	*.43:59	Pal. Fol. N9; Inscr. M. F5; N5; W. B6

11.	III.	*.196v.?.43:59	Pal. 5 Kayab frag.
13.	III:	*.36.59	Pal. T. 18, Tab. B18
15.	III.	*:59	Tik. 26, F7
4.	III.	*.?:59	Pal. Sun, N6
10.	III:	*.?	Pal. T. 18 (Blom)
9.	head?.124:	*.116?:140.	Pal. Ruz 1, Q16
12.	III? or 118?.	*	Tonina 26, B8
14.	III.35.	*v?:59	Carac. 16, B14

Probably the three dots are not numerical. The example from Tonina is not too clear. The glyph from Caracol substitutes the curved "ladder" for the infixed crossed bands, a substitution which occurs also with Glyph 561 (sky glyph).

GLYPH 598 (Impinged bone)
(23 Examples; Sheets 243, 244)

1.	1:	*:23	Cop. J, E. 44
3.	58:197?:	*:23	Cop. J, E. 28
9.	92.	*:23	Pal. Fol. M15
19.	92.	*:23	Tik. 5, A12
2.	204:	*	Cop. J, E. 48
18.	204.35:	*:23?	Tik. L. 3, F6
15.	528P?.	*:23	Quir. H, N2
7, 8, 10–14, 16, 22.		*:23	Pal. Cross, B15; Fol. L15; Sun, N15; Pal. A, pier; D, pier; Ruz 1, D3; Peñafiel tablet; stone frag.; T. 3, N. stucco
23.		*.23	Peto jaguar bowl
6.		*:23	Cop. Alt. St. 13
17.		*:116	Yax. L. 26, Y′
4.		*.187	Cop. 6, C7
5.		*?.?	Cop. 1, D2
20.		*:?	Carac. 1, D3
21.	126.67:	*?	Xcocha capital front

At Palenque, where this glyph occurs with greatest frequency, it follows the sky glyph (561) with *al* (23) postfix. In two instances at Palenque (Fol. M15; House D, Pier d), there is no doubt that the central element is a jawbone. In other cases the central element is the head of a long bone. No. 21 conforms in appearance, but is on its side; it may be something quite different. At Yaxchilán, Glyph 598 is associated with Caban (Glyph 526; see entries under that number). Caban (earth) and the sky glyph are in an intimate relationship.

GLYPH 599
(5 Examples; Sheet 245)

4.	*	Cop. T. 11, E. door, A4
5.	*	Tik. 5, A12
1, 3.	*	P.N. Thr. 1, I1; F'6
2.	*:23	P.N. Thr. 1, F'2

The three examples from Piedras Negras Throne 1 are in the same clause comprising this glyph with a shell and quincunx element before it and a winged cauac after it. The Tikal example seems to have a kin element infixed.

GLYPH 600 (Fasces)
(17 Examples; Sheet 282)

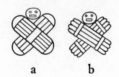

a   b

11.	12.	*.23:87	Cop. B', B1
2.	198? or 260?:	*[87]:23	Cop. J, E43
16.	291?.	*.87?	Tik. 11, C3
15.	117.	*:87:4	Yax. L. 25, G2
3–6.		*.4:87	Cop. 11, A2; Q, B2; A5; H.S., Frag. Gxiia
10.		*:4:87	Cop. Rev. Stand, Step D'
12, 13.		*.4:87	Quir. J, D16; F, B7
1, 8, 9.		*:87:?	Cop. B, B11; H.S., Step E; Q
7.		*.?:87	Cop. T. 11, N. door, W. pan.
14.		*.23:87?	Quir. P, Cart. 7
17.		*:?	Tohcoh painted jamb

There is some doubt as to whether the top element is the number seven or a small face; there are examples of both. One is reminded of the similar sign in the earplug of the jaguar god of the number seven. Affix 87, the *te* sign, is present in all cases, presumably to indicate that the bundles are of wood. One is tempted to see in either this glyph or Affix 150 a possible connection with the symbol of the Aztec *xiuhmopilli,* the bundle of the years.

GLYPH 601 (*Cuch*)
(71 Examples; Gates' Glyph 301; Zimmermann's Glyph 1363)

1, 2.	149.67.	*	D. 8b (twice)
3, 4.	1.149.67.	*	D. 9b (twice)
5–10.	67.	*.181	M. 40b (twice); 41a (twice); 41b; 58c
11–12.	67.	*.181:25	M. 41b (twice)
13.	III:	*.181.25	P. 9c
14.	III.	*:25	P. 5c
68.	25.527:	*	M. 94d
15–18.	1.528:	*	D. 17b; 18c; 19c; 25a
19–28.	1.528:67.	*	D. 16b (twice); 17a; 17b; 17c; 18c; 19c; 26a; 27a; 28a
29.	1.528:67?	*	D. 16a
30–33.	10.528:67.	*	D. 18c; 20c (thrice)
34.	10?.528:67.	*	D. 16a
35.	13.528:67.	*	D. 19c
36.	115.	*	M. 92c
37, 38.	115.614:	*	P. 15a; 15b
39–43.	115.614:	*	D. 28b; 35a; 35c; 41c; 44a
44–63.	115.192:	*?	Zimmermann lists 20 examples in Madrid
64.	614:	*	M. 59b
65.	21.115.614:	*	D. 38c
66, 67.	207.115.614:	*	M. 103c (twice)
69.	662?.614:	*	D. 36c
70.	?.667:	*	M. 85e
71.	?	*.181:145	P. 10d

This is the well-known *cuch* glyph, the meanings of which as "burden," "office," "charge," or "prophecy" are established beyond cavil. The main element is usually compounded with the *te*, "wood," symbol (87), the cauac sign (528) or the thatch signs (192 and 614).

As noted under Glyph 614, it is often hard to distinguish between Glyph 614 and Affix 192, particularly in the Codex Madrid. Nos. 44–63 are listed by Gates as 115.192 M.S. without any other attached element. Zimmermann, on the other hand, considers them to be 115.614:601 (in both cases reduced to my system of numeration). The drawings are so wretchedly done that either epigrapher could be correct. As a compromise between the two interpretations, I list them as 115.192:601.

GLYPH 602 (Hatched with line of dots)
(31 Examples; Sheets 276, 281, 339)

31.	1.	*:25.?	Jade head, Br. Mus.
14.	1.	*:25:178 or 142	Yax. L. 46, F′ ′8
2.		*.25:178	Carved shell, Tuxtla Mus.
3, 10, 11.		*.25:178	Pal. Inscr. E. S12; Pal. House C, eaves; carved I.S. pot
17–26, 30.		*P.25:178	Pal. Inscr. W. F5; J5; N2; Ruz 1, G7; J13; P11; H.S., A5; A6; C6; Sub. Alt. J; T. 4, sculpt. stone 2, C1
27.		*P.25:139	Pal. stucco frag. in Bodega
28.		*P.178:25	Miraflores Tab.
7.		*:25:178	Pal. Inscr. W. A3
9.		*.25?:178	Pal. Inscr. W. G3
15.		*.25:178?	Pal. Sarcoph., W. edge
1.		*:25:?	Pal. Sarcoph., Gl. 41
4–6.		*.205:178	Pal. Inscr. Mid. F8; H3; K2
8.		*[205?]:?	Pal. Inscr. W. F2
12.		*.103?:23	Yax. 19, A7
29.		*:126.501:25	Pal. Fol. sculpt. stone A10
13.	12.	*.?:23?	P.N., L. 2, Z2
16.	204.	*:671	Jonuta 1, A2

As previously noted, this glyph is probably a lower Usumacinta basin variant of

Glyph 586. The replacement of the comb element by the fish head has an interesting parallel in the case of Glyph 586 at Chichén Itzá. The personified examples are identified by the hatched areas on the best-preserved faces, the similarity of affixes, and the clause associations (usually they follow the shield glyph and precede one of several glyphs—(dragon, wavy bone, etc.) with Affix 168.

For further examples of Glyph 602, see under Glyphs 501 and 671.

GLYPH 603
(2 Examples; Sheet 274)

1.	19.	*:181?	P.N., L. 2, I′1
2.		*:?	Bonam. L3, A4

This glyph may be regarded also as Affix 93 (fire and smoke) used as a main sign.

GLYPH 604
(57 Examples; Sheets 264, 265, 274; Gates' Glyphs [in part] 319, 343, 359;
Zimmermann's Glyph 1302)

28, 29.		*	Cop. T. 11, Step 22; O′, A3
35, 36.		*	Pottery box supports, Carcha & Chajcar
56.		*?	Nar. 29, F17
33.		*	Carac. Alt. 12, 1–4
1–14.		*	Beyer 1–14
30.		*	Pal. T. 18, stucco
37.		*	D. 33a
39–44¹.		*	M. 80b; 81b (4 times); 96b
15, 16.		*.*	Beyer 604; 605
32.		*:*	Nar. 32, Z4
46¹.		*.*	D. 16c
47¹.		*.*	M. 110c
48¹.		*.*	P. 2b
57.	1.	*:117	Dzib. 19, A2

25.	1.	*	Cop. F′, C2
22.	25?	*:219	Beyer 606
49[1].		*:219	M. 40a
50[1].		*.219	D. 13c
51[1].	1.19.19:	*.130	P. 4d
38[2].	62:	*	M. 94c
52.	96.	*?	D. 32a
53[2].	526.526af:	*.671	M. 88c
55.	?	*	Nar. 29, E14
54.		*.60?	El Cayo, L. 1, H1
26.		*:60?	Cop. T. 21a, I
23, 27.		*:61	Cop. R, C1; T. 11, Step 7
45[1].		*.82?	M. 96b
24.		*?.130	Cop. 4, A9
20.		*.136?	Beyer 144
21.		*:136?	Beyer 145
34.		*.181	Carac. Alt. 12, E1
31.		*.181:114?	Nar. H.S., L2
17–19.		*.291	Beyer 141–43

[1] Lacks hachure.
[2] Lacks prefix 149.

Examples from the codices without hachuring of the central element are included, but the absence of that feature may affect the meaning. Most of the examples from Copán occur in a five-glyph phrase. In the codices the glyph without hachure seems to be that of the quetzal; with Glyph 219 affixed, the glyph may represent some species of vulture (identification proposed some sixty years ago by Cyrus Thomas).

GLYPH 605
(2 Examples; Sheet 240)

1.	167:	*	Jonuta 2, B2
2.		*:61:302	Jonuta 2, A2

A rare glyph with rare affixes.

GLYPH 606 (Shell)
(50 Examples; Sheets 233–36)

a   b

28.	44:110.	*:23	Pal. Sun, P5
42.	110.44:	*:23	Pal. Cross, S2
34.	110.168:44:	*	Pal. Fol. E9
41.	40v.168:44:	*	Pal. Cross, Q9
13.	44?:	*	Pal. 96 Gl. L5
33.	78?:	*	P.N. 12, B19
44.	89:	*.181	Pal. Fol. E9
2.	126?:	*?	Cop. 12, D7
29.	?.232.125:	*	Yax. L. 37, T5
43.	565af:	*?:23?	Pal. Cross, J1
20.	I.	*:23	Pusil. M, C7
1.	IP:	*:23	Cop. H.S., Step G
18.	I.	*?:?	P.N. 3, C7
38.	I?:	*:23	Carac. 1, F3
19.	1.I:	*:23	Pusil. E, C4
21.	1.I:	*.23	Nar. 24, D8
22.	3.I.	*:23	Tik. L. 3, H5
23.	3.I.	*.23	Tik. L. 4, E1
12.	3.I:	*:23	Pal. 96 Gl., I8
25.	11:I:	*	Pal. Sarcoph., Gl. 55
3.	11:I.	*:23	Pal. Fol. N17
16.	11:I.	*:23?	Pal. Fol. Sanct. A10
50.	136.?:	*.136:?	Carac. 3, C9
6, 7.	191.I:	*:23	Pal. Inscr. W. A1; M. F7
14.	204.I:	*:23	Pal. Cross, E. Pan. B1
17.	204.I:	*:23	Yax. 10, H1
4.	204?.I:	*:23	Pal. Sun, M5
9.	232.I:	*:23	Pal. Ruz 1, D14
8.	125:669b:130.I:	*:23	Pal. Inscr. W. S11
24.	?.I:	*?:23?	Moral., 2, B11
30.	?.	*:23	Yax. L. 47, G3
35.	?.	*:23	Nar. 13, H1
37.	?:	*?:23?	Carac. 17, B3
47, 48.		*[508]	P.N. Thr. 1, I1, F'6
49.		*[508]:23	P.N. Thr. 1, F'1

5, 10, 11, 15.		*:23	Pal. Sun, C2; Ruz 1, C6; D4; T. 18, detached stucco
39.		*:23	Calak. 51, F4
26, 31.		*:23	Yax. L. 25, M2; 18, C1
36.		*:23	Ixkun 2, D4
27.		*.24:23	Yax. L. 25, T2
32.		*.59:23	Yax. L. 32, G1
45.		*:23.173 or	variants of half
46.		*:23.74:173	period glyph
40.		*.248	Uaxac. sherd 4781

Glyph 606 resembles rather closely the codical form of the day sign Men (Glyph 613), but this resemblance is seemingly fortuitous; Glyph 606 does not appear in the codices. There seem to be reasonable grounds for supposing this sign to be derived from drawings of a conch shell. Examples 45 and 46 are two of a series of combinations of Glyph 606 and Affixes 74 and 173 to indicate half completion (Thompson, 1950, pp. 192–93). The many occurrences of this glyph with a co-efficient of one present an interesting problem.

It should be noted that the clenched fist (Glyph 672) is distinguished from other hand signs by the infixing of 606. The whole may signify something like completion of a period.

See also under Glyph 173.

GLYPH 607
(20 Examples; Sheet 253; Zimmermann's Glyph 1369 [one example])

a   b

11.		*	Beyer 197
14.	1.	*:93	D. 6b
13.	1.	*:93	M. 42c
1.	1.	*:580	Beyer 583
7.	13.67:	*.24	Beyer 590
9.	89.67:	*.24	Beyer 72
10.	89:67.	*:24	Beyer 73
6.	228.67	*.24	Beyer 589
3.	228	*:511	Beyer 582
5.	513.67	*:24	Beyer 588

4.	513:	*:580	Beyer 584
8.	89:	*.130	Beyer 51
12.	125.	* ?:130	Beyer 52
14.	126.	*:758:246	Beyer 593
15.		*.758:126?	Beyer 592
19.	?.	*	Bonam. Rm. 2, judgment
17.	IV.93:	*.178	Quir. A, D7
18.	IV.118?.93:	*:141?	Quir. J, H8
20.		*.IV:59	Kabah mur. Becker
13.		*:580	Beyer 586
16.		*:608.178	Beyer 594

This closely resembles the *hax*, "drill," glyph (589) except that it is on its side. The two examples from the codices and the two from Quiriguá seem to confirm this, for they have the same smoke or flame affix (93) as Glyph 589. Moreover, two of them, like examples of Glyph 589, are combined with the jade symbol, presumably to represent drilling of jade. Incorporation of the number four at Quiriguá and Kabah is interesting. The Kabah example is reversed, and that may account for the postfixing of the numerical coefficient.

For further examples of Glyph 607, see under Glyphs 580, 713, and 758.

GLYPH 608 (Beyer's Mollusk)
(23 Examples; Sheet 270; Gates' Glyph 342; Zimmermann's Glyph 756)

1.	90.	*	M. 22b
2–4.	149.	*	M. 20d (twice); 21d
13–15.	229.	*:188	Beyer 86, 88, 92
16.	229.	*:188?	Beyer 89
19.	229:	*:188	Beyer 87
17.	?.229.	*.130:188.136	Beyer 90
18.	229:	*.130:188:136	Beyer 91
20[1].	229.	*.188:130:136	Beyer 93
21[1].	229.	* ?.?:130:136	Beyer 94
22.	1000?:	*:23	Beyer 97
23.	679:1000.	*:697	Beyer 98
5–8.		*.149	D. 6b; 7b (thrice)
9.		*.149	M. 100c
10.	?	*.149	M. 10b

11.	*.568	D. 50f
12.	*.head	D. 50e

[1] In these two examples Affix 229 is postfixed to the bottom of the previous glyph (568), which it usually follows at Chichén Itzá.

Several identifications of this glyph have been suggested, notably that of Barthel (1955a). For convenience I use the early Beyer name pending agreement on the meaning of the glyph.

For further examples of Glyph 608, see under Glyphs 568 and 607.

GLYPH 609 (Jaguar pelt)
(16 Examples; Sheet 232; Gates' Glyph 333; Zimmermann's Glyph 1356)

a   b

14.	128:	*:23?	Pal. House E, mur.
15.	204:128:	*:23	Tila B, A7
10.	155:	*	M. 37b
11–13.	155:	*:126	M. 34b; 35b; 36b
5.	168:	*	D. 21c
6–8.	168:	*.130	D. 11c; 14c; 21b
9.	172.168:	*	D. 58b
3.	751.284:	*	Carac. 16, D18
1.	?:	*.23	Yax. L. 26, L'2
4.	1000.	[*]1031	Tik. L. 4, F3
16.		*:142?	Cop. D, B4
2.		*:65	Tik. L. 3, B7

Sculptures of jaguar pelts draped over daises leave little doubt that this glyph represents a section of jaguar pelt. Nos. 14–16 are rare variants of Glyph F of the lunar series, probably used because of the close association of the jaguar with darkness and the underworld. There are some grounds for supposing a somewhat similar association in Codex Dresden. In No. 4, the long-nosed god without lower jaw (sometimes god of the number thirteen) wears this glyph element on his head.

GLYPH 610
(17 Examples; Sheets 4 and 225; partly Gates' Glyph 340; partly Zimmermann's Glyph 1359)

1, 2.	86:69:	*	Pal. Sun, C12; Inscr. E. R5
5.	86:69:	*:23	Pal. T. 18, Tab. D11
4.	86:69?:	*:23?	Yax. L. 17, B3
3.	69:	*:23	Yax. L. 15, F3
42.	86:69:	*:142	Pal. Fol. C10
49.	109.	*:102:59	Pal. Inscr. M. N6
43, 46.	113.	*:138?:59	Pal. Fol. L8; Sun, N10
41.	115.	*:138?:59	Pal. Cross, D12
62.	115.	*:?:102	Pal. H.S., D6
6.	III:	*.181	P. 9d
7.		*.250	M. 20d
8.		*.533:277?	M. 61c
9.		*.586	D. 53b
10.		*.?	M. 21a
11.		*(on side).47	M. 8a

Glyph 610 appears in a few instances prefixed to heads of animals and gods. Nos. 6–10 are listed by Gates and Zimmermann as Glyphs 340 and 1359 respectively.

When this glyph is vertical and does not have a ragged edge, it is here classified as Glyph 610; with a ragged edge it is listed as Glyph 283, an affix which sometimes functions as a main element. An exception is No. 11. It is quite likely that Glyphs 610 and 283 are the same glyph, but it is best to keep them separate until that is proved.

GLYPH 611 (Number 8)
(9 Examples; Gates' Glyph 318; Zimmermann's Glyph VIII)

1.	25?.62:	*:140	M. 35b
2, 3.	84:	*	D. 36b; 39c
4.	84:544.	*	D. 65a

| 5, 6. | 33.85: | * | D. 67a, 68a |
| 7, 8. | 86: | * | Cop. I, C6; Alt. of I, Gl. E |

As I have noted (1950:272), this is probably a symbol of the maize god, who is the deity of the number eight (bar and three dots). The two examples from Copán, probably a sculptor's conceit, represent the number eight and are regular numerical affixes. Small decorative elements appear to the left and right of the main glyph when there is no affix to the left. There can be little doubt that they represent maize leaves. They are absent at Copán.

GLYPH 612 (Men semblant)
(85 Examples; Gates' Glyph 25; Zimmermann's Glyph 731a)

1, 2.		*	M. 23a; P. 8b
3.	1.	*	M. 21c
4.	1.	* :542	M. 91a
5.	69?:	*	M. 100d
6.	71:548.116:	*	M. 104b
7, 8.	73:	*	D. 4a; 8a
9.	74:	*	M. 22c
10–13.	124:	*	D. 62e; 62f; 63a; 63b
14, 15.	145:	*	D. 62c; 67a
16, 17.	109.145:	*	D. 69e; 70a
18.	153:	*	M. 21c
19–69.	168:	*	Zimmermann lists 51 examples (42.731a) in all codices. Gates' figure is higher.
78.	168?:	* :25	M. 107c
70–74.	168:	* .130	M. 20a; 20b; 23d; 99a; P. 17b
75.	168?:	* .130?	M. 21a
76.	25.168:	* .130	M. 73b
77.	51.168:	*	D. 68b
85.	V.168:	*	Acanceh tomb mural
78–80.	267:	*	D. 8a; M. 86b; 87a
81.	1?267:	*	M. 24a
82.	1.612:	*	M. 91a

83.	?	*	M. 52a
84.		*.1016?	M. 90c

See discussion under Glyph 613; see also under Glyph 542.

GLYPH 613 (Men)
(97 Examples; Gates' Glyph 15; Zimmermann's Glyph 731)

97.		*	Day sign Men in codices
1.		*	P. 8b
2.		*	M. 26b
3.	1.	*	M. 95d
4, 5.	1.	*:23	D. 14a (twice)
15.	25.30:	*	M. 66a
57.	30:	*.head	D. 53a
6–12.	31:	*	D. 6b; 8c; 17a(?); 17c; 19b; 21a; 23a
13.	31:	*	M. 33a
14.	17.31:	*	D. 66b
15.	69:	*	D. 40a (picture)
16.	69:	*	P. 18e
17.	69?:	*	D. 17a
18.	1.69:	*	M. 41a
19, 20.	59.69:	*	D. 37c; 37c (picture)
21, 22.	59.69:	*	M. 40a; 41a
96.	62.	*?	M. 34c
23, 24.	96.69:	*	D. 69b; 69b (picture)
25.	96.69?:	*	D. 40a
26.	96.69:	*?	M. 11c (picture)
27.	103.69	*	M. 11c
28, 29.	207.69:	*	M. 40a (twice)
30.	552af.69:	*	M. 41a
33–34.	96.	*:23	M. 100d (twice)
31.	96.74:	*	D. 40a
32.	96.296:	*	D. 65b
56.	142v:	*	P. 23a
35.	109.145v:	*	M. 10b
36.	1027.145:	*	M. 102d
37.	1047.145:	*	M. 102d
93.	145:103:	*	M. 100d

38.	168:	*	D. 17b
39–51.	168:	*	M. 11b; 11b; 24c; 25a; 25c?; 53b (thrice); 55a; 95d; 97b; 97b; 107b
52.	168:	*.59	D. 8b
53.	168:	*.612af	D. 33c
54, 55.	1.168:	*	M. 96d, 98b
56.	210:	*	M. 36b
94.	233:	*?	D. 36b
58–87.	267:	*	30 examples in three codices. See Zimmermann 43:731
88.	17.267:	*	D. 73b
89.	87:283.	*	D. 37b
90.	VII:288:	*:47	M. 36b
91.	85?:521:	*:47	M. 35a
92.	IX?.	*?:59	P. 16c
95.	526:	*?:	M. 110c (picture)

Glyphs 612 and 613, it is rather widely supposed, are most probably variants of the same glyph, for in large part they take the same affixes and appear to be interchangeable. Nevertheless, the fact that certain affixes are found with one glyph but not with the other may indicate differences in meaning. With the Affix 145, Glyph 613 is the name of the old goddess of weaving. Glyph 612 has the same combination with the chac affix (109) sometimes added. No. 92 is probably a badly drawn glyph of Bolonyocte.

267:613 is a fairly common augural glyph of evil character, and is particularly common in passages involving the moon goddess, Ixchel, but is not found in connection with weather almanacs.

See also under Glyph 648.

GLYPH 614 (Thatch)
(79 Examples; Sheet 283; Gates' Glyphs 301.4, 301.5, 431; Zimmermann's Glyph 1306a)

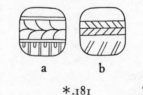

a   b

79.	79:	*.181	Tik. 31, D27
55–60.	80:	*.181	D. 52b; 61a (twice); 69f (thrice)

1–21.	208:	*	Beyer 203–206, 545–61
63–78.		*:515	See under No. 515 for accompanying prefixes
22–54.		*:601	See under No. 601 (Nos. 37–69) for accompanying prefixes
61.		*:115.515.59	Beyer 562
62.		*:115.515:59?	Beyer 563

In some of the 614–601 compounds, Glyph 614 and Affix 192 seem to be interchangeable, and, indeed, the main part of Glyph 614 is Affix 192. Details are often not too clear, and it has seemed best to group all together under Glyph 614. Similarly, some of the examples from Chichén Itzá may be replaced by Glyph 679, as noted by Beyer (1937, pp. 75 and 116). Nevertheless, it is a shade more probable that these weathered examples represent Glyph 614, and they are thus catalogued here.

The 614–115–515–59 compounds are interesting, for, although the design of the burden part is somewhat unusual, they supply an interesting link between Chichén Itzá and the three codices because of their close parallelism with the 115–614–601 compounds. No. 79 suggests that Affixes 79 and 80 are the same.

For further examples of Glyph 614, see under Glyphs 17, 515, 601, 683.

GLYPH 615 (Twisted reed)
(1 Example)

1.	?.	*	Sayil Str. 3B1, Gl. 20

The twisted-reed plaiting is the most important element of the month glyph, Pop, and in a somewhat more elaborated form is a common art motif.

GLYPH 616
(16 Examples; Sheets 238–39)

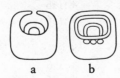

a   b

12.	74:?:	*.181:116	Cop. C, A12
6.	229.	*:47	Pal. carved pot, F4

14.	229.	*	Acasaguastlán carved jar, Fig. 48
2.	229.	*:67	Beyer 630
15.	229.	*:125	Hondo bowl. Guat. Seler
1.	229.	*:126	Quir. J, E1
16.	229.	*:126	Uxmal Ball Crt. W. ring
9.	229.	*P:126	Quir. J, G1
10.	229.	*:126	P.N. pottery drum
3.	25.229.	*:178	Holmul cyl. jar
8.	229?:?:	*.?:126?	Quir. I, C5
4, 5.		*:121? or 116?	Cop. T. 22, Step 6; O', F3
11.	229.III:	*:69:254	P.N., L. 12, F1
7.	VI:	*?:?	Quir. P, P3
13.	282.126:	*:130	Cop. U, Q4

The personified form of Glyph 616 is recognized by its position and affixes, and by the element on the crown of the head.

GLYPH 617
(30 Examples; Sheets 237–39)

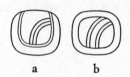

a   b

30.	74:	*:142	Xcalum. N. build., Frag. B
1, 2.	125.	*:142v:139	Yax. L. 22, B3; L. 47, G1
3.	125?.	*:?	Alt. Sac. 4, C6
23, 24.	229.	*:125	Tort. 1, A3; A4
5.	229.	*:126?	Cop. Alt. of 13
26.	229.	*:125	Pusil. round-based vase
6.	229.	*:126	Alt. Sac. 9, E3
7.	229?:	*:126	Nar. H.S., Y1
8.	V?.229.	*:126	Uaxac. I.S. vase, 8
9, 17.	229.	*:126	Uaxac. sherds 3112, 4977; Smith
11.	229.	*:?	Holmul tripod plate, Gl. 5
18.	229.	*:126	Blowgun vase
27.	229.	*:126:360	Tik. 31, A12
17.	?.229.	*:126	Carac. conch god vase

13.	229.	*:130?:202	Cop. brown ware tomb 2–38
15.	229.	*:130	Cop. quetzal vase
22.	229.	*:142	Acasaguastlán carved brown, Fig. 48b
16.	229?	*:?	R. Hondo vase (Gann)
21.	V	*	Glyph G5
19.	V.48:	*:125	Pal. Fol. detached gl.
20.	V.?:	*?:126	Pal. Cross detached gl.
29.		*:126:23	Tik. 31, C19
4.		*:142.?:?	Pal. Inscr. W. A12
28.		*:126:360?	Tik. 31, G15
10.		*:241	Uaxac. sherd 3112
12.		*:200	Uaxac. stuccoed jar

The occurrences on pottery seem to represent meaningless copying by one potter of the work of another. Nos. 9 and 10 may represent the toothache moon glyph, but more probably they are bad copies of Glyph 617 by an artist who did not understand what he was copying. In a few cases, notably No. 17, the curved lines have become vertical, a process frequently occurring with Glyph 679.

GLYPH 618
(3 Examples; Sheet 244)

1.	?	*:grotesque head	Xcalum. S. build. W. jamb, A3
3.		*.23	Peto jaguar vase
2.		*.56	Xcalum, S. build., E. front pan.

Glyph 833 conceivably is a variant of Glyph 618.

GLYPH 619 (Crossed bands on side)
(4 Examples)

4.	1?.	*:?	Tabi 1, G
1, 2.	181.	*:70	Sayil Str. 3B1, Gl. 5, 7, 26
3.	13?.544:	*.?	Xkichmook, Pal. Rm. 11, roof painting

Nos. 3 and 4 have complete cartouches.

GLYPH 620
(1 Example; Sheet 223)

1.	513af:79:	*.116	Cop. S, Gl. I

Only one surviving example. Perhaps a tun sign.

GLYPH 621
(3 Examples; Sheet 223)

1, 2.	79:	*.116:130	Cop. U, N5; G2, A2
3.	130.168:217.	*?	Pal. House C, basement

Perhaps a tun sign. The example from Palenque may be something else. Only a drawing is available, and that shows strange flanking elements.

GLYPH 622
(8 Examples; Sheet 622)

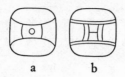

a   b

1.		*	Cop. Z, F1
2.	165.	*:77	Form of Glyph X
3.	165.	*:26	Form of Glyph X
4.	228.	*:*	Pal. Inscr. W., C10
5.	228?.	*:181?.?	Form of Glyph X (Cop. 2)
8.	229.	*:25	Jade head, Br. Mus.
6.		*.580	Yax. Str. 44, Y6
7.	12:	*:580	Yax. 18, A5

GLYPH 623 (Cross-bones)
(8 Examples; Gates' Glyph 354)

1–5.		*	M. 105a (picture); 105b; 105c (picture); 107b; 110b (picture)
6.		*	M. 103b (picture)
7.	506:506.506:	*	D. 28b (picture)
8.	III.	*	D. 103b

There is a distinct possibility that this glyph is a basic element of Glyph 624 (shield), although no examples from the Central Area are known. The cross-bones without the surrounding circlets appears as an infix and is given the number 623 (see Glyph 765). Nos. 6 and 8 lack the blackened area.

GLYPH 624 (Shield)
(58 Examples; Sheets 155–58; Gates' Glyph 437; Zimmermann's Glyph 1372)

	a	b	c

<table>
<tr><td>32.</td><td></td><td>*.?</td><td>Uaxac. mur. G5</td></tr>
<tr><td>30.</td><td></td><td>*[533]</td><td>Yax. L. 27, C2</td></tr>
<tr><td>38.</td><td></td><td>*[533?]</td><td>Cop. H.S., Frag. Gxii</td></tr>
<tr><td>47–49.</td><td></td><td>*[533]</td><td>M. 16b; 17b; P. 2d</td></tr>
<tr><td>39.</td><td>1.109?:</td><td>*[533.217]</td><td>Tik. L. 4, B4</td></tr>
<tr><td>35.</td><td>1.109?:</td><td>*[533]</td><td>Nar. 23, G14</td></tr>
<tr><td>36.</td><td>3?:109?:</td><td>*</td><td>Nar. H.S., B1</td></tr>
<tr><td>41.</td><td>11?:?:</td><td>*[533]:139?</td><td>Tamar. H.S. 2, E16</td></tr>
<tr><td>50.</td><td>58:</td><td>*.548:24</td><td>P. 5c</td></tr>
<tr><td>51.</td><td>58?.</td><td>*[533]</td><td>P. 4d</td></tr>
<tr><td>57.</td><td>544:12.58:245:</td><td>*[533]</td><td>Yax. L. 10, A6</td></tr>
<tr><td>3, 11, 12, 20,
22, 23, 27, 28.</td><td>74.184.</td><td>*a</td><td>Pal. Sun, L5; Inscr. W. G3;
I5; Ruz 1, P19; 96, Gl.
C1; K7; Cross, W. pan.
6; Del Río Slab</td></tr>
<tr><td>8, 16, 18, 25, 26.</td><td>74:184.</td><td>*a</td><td>Pal. Inscr. W. A3; S2; T12;
Ruz 2, B1; Pal. House C,
Eaves E1</td></tr>
<tr><td>4.</td><td>74.184.</td><td>*a:178</td><td>Pal. Inscr. E. R11</td></tr>
<tr><td>21.</td><td>74.184.</td><td>*aP:178</td><td>Pal. 96, Gl. B3</td></tr>
<tr><td>2, 7, 24.</td><td>74.184.122.</td><td>*a</td><td>Pal. Cross, J1; Inscr. Mid.
G3; H.S., A5</td></tr>
<tr><td>14.</td><td>74.184.122?</td><td>*a</td><td>Pal. Inscr. W. O2</td></tr>
<tr><td>6.</td><td>184.122:</td><td>*a</td><td>Pal. Inscr. Mid. E8</td></tr>
<tr><td>13, 43.</td><td>184.</td><td>*a</td><td>Pal. Inscr. W. L5; Fol.
Balustr. J2</td></tr>
<tr><td>15, 17.</td><td>184:</td><td>*a</td><td>Pal. Inscr. W. R2; S6</td></tr>
<tr><td>5.</td><td>184.</td><td>*a:178</td><td>Pal. Inscr. M. C4</td></tr>
<tr><td>1.</td><td>184?:</td><td>*a:178</td><td>Pal. Cross, K4</td></tr>
<tr><td>9.</td><td>74?:184?:</td><td>*a</td><td>Pal. Inscr. W. F2</td></tr>
<tr><td>10.</td><td>74.184.</td><td>*b</td><td>Pal. Inscr. W. E5</td></tr>
<tr><td>19.</td><td>74:184:583.</td><td>*[537]:178</td><td>Pal. Ruz 1, C12</td></tr>
<tr><td>40.</td><td>184.583:</td><td>*[533]</td><td>Pal. Sarcoph. 8</td></tr>
<tr><td>46.</td><td>112.</td><td>*a</td><td>D. 60c</td></tr>
<tr><td>52.</td><td>112:</td><td>*[533]</td><td>P. 6c</td></tr>
</table>

37.	204.	*[533]	Tik. 17, G4
59.	204?:?:	*	Dos Pilas 2, D4
29.	232.44:666:	*[533]	Yax. L. 25, D1
41.	1.257:	*[533]	Tort. 6, D4
56.	1:257:	*[533]	Tort. 6, A11
42.	501:	*[533]	Dos Pilas 2, C4
33.	?.	*[533]	Alt. Sac. 4, B12
31.	?.	*[533]	P.N. 43, A1
34.	?.3:	*[533]:139	Pusil. D, C14
53.	?.	*[533]	P. 3c
54.		*.?	M. 34d
55.		*c:178	Beyer 614
58.		*a.531	P.N., L. 3, U6

The associations of this glyph at Palenque, where it is so common, are not clear. Sometimes it appears close to records of 4 or 5 katuns; often it is followed by the hatched dot (Glyph 602) compound. The presence of Affixes 74 and 184 is of interest. Nos. 19 and 40 show that the propeller element is really an infix. The variant with checkerboard infix (No. 55) is of interest, because that same element, when it forms a separate glyph (594), usually takes the same pair of Affixes 74 and 184. In the case of No. 57, the substitution of 544:12 for the common 74.184 is of interest.

GLYPH 625 (Turtle shell)
(9 Examples; Sheet 273; Gates' Glyph 432.1.1; Zimmermann's Glyph 1304)

3.	1:	*	Beyer 581
1, 2.	1.	*:103	D. 2d; 2d
8.	13.	*:7?	Beyer 580
5.	1.58.	*:501	Beyer 577
4.	1.58.	*?:116	Beyer 578
6.	92.58:	*:116	Beyer 576
7.	92:	*:24	Beyer 579
9.	89 or 92.	*:116	Beyer 169

GLYPH 626 (Turtle Carapace)
(31 Examples; Sheet 272; Gates' Glyph 367; Zimmermann's Glyph 726)

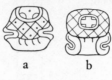

a   b

15.	12:	*	Cop. R, G1
1.	12:?.	*:25.head	Beyer 167
2.	25.?:	*.25:130	Beyer 166
10.	63:	*	D. 41b
11.	63:	*	P. 6b
19–22, 24.	64:	*	P.N., L. 3, Z4; L. 2, I1; X6; X10; 1, K8
23.	64:	*	Xultun 18, A2
12.	64:	*	D. 60a
16, 17.	94:	*	Yax. L. 49, P6; L. 37, Q6
3.	136:	*:589	Beyer 168
4.	136:	*:24	Beyer 575
5, 6.	130:136:	*	Beyer 163; 164
7.	130:136:	*:136	Beyer 165
25.	1000.168:	*:130	Poptun frag. Sculpt.
29.	12:168:	*	Tamar. H.S. 2, F6
26–28.	168:	*	Aguatec. 1, B13; D4; A9
8.	178:	*	Beyer 574
18.	206.	*:87	P.N., L. 3, W1
9.	552af.136:	*:130	Beyer 168a
31.	74:	*	Mac variant at Yax.
13.	XIII:74:	*	D. 69c
14.	?.	*:23:60	Beyer 573
30.	?:	*?	P.N. 11, F7

No. 13 may represent the month glyph Mac. Note that there are certain resemblances between this glyph and the fish head used in some variants of the month
Mac. Note the presence of the Kan cross in the best-preserved example at Chichén
Itzá, and in three from Piedras Negras. This is further evidence for accepting the
identification of this glyph as a turtle carapace, first made by Beyer (1931). The
three from Aguateca occur in a phrase.

In view of the undoubted examples of Glyph 626 used as Mac at Yaxchilán
(Lintels 24, 25, and 43), it is of considerable interest to note that *mac* means inter
alia turtle carapace (see under *concha* in the Vienna and Solis Alcalá dictionaries).
This is a clear example of rebus writing.

GLYPH 627 (Fly Wheel)
(8 Examples; Sheet 159)

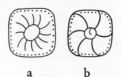

a   b

	a	b	
2.	1024.114:	*:19	Pal. Ruz 1, D15
5.	327:	*:279	Cop. T. 11, Step Gl. 6
6.	?.327:	*	Site Pal. X, 1, A1
3.	590.	*.*	Beyer 110
4.	165v.590:	*.*	Beyer 108
8.	27.635:	*.*	Sayil Str. 3B1, Gl. 8
1.	Head.	*.*:?:?	Cop. H.S., Step V
7.		*.575af:1021	Tort. 6, H5

Glyph 627 resembles the Aztec sign for day. In the four cases where Glyph 627 is duplicated, it may be serving as a postfix.

GLYPH 628
(5 Examples; Sheet 162)

a   b

	a	b	
2.		*b	Cop. H.S. Gxiig
4.	79:	*a:IX	Cop. A, A10, Gl. A
5.	79:	*a:X	Cop. N, A14, Gl. A
3.	203.	*	Cop. H.S., Step A
1.	211:	*a	Cop. A, F6

The clue to the meaning of this glyph is that twice it replaces the moon sign in Glyph A of the lunar series. Compare with the example of Glyph X on La Florida Stela 1. Note resemblance to Glyph 629.

See also under Glyph 713.

GLYPH 629
(4 Examples; Sheet 163)

3.		*?	Pal. frag. of yoke
1.	223:	*	P.N. 40, front bottom
2.	VII.223:	*	P.N. 40, front bottom
4.	324:	*?.181	Tort. 6, C6

Note resemblance to Glyph 628.

GLYPH 630 (Double comb)
(56 Examples; Sheets 193, 194)

52.		*	Lacanja 7, F3
46.		*	Sacchana 2, C2
40.		*-181	Pal. Sarcoph. lid top
23.	1:	*	Cop. J, E. 29
39.	1:	*-181	Kuna L. 1, D4
2.	1.	*-181:142	Pal. Tower S. Scribe, E5
56.	11.	*-181:126:130	Aguatec. 1, A7
35.	13:	*-181:130?	Nar. 32, N2
51.	89:	*-181	Quir. I, C8
26.	128 or 125:181.	*:130?	Yax. L. 33, E1
7.	181.	*:130	P.N., L. 3, V'1
30, 31, 32, 33.	181.	*:130	Tik. 5, D11; 16, B3; L. 4, D4; F10
29.	181:	*:130	Tik. L3, H8
19.		*.181	Xcocha
4, 28.		*-181:142	Yax. L. 3, F4; L. 42, D2
45.		*-181:142	Pal. Sarcoph. leg
14, 16.		*.181:139	Xcalum. S. build., E jamb; N. build., W. col.
41-44.		*-181:178	Xcalum. I.S. build., rt. col.; lt. col.; rt. jamb.; lt. jamb

13, 15, 17.		*.181:178	Xcalum. S. build. W. jamb; W. col.; N. build., Serpent, Gl. 10
9.		*–181:?	P.N., Alt. 1, O′3
36.		*–181:178	Kuna L. 1, I5
37.	?:	*–181	Kuna L. 1, K4
5.	1000.	*–181:142	Yax. L. 13, D3
38.	1000.	*–181:142	Kuna, L. 1, J4
3.	1000.	*–181	Yax. L. 14, C3
6.	1000?.	*–181:130?	Yax. 7, C8
11.	1000.III?:	*–181:?	Nar. 8, B2
1.	1000.	*–180	Pal. 96, Gl. K1
20.	202:	*	Cop. A, H10
22.	202.	*	Cop. J, E. 44
27.	202:	*.181:?	Nar. 23, F18
24.	202:	*:219	Cop. H.S., Frag. Gxiih
18.	1:202.	*:130	Halakal L. 1, G7
47.	202:1000.	*–181	Cop. M, C9
8.	228.	*:?	P.N. 15, C13
34.	228?.	*	Uaxac. Tzakol stucco jar
48.	150.?.	*:683P	Cop. A, D7
54.	756.	*:?	Pal. T. 4, N. Sculpt. stone 1, C1
50.	?.	*–181:88?	El Cayo L. 1, F4
12.		*.60:23	Xcalum. I.S. build., rt. lint.
21.		*.114:25	Cop. J, C3
53.		*:178	Lamb site L. 1, E2
10.		*–181?:?	P.N. Alt. 1, O′4
25.		*:219?	Cop. T. 21a, C
49.		*.88?:245?	Pal. Inscr. E. O9
55.		*.683:142	Peto jaguar vase

In almost every case the original glyph, comprising two comb elements with two vertical bars or an ornamental bone set between, is combined with the lunar sign, or carries with it this affix (Glyph 181) prefixed, infixed, or postfixed. A hyphen indicates where the two elements are combined to form a compound glyph.

Other affixes are rare. Affix 202 is prefixed in five cases which are distributed from Copán to Yucatán. This same element as a main glyph precedes number twelve. The presence of Affix 202 usually is balanced by the absence of the moon sign.

We find the compound with youthful head, apparently of the number one, or the moon goddess, affixed in examples from the Usumacinta drainage. It is not unlikely that here the portrait of the goddess of the moon, *u*, stands for the possessive *u*.

This glyph is not common, but it has a wide distribution throughout the Maya area, although it is not found in any of the three codices.

See also under Glyph 683.

GLYPH 631
(1 Example)

The one appearance of this glyph is on Madrid page 34 in the upper picture dealing with ceremonies for Cauac new years. It stands above a Cauac sign. Conceivably it is a badly drawn representation of some common affix. In the same position on pages 35 and 36 of Codex Madrid, which also cover new year ceremonies, the Cauac glyph has respectively an Akbal and a Chac affix.

GLYPH 632 ("S" design)
(18 Examples; Sheet 154; Gates' Glyph 352; Zimmermann's Glyph 1309)

4–7.		*	M. 11b; 35d; 36d; 37b
11.	47.	*:140	D. 52b
13.	58.	*	M. 34d
8.	58.	*.1	M. 37d
9.	95.	*:136	D. 41b
10.	95.	*:140	D. 38a
12.	181.168:	*	D. 68a
17, 18.	240:	[*]747	Yax. L. 35, V4; L. 49, N2
14[1].	513af:	*:*	Beyer 627
15[1].	VI:	*	Quir. P, P2
16[1].		*P:23?	Quir. G, N2
2, 3.		*:125?	Nar. 21, A6; 13, G9
1.		*	P.N., L. 2, G'1

[1] These examples are not encircled with circlets.

Glyph 632 also appears as an affix (see Glyphs 544, 561, and 747).

GLYPH 633
(2 Examples)

1.	1.	*	Sayil Str. 3B1, Gl. 14
2.	142:	*.59	Sisilhá, lt. jamb 2

Conceivably the second example is something else.

GLYPH 634
(6 Examples; Sheet 230)

1.	151.1:	*:24:136	Pal. House C, Eaves B1
2, 3.	?.	*	Yula (Beyer 24, 25)
6.		*:565	Tik. 31, J4
4.		*.181:19	P. 10d
5.		*.747[501]?:	Cop. K, Q2
		142	

This is a composite glyph, the main element being Affix 23. Nos. 2 and 3 follow the head of God C.

GLYPH 635
(2 Examples; Photographs)

1.	27.	*:627.627	Sayil Str. 3B1, Gl. 8
2.	1010?.	*	Sayil Str. 3B1, Gl. 28

GLYPH 636
(1 Example)

1.	136.	*	Sayil Str. 3B1, Gl. 1

GLYPH 637
(1 Example)

1.	1.	*	Sayil Str. 3B1, Gl. 3

Conceivably this represents a variant of Glyph 504 (Akbal), but not used here as a day sign.

GLYPH 638 (Yucatec Lamat)
(9 Examples; Gates' Glyph 8; Zimmermann's Glyph 1328)

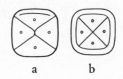

a   b

1.		*	Lamat in codices and Chichén Itzá
2.	12. or 134v.	*	Sayil Str. 3B1, Gl. 15
4, 5.	V.125:	*	Pal. Cross, detached glyph
6.		*.*:25	Beyer 570
7.		*:8	Beyer 565
8.	1.	*:8	Beyer 564
3.		*.?	Sayil Str. 3B1, Gl. 12
9.	1010?.	[*]	Sayil Str. 3B1, Gl. 22

GLYPH 639
(1 Example)

1.   1.   *:7?   Sayil Str. 3B1, Gl. 23

Possibly this belongs with one of the Ahau variants.

GLYPH 640
(1 Example)

1.   181.   *   Sayil Str. 3B1, Gl. 16

GLYPH 641
(1 Example)

1.   ?.   *:321   Sayil Str. 3B1, Gl. 18

GLYPH 642
(8 Examples; Sheet 306)

2–6.   1.67:   *.2 or 24   Xcalum. S. build., W. Col.
                                          A1; W. Pan. A2; Lint.
                                          Front A1; N. build., W.
                                          Col. A1; I.S. build., Rt.
                                          Col. A2
1.   67.1:   *.2 or 24   Xcalum. S. build., E. Jamb
                                          A2

[251]

7.   67:   * :?   Xcalum. I.S. build., Lt.
                                        Jamb A3
8.   122.?:   * ?:?   Cop. 3, B9

Perhaps a highly stylized head.

GLYPH 643
(1 Example; Sheet 308)

1.   32.   *   P.N. Thr. 1, H4

Conceivably this is a variant form of Glyph 530.

GLYPH 644 (Seating)
(55 Examples; Sheets 284, 285, 305, 338)

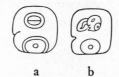

a   b

54.	1.	* ?	Covarrubias *sub judice* B1
52.	11.	* :247?	Pal. Inscr. tomb, jade ear-plug
41.	125.	* :130	Pal. Inscr. W. J9
17, 18.	165.	* :59	Pal. Sarcoph. lid.
19.	165 or 61.	* :59	Pal. Sarcoph. leg
21.	165.	* ?:59?	Pal. Inscr. E. R2
24.	204?.	* :59?	Pal. Inscr. E. C10
22.	204?:	* ?:59	Pal. Inscr. M. D1
37.	204.	* .126?:201: 140	Pal. 96, Gl. D7
20.	205.	* ?:59	Pal. Inscr. E. T7
10.	1013.	* :59	Pal. Ruz 1, C7
5.	741.	* .116	Cop. T. 22, Step 16a
55.		* :88	Kuna L. 1, N3
4, 45.		* :130:116	Cop. H.S., Step M; J, E26
53.		* .116:130?	Tort. 1, A4

[252]

23, 25.		*.130:116 [125]	Pal. Inscr. E. A11; G6
16, 32.		*.116:130 [125]	Chinikiha Thr. 1, Z2; F'1
26, 27, 29.		*.116:130 [125]	Pal. Inscr. E. L3; L10; R10
48.		*.116:130:125	Tort. 6, F4
11.		*:116:130	Yax. 12, C2
49–51.		*.116:130	Tort. 6, B7; B9; D10
6.	Missing	*:116:130?	Cop. H.S. Gxiiim
42, 47.		*.116:130	Cop. L, A3; T, back
43.		*:130:116:126	Cop. U, K2
44.		*.126:130:116	Cop. U, O4
46.		*:126	Cop. C, A10
12.		*.*:116	Yax. L. 31, J5
13.		*.88:178[125]	Tik. L. 4, F9
28.		*.88:178 or 116[125]	Pal. Inscr. E. M12
8.		*.178:88:125	Pal. Fol. N7
9.		*.88:130? [125]	Pal. Sun, A14
30, 31.		*.125:24	Pal. Inscr. W. R8; T7
15.		*.88:140v? [125]	Tik. 22, B1
3.		*:131	Cop. H.S., Step Q
2.		*:178?:?	Cop. H.S., Step E
7.		*:178?	Los Higos 1, C1
38, 39.		*:180	Pal. 96 Gl. F3; H2
36.		*.180:140	Pal. 96 Gl. D5
1.		*.181:178	Cop. H.S. Gxiiim
14.		*.181:140	Tik. 21, B4
40.		*:201:?	Pal. 96, Gl. G5
33.		*.528.116 or	Seating of haab gl.
34.		[*]528.116	Seating of haab gl.
35.		*.month sign	Seating of month

Because of the use of the glyph with month sign in positions which can be proved to fall the day before the first day of the month, it is very likely that the sign corresponds in meaning to "seating of," as previously noted (Thompson, 1950, pp. 119–20).

Nos. 13–15, 42–47, and probably No. 11 lack the little head, but otherwise conform to the type and are used in a similar way.

For further examples of Glyph 644, see under Glyphs 528 and 782.

GLYPH 645
(2 Examples; Sheets 308, 415)

1.	11:	*.203:24	P.N., L. 12, M1
2.	1000?.	* ?:?	Carac. 16, D13

GLYPH 646
(2 Examples; Sheet 308)

1.	1:228:	*.87	P.N. 25, G2
2.	12.	*or 544:23	La Mar 2, C1

GLYPH 647
(1 Example; Sheet 308)

1.	23.129?:	*	P.N., L. 3, X2

GLYPH 648 (Kaz)
(123 Examples; Gates' Glyph 142; Zimmermann's Glyph 705)

79–84.		*	M. 29b; 53b; 55a; 84c; 85c; 90b
67–70.	1.	*	M. 26d; 63c; 89b; 90b
91–93.	1.	*:24	P. 22a; 24a (twice)
1–62.	1.	*:25	In all three codices. See Gates or Zimmermann.
63.	1.	*.25	M. 103b
64.	1:	*:25	M. 24a
71–76.	10.	*:25	D. 14b; 16c; 17a; 18c; 21b; 22a

65, 66.	10.	*:10	D. 12b; 13c
77.	13.	*:25	D. 11a
78.	13.	*:59	D. 17c
115–118.	19.	*:25	D. 72b; c; 73a; c
86.	25.	*	M. 54a
119–123.	25.	*:25	M. 50c; 90a; 92c; 96c; 112b
85.	25.	*:114?	M. 69a
104.	58?.	*	M. 55b
87.	115.	*	D. 54b
88, 89.	115.	*	M. 54b; 88a
90.	115.	*:140	D. 65b
94.	172.	*:25	D. 47f
95.	172.	*:25	M. 90a
96[1].	181.	*:?	M. 87c
97–100.	181.	*:25	M. 64c (twice); 83c; 87a
101.	267:613.	*	D. 53a
102.	III.567.	*	D. 69a
103[2].	VIII.	*	M. 87c
105–107.		*:25	M. 15a; 28c; 96c
108.		*.227	D. 72b
109.		*.526:138	D. 44b
110.		*:25.548:24	D. 72c
111.		*:140.548:24	P. 5c
112.		*?:548	P. 5c
113.		*:25.567	D. 65a
114.		*.1006a	D. 45c

[1] Main sign in vertical position apparently because of lack of space.
[2] The numerical coefficient may not belong with this, but may be part of the structure of the badly damaged almanac which the glyphs illustrate.

This is the "misery" or evil-tidings glyph, which appears to correspond to the Yucatec word *ƙaz*, "evil" (Thompson, 1950, pp. 268–69; 1959). It is one of the commonest augural glyphs in the codices.

See also under Glyph 561.

GLYPH 649
(1 Example)

1.	*.?	Xcalum. S. build., W. Pan. C2

GLYPH 650
(1 Example)

| 1. | 1. | *:139 | Xcalum. S. build., W. Pan. B2 |

Perhaps this represents a branch of a tree or a flower.

GLYPH 651
(1 Example; Sheet 307)

| 1. | 12: | *.87 | Yax. L. 18, C1 |

This resembles an inverted Kankin, but the shape suggests a different derivation.

GLYPH 652
(11 Examples; Gates' Glyph 4.24 and 4.25 in part)

1.	*:103	M. 108a
2.	*.*:103	D. 40c
3.	*:103:135v	M. 8, rt. col.
4, 5.	*:506	M. 49c; 98a
6, 7.	*:506.506:103	M. 68a; 103b
8.	*:506.506:686	M. 106a
9.	*:506.501:686b	M. 51b
10.	*:686b	M. 106c
11.	*.668:506.506.506:686	M. 12b

This glyph from its associations undoubtedly represents some form of offering, and because of the presence of Glyph 506 in its interior, it presumably represents some form of maize; conceivably the serrations indicate the ears of corn.

GLYPH 653
(1 Example; Sheet 305)

| 1. | 89: | * | Pal. House C, Eaves A1 |

GLYPH 654
(1 Example; Sheet 309)

| 1. | | *:74 | Xcalum. S. build., W. Front Pan. D1 |

GLYPH 655
(2 Examples; Sheet 310)

| 1, 2. | 74: | * | Xcalum. S. build., Rear Lint A2; N. build., Frag. R |

GLYPH 656
(2 Examples; Sheet 310)

| 1. | III.XVIII: | * | Xcalum. N. build., Frag. E |
| 2. | XV: | *v | Uaxac. mur. M1 beneath hut |

Note the similar glyph, but placed horizontally, which is repeated three times, on the Olmec stela at Piedra Labrada, near Coatzacoalcos, Veracruz (Blom and La Farge, 1926–27, Fig. 38).

GLYPH 657
(5 Examples; Sheets 260, 308)

a   b

1.	1.21?:	*.24?	Cop. B′
2.	61:	*?.204?	Xcalum. I.S. build., Lt. Col. A3
3.	86:	*	P.N. 12, D11
4.		*?:287	Cop. Alt. St. I, L
5.		*?:200	Tort. 6, D1

Perhaps the second example does not belong here. The Copán and Piedras Negras examples seem to show a naturalistic snake.

See discussion under Glyph 737.

GLYPH 658
(1 Example)

1.	19v.?.11:	*:102	Beyer 107

Beyer believes this is a jawbone. It should be compared with Glyph 590.

GLYPH 659
(1 Example; Sheet 248)

1.	*:23	Cop. T. 11, Step 20

GLYPH 660
(1 Example; Sheet 311)

| 1. | 21. | *:61 | Yax. L. 18, C5 |

GLYPH 661
(1 Example; Sheet 311)

| 1. | 229.168: | * | Yax. L. 9, C3 |

GLYPH 662
(10 Examples; Gates' Glyph 45.10; Zimmermann's Glyph 1318)

10.	1:	*:27	M. 34b
1–3.		*:544	M. 85b (thrice)
4–6.		*:544.116	M. 85b (thrice)
7.		*:*.679	Beyer 497
8–9.		*:*:8?.679	Beyer 495, 496

It is a little doubtful that Nos. 7–9 are, indeed, examples of Glyph 662; No. 8, in particular, resembles the Cimi percentage sign very closely. It is possible that the glyph is not a main sign, but only an affix. The oval shape argues in favour of a main sign, but the facts that the glyph never stands alone or with obvious affixes and that the main element may be doubled argue for the belief that this is an affix. Compare also with Glyphs 663 and 723.

GLYPH 663 (Seed)
(70 Examples; Gates' Glyph 337; Zimmermann's Glyph 1317)

1.	1.	*:23	D. 24b
70.	1.	*b[1]:47	M. 36a
2.	84:	*	P. 5a
3.	84:115.	*.115	P. 23a
4, 5.	84:115.	*.115	D. 73b; 72c
6.	84:115.	*.115	M. 11a
7–9.	85:115.	*.115	D. 34b; 50d; 71b
67.	85:115.	*.103	M. 36b
• 14.	99.84:	*a[2].115	D. 44b
22, 23.	116.84:115.	*a.115	D. 43c; 45b
10.	172.	*	P. 23a
11.	172.	*:23	D. 55a
20.	172.	*?:23	D. 49d
12.	172.84:	*	D. 72c
13.	172.84:115.	*.115	D. 45b
15, 16.	172.85:	*	D. 25b; 73b
17–19.	172.85:115.	*.115	D. 39b; 40b; 46d
21.	172.85:	*a:680	D. 56a
24.	85:	*.521	D. 48e
25.	84 or 85:115?.	*?.115	D. 73a
26.	84:1022.	*	P. 11c
65.	277?.85:	*b	M. 34d
27.	90.	*:23	D. 48e
28, 29.	168:115.	*.115	M. 68a; 71a
30.	168:115.	*.115[130]	M. 69b
31.	172.168:	*:130	P. 5c
32.	172.192:	*	D. 58b
33.	207.130:	*	P. 22d
36, 37.	526.	*	D. 42b picture; 56a
63.	526.	*b	M. 34d
38.	526:	*	D. 60b
34.	526:251.	*:23	M. 37d
47–50.	526:251.	*:23	D. 33b; 40c; 71c; 73a
62.	526:251.	*:23	P. 23a
68, 69.	526:251.?:	*b	M. 29c (twice)
64.	526:251.	*b:face	M. 34d

66.	526:251?.	*b.309:308	M. 35d
40–42.	59.526:251.	*:23	D. 35b; 38b (twice)
43.	91.526:	*	P. 8c
44.	91.526:251.	*:23	D. 39b
45, 46.	96.526:	*	D. 34b; 35b
55.	172.526:	*	D. 60b
51.	172.	*.526:23	P. 23a
52.	172.526:251.	*:23	P. 24a
53, 54.	172.526:251.	*:23	D. 57a; 71a
56.	181.526:23.	*:251	M. 90a
57.	181:	*:251.526:23	P. 5c
39.		*.526	D. 38b picture
58.		*:23.526:251	D. 66a
59, 60.		*:23?.526:251	M. 77e; f
61.		*:23.526:251	P. 3b
35.		*:?	M. 2b

[1] *b. Examples in which the vertical line is set diagonally. The associated signs make it very probable that these are merely poorly drawn examples of Glyph 663. The element which is shown by Affix 115 as prefix and postfix probably is a general sign for vegetation.

[2] *a. Examples which lack the vertical line, but which from context or affixes almost certainly represent the same glyph.

There seem to be good grounds for identifying this glyph as the sign for seed (Thompson, 1950, p. 271). Combined with Glyph 526 (caban, the earth glyph), the glyph surely indicates milpa. Indeed, on Dresden 38b, God B is pictured walking over this compound digging stick in hand. The interchangeability of Affixes 84 and 85 suggests either carelessness in drawing or that the two signs have the same significance and are merely variants of the same sign for maize.

The glyph, like others of an agricultural nature, is not found in the monumental inscriptions of the Classic period.

For further examples of Glyph 663, see under Glyph 558.

GLYPH 664
(1 Example)

1.	?:277?:	*	Xcochkax jamb frag.

This glyphic element, the mat pattern, is the chief element of Glyph 551, the month sign Pop.

GLYPH 665 (pseudo Chuen)
(10 Examples)

1.	1.	*:23	Tik. 31, G18

The remaining nine examples, all from Palenque, are listed under Glyph 713, with which they are compounded.

GLYPH 666 (back of fist)
(12 Examples; Sheets 319, 368)

1.	19.86:	*[521]	Pal. jade earplug
2.	49:	*inv.	D. 25a
3.	53.	*:122inv.	Chinkul. marker, Gl. 14
10[1].	93.	*	Cop. H.S., Frag. Gxiig
4.	196?:122:	*:783.783	Carac. 17, C5
5.	89.153:	*	Cop. T. 11, S. door, W. pan., A6
6.	116?:	*	Quir. U, A7
7.	?	*inv.	Yax. Str. 44, S.E. Step V4
12.		*.19	P.N. sherd. Butler, 1935, Pl. 3, 11
11.		*:23	M. 37b
8.		*inv.:513?	Beyer 466
9.		*inv.:?	Beyer 467

[1] There seems little doubt that this is the artist's free treatment of the 93–672 compound.

For further examples of Glyph 666, see under Glyphs 501 and 624.

GLYPH 667 (inverted fist)
(114 Examples; Gates' Glyph 141; Zimmermann's Glyph 167)

1–12[1].		*:*	M. 43b (7 times); c (5 times)
13–16.	1.	*:*	M. 43b (twice); c (twice)
17.	1.	*:19	D. 33c
18.	1.	*:24	M. 96b
19.	1.	*:47	D. 37c
26–47.	1.	*:130	D. 30c to 39c (22 times)
20–24.	13.	*:780	M. 38a (twice); 39a (thrice)
25.	15.	*:23	D. 42a
48–52.	15.	*:47?	D. 29c (thrice); 40a; 41b
53, 54.	15.	*:47?	M. 85c; 87c
55–68.	15.	*:130	D. 30c; 31c; 32c; 40a; c (thrice); 41a; c (thrice); 42a; 43a (twice)
69.	15.	*:736	M. 87c
70.	1.15.	*:130	D. 38c
79–90.	15.	*:308	P. 15–18 (12? times)
71.	74.	*.146:19	D. 46f
72–75.	115.	*P?	M. 10c (twice); 11c (twice)
77.	115.	*P?276	M. 11c
78.	115.	*?.276	M. 58b
76.	130[115].	*:126	M. 40c
91, 92.	181.	*.276	M. 83c (twice)
93.	181.	*:15?	M. 86c
94–96.	238.	*	M. 84c (thrice)
99.	238.	*:19	D. 33c
97, 98, 104–114.	238.	*:23	D. 65b to 69b (13 times)
101.	head	*	M. 11c
100.	III?.	*:19	M. 41b
102.	?.	*:601	M. 85c
103.		*:24	M. 96b

[1] It is probable that the **u** bracket, Affix 1, is not present in these examples because of lack of space. It appears with the first and last examples in each row, and the same procedure is followed with the adjacent glyph (283.558). If this supposition is correct, we have an interesting case of the kind of short cut used by scribes the world over.

The most carefully drawn examples clearly show an inverted hand with an unusual infix. I have labeled as Glyph 780 a few signs with hook infix which both Gates and Zimmermann include with the regularly drawn examples of my glyph. Possibly these should be regarded as Glyph 667 with glyphic element 19 infixed.

For further examples of Glyph 667, see under Glyphs 601, 736, and, as noted, 780.

GLYPH 668 (Glyph of God B)
(207 Examples; Sheet 346; Gates' Glyph 77; Zimmermann's Glyph 169)

1–7.		*	Gates' Gl. 77 except 1.
8–139.		*.103	Gates' Gl. 77.1; 119 in Dresden; 8 in Paris; 13 in Madrid
140–145.		*:103	Gates' Gl. 77.1a; 1 in Dresden; 5 in Madrid
182.		*.103:528	M. 37a
183.		*.103.679	D. 33c
146.	1.	*	M. 98b
147.	1.	*.103	M. 18a
148.	1.	*:?	P. 11d
149, 150.	12.	*.	M. 89a; 89a
151, 152.	14.	*	M. 21a; 21c
153.	15.	*	M. 11b
154.	15?.	*	M. 20c
155.	17.	*	D. 44a
156, 157.	17.	*.103	D. 34a; 62
158.	17?.	*:103	P. 18f
205.	23inv.?:	*	Uxmal 20, A3
159–163.	24.	*	M. 29b; 29b; 62a; 92b; 93d
164.	24:	*	M. 25c
165.	25.	*?:130	M. 99b
181.	25.	*:548.24	P. 3b
166, 167.	58.	*	D. 32b; 38b
168.	58.	*	M. 24d
192.	59.	*:526	M. 8a
169, 206, 207.	70.	*	M. 28d (thrice)
170.	?.	*	M. 28d
171.	90.	*	M. 94d

172.	95.	*	P. 18c
173.	95.	*	M. 28b
174–176.	95.	*:103	D. 33b; 43a; 70
177, 178.	109.	*	D. 39b; 42a
179, 180.	109.	*	P. 4d; 10b
201.	109?.	*	M. 28b
184.	238.	*:103	P. 16b
185, 186.	281.	*	D. 34b; 38b
187.	281.	*:103	D. 43a
188.	281.103:	*	M. 28b
196.	?.	*.23:?	Beyer 251
200.	90:558.	*:103	D. 60a
189.	III.	*.24	M. 72b
190.	III.	*.103	M. 68b
191.	III.	*.181:283	M. 41a
202.	652.	*:506.506.506	M. 12b
203.	?.	*:103?	Uxmal Ball Crt. W. ring
193.		*:23	Beyer 250
197.		*.74?	M. 82c
194.		*:102	Beyer 249
204.		*:103?	Uxmal Ball Crt. W. ring
195.		*.580	Uxmal, Monjas capstone
198.		*.24:?	M. 96b
199.		*.?	M. 89a

This sign is the name glyph of God B, and perhaps was sometimes used also to denote other deities. It is confined to the codices, particularly Codex Dresden except for three examples at Chichén Itzá and four at Uxmal. This distribution serves to confirm that the surviving codices originated in Yucatán.

GLYPH 669 (death fist)
(182 Examples; Sheets 327–32; Gates' Glyph 23; Zimmermann's Glyph 166)

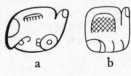

a   b

73–77, 85, 86.	*a¹	Beyer 1; 3; 5; 8; 10; 13; 14
37.	*b	P.N., L. 2, T2
78–83.	*b	Beyer 2; 4; 6; 7; 9; 11
55.	*a:*a	Beyer 229
108.	*a.*a	P. 18b

56.		*b:*b¹	Beyer 230
57, 95.		*b.*b	Beyer 231; 23
128.	1.	*a.71?	D. 2d
119.	1.	*a.181	P. 6b
106.	1?.	*b:8	Beyer 247
4.	11.	*b:24	Pal. Fol. E7
47.	12.	*:*b	Beyer 221
99.	13.	*:8	Beyer 27
107.	13.	*b:23	Beyer 248
23.	23.	*b:130	Pal. Inscr. W. Q5
177, 178.	25.	*a:130	M. 99b (twice)
130.	24.	*a	M. 64b
48.	35.12.568.	*a	Beyer 222
31.	44:	*a	P.N. 12, A18
26.	44:	*b	Yax. 21, A4
29.	1?:44:	*a	Yax. L. 45, T6
28.	1.44:	*b.586:25:178	Yax. L. 46, F' '8
84.	53.	*a	Beyer 12
50.	53.	*:*b	Beyer 224
49.	59.	*.*a	Beyer 223
175.	60.131?:	*a	Chajcar pottery box
176.	60.?	*a	Carcha frag. of box
32–34.	74.	*a:130	Nar. 32, A'1; Y2; Y5
120–122.	74:	*a.130	D. 14b (thrice)
114.	1.74:	*a	D. 13b
118.	1.	*a:74	D. 2d
124.	1.130:	*a:74	P. 10b
123.		*a.130:74	D. 15c
115–117.	10.74:	*a	D. 13b (twice); 15c
125–127.		*a:130	D. 12c (thrice)
70.	92.	*b:558	Beyer 234
14.	92.	*b:683	Pal. Inscr. M. A9
132, 133.	1.96:	*a	M. 14a (twice)
173.	1.109:	*a.181	D. 8c
109.	13.109:	*a.181	D. 8c
65.	122:	*b	Beyer 244
94.	122:	*?	Beyer 22
63.	1:122:	*a	Beyer 242
64.	1.	*a[122]	Beyer 243
59, 60.	12:122:	*b	Beyer 238; 239
58.	53.122:	*a	Beyer 237
62.	59?.	*a.122	Beyer 241
61.	129?.122:	*a	Beyer 240

66, 87, 88, 93, 96.		*b:122	Beyer 245; 15; 16; 21; 24
89, 90.		*a.122	Beyer 17; 18
91, 92.		*.122	Beyer 19; 20
67, 97.		*b.122	Beyer 246; 25
172.	163.122:	*a.155:595	D. 67a
5–8, 11–13, 15–21.	125.	*b:130	Pal. Inscr. E. A7; E11; J6; K7; R4; Q7; S10; M. C5; C8; F1; I4; J10; K3; L9
9, 24.	125:	*b:130	Pal. Inscr. E. O4; W. S11
180.	125:	*bv:130	Carac. 3, D13b
10.	228?.125:	*b:130	Pal. Inscr. E. P11
30.	129:	*	Yax. 18, B3
112.	131:	*a	Yax. L. 16, A3
110.	131 or 130.	*b	Alt. Sac. 4, D6
111.	131 or 130.	*[528]	Seib. 10, A6
113.	12.131:	*a	Yax. L. 16, E1
71.	133:	*b.558	Beyer 235
163.	25.202:	*a	M. 99d
164.	25.202?:	*a	M. 104d
25.	204.	*b:24	Pal. Madrid Tab. 2
51–54.	211.	*a:*a	Beyer 225–28
98, 104.	211.	*b	Beyer 26; 45
69.	211.	*a:558.24	Beyer 233
68.	211.	*a:558.35	Beyer 232
22.	228.	*b:595:142	Pal. Inscr. W. C6
27.	232?.	*?:57	Yax. 18, A13
170.	238:	*a	P. 15b
2.	258?.	*.126:142: 288?	Cop. K'', B1
134.	59.509:	*a	M. 40c
179.	679af.	*a	Tort. 6, D11
169.	679af.558:	*a	D. 21b
167.	715.	*a	M. 64b
151–157.	715:	*a	M. 106b; 107a (6 times)
135–150.	1.715:	*a	M. 96b (thrice); 103b (thrice); 104a (twice); 104b (twice); 105b (4 times); 106b
166, 171.	715:	*a.1	M. 104b (twice)
158–160.	1.715:	*a.181	D. 15b (thrice)
161, 162.	10.715:	*a	D. 15a; 16b
174.	1000:	*?	Yax. L. 28

103.	1008.	*b	Beyer 31
100–102.	1000?.130?.	*b:71	Beyer 28–30
129, 131.	I.	*a	M. 40a; 41a
168.	XII.168:	*a	M. 41c
35.	?.?:	*a:178	Nar. 32, A'4
165.		*a:62	P. 6c
181.		*a.117	Tik. jade B2
41.		*:117.178	Beyer 217
43–45.		*a.117.178	Beyer 215; 218; 219
46.		*a.117:178	Beyer 220
42.		*a.746[178]: 117	Beyer 216
1.		*.*b:126	Cop. F', A2
3.		*b:130	Pal. Fol. B17
182.		*a:142	Tik. jade A6
105.		*b.178.683	Beyer 71
38.		*b.181:178	Xcalum. I.S. Build., E. Col. B1
36.		*a:285?	Chama. Carey vase, F1
40.		*?.1:2?	Xculoc, Cent. lint., H.
39.		*b:?	Xcalum. N. build., Frag. W
72.		*b.558:35	Beyer 236

1 "a" denotes the infix is the comb; "b" that it is a cross-hatched area. Present evidence would indicate that the change of infix does not affect the value of the glyph.

At times the glyph seems to substitute for the smoke fist in clauses to do with period endings. At Chichén Itzá it is commonly associated with the moon. In the codices, where the comb alone is infixed, it is commonly an action glyph. The death elements do not seem to make it a glyph of ill omen.

For further examples of Glyph 669, see under Glyphs 501, 509, 528, 552, 558, 563, 586, 595, 606, 679, 683, 715, and 757.

GLYPH 670 (Hand with glyph in angle)
(92 Examples; Sheets 131, 340–42; Gates' Glyph 427; Zimmermann's Glyph 161)

52.	19:	*	M. 107b
22.	19:	*	Bone figurine (Caso)
86.	19:	*	Rossbach coll. Lothrop, 1936

53.	19:	*.120:140	D. 14c
54.	19:	*.?	P. 18b
55.	1.19:	*:130	D. 67a
92.	1.19?:	*:?	Carac. Alt. 13, Gl. 32
56.	47.19:	*.120	D. 2d
87.	122.19:	*	Uaxac. Str. 18, mur.
29.	125.19:	*	P.N. 6, B15
88.	125.19:	*:360	Tik. 31, B23
76.	125.19:	*:246?	Pal. Inscr. W. O11
35.	125.19:	*:125?	Tik. 17, H5
85.	125.19:	*	Cop. 20, C4
21.	125?.19:	*	Pal. Inscr. W. S3
84.	125?.19:	*	Alt. Sac. 18, A11
57.	126.19:	*.120	M. 102b
51.	24?:	*.120	M. 65b
24.	1:98:	*:142	Pal. T. 18, stucco
19[1].	125?.inv:	*	Cop. 3, B7
67.	126?.504 or 520?:	*.120	M. 65a
91.	?.155:	*.365.74	Tik. 31, B22
68.	511:	*:103	M. 37c
13[1].	533:	*:?	P.N., L. 2, O2
1[1]–3[1].	533:	*:114	Cop. J, A3; B7; D7
89.	1.533:	*:130	Tik. 31, E12
11[1].	1.533:	*:131 or 130?	P.N. 3, E3
6[1].	59.533:	*	Yax. L. 42, B2
10[1], 15[1].	59:533:	*	Yax. L. 3, C2; L. 1, C1
16.	Head.32:533?:	*:59	Yax. L. 2, I2
12[1].	93.533:	*:130	P.N., L. 2, H1
5[1].	211.533:	*:130	Pal. Ruz 1, H11
43.	534:	*	Calak. 89, D4
58.	534:	*.24.103	M. 37d
59.	534:	*:126	P. 5c
4[1].	1.534:	*	Cop. Q, F6
38[1].	87?:534?:	*	Ixkun 2, C9
9.	89:534:	*	Yax. L. 10, C1
8[1].	126:534:	*	Yax. L. 10, F5
46.	126:534:	*	Bonam. 1, I1
47.	126.534:	*	Carac. 16, B19
7[1].	126:534:	*:130?	Yax. L. 10, A2
14.	679.534:	*.130	P.N., L. 2, W4
33.	?.534:	*	Tik. 5, C8
36, 37.	125.535?:	*:141	Tik. 3, C7; 13, B4

48.	32.544:	*:254	Yax. L. 22, A4
49.	125.32.544:	*:254	Yax. L. 47, G4
50.	87?.544:	*:?	Cop. F, A10
73.	561c:	*.?	Beyer 334
63.	53.561c:	*	P. 5b
66.	59.561c:	*	P. 6b
26.	59.125:561:	*:178?	Yax. 18, C5
17.	125:561d:	*	Cop. B, A13
42.	125:561:	*:139	Xcalum. S. build., W. pan.
20.	125.561:	*:88	Pal. Inscr. E. P10
44.	125.561?:	*	Kuna L. 1, J1
60, 61.	286.561c:	*	D. 65b; 58b
72.	286.561:	*	D. 24a
62.	286.561e:	*:140	D. 54b
64.	I.286.561c:	*	D. 53a
65.	I.561c:	*	P. 7b
90.	?.155:	*:561g.365.74	Tik. 31, M2
69.	584:	*	D. 33c
39.	584:	*.612 af:?	Kabah sq. alt.
25.	756:	*	Pal. T18, stucco
41.	125.1002:	*:178	Pal. Cross balustr., K1
40.	125.1007:	*:178	Pal. Fol. balustr., K1
75.	125.1007:	*:126?	Pal. Cross, K5
71.	1016:	*.120	M. 93c (north var.)
81.	IX: or .35.1016:	*	Glyph G1
82.	IX: or .36.1016:	*	Glyph G1
70.	122.1020:	*	D. 65a
28.	1.?:	*	Seib. 9, C3
23.	1.?:	*:130	Quir. J, H5
30.	1:?:	*:?	La Amelia H.S., K1
45.	11.?:	*:?	P.N. 1, K15
31.	13.?:	*:?	La Amelia H.S., G1
34.	59.?:	*:87?	Tik. Alt. V, Gl. 16
74.	125:?:	*.141?	Cop. 8, A6
27.	125.?:	*:178?	P.N. 14, A15
83.	126.?:	*.114?:23?	Ikil L. 1, H
18[1].	?:	*	Cop. 3, B7
32.	?:?:	*:?	Nar. 32, U3
77–80.	?:	*	M. 87b; 88b (thrice)

[1] Examples apparently in close association with C.R., D.N., or P.E. dates.

The compound with the sky sign (561) resting on the hand has a very wide distribution. No. 90 is of interest, for here the sky sign is beneath the hand, not resting on it. This suggests that there is no special significance attached to the position in the angle of the hand.

GLYPH 671 (Manik hand)
(196 Examples; Sheets 139–42, 336–38; Gates' Glyph 7; Zimmermann's Glyph 160)

171.		*	Day sign Manik
137, 138.		*	M. 79c; 91a
5.		*[544]	Nar. 22, C14
66.		*[107?]	P.N., L. 3, T′1
61.		*:*	Quir. Str. 1, miscell. frag.
179.		*:*?	Poptun plate. Shook & Smith
89–97.	1.	*:*	D. 4c (thrice); 5b; 5c; 6b: 7b (thrice)
141.	1.	*:136	M. 41a
48.	3.	*[544].116	Cop. 10, E9
53.	11:	*:59	Pal. Cross, O6
55.	11.	*.2:59:116	Pal. Fol. O8
71.	11.	*:130?	P.N., L. 2, Z1
142–144.	12.	*	M. 40b; 41b; 41b
183.	12.	*:88	La Mar 1, F1
145, 146.	12.	*:136	M. 40b; 41b
147.	12.	*.130:136	D. 65b
81.	12.125:44.	*	Beyer 464
80.	12.142?:	*	Nebaj. Fenton vase, B5
98, 99.	13.	*:*	D. 5b; 6b
124.	15.	*:*	D. 6b
39.	16.	*:47	Xculoc, S. lint., C, E
15.	16.	*[544?]:116	Yax. L. 9, C2
57.	16.	*.126:141:178	Cop. U, P4
33.	16.60:	*:82	Quir. E, C19
4.	16.60:	*[544?]:116?	Nar. 29, F14
82.	60.16:	*:103	Beyer 465
79.	16?:60:	*.?	Ixlu Alt. 2, F2
185.	16?.86:	*	La Mar 1, B9

14.	16.168:	*[544]	Yax. L. 58, D3
16.	16.?	*	Tik. Alt. V, Gl. 30
174.	59.16?:	*	Yax. L. 17, A2
59, 60.	17.	*	Cop. Quetzal vase; R. Hondo deer vase
45.	17:	*:86	Cop. D'5
38.	17.	*:47	Xculoc, S. lint., C1
148.	17.	*:186	D. 71b
72.	1.17?:	*	P.N. support, B2
28.	17.86:	*:140	Pal. Ruz 1, R13
44.	17.86:	*	Cop. J, E. 30
47.	17.86:	*:178	Cop. 7, D9
193, 194.	17.86:	*	Aguatec. 1, D6; 7, E1
56.	17.86:	*	El Cayo L. 1, C15
78.	17?.86:	*	Ixkun 1, J7
52.	17?.86:	*:?	Cop. 19, D7
68.	86:	[*]17?:178	P.N. 3, D3
49.	17:130?:	*	Cop. F', A4
156.	VI.17:	*	D. 48b
157, 158.	VI.168:17:	*	D. 34c; 48c
159.	VI.168:17:	*	M. 42c
160.	VI?.168:17:	*	P. 10b
161.	VI.168:17:	*.130	P. 9b
162.	VI:168:17:	*:130	P. 4d
13.	17.?:	*[544?]:116	Yax. L. 58, C1
176.	19:	*	Nar. 21
177.	19:	*.23:178?	Tuxtla Mus. shell
178.	?:19:	*:19?	Kabah sq. alt.
180.	19:	*	Pal. Inscr. W. N1
74.	44?:	*:122	Seib. H.S., K1
166.	58.	*	M. 20d
173.	58?:	*:88:126	Quir. E, D15
139.	59:	*.181:25	D. 33c
42.	60:	*	Cop. K, N2
46.	60:	*[544].116	Cop. 11, A6
190.	60.	*:125	Yalloch cyl. jar
175.	1.60:	*	Nar. 19, A3
31.	12:60:	*	Pal. Ruz 2, E2
70.	12.44?:60:	*	P.N. 12, Capt. Gl. 23
181.	68.	*[544].116	Cop. 10, B9
11.	74.184.198?:	*	Jonuta 1, A3
36.	?.86:	*.165?	Quir. Alt. P, W1
29.	?.86?:	*:125	Pal. Ruz 1, R13

172.	59?:86?:	*:122	Yax. L. 10, D8
187.	88.	*	Chipoc, Fig. 15d
69.	90.	*:*	D. 11b
101–122.	91.	*:*	D. 4a–10a (20? times); 11b; 11b
123.	12.91:	*	D. 22a
136.	207.91.	*:*	D. 11a
100.	715.91:	*	D. 2a
165.	95.	*	M. 20d
167.	109?.	*	M. 20d
149.	112.	*.103:276	M. 38a
182.	115?:	*	Cop. H.S., Frag. Gxiih
73.	134[110]:	*	Tuxtla Mus. shell
164.	157:	*	M. 25a
24.	168?:	*[544].130:116	Bonam. Rm. 2, I.S.
195.	17.168:	*	Aguatec. 2, F4
67.	35.168:	*.584	P.N. jade jaguar head
40.	126.168:	*:87:316	Yax. L. 21, D1
76.	174:	*.61	Tik. L. 2, B11
77.	174:	*.?	Tik. L. 4, E12
65.	178:	*	Yax. L. 58, D1
170.	194? or 207.	*:23	D. 35c
54.	204.	*.2:59:116	Pal. Fol. O8
41.	204.602:	*	Jonuta 1, A2
7.	204.?:	*	Nar. 30, C9
186.	205.	*	Hondo, Guat. bowl. Seler
37.	207:	*	Yax. L. 31, J4
125–128.	207.	*	M. 21d; 22d (thrice)
129.		*.207	M. 21d
130–132.	207.	*:47	D. 10b; 10b; 32b
133, 134.	207:	*.47	D. 33b; 34b
135.	207:	*:126	D. 35b
168.	281.	*	M. 21d
23.	281.116:	*	Nebaj. Fenton vase, B2
152.	296.	*:126	M. 102d
153.	296.	*.126:126	M. 102d
62.	317:	*[528]	Nar. H.S., Y1
63.	12.317:	*[528]	Nar. H.S., L3
64.	12.317?:	*[528]	Calak. 51, D3
50.	318:	*	Sayil Str. 3B1, Gl. 11
169.	319:	*	M. 21c
154.	526.526af:604.	*	M. 88c

191.	527af:?:	*	Dos Pilas Sculpt. C, B6
84.	548:	*.?	M. 63a
163.	552v.	*:24	D. 48d
26.	679.	*	Pal. Inscr. W. A10
83.	679:	*	M. 35c
27.	679.	*:102	Pal. Inscr. W. D2
32.	679.	*.130?	Pal. Cross, W. pan., H1
151.	1.715:	*	M. 103a
188.	?	*	P.N. sting ray 4
75.	?.?:	*	La Amelia H.S., F3
155.	?.?:	*	Nar. 30, G13
10.	?:	*	Nar. 32, W5
35.	?:	*	Quir. M, C1
8.	?.	*:126	Nar. 30, F4
9.	?.	*.?	Nar. 30, E9
1.		*[544]:116	Yax. L. 10, C2
3.		*[544]:116	Pusil. D, D4
6.		*[544]:116	Nar. 22, H12
17–22.		*[544]:116	Beyer 352–57
25.		*[544]:116	Pal. Sun, N9
43.		*[544?]:116	Cop. U, M2
2.		*[544].116	Tuxtla Mus. shell
34.		*[544]:116: 126	Quir. F, D17
12.		*[544].116: 184	Xultun 18, A8
189.		*[544?]:116	P.N. sting ray 3
58.		*.130:24?	Cop. T. 21a, D
51.		*.178?	Kabah mask trunk
196.		* or 217.181: 82	Carac. 3, C11b
140.		*.181	D. 25b
184.		*(horiz.).?: 188	Yax. L. 49, O3
150.		*:241	P. 7d
30.		*:316:?	Pal. H.S., D1
85–88.		*.679:103	M. 93c (four times)
192.		*:?	Dos Pilas H.S. 2, E8

The hand in this position occurs very frequently both as a main sign and as an affix. For various reasons it has seemed best to assign a number to the affix (219) which is different from that of the main sign. Note the frequency of the kin (544) infix and compare with the compound for west.

For further examples of Glyph 671, see under Glyphs 553, 575, 604, and 744.

GLYPH 672 (fire fist)
(87 Examples; Sheets 322–27)

41, 52.	93:	*	Quir. P, Cart. 2; 7
53.	93:	*	Yax. 11, G4
74.	93.	*	Holmul V tripod, Gl. 2
3, 20.	93.	*	Cop. 7, A12; 12, A12
81.	93?:	*	Kuna L. 1, L3
45, 46, 54, 55.	93.	*:142	Yax. L. 25, I1; 12, A3; 18, A12; L. 52, D1
49, 50, 58.	93:	*:142	Yax. Str. 44, Step X3; V4; L. 10, F5
63.	93:	*:142	Tik. L3, F4
64.	93.	*:142	Tik. L4, E5
23, 24, 27, 28, 30.	93.	*:142	Pal. Fol. M8; Sun, O4; Inscr. W. B2; C4; House C, Plat. D1
16, 17, 21, 83.	93.	*:142	Cop. T. 22, Step 15; T, C2; H'', A2; T. 11, Rev. E'1
13, 15.	93:	*:142	Cop. T. 11, Step 1; H.S. Gxiil
31, 38.	93:	*:142	Quir. A, C6; G, O'1
32, 35, 36, 40, 43, 44.	93.	*:142	Quir. C, D14; J, C17; E8; H, A2; Alt. O, I'4; N'4
60.	93.	*:178	Bonam. 2, F4
61.	93.	*:178?	Pusil. D, D3
66.	93.	*:178?	Ixkun 1, V1
68.	93?.	*:178	Ixkun 1, P1
77.	93:	*:181	Calak. 89, C8
4, 6, 71.	93:	*:255	Cop. P, D11; 10, E8; T. 11, reused stone, H1
7.	93.	*P:255	Cop. P, A11
42.	93.	*:255?	Quir. P, Cart. 12
47.	93.	*:288	Yax. 12, F2

[275]

12.	93.	*:288	Cop. T. 11, frag.
22.	93.74:	*:142	Cop. 12, D6
1, 2, 10, 11.	93.74:	*:255	Cop. 9, B11; E9; 2, A6; C9
56.	93.74:	*:255?	Yax. L. 34, I8
76.	93.74:	*:288	Cop. Md. 2, K1
8, 9, 14, 75.	93.	*:74	Cop. 8, D3; 6, C4; T. 11, Step 14; brown-ware Longyear 103d
18.	93:	*.74	Cop. A, F4
67.	93.	*:74	Ixkun 1, K6
5.	93.	*:74:288:142	Cop. 10, G6
78–80.	93.	*:74?	Kuna L. 1, C3; J1; M6
33, 34.	93:	*:74?	Quir. E, B9; A16
70.	74?:93:	*	Carac. 1, H2
59.		*:74:142	Yax. L. 46, H''3
57.	74:278:	*	Yax. L. 10, B5
52.	74:	*:?:?	Nar. 12, E1
69.	93.168:	*	Carac. 6, D21
72.	93.168:	*:	Nar. 12, C2
62.	93.168:	*:288	Nar. H.S., I1
73.	93?.168:	*:130	Nar. 10, B3
25, 26.	93.28:	*	Pal. Inscr. M. D3; K1
87.	93.IV:	*:74	Quir. E, C12
65.	IV.93.28:	*:142	Moral. 2, D4
86.	IV.28:548:	*	Cop. 3, A9
84.	V:28:93	*	Quir. P, C7
29.	V.28?:93.	*	Quir. Alt. P, X1
85.	V.28:93?.	*	Quir. P, Cart. 8
48.	V:28:548:93?.	*?	Quir. Alt. O, B'1
37, 39.	93:	*:?	Quir. G, A'2; T'1
82.	93.?:	*	P.N. 25, I6
51.	?.93:	*	Yax. Str. 44, Step C4
19.	?.93:	*:?	Cop. V, E1

This fist with its three circles, the ancient Maya symbol of fire, almost invariably carries Affix 93, which with little hesitation can be identified as sparks and smoke (cf. Glyph 589). Accordingly, there is little reason to doubt that the glyph stands for an action connected with fire, such as to light fire, to burn copal, etc., but the action may in some cases be used as a rebus. The glyph often follows or, rarely, precedes a katun sign (Nos. 2, 6, 11, 27, 31, 32, 38, 46, 47, 49, 53, 62, 65, and 69–71). In a few instances it is associated with the death god and occasionally with the 504–712 compound or the count of the year and world direction phrase.

The absence of Glyph 672 from Yucatán and the hieroglyphic codices is of interest, and serves to confirm the assignment of the three surviving books to Yucatán.

GLYPH 673 (fist palm forward)
(38 Examples; Sheets 317–19)

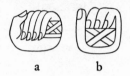

a   b

32.		*	Xcalum I.S. build., Lt. Col. B4
34.		*	R. Hondo blowgun bowl
18–20.		*[552]	Beyer 460–62
1, 2.	25.	*[552]:74	Pal. Creation stone, C1; C2
12.	53.	*[552]:59	Beyer 52
7.	12.168:	*	Yax. 18, B6
3.	115.168:	*[552].60:?. 585	Yax. L. 37, R6
35.	279.	*	Cop. Q, D2
33.	315:	*[552]:145	Xcalum. N. build., E. col., A3
4.	315:	*[552].59	Xcalum. S. build., W. jamb, A1
8, 11, 21–25.		*[552].59:138	Beyer 39; 42; 449–53
5, 6, 9, 10, 13, 14, 26, 27.		*[552].138:59	Beyer 26; 27; 40; 41; 101; 102; 454; 455
28.	59.	*[552]:138	Beyer 456
29.	59:	*[552?].138	Beyer 457
36.		*[552].60: 188?	Pomona, Stann Creek. Jade earplug
15–17.		*[552]:110	Beyer 112–14
31.		*[552].580	Beyer 459
30.		*[552]:580	Beyer 458
37.	?.	*	Pusil. bowl
38.	58:278?:552.	195:219M.S.	Cop. K, N2

The last line (No. 38) almost surely represents an alternative way of writing 673[552]. The predominance of this compound 673[552] at Chichén Itzá is of interest, and its appearance also at Palenque, Yaxchilán, and Xcalumkin is prob-

[277]

ably indicative of glyphic influences. Except for No. 35, which is somewhat different from the rest, only the examples on pottery lack Infix 552.

GLYPH 674
(3 Examples; Sheet 311)

1.	1.71:	*:1040	Yax. L. 21, B8
2.	769:	*?	Pal. House C, basement, D1
3.	78?.	*	D. 39b

GLYPH 675
(3 Examples)

1.	46.129:	*	Glyph G2
2.	34.122?:	*	Glyph G2
3.		*.122?:513?.	I.S. Intro. glyph

GLYPH 676
(14 Examples; Sheets 160, 161; Gates' Glyph 334; Zimmermann's Glyph 1315)

14.	12:	*:178	Tort. 1, A2
5.	1.17:	*	Yax. 12, G2
7.	17.	*	D. 56a
8–10.	17:	*	D. 51b; 55a; 57b
13.	74?:	*	Ikil L. 2, J
6.	204.	*P	Pal. T. 18, stucco gl.
12.	1030.23:	*:178	Pal. T. 18, stucco gl.
11.	VI.VI:	*	D. 10a
4.	3.VII:	*:178	Yax. L. 49, O4
1.	3.VIII:	*:178	Yax. L. 37, Q1
2.	3.IX:	*:178	Yax. L. 37, Q7
3.	3.IX?:	*:178	Yax. L. 49, M7

Morley (1937–38, II, 382) identifies this glyph as the day sign Oc in its occurrences with coefficients on Lintels 37 and 49 at Yaxchilán. Nevertheless, no day sign ever has Affix 3 attached to it. Moreover, the resemblance he saw to forms of Oc in the codices are fortuitous, for those represent a dog's ear, as has been long known. Morley seems to have been unaware of the examples of Glyph 676 in Codex Dresden, notably in the eclipse table. Whatever meaning this glyph may have, it certainly is not Oc.

Affix 274 so closely resembles Glyph 676 that it is probable they are one and the same sign.

GLYPH 677
(1 Example)

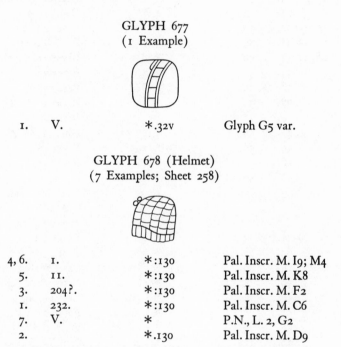

1.	V.	*.32v	Glyph G5 var.

GLYPH 678 (Helmet)
(7 Examples; Sheet 258)

4, 6.	1.	*:130	Pal. Inscr. M. I9; M4
5.	11.	*:130	Pal. Inscr. M. K8
3.	204?.	*:130	Pal. Inscr. M. F2
1.	232.	*:130	Pal. Inscr. M. C6
7.	V.	*	P.N., L. 2, G2
2.		*.130	Pal. Inscr. M. D9

The single appearance of this glyph at Piedras Negras makes it fairly obvious that this represents a headdress, for in the accompanying sculptured relief six spearmen with helmets of exactly the form of the glyph, but crowned with plumes, kneel before a chief, who may be wearing yet another of these helmets. This lintel at Piedras Negras is earlier than the inscriptions at Palenque, and so the glyph may have originated at Piedras Negras and been borrowed by Palenque. Other examples of interchange of glyphs between the two sites have been noted.

GLYPH 679 (Forward)
(78 Examples; Sheet 286; Gates' Glyph 328; Zimmermann's Glyph 1333a)

	a	b	c	d

79.			*	Tort. 6, A10
25.			*	Xcalum. S. build., W. col.
4.			*?	Cop. J, B4
41, 42.	59:		*	Beyer 491; 492
29–31.	59:		*.8	Beyer 33–35
28, 32, 34.	59.		*:8	Beyer 32; 36; 39
33.	59.		*.8	Beyer 37
38.	59.		*:8?	Beyer 42
37.	59.		*.8?	Beyer 40
40.	1?.59:		*	Beyer 490
20, 21.	59.		*:25:135	Nar. 32, Z2; Z5
35.	59:		*:205?	Beyer 38
36.			*.59:8?	Beyer 41
68.	59.202?.		*	P. 17b
24, 26, 27.	136:		*.59	Xcalum. S. build., E. jamb, A4; W. col., A5; N. build., Frag. U
49–51.	67:		*	Beyer 499–501
62.	74.		*:103	P. 5c
15.	79:		*.181:23.23	Pal. Peñafiel Tab. B2
59.	*.79:		*.116	Retiro slate pendant
56.	79:		*?.116:130	Cop. U, N5
57.	79:		*.116:130	Pal. Ruz 1, V1
58.	79:		*?.116:130	Quir. B, Block 12
16.	127?.		*:129:2?	Cop. D', 6
74.	168:		*:?	Tik. 31, B25
19.	178?.213?.		*	P.N., L. 3, A'5
63.	277:		*	P. 6c
64.	277.		*:74	P. 9c
65.	277.		*.103?	P. 11d
45, 46.	662:662:8?.		*	Beyer 495; 496
47.	662:662:		*	Beyer 497
48.	662?:		*	Beyer 498
60.	1000.		*:306	Uaxac. incised red bowl
73.	1042:		*	Cop. I, D3

55.	125 or 126. 1042:	*	Beyer 505
52–54.	1042?:	*	Beyer 502–504
23.	756:200.	*:23	Cop. 10, C9
39, 43.	?:	*	Beyer 81; 493
22.	?.	*:?.	Ixkun 2, C5
66.		*:62	P. 10c
1, 2.		*:65:130 or 129	Cop. J, A2; A3
3, 5–8.		*:65:130 or 129:178	Cop. J, B3; B5; A6; A7; A8
9–11, 13, 14.		*.130 or 129: 65.178	Cop. J, C2; D2; D4; D6; C7
12.		*.130 or 129: 65:181.178	Cop. J, D5
61.		*:103	M. 95c
18.		*.116:125: 129?	Yax. L. 18, B1
75.		*.117:23	Tik. 31, P1
67.		*:219	M. 35c
69.		*:273	M. 35b
78.		*:510	Tort. 6, A11
70.		*.558:669	D. 21b
71.		*.513:59	count forward glyph
17.		*:?	Yax. L. 47, F7
44.		*.?.?	Beyer 494
72.		*.738:59	Count forward Gl. P
76.		*.1081	Tik. 31, E22

The use of Glyph 679 with 513 or 738 and 59, proved mathematically to occur only with a forward time count or with the later in time of two dates (Thompson, 1944), establishes beyond doubt the general meaning usually assigned to this glyph in the inscriptions of the Classic period. The glyph is also used as an affix of other main signs. Furthermore, it serves as the headdress of a death god (Glyph 1041) and may also be affixed to the pictorial glyph of Mam, the old god of the under-world. The glyph may be the one in Landa's alphabet representing the sound *i*. It is just possible that the examples from the codices represent a different glyph.

Glyph 679 is used more often as an affix than any other main sign. For further examples, see Glyphs 82, 502, 506, 507, 513, 516, 526, 550, 552, 556, 558, 563, 565, 573, 575, 580, 585, 586, 608, 662, 668, 669, 670, 671, 683, 684, 695, 700, 710, 713, 714, 738, 740, 765, and 803.

GLYPH 680 (God M's glyph)
(21 Examples; Gates' Glyph 148; Zimmermann's Glyph 102)

1.		*	Variable element in Glyph C.
2.		*	D. 16b
3–18.		*	M. 15b; 52a; 53a; 53b; 54b; 54c; 55a; 55b; 88a; 88a; 90a; 91a; 98b; 99c; 104b; 107a
20.		*	I.S. intro. gl. for Uo. Pomona
21.	172.85:663:	*	D. 56a
19.	VI?.	*	M. 53a

The long-recognized name glyph of God M. The substitution of this glyph for the usual head of God 7 as patron of the month Uo on the newly discovered monument at Pomona Tabasco, opens up many possibilities.

GLYPH 681
(1 Example)

1.	165?.	*	Glyph X3 var.

GLYPH 682 (Moon)
(55 Examples; Gates' Glyph 59; Zimmermann's Glyph 147)

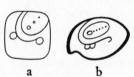

a   b

1.		*	D. 70c
2–9.	1.	*:25	D. 24a (twice); 25b; 48f (twice); 49e; f; 58
10.	1.	*?:25	D. 46f

21.	15.	*:17	D. 49d
11.	58:	*.130	P. 3d
12.	IX:90.	*	D. 26c
13.	XVI.90:	*	D. 27c
14.	XV.91:	*	D. 28c
15.	XVI.93:	*	D. 26a
16, 17.	V and VI.93.	*:87	D. 27a; 28a
18.	?.96:	*	P. 3b
19.	130.	*:*.130	P. 8d
20.	172.	*	D. 46d
22.	181:	*:130	M. 96c
23–29.	190:	*:25	M. 97b (thrice); 98b (4 times)
30.	283?:	*	D. 54a
31–40.	326.	*	D. 38b; 39c; 53a; 55a; 56a; 57a; 58b; 66a (twice); 74a?
41, 42.	326.	*	P. 4b; 10c
43.	?.	*:276?	M. 89b
44, 45.		*.103	D. 31a; 73a
46.		*.103:23	D. 61a
47–50.		*:130	M. 95c (4 times)
51.		*:140	D. 53b
52.		*.526:138	M. 60c
53.		*.130:526	M. 37b
54.		*:314?	M. 96d
55.	number: or.	* or *.number.	Moon sign used as symbol for 20

Glyph 682 is the counterpart in the codices of Glyph 683, found only on the monuments. Both function as symbols of the moon and also as the numeral twenty. See also under Glyphs 526, 528, and 584.

GLYPH 683 (Moon)
(237 Examples; Sheets 271, 294–305)

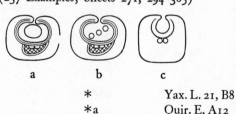

	a	b	c

113.		*	Yax. L. 21, B8
187.		*a	Quir. E, A12
85, 107, 158.		*aP	Quir. D, B24; G, P'2; P'2

27.		*a	Pusil. P, D5
70.		*a	Seib. 8, A6
231.		*b	Dos Pilas H.S. 2, F4
88.		*bP	Quir. G, I'1
114.		*[178]	Yax. L. 21, C6
29.	1.	*b:61	Nar. L. 1, E1
37.	1? or 6?	*a	Yax. L. 46, F''4
153.	1?.	*a.23	P.N., L. 3, F''1
222.	2?.	*a:?	Poco Uinic 3, B15
188.	12:	*[178?]	Beyer 362
76.	12.	*[178?]:82?	Ixlu Alt. 2, B4
48, 195.	12:	*a	Yax. L. 31, J1; 11, C15
46, 47, 52, 53, 54, 59, 62, 64, 65.	12.	*a:109	Yax. L. 16, F4; L. 30, H2; L. 33, H7; L. 52, D2; L. 42, F4; L. 3, E2; L. 2, N1; 11, J1; L. 43, C1
223.	15?.	*b	Xlabpak 4, B1
215, 216.	109:	*[178]:87	Yax. 6, C8; 3, A6
217.	109.	*[178]:87	Yax. L. 45, U5
38.	12.1?:	*a	Yax. 1, F11
118.	23.	*:102	Beyer 152
116, 117.	23.	*:102?	Beyer 150, 151
119–122.	[23.]¹	*:102	Beyer 153–156
228.	23?.	*	Chajcar carved vase. Dieseldorff, 1926–33
68.	23.130?:	*[178?]	P.N. 1, G5
66.	23:130?:	*[178?]	P.N. 3, D2
23.	23.131?:	*b	P.N. shell, I2
234.	23.131:	*b	Aguatec. 2, E2
75.	24inv.:	*a	Ixkun 2, C4
69, 72.	35:	*a?	Seib. 8, A4; 11, E1
71.	35?:	*	Seib. 9, D2
161.	38?.	*bP	Bliss conch god vase
189.	44?:	*?	Carac. 1, G3
35.	1:57:	*a	Yax. 20, E6
98.	58.	*b:24	Pal. House C, platform
99.	58.	*b:?	Pal. H.S., C5
214.	58.291:	*b.?:142?	Pal. Ruz 1, D2
97.	59.	*	Yax. Str. 44, Mid. Up. Step C4
115.	59.	*b:130?	Yax. L. 9, B1
112.	59.74:	*b	Pal. T. 18, stucco
152.	59.131?:	*a:142	Yax. L. 53, E2

151.	59.131?:	*a?:130:142?	Yax. L. 53, C1
167.	?:131?:	*b	Nar. 12, F4
179.	61:	*?	Carac. conch god vase
174.	16:61:	*b:125	Cop. J, A8
79.	74?:	*b:23	Xcalum. N. build., Frag. J
192–194.	79:	*[178]	Pal. Fol., balustr., K2; Sanct. jamb, B12; Cross balustr., K2
19.	79:	*[178?]	Pal. Sun, N14
18.	679af.79:	*[178]	Pal. Fol. O16
10.	103.	*[178?]:142	Yax. 21, G6
16.	103:	*[?]:142	Xcalum. S. build., E. col., A5
139, 150, 197.	1.103:	*:178	Beyer 23; 165; 365
184.	511:103:	*b	Cop. H.S., Frag. Gxiik
237.	122?.	*	Coba 1, front D7
91, 36.	125:	*a	Yax. L. 33, E1; L. 40, C2
224.	125?.	*:130?:?	Comal. tomb E3
67.	1.125.	*b:130?	P.N. 12, B8
24.	126.	*b:47	P.N. 12, Capt. 28
142.	126.	*b:130[178?]	Beyer 108
144.	126.	*b.178:130	Beyer 110
145.	126.	*b.130:178	Beyer 111
195.	126.	*.130:24	Beyer 363
148.	230?.126:	*:178	Beyer 164
143.	126?.	*b:130[178?]	Beyer 109
105.	128?:	*a	Quir. E, A12
104.	131:	*b	Cop. R'', B1
180.	131:	*b:142	Cop. Z, C1
90.	4.131:	*bP	Pal. T. 18, stucco
128–130, 133, 134, 138.	133:	*:130	Beyer 15–17; 20; 21; 23
132, 136.	133:	*.130	Beyer 19; 22
148.	?.133?:	*:178	Beyer 164
135, 137.	1.133?:	*:178	Beyer 21; 22
140.	I.133:	*.254v:130	Beyer 104
141.	I.133:	*:130:254	Beyer 105
92.	148.203:	*b	Carac. 6, F23
108.	220.	*:87	Yax. L. 16, F1
43.	228.	*:47	Chajcar pottery box frag.
14.	228?.	*b:103	P.N., L. 3, B'1
80.	229.	*b:126	Nebaj. Fenton vase
45, 50, 51,	229.	*c:109	Yax. L. 41, E1; L. 21, D8;

A Catalog of Maya Hieroglyphs

55–58, 61, 63.

L. 8, B7; L. 39, D3; 15,
D2; L. 6, F1; L. 5, A4;
L. 1, A6; L. 13, E4

49.	229:	*a:109	Yax. L. 31, K1
60.	229:	*b:?	Yax. L. 3, J1
106.	229.	*a:125?	Quir. I, D9
83.	229.	*P:24?	Pal. Inscr. W. D6
214².	229.	*:125?	Carac. 16, CD5
77.	229?	*[178?]:178	Ixlu Alt. 2, B4
94.	229?.	*b:23?	Carac. 19, Frame 1
21.	229.25:	*a	Pal. Inscr. E. M8
96.	230.	*bP:178?	Miraflores Tablet
110.	230.57:	*a	Yax. Str. 44, X2
177.	249:	*:111	Cop. R, G2
173.	16:249:	*b	Cop. J, A4
206.	271:	*	Rare form of Glyph A, Copán
32.	278:	*b	Jonuta 2, A2
178.	299:	*b:142	Cop. 9, F4
131.	310.	*.130	Beyer 18
163, 168.	320:?:	*	Nar. 12, C9; D12
219.	1.510.	*:12	Pal. 96 Gl. E7. D.N. intro. gl.
171.	511:	*b	Beyer 366
232.	529:	*b	Dos Pilas H.S. 2, D5
205.	13.534:	*b	P.N. pottery drum frag.
185.	580:102:	*b	Cop. H.S., Frag. Gxiil
186.	614.	*	Beyer 367
74.	630af?:	*a	Tik. L. 3, E1
81.	150?.630:	*bP	Cop. A, D7
17.	679af.68:	*b	Pal. Cross, R5
84.	679af.168?:	*bP	Quir. D, B22
93.	126:68:679af.	*bP	Pal. T. 18, stucco
20.	679af.764:	*a	Pal. Sun, Q13
218.	669:178.	*	Beyer 71
3–8.	I.	*a:102	Pal. Inscr. M. D6; C10; E3; J5; K4; L10
33.	I?.	*b:102?	Moral. 2, E10
101.	I:130? or 87?:	*	Pal. Ruz 2, A3
31³.	1.I:	*a:130	Tik. 17, G1
15.	I?.	*b:24	Xcalum. S. build., W. pan., C1
11.	12.I:	*a:102	Yax. Str. 11, R2

169.	III:	*a:?	Nar. 12, F9
100.	III:130? or 87?:	*b	Pal. Ruz 2, A2
166.	IV:	*:130?	Nar. 12, D16
182.	IV.87.	*b:130	Cop. T. 11, Step 8
87.	IV:	*bP:125	Quir. G, Q'2
159.	V:	*bP:?	Quir. G, Q'2
211.	93.V?:	*b	Pal. Fol., detached glyph
212.	V.?:	*?	Pal. Cross, detached glyph
28.	VP?.	*.	Nar. 30, C15
30³.	204.VII:	*a	Tik. 5, A6
170.	VIII:	*a	Nar. 21, B12
236.	VIII.	*a	Tik. 25, C4
229.	VIII:	*a:130.511	Tik. 31, F12
157.	VIII.	*a:279	Nar. 13, F15
220.	IX.16?:	*b	Carac. 19, Frame 2
172.	IX.573?:21:	*[178]	Cop. A, E6
213.	X.I?.	*?	Nar. 8, A3
44³.	head?.IX:	*a:130	Tik. 22, A5
198.		*a:IX or X or.	Glyph A, lunar ser.
199.		*a:102:IX or X	Glyph A, rare var.
200.		*[head].	Glyph A, rare var.
82.	XI:	*aP:24	Quir. G, R'1
40³.	XVI:	*a	Alt. Sac. 9, F7
155³.	1.XVIII or XVI:	*a	Nar. 24, D3
201.	Variable I–IX:	*a:126 or 82 or 246	Glyph E, lunar ser.
202.	Variable I–IX: 34 or 35:	*:126 or 82	Glyph E, lunar ser.
207.	Variable zero– XIX.	*:126	Glyph E as distance number
203.	No? num. coeff. 271:	*b:126	Cop. I, new moon?
191.	1000.	*a:102	Yax. 4, G1
109.	1000.?:	*a	Yax. L. 14, G1
103.	1000.?:	*b	Pal. Tower, S. scribe, A3
221.	1000.	*b:575	Pal. T. 18, stucco
126.	1051a.	*.102	Beyer 160
125.	1051a.	*:102	Beyer 159
124, 127.	1051a.	*:?	Beyer 158; 161
12.	1044.	*[202]:102	Yax. L. 1, G1

183.	1030.	*[178]	Cop. Alt. of E, E1
22.	741?.?:	*a	Pal. Inscr. E. S5
102.	?:	*	Pal. Ruz 2, B2
25.	?:	*	P.N., L. 2, C'1
233.	?:	*b	Dos Pilas H.S. 2, C6
154.	?.	*b:?	P.N., L. 3, B'5
95.	?.	*b.?:130?	Miraflores Tablet
89.	?:	*bP	Pal. T. 18, stucco
225.	?.	*aP:?	Comal. tomb, A3
39.	?:	*a:?	P.N. 12, B14
41.	?.	*a:?	P.N. 8, U2
190.	?.	*a:?	Carac. 15, E4
160.	?:	*b	Nar. H.S., R2
235.	?:	*b	Tamar. H.S. 1, I2
162.	?:	*[202]	Nar. H.S., E1
78.	?:	*[178]	Xcalum. S. build., W. jamb, A6
111.	?.	*b.130:82	Pal. T. 18, stucco
165.	?:?:	*	Nar. 12, E8
156.	?.?:	*[178?].?	Nar. 24, D3
175.	?:?:	*b	Cop. J, C1
26.	?:?:	*b	P.N. 8, C15
73.		*:24?	Seib. 11, B2
86.		*aP:24?	Quir. G, Q1
1.		*a:102	Cop. T. 22, Step 12, A1
2.		*aP:102	Cop. T. 22, Step 12, A2
164.		*:?:102?	Beyer 162
13.		*:103:215	P.N. Str. 1, C'5
42.		*b:126.	Uaxac. I.S. vase
146, 147, 149.		*:130	Beyer 163–65
181.		*a:130?	Cop. H.S., Step D
230.		*b:178	Tort. 7, B3
123.		*:178?	Beyer 157
176.		*a.181:125	Cop. J, D3
34.		*b:215	Cop. 12, A13
238.		*:?	Coba 1, back C13
9.		*b.?:?	Pal. Ruz 1, Q15

[1] Affix 23 is postfixed to the preceding compound, but it is probably meant to be read with the moon sign.

[2] Unusual infix.

[3] In these cases the moon glyph precedes Glyph 573 (*hel*) with Affix 21. It is highly likely that in these contexts it has the numerical value of 20.

Note that the codical form of the moon glyph is assigned the number 682. Glyph

683 appears in clauses at Palenque, Yaxchilán (Thompson, 1950, Figs. 3 and 46) and at Chichén Itzá (Beyer 1937, Groups 2, 3, 26, 28, 39, and 40). Often the kin sign (544) is prefixed to the macaw glyph (744), and the moon signs (683 or 181) are sometimes prefixed to the eagle glyph.

For further examples of Glyph 683, see under Glyphs 17, 58, 510, 528, 573, 590, 630, 666, and 669.

GLYPH 684 (Toothache)
(58 Examples; Sheets 333, 334; Gates' Glyph 59.13; Zimmermann's Glyph 147 [in part])

a   b

1.		*	El Cayo L. 1, E4
2, 5.		*	P.N. Thr. 1, G′3; 15, B1
15.		*	Yax. L. 30, H5
54.		*	Dos Pilas Sculpt. C, B2
14.		*	Cop. T. 11, Step 12
13.	1:	*?	Yax. 20, D1
21–26.	1.	*	M. 90a; 91a (4 times); 92a
11.	168:	*:188	P.N. 16, C5
6, 7.	1?.168:	*?:178	Pusil. E, C3; D6
8.	59.168:	*	Nar. 20, A4
3.	59.168:	*:188	P.N. Alt. 2, E2
55.	59.168:	*	Aguatec. 1, B12
9.	168:	*.59:188?	Nar. 6, A3
51.	179[50].11?:	*:125?	Tik. 5, B9 (knot in center)
12.	180?.	*	Yax. 11, C4
17–20.	181.	*	M. 92a (twice); 93a (twice)
27.		*:53	Cop. 9, C9
16.		*.181	D. 67a
10.		*:126	Seib. 7, A2
4.		*:126v	P.N., L. 3, A′1
28.	?:	*[561]:?	Tort. 6, D5
		ANIMALS	
31.		*	P.N., L. 2, K′1
43–47.		*	D. 23b (5 times)
34.	35?.	*	Cop. 9, F3
41.	59:	*	Yax. L. 26, K′1

52.	59.	*.181	Tik. 4, A5
28.	168:	*	P.N. 25, I8
29, 50.	1?.168:	*	P.N. 25, I12; A15
48.	59.168:	*:188?	P.N. 36, B8
57, 58.	59.168:	*.181	P.N. 11, E7; 14, B11
33.	281.23:	*:142	Pal. Sarcoph., Gl. 19
36–38.	281:23.	*:142	Pal. Cross, S15; Sun, P4;
			Ruz 1, P9
39.		*[281]	Pal. Ruz 2, A3
40.	679af.	*.181:217	Pal. carved I.S. pot, G1
53.		*[281]:142	Pal. Sarcoph., W. side
42.		*.181	D. 23b
56.		*.181	P.N. 8, I3
35.		*.88?.126	Cop. F', C3
32.		*?.181	Bonam. 2, C1
49.		*[747].116.	Tort. 6, G4
		125	
30.		*.?	P.N., L. 2, X9

The animal heads are included because they appear in some cases to function in the same way as the tied-up moon glyph. In many cases (Nos. 1–3, 8–12, 14, 15, 32, 33, and 48) the glyph follows a C.R. date immediately or with one glyph intervening; more rarely (Nos. 4, 28–30) the association is with a D.N. The presence of Affixes 168 and 188 in a few examples is of interest because 168 and 188 form a separate glyph which follows, usually directly, Glyph 684 (Nos. 2, 4, 5, 12, 15, 30, 32, and 41). These examples are confined to the Usumacinta drainage, but Example 35, from Copán, is preceded by a compound with Affix 188 as the main element.

The associations of the glyph in the codices are entirely different. No. 28 is the tied-up sky sign (Glyph 561). Affix 59 with number 52 may be merely a forehead ornament.

GLYPH 685 (Pyramid)
(7 Examples; Sheet 247; Gates' Glyph 402; Zimmermann under 1333a)

6.	1?.	*:23	Tik. 26, Rt. side
3.	12.V:	*.4	Pal. 96 Gl. A4
4.	12.V?:	*.4:23	Pal. Ruz 1, I14
5.	90.	*:23	P. 8b

1.	188.74:	*:4	Pal. Cross, I1
2.	188.74:	*:4?	Pal. Sun, E2
7.	?:	*:23	Cop. H.S. Gxiih

This glyph appears to represent a pyramid with stairway on the front.

GLYPH 686 (Pottery vessels)
(17 Examples; Sheet 304; Gates' Glyphs 333, 434, 438)

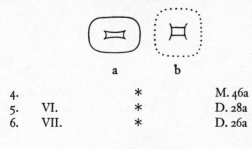

a   b   c

1, 2.		*	Beyer 82; 83
3.	head:	*?	Beyer 628
4.		*	M. 86c (drums)
5.	19:	*	M. 86c
6, 7.	44v:	*	M. 2b; 3b
8.	44:	*[526]	D. 29c
15.	238.	*	M. 43b
9–13.	506:	*	M. 34a; 95b; 104b; 105b; 106c
16.		*[501]	D. 34c
14.		*[533]:47	M. 34c
17.		*:59.301	D. 39a

Nos. 1–3 are on their sides; 9–13 are a sample of offerings for the deities placed in bowls. Simpler forms of pottery dishes are covered by the number 686, but are not illustrated.

For further examples of Glyph 686, see under Glyphs 577, 652, 799, and 839. In all cases bowls are the containers of these offerings.

GLYPH 687 (Ich)
(16 Examples; Sheet 242; Gates' Glyph 341; Zimmermann's Glyph 1316)

a   b

4.		*	M. 46a
5.	VI.	*	D. 28a
6.	VII.	*	D. 26a

7.	XI.	*	D. 27a
8.	IX.	*.24	D. 25a
9.	?:	*.	M. 56a
3.	136:	*	Chajcar pottery box frag.
11.	149v:	*	
14, 15.	181.	*.557	M. 84b (twice)
16.	181.557:	*	M. 84b
10.		*.130:190?	M. 62c
11, 12.	582:	*	M. 96d; d
13.	1.582:	*	M. 96d
1, 2.		*:142	Bonam. Rm. 1, dance impersonators

This element more often appears as part of the very common "Ben-Ich" (168) affix.

For other examples of Glyph 687, see under Glyphs 501, 507, 548, and 580.

GLYPH 688
(3 Examples; Sheet 257)

1.	25:	*	Xcalum. S. build., S. jamb A5
2.	741.25:	*	Xcalum. S. build., W. col. A3
3.	missing	*	Xcalum. N. build., Frag. A

A glyph apparently confined to Xcalumkin.

GLYPH 689
(4 Examples; Sheet 261)

3.	12:	*	Xcalum. I.S. build., Rt. Lint. D1
4.	1.125:	*.130:?	Tulum 1, A12
1, 2.		*:229	Xcalum. S. build., W. col. A3; Rear Lint. E1

[292]

The top part of this glyph resembles closely the top part of Glyph 504 (Akbal), although this is not readily apparent in the illustration.

GLYPH 690
(6 Examples; Sheet 271, 406)

1, 2.	74:	*a	Xcalum. S. build., W. Pan. C1; E. Pan. B1
4.	12.248:	*b	Xcalum. N. build., Serp. Gl. 11
3.		*?.53?:116	Xcalum. N. build., Serp. Gl. 6
5.		*b:?	Xcalum. N. build., Serp. Gl. 24
6.		*?.?	Xcalum. N. build., W. Col. A2

Conceivably all are local variants of Glyph 501 (Imix).

GLYPH 691
(1 Example)

| 1. | *:23 | Xcalum. I.S. build., Rt. Col. B5 |

Affix 23 most irregularly has the two little circlets arranged almost one above the other instead of horizontally. Compare with Glyph 733 and with supposed Calli signs at Xochicalco and at Río Grande, Oaxaca.

GLYPH 692 (Mol semblant 2)
(4 Examples; Sheet 316)

3.	168:	*.116:30	Cop. A, F5
1.	38:168:	*:142	Seib. 8, A5b
2.	?:	*:24?	Seib. 11, G3
4.	18.	*?.181:178	Uaxac. 13, A4

GLYPH 693
(2 Examples)

| 1. | | *:? | Xcalum. I.S. build., Rt. Col. B6 |
| 2. | | *.181:? | Xcalum. I.S. build., Lt. Lint. Gl. C |

GLYPH 694
(1 Example)

| 1. | 110. | * | P.N., L. 2, P2 |

GLYPH 695
(5 Examples; Sheet 315)

4.	18.	*?.181:178	Uaxac. 13, A4
1.	312.13:32:	*:2?	Jonuta 2, B4
2.	74:	*?:136	Pal. Fol. G8

5.   154.?:   *:88   Quir. E, A21
3.   679.   *?:117?   Pal. Inscr. W. J1

A miscellany which may not belong together.

GLYPH 696
(3 Examples)

1.   *   El Encanto 1, C14
2.   VII.   *:552?   Cop. Ball Crt. marker,
                                           lower S.
3.   IX.   *:552?   Cop. Ball Crt. marker,
                                           lower N.

GLYPH 697
(1 Example)

1.   679:1000.608:   *   Beyer 98

GLYPH 698
(4 Examples; Sheets 311, 316)

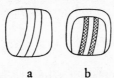

a   b

4.   12.   *:501   Yax. L. 18, D4
2.   108?:   *   Seib. H.S., G2
1.   109.513:   *   Yax. L. 18, C4
3.   122[19]?:   *:141?   Yax. L. 47, A5

GLYPH 699
(3 Examples; Sheet 262)

1–3.   *   Xcalum. N. build., E col.,
               B4; Frag. C; Frag. L

The top part is probably Affix 74 fused to the main sign. The whole is reminiscent of the half-period glyph, but the resemblance may be fortuitous.

GLYPH 700 (legs)
(9 Examples; Sheet 263)

1–6.	168:	*	Yax. L. 37, R1; R7; L. 35, V1; L. 49, N3; N7; P4
7.	168:	*.116:126	Pal. Ruz 1, K7
9.	228.168:	*.116:126	Pal. T. 18, Tab. C11
8.	679af.168:	*.116	Pal. T. 18, Tab. D6

The six examples at Yaxchilán come from lintels in a single building, and are of quite early date, probably 9.5.0.0.0, and they follow in several cases Glyph 623. The three examples at Palenque occur in texts dating from about two hundred years later. They have postfixes and in two cases follow C.R. dates. One is reminded of the Aztec glyph of human legs to represent the sound *tzin*, and Glyph 701 is also very similar.

The Yaxchilán examples occur in phrases of five glyphs.

GLYPH 701 (crossed legs)
(5 Examples)

| 1. | 181: | * | Glyph X, Form 4 |
| 2. | 731?: | * | Glyph X, Form 4 |

3.	1044:	*	Glyph X, Form 4
4.		*:181	Glyph X, Form 4
5.		*:1044	Glyph X, Form 4

All five forms of Glyph X seem to have the same value. Perhaps Glyph 701 is used as an affix with Glyph 526 (Caban) at Palenque (see Nos. 80–82 under Glyph 526).

GLYPH 702 (legs and loin cloth)
(2 Examples; Gates' Glyph 370; Zimmermann's Glyph 103)

1.	1.85:	*	P. 5a
2.	35?.85:	*	S. Rita mural, north wall

The occurrence of this rare glyph at Santa Rita and in Codex Paris is of considerable interest. It was first noted by Zimmermann. At Santa Rita the glyph is associated with a tun 1 Ahau; in Codex Paris with the tuns 7 Ahau, 1 Ahau, and 8 Ahau.

GLYPH 703 (headless seated figure)
(7 Examples; Sheet 293)

2.		*	Pal. House C, eaves
3.		*	Aguas Cal. 1, C10
5.	99.	*:8?	Beyer 472
1.	1000.168:	*	Pal. Ruz 1, F13
4.	1000?.	*	Carac. 16, D14
6.	head?.	*	Bonam. Rm. 1, attiring left batab
7.	II.16:	*?:87	Pal. Inscr. W. N7

The severed neck carries a design reminiscent of Affix 188. At present there is no evidence whether this resemblance is significant. Glyph 703 may be related to Affixes 226 and 227, the scale of which does not make it obvious whether a head is supposed to be present. No. 7 may be something quite different; the crouching position of what appears to be the body and the affixes are atypical.

GLYPH 704 (headless bust)
(5 Examples; Sheet 353)

1.	86:	*	Pal. T. 18, B18
2, 5.	86:	*:140	Pal. Fol. D13; Ruz 1, F9
4.	86:	*v:140	Pal. Inscr. W. M1
3.	86:	*?:140	Pal. Sun P10

Nos. 2–5 have an element on each side, which often forms part of Affix 86, and which may represent corn tassels. Conceivably this glyph represents the maize deity. It is confined to Palenque.

GLYPH 705
(1 Example)

1.	1.	*.?.116.	Beyer 471

This damaged glyph appears to represent the lower half of a human body.

GLYPH 706
(1 Example; Sheet 316)

1.	?	*	Pusil. D, G12

GLYPH 707
(2 Examples; Sheet 316)

1.	113.117?:	*	Pusil. D, E5
2[1].	16:	*?	Yax. L. 10, B4

[1] Conceivably a badly carved Glyph 683. See Glyph 826.

GLYPH 708
(2 Examples; Sheets 316, 405)

1.	61?:	*:130.	Pusil. E, B8
2.	86:	*	Cop. 10, E4

GLYPH 709
(8 Examples; Sheet 367)

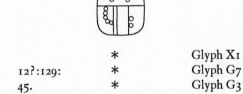

1.		*	Glyph X1
2.	12?:129:	*	Glyph G7
3.	45.	*	Glyph G3
6.	174:	*	Quir. D, C21
8.	174:	*	Yax. L. 35, V3
5.	1:174:	*.102	Cop. Z, C2
7.	?:174:	*:1?	Quir. F, B13
4.		*.1010?	I.S. intro. gl. for Pax

The head before which Glyph 709 stands to form the I.S. introductory glyph for the month Pax seems to have certain feline characteristics and to lack a lower jaw. For discussion see Thompson, 1950, pp. 116 and 209.

GLYPH 710 (inverted hand)
(55 Examples; Sheets 343–45)

44¹.		*²	Carac. 1, F11
32³.	1.	*	Ixkun 2, D10
23.	1.	*²	Alt. Sac. 9, E4
24.	1.	*²	Bonam. 3, A3
33³, 34.	1.	*²	Ixkun 1, A2; J6
45¹.	1.	*²	Nar. 19, A2
26.	1.	*⁴	Nar. 13, F11
27³.	1.	*⁴	Nar. 22, G12
43³.	1?.	*²	Carac. 6, E18
1³.	1.	*²:88	Cop. B, B7
6¹, 10³.	1.	*²:93	Quir. A, D5; J, B16
28³.	1.	*²:93	Nar. 14, E12
8¹.	1?:	*:93:130	Quir. E, D19
51³.	1:	*².93	Aguatec. 2, G3
52³, 53³.	1:	*²:93:136?	Aguatec. 1, A2; D2
18³.	1.	*²:110:130	Quir. Str. 1, P'
47³.	1?.	*.93?:110:130	Ixlu Alt. 2, A4
19.	?:	*²:110:130	Quir. Str. 1, V'
37³.	1.	*²:110?:130	Ixlu 1, A3
30.	1.	*²:130	Tonina 8, D2
7³, 11³, 16³.	1.	*²:130	Quir. C, C13; D, D18; Alt. O, R2
13³.	1:	*²:130	Quir. P, C4
36³.	1.	*²:130	Ucanal 1, B2
35.	1.	*²:130	Honradez 4, C2
46.	1.	*²:130	Carac. Alt. 12, I2
31.	1.?:	*:?	Tonina 8, Side B
12¹.	1.	*:136	Tonina 7, Gl. 8
4³.	11.	*²:130?	Pal. Ruz 1, E19
25.	12:	*²	Pusil. D, F7
2³.	93.	*²:88	Cop. J, W32
48.	57:	*.?.?	Beyer 468
22³.	230.	*²:88	P.N. 40, C15
21.	?:	*:142?	Caribe 1, B3
14³.	?:	*:130?	Quir. K, D6
50.	?:	*v	Covarrubias *sub judice* A2

15.	?:	*.?	Ixkun 1, A5
17[1].		*[2]:93	Quir. I, A4
20.		*:130:93	Seib. H.S., G1
38[3].		*[2]:130	Yaxha 13, A3
39[3].		*[2][679].93	Tik. 21, B5
42[3].		*[2][679].93: 125?	Tik. 22, B12
29[3].		*[2][679?].93: 136?	Tik. 19, B13
9[3].		*:93:88	Quir. E, B18
41.		*:88	P.N. 40, A17
49, 50.		*.87	Dos Pilas 11, A3; 3, C3
51.		*?:102?	Tik. jade B6
40.		*:142	Yax. L. 26, K'1
3.		*:?	Cop. 23, H6
5.		*:?:?	Cop. H.S., Step R

[1] Precedes a C.R. or period glyph.
[2] Circlets falling from between forefinger and thumb.
[3] Follows immediately or with one or two glyphs interposed a C.R. or period glyph.
[4] Unidentified object between forefinger and thumb.

The hand is apparently scattering either grains of maize or drops of water. The many associations with dates are probably significant.

GLYPH 711 (part-closed hand)
(4 Examples; Sheet 406)

1.	12:	*	Beyer 177
4.	13.	*:178	La Mar 1, E3
2, 3.	25.178:	*	Beyer 119; 120

Compare Glyph 711 with the inverted examples of Glyph 666. One hesitates between the two categories.

GLYPH 712 (Pseudo inverted fist)
(46 Examples; Sheets 27–29)

28¹.	1.	*	Pusil. E, C10
3².	1.	*	Cop. O, U3
23¹.	1:	*:81?	Yax. L. 10, D6
19.	?:1:	*:314	Yax. L. 24, B′1
46.	16:95.	*:?	Carac. 3, B19b
20¹.	59:	*:24	Yax. L. 24, D′1
18¹.	59.	*:314:24	Yax. L. 24, Z1
24.	84?.	*	Yax. L. 10, F7
33².	1.126:	*:81?	Kuna L. 1, D6
10¹.	?.129?:	*:81	Cop. F, B9
15¹.	204.	*:81	Pal. Sun, D11
9¹.	3:757:1?.	*:81	Cop. P, D5
29.	?.	*:81	Tik. L. 3, G8
26¹.	1:	*[504]	Yax. 7, C6
5.	1.	*:81.125.504: 24	Cop. 7, A11
12.	1.	*:81.125.504: 4?	Cop. 12, A12
13¹.	11:	*[504]:81:24	Pal. Cross, E3
16².	12.	*[504]:81:24	Pal. Inscr. W. K3
27.	12?.	*[504]:24	P.N. 25, F1
1¹.	13.	*:81.504.82	Cop. 6, D9
8¹.	13.	*:81.125:504: 24?	Cop. I, C5
39.	74:	*[504]	Pusil. D, D14
40.	74:	*[504].82	Yax. 18, B5
2.	89.	*[504].24:81	Cop. 6, C2
21².	89.	*:81?.59.122: 504:82	Yax. 18, A10–11
7.	89:	*:81.59:504: 24	Cop. P, A10–B10
30.	89.	*.81.59.126: 504:24	Tik. L4, D3–C4
14.	89.11:	*[504]:81	Pal. Fol. L12
37.	122.	*[504]	P.N., L. 2, B′1
38.	122:	*[504]	P.N., L. 2, I2

17.	228.	*[504]:24	Pal. Tower, Sub. 2, C1
41.	228:	*.228:504:24	Pal. Tower, Sub. 1, B1
32.	228?.	*[504]	Nar. 35, D11
44.	229.	*[19]:125	Chipoc Fig. 15d
6[1].		*.125?.504?	Cop. 10, F3
45.	544.186?:	*[504]	Tik. 31, B9. Unusual form of Gl. G9
22, 25[2].	?:	*:81?	Yax. 11, J2; L10, F6
36.	?.	*:81	Ixkun 1, K4
43.	?.	*:?	Alt. Sac. 4, C6
11.	?:?:	*	Cop. H.S., Step G
34.		[*] mouth of grotesque	Yax. L. 10, F6
35.		*:81	Tik. L4, F4
31.		*:?	Moral. 2, D3

[1] Preceded by Glyph 757 or possibly in some cases Glyph 758.
[2] Preceded by Imix glyph.

This glyph resembles an inverted fist, but must be something else, for the "thumb" element sometimes projects in an unnaturalistic way and in no case shows a thumbnail. The series with Glyph 504 (Akbal) either infixed or following is of considerable interest because of its wide distribution. No. 45, an early substitution for the normal Glyph G9, confirms the identification of this as the night sun in the underworld.

GLYPH 713 (flat hand)
(109 Examples; Sheets 347–52; Gates' Glyph 426.1; Zimmermann's Glyph 163)

a   b

32.	3:	*.165:302	Cop. 9, C6
28.	16:	*.61:606	Cop. 9, F10
72.	19?.	*.181	Nar. 13, G8
64.	24:	*.181	Huehue. I.S. vase, C9
105.	24:	*.181	Cyl. jar, Petén. Thompson, 1954
78–82.	24:	*	D. 46b (4 times); D. 50b
83–103.	24:	*.181	D. 24b; 46e; 47–50 (19 times)

71.	59.	*.181:102?	Seib. 12, B4
22, 25.	60:	*:?	Pal. Ruz 2, H4; 1, Q14
20.	1:60:	*:?	Pal. Ruz 1, K10
77.	1.60:	*:121	Tonina 7, C3
17.	11.60:	*:12	Pal. Fol. M12
23.	50 or 58.60:	*:246?	Pal. Ruz 1, R5
24.	122:60:	*	Pal. Ruz 2, C2
16.	204.60:	*:121	Pal. Cross, O12
21.	232.60:	*:82	Pal. Ruz 1, O10
18, 19, 40.	679af.60:	*	Pal. Fol. O2; Inscr. W. E4; Ruz 2, A5
26.	?.60:	*	P.N. 14, A14
36.	62:	*.181	M. 67a
61.	121:	*.181	Moral. 2, C10'
12.	121:	*.181	Pal. Ruz 1, O1
13.	121:178:	*.181	Pal. Ruz 1, U4
15.	121:	*.181:126	Quir. J, F4
29.	121:	*:130	Cop. T. 11, E. door, N. panel
65, 66.	121:	*.181	Xcochkax jamb frags.
63.	121:	*.181	Xcalum. S. build., E pan., A1
57.	679af.121:	*.181	Yax. Str. 44, Mid. Step D11
2, 3.	121:	*.116:130	Pal. Sun, P3; P7
35.	16:121:	*:114?	Yax. Str. 44, Mid. Step D10
11, 62.	151:	*.181:136	Pal. Ruz 1, E8; T. 18, B17
4.	228?.151?:	*:136	Pal. Inscr. M. I2
70.	170:	*.165	Uxmal Monjas capstone
104.	74.184.	*.165?:142	Cop. G', C3
10.	225.	*	Nar. 13, G12
69.	1?.225.	*	Nar. 24, B17
55.	50.522:	*.126:136	Pal. Ruz 1, P18
50.	50.526?:	*.181	Pal. Cross, L3
67.	533?:	*.181	Xcocha frag.
76.	?.533?:	*	Nar. 25, B9
30.	546?:	*	Alt. Sac. 13, D6
106.	548:	*.181?	Chipoc, Fig. 15d
9.	575:	*	Pal. Inscr. W. J4
6.	59.575:	*	Pal. Inscr. W. B11
8.	16:59:575:	*	Pal. Inscr. W. D8
7.	191.59:575:	*:130	Pal. Inscr. W, C3
5.	228.59:575:	*:130	Pal. Inscr. W. A7

107.	359:575:	*	Tik. 31, C20
33.	16.628?:	*	Pal. Ruz 1, F7
44, 51, 52, 53.	50.665:	*	Pal. Cross, O4; Q15; E3; Sun, L2
41, 45, 47, 49.	679af.50:665:	*	Pal. Cross, F7; R6; R16; T17
42.	679af.50:665?:	*	Pal. Cross, P1
48.	679af.?:	*	Pal. Cross, T3
1.	679af.11?:?:	*	Pal. Cross, C3
43.	679af.1000:	*	Pal. Cross, Q7
54.	679af.1010.23:	*	Pal. Inscr. W. S9
56.	1010.181:	*	Pal. H.S., A6
46.	35.50.1016:	*	Pal. Cross, S11
34.	12.136?:1016?:	*	Quir. Alt. P, T1
108.	II.	*:23:126	Xcalum. unusual Gl. D
37.	?:	*.181	Alt. Sac. 4, A12
14.	?:	*:178	Cop. 16, B3
27.	?.	*:565af	Quir. Alt. P, W2
39.	?:	*.23?	Nar. 30, A5
38.	?.?:	*	Nar. 24, D2
74.	?.	*:?	Bonam. Rm. 1, attiring scene
31.	?.?:	*.?:130	Cop. Alt. of St. I, k
58, 59.		*.181:24	Nar. 24, C7; 29, F8
60.		*.181:24?	Nar. 29, G12
68.		*.181:24?	Quir. L, Gl. 2
109.		*.126:181	Nar. 13, unusual Gl. D
73.		*.165:575	Tik. L3, C7
75.		*.165?:575	Alt. Sac. 4, B8

The line between Glyph 713 and Affix 217 is not sharp. The outstretched hand also serves, perhaps as a main sign, with the various forms of Glyph C of the lunar series.

See also under Glyph 744.

GLYPH 714 (hand grasping fish)
(30 Examples; Sheets 371, 372; Gates' Glyph 293.1; Zimmermann's Glyph 758
[in part])

15, 18.		*	Yax. L. 38, A2; L. 39, A2
26–28.		*	P. 5d; 7d; 9d?
30.		*	D. 44a (picture)
16.	I.	*	Yax. L. 40, A2
4.	I.	*	Cop. Y, F2
17.	I.	*	P.N., L. 2, M1
25.	I.	*	D. 65a
3.	I:	*:130	Cop. 8, B2
10.	I:	*:130	Yax. L. 25, F1
5.	II.	*:130	Pal. Cross, O9
21.	II.?:	*	Tik. L. 4, C3
7.	105.	*.35	Pal. Fol. M10
6.	204.	*	Pal. Fol. C9
13.	679af.	*	Yax. L. 15, F2
2.	679af:	*:130?	Cop. I, C1
19.	I.	*.121?	Motul S. José 1, A4
29.	III:	*	P. 8c
22.	IX.	*	Yax. Str. 44, Mid. Up Step C12
23.	IX.	*.181	Quir. J, E5
24.	IX.	*?.181	Tonina 20, E1
20.		*:25:136	Beyer 469
1.		*.87:126	Cop. 6, D5
11.		*:130[126]	Yax. L. 25, M1
8.		*.138:130	Pal. Sun, O13
12, 14.		*.181	Yax. L. 14, A2; L. 15, A2
9.	?.	*?.?	Quir. Alt. L, Gl. 2

This glyph very frequently precedes a glyph of one of the deities, particularly the long-nosed god, but these associations may be fortuitous.

GLYPH 715
(36 Examples; Gates' Glyph 312; Zimmermann's Glyph 1300)

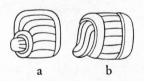

1, 2.	1.	*	M. 110 (twice)
3.	1.12:	*	D. 61a
4.	1.	*:219	M. 103c
5–20.	1.	*:669	M. 96b (thrice); 103b (thrice); 104a (twice); 104b (thrice); 105b (4 times); 106b
21–23.	1.	*:669.181	D. 15b (thrice)
24, 25.	10.	*:669	D. 15a; 16b
26–32.		*:669	M. 106b; 107a (6 times)
33.		*.669	M. 64b
34.		*:669.1	M. 104b
35.	47.	*.181:23	P. 10b
36.		*.501:136	D. 34c

As Gates wrote, a glyph that is a mere hollow outline quite challenges one's imagination.

See also under Glyph 671.

GLYPH 716
(14 Examples; Sheet 321)

a   b

11.	168:	*	Tamar. H.S. 2, F8
12.	168?:	*:130?	Tamar. H.S. 1, E4
6–8.	32:168:	*	Aguatec. 1, A10; A14; D5
4.	36?.168:	*.130	Dos Pilas H.S. 4, C4
3.	38.168:	*.130	Seib. H.S., N2
5.	38.168:	*:130	Aguatec. 7, D2
9.	38?.168:	*.130	Aguatec. 2, G5
13.	38?.168:	*	Tamar. H.S. 1, I3

1, 2.	38?.168?:	*:130	Amel. H.S., C1; J3
10.	43:168:	*	Aguatec. 1, A6
14.	?.168:	*	Seib. H.S., G2

This appears to be the "emblem" glyph of several sites in the Pasion drainage; its distribution may indicate the approximate bounds of a city-state of that area. It seems to converge with Glyph 778.

GLYPH 717
(1 Example; Sheet 311)

| 1. | ?. | *:102 | Xcalum. S. build., W. jamb. A4 |

GLYPH 718
(2 Examples; Sheet 319)

| 1. | * | Nar. 24, C16 |
| 2. | * | Tik. 31, A21 |

GLYPH 719
(1 Example; Sheet 319)

| 1. | * | Nar. 24, D9 |

GLYPH 720
(2 Examples; Photographs)

| 1, 2. | * | Sayil, Str. 3B1, Gl. 9, 29 |

GLYPH 721
(5 Examples)

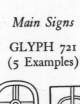

a   b

1.		*a:110	Kabah square alt.
2.		*b	Celestial band, D. 54b
3, 4.	?.	*v	Chipoc, Fig. 3
5.		*?:216	Br. Mus., Fenton tripod bowl

The examples on the Chipoc pottery vessel may be something different as they have a dot in each of the four quarters. Yet, they are not Glyph 510.

GLYPH 722
(1 Example)

1.   ?:319?:   *   Kabah square alt.

GLYPH 723
(1 Example; Gates under Glyph 337; Zimmermann under Glyph 1317)

1.   1.   *:47   M. 36

Perhaps merely a misdrawn Glyph 663, but Affix 47 does not occur elsewhere with Glyph 663, and note the horizontal line at the top, atypical of Glyph 663 but appearing in Glyph 724.

GLYPH 724
(1 Example; Gates' Glyph; Zimmermann's Glyph 1314)

| 1. | 74. | * | D. 8a |

GLYPH 725
(1 Example; Gates' Glyph 338; Zimmermann's Glyph 1377)

| 1. | | * | P. 23a |

The glyph is in a section facing to the right and so has been reversed in this drawing.

GLYPH 726 (Chicchan)
(3 Examples; Gates' Glyph 5; Zimmermann's Glyph 1325)

1.		*	Form of day Chicchan in codices
2.	115.	*	D. 34b
3.	115.	*:116	M. 37a

See Glyph 1022, which is the personified codical form of Glyph 726, and also Glyph 1002.

GLYPH 727

(2 Examples; Gates' Glyph 357.6; Zimmermann's Glyph 1343a)

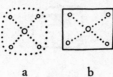

a   b

1.   47.   *a:84   D. 56b

2.   *b   In celestial band. D. 52b

Probably these are variants of Glyph 544 (kin).

GLYPH 728

(1 Example; Gates' Glyph 368; Zimmermann's Glyph 1376)

1.   *   D. 20b

Perhaps this is Affix 157 used as a main sign.

GLYPH 729

(1 Example; Gates' Glyph 317.2; Zimmermann under Glyph 1373)

1.   *   M. 26d

GLYPH 730

(2 Examples; Gates' Glyph 339a; Zimmermann's Glyph 1308c)

1.   *   D. 55b

2.   *:143v   D. 57a

GLYPH 731
(25 Examples; Gates' Glyph 93; Zimmermann's Glyphs 113, 704)

2, 3.	234.	*	M. 34d; 73b
4.	234.	*:60?	M. 72a
5.	234.	*:60?:?	M. 41b
6.	234.	*:149?	M. 70b
7.	234.	*:528	M. 85c
8.	326.	*	P. 5d
9.	534:	*	M. 91c
10.	II.	*:130	D. 46f
11.	III.59:	*	D. 48f
12.	VII.	*:59	D. 49f
13.	VIII.62:	*	M. 85b
14.	X.234.	*:140.	M. 66a
15.	X.	*:521	D. 50f
16.	XIII.561c:	*	D. 7c. Muan glyph
1.	283:563b.104:	*	D. 68b
17.	?:?:	*	M. 34b
18.		*.24.23:19	D. 39c
		M.S.	
19.		*:130	M. 37a
20.		*.47:59	P. 5c
21–25.	24.	*?	M. 22a; 23a (4 times)

The head corresponding to Nos. 21–25 has dots outlining the horizontal omega, and may not be Glyph 731. Zimmermann gives it a separate number (113).

See also under Glyph 701.

GLYPH 732
(3 Examples; Sheet 359)

3.	*	Beyer 569
1.	*.337	stamped pottery base, Chajcar
2.	*.337	stamped pottery base, Carcha

Nos. 1 and 2 from Carnegie Institution of Washington negatives 52–1–36 and 52–1–61.

GLYPH 733
(8 Examples; Sheet 306)

8.	1.124:	*:88	Tik. 31, B21
3.	1:122:	*	Nar. 12, G5
4.	4.122:	*:23	Uaxac. bowl. Bur. A31
1.	59.80?:	*:126?	Tik. L. 2, D1
2.	80?:	*.113:126?	Tik. L. 2, A11
5.	122:	*:130?:92?.	Yax. L. 21, A8
6.	510 or 1.122:	*:88	Uaxac. sherd 3506
7.	168?:	*:102 or 103	Carac. Alt. 12, 1.7

It is interesting to note that this rare glyph, apparently confined to the Petén and neighboring Yaxchilán, appears on a pedestal bowl from a late Tzakol burial at Uaxactún. This would suggest that the bowl in question was of regional workmanship. No. 8 has an interesting rearrangement of the interior details.

GLYPH 734 (Head with Kin infix)
(17 Examples; Gates' Glyph 46; Zimmermann's Glyph 700)

1.	115.	*	M. 81c
2.	115.	*	P. 10b
3, 17.	115.	*:24	M. 103b; 112c
4–8.	115.	*:24	P. 6b; 7c; 8b?; 23a; 24a
9–12.	115.	*.116	D. 61a; 67b; 68b; 69b
13, 14.	115.	*:116	M. 65a; 65b
15, 16.	115.	*:276	M. 101c (twice)

See Glyph 735. Nos. 9 and 12 are preceded by heads corresponding to the numbers six or sixteen, and appear to represent the time period *kin*, "day."

GLYPH 735 (Head with Kan infix)
(8 Examples; Gates' Glyph 46; Zimmermann's Glyph 701)

1, 2.	115.	*:24	D. 8c; 9c
3–5.	115.	*:116	D. 4c; 6c; 9a
6.	115.	*.142	M. 50c
7.	115.	*:276	M. 58b
8.	115.	*:?	M. 87b

It seems probable that Glyphs 734 and 735 are one and the same, for they take the same affixes and are distinguished only by the infix, *kin* in one case, *kan* in the other. However, the two—sun and yellow—are close in meaning, as they are in design, and in sound, for, according to Raymond H. Thompson, the people of Lerma, Campeche, call a stool, normally *kanche, kinche*.

GLYPH 736 (Death)
(266 Examples; Gates' Glyph 6; Zimmermann's Glyphs 151, 152)

	a	b	c
1.		*	Day *Cimi* in codices
2–11.		*	M. 10c; 36c (twice); 52a; 54b; 61b; 80a (picture); 90b; 93d; 95b
12.	1.	*	M. 58b
13.	1.	*:1	M. 35b
14, 15.	1.	*:25	M. 34b; 91b
16.	1?.	*.181	M. 58b
17.	13.	*.140	D. 17c
18.	14.	*	M. 89b
19–21.	15.	*	D. 4b; 22c; 23b
22–87.	15.	*	M. (66 times)
88–91.	15.	*	P. 4d; 5d; 6d; 7c
92.		*.15	M. 23d
93.	15.	*:13	M. 39a

[314]

94–96.	15.	*:19	M. 38b; 38c; 81c
97–99.	15.	*:24	M. 63b; 63c; 70b
100.	15.	*.24	M. 29c
101–215.	15.	*:140	D. (45 times); M. (49 times); P. (21 times)
216.	15.	*[509]:178	D. 28a
217.	1.15.	*.24	M. 36d
218.	1.15.	*:140	D. 2c
219, 266.	1.15.	*:140	M. 66a; 68c
220–221.	1.15.	*:140	P. 2b; c
222.	15?.	*:758:110	P. 10c
223.	17.	*	M. 34b
224.	24.	*	D. 11a
225–233.	24.	*	M. 25a; 52b; 79b; 88b; 91b; 92b; 100a; 101d; 108c
234.	24.	*:103	M. 28d
235.	25.	*	M. 52a
236.	25.15.	*:140	M. 67a
237.	25.15?.	*	M. 67b
238.	58.109:	*	D. 18c (epilepsy glyph)
239, 240.	90.	*	M. 69a; 93d
241–243.	172.	*:13	M. 40a; 40b; 41b
244.	172.15.	*:178	D. 57a
245.	1.227.	*:*	M. 36d
246.	234?:	*:534	M. 35d
247.	236:	*	M. 88c (picture)
248.	238.	*?:140	M. 11c
249.	1.270.	*.181	M. 59b
250.	506.	*	M. 24c (The maize has died.)
251.	15.533:	*	M. 98b
252.	15.667:	*	M. 87c
253.	811:276?.	*:8	M. 35d
254.	X.	*.130:136	M. 67b
255.	[X.]	*	M. 89d (10 transferred from glyph 1050)
256.		*:140	M. 111c
257.		*:140.548:23	D. 72a (a year of death)
258–261.		*:140.548:23	P. 5d; 9c (twice); 11b (same)
262, 263.		*.181	M. 58b; 59b?
264.		*.*:186	P. 4c
265.		*:186	M. 50c

The death glyph is so frequently given because of the generally pessimistic tone of the divinatory almanacs and prophecies.

For further examples of Glyph 736, see under Glyphs 227, 533, 534, and 548.

GLYPH 737 (Snakes and Larvae)
(7 Examples; Gates' Glyph 276; Zimmermann's Glyphs 729, 759, and 1363)

1.		*	D. 43b
3.		*	M. 28c
7.		*[?]	Tik. 31, I3
2.	59.	*	D. 54a
6.	61:	*	Tik. 31, M3
4.	1047.	*	P. 6b
5.	?.	*	Uxmal col., Alt. B5

No. 5 apparently represents a naturalistic snake with looped body and head and tail almost meeting at bottom. No. 4 is probably a rather similar treatment, the front and end halves of the snake forming a sort of St. Andrew's cross (cf. Glyph 657). No. 3 probably represents a larva, to judge by the accompanying picture, although the head might represent almost any member of the animal kingdom. No. 6 is a headless snake, and its form shows that Beyer was correct in identifying Affix 155 as the body of a snake. In No. 7 the snake is draped around a weathered element. The examples under Glyph 657 are differentiated from those of Glyph 737 by the presence of a cartouche.

GLYPH 738 (Fish)
(75 Examples; Sheets 379–83; Gates' Glyph 293; Zimmermann's Glyph 758)

	a	b	c
19.		*a	Xcalum. N. Build. Frag. V.
27.		*a	Mexicanos, Salv. carved vase.
28.		*a	Cop. Carved brown vase. Lothrop

68.		*a	Uaxac. mural O5
26.		*a	Uaxac. tripod. Smith fig. 1b
69.		*b	Chajcar carved vase. Dieseldorff 1926–33
49–54.		*	D. 23b; 29b; 40c; 44a; 27c and 44c pictures
67.		*	Poptun tripod bowl
24.		*	Cop. tripod vase lid. Longyear 117
3, 13.		*	Cop. Y, B2; 6, C2
29, 36.		*	Pal. Inscr. W. A11; T. 18, A18
34, 35.		*	P.N., L. 2, S2; H2?
55.		*	I.S. intro. gl. variable for Zotz'
4.	60:	*a:23	Beyer 133
7.	60:	*a:head	Beyer 135
17.	60 or 71?:	*a	Beyer 395
16.	61.	*a.24	Chilib squash vessel. Gl. 1
10.	82?	*a	Cop. T. 11 Step 26.
11.	12.?528?.84:	*	Cop. 13, F4
37.	115?:	*	P.N. 3, F5
5.	122:	*inv.:130	Cop. P, A11
56.	124:	*[552]	Pal. Inscr. M. D8
57.	16.124:	*[552]	Pal. Inscr. M. L7
15.	126.168:	*	Tik. L. 4, B6
1.	211.178:	*a^1:74	Cop. A, E8
65.	184:	*[552]	Yax. L. 10, E8
61, 63.	184.74.126:	*c^2[552]	P.N. 12, A13; 15, B3
58, 59.	184.74.126:	*c^2[552?]	P.N. Thr. 1, J1; G'4
60.	126.?:	*c^2[552?]	P.N. Thr. 1, K'6
62.	?.126:	*c^2[552]	P.N. 12, D17
64.	126.?:	*c^2[552]	P.N. pottery drum frag.
71–74.	229.	*c^2:125	Tort. 6, A6; A13; E11; D2
46.	331.	*a^1	Carac. bowl
39.	546:544.332:	*c^2:12	Tik. L. 3, A5
40, 42.	4?:126.332?:	*	Tik. Alt. V, Gl. 6; 14
38.	333.	*c^2	Nar. 24, E12
45.	21:528:507?.	*c^2	Chilib squash vessel, Gl. 3
44.	544:116.	*?	El Porvenir frag.
48.	679af. or:	*. or:59	Posterior date indicator P.
30.	679af.	*:102	Pal. Inscr. W. C8
66.	?.	*:181	Pal. T. 4, sculpt. stone 1, B1

41.	?:	*.181	Tik. Alt. V, Gl. 17
9.	?.?:	*	Cop. H.S., Step O
12.		*c^2:24?	Cop. 12, B12
47.		*c^2.59:126 or *c^2.126:59	Anterior date indicator P.
32, 33.		*c^2.59:120	Quir. D, B20; A, C4 (not normal date indicators)
18.		*a^1:102	Chajcar box 52–1–43
2, 31.		*:102	Cop. 8, D5; U, T5
6.		*?:102 or 103?:IX	Cop. H.S., Step M.
43.		*a^1:103	D. 31b
20, 21, 22.		*a^1.130	Uaxac. I.S. vase; sherd 3124; Cop. vase Longyear fig. 103d
75.		*b:130	Uaxac. Tzakol stucco jar
25.		*c^2.130	Cop. vase, Longyear Fig. 117a
23.		*c^2:130	Cop., Longyear, 117i''
14.		*:130	P.N., L. 3, P2
70.		*b.148:77	Tik. 31, K3
8.		*:?	Cop. H.S., Step N

[1] a, more naturalistic types.
[2] c, curl at corner of mouth.

There is great variation in the appearance of these fish glyphs from the naturalistic to the highly conventionalized. The latter can be recognized by the barbules which sweep up in front of the forehead and down behind the mouth. A fin projects at the back of the head, and sometimes there is a deep indentation in the top of the head between barbule and fin which results in a superficial resemblance of the glyph to the codical form of Glyph 671 (Manik). Note the glyph of the Fish god (1011) and Affixes 203 and 204. With some hesitation I included Nos. 58–64, but, despite their aquiline noses, they are close to Nos. 56 and 57, which are definitely frogs. On the whole, they seem to fit type c, characterized by the curl at the corner of the mouth. No. 65, which is highly conventionalized, appears above the glyph of a frog. Could this group represent some creature which in Maya eyes had the features or characteristics of both frog and fish?

Nos. 71 to 74, all on the same monument at the remote site of Tortuguero, are of particular interest. Those at A6, A13, and D2 lie between D.N. and C.R. date reached, but E11 follows a C.R. date from which a count backward has been made. Affix 229 rather clearly has some such meaning as "expiration" for it is the equivalent of Affix 12; the fish head has the meaning of count. Accordingly, the compound almost certainly means something like the completion of the count, and is the same as the count forward (679–738–126) compound. Its occurrence with the later of sets of paired dates strengthens this identification.

See also under Glyph 756.

GLYPH 739 (Turtle and carapace)
(33 Examples; Sheet 384; perhaps Gates' Glyph 293.4.2; perhaps Zimmermann's Glyph 763 in part)

a   b

$4^1, 25^2.$		*	Cop. T. 11, S. door, E. pan., B2; A, A6
3.	120?.	*	Cop. J, E. 15
$13^2.$	II.	*	Yax. L. 46, C′′
12.	II.	*.120	Yax. 6, E2
$21^2.$	III.	*	Yax. Alt. 3, J
$22^2.$	III.	*?.120	Yax. L. 20, D1
$24^2.$	VI.	*.120	Yax. 11, B′9
$28^2.$	VI?:	*	Lacanhá 7, A7
23.	VI–VIII.	*	Yax. Alt. 6, J
$14^2.$	IX.	*	Yax. 6, A6
$26^2.$	XP?.	*	Xcalum. I.S., AB10
$27^2.$		*:120	Tila B, B7
$5, 6^1.$		*.120	Pal. Conde stucco gl.; carved I.S. pot
$8^1, 10^1, 11,$ $15^2–20^2.$		*.120.	Yax. L. 30, F4; 4, A4; 1, E5; L. 29, B9; Str. 44, Mid. Step A6; L. 21, A5; L. 56, E1; 11, P1; 1, C5
1.		*:120	Cop. K, P1
$9^1.$		*:120	Yax. 11, C′8
2.		*.120	Cop. B, B10
29.		*.120	Tik. 11, D3
$7^1.$		*.120?	Quir. K, C1
30, 31.		*?:102	M. 103b (twice)
32, 33.		*?:506	D. 29b; 34a

[1] Occurs in the 819-day count (Thompson, 1950, p. 212). No. 5 may belong in this series.
[2] These occur in lunar series, the so-called Glyph Y. In many cases they are preceded by Glyph

585 (the quincunx) often personified and with a numerical coefficient. This is the so-called Glyph Z of the lunar series. It is possible that it here corresponds to a numerical classifier and it and its numerical coefficient should be read with Glyph 739.

The identification of the glyph with a turtle is not beyond question, but the tail and the flippers support the suggestion (cf. drawings of turtles on Madrid 17a and 17c).

GLYPH 740 (Up-ended frog)
(93 Examples; Sheets 373–77)

5.		*	Cop. T., east (below figure)
71.	1.	*.23:217	Pal. Inscr. M. F4
73, 74.	11:50.	*:23:178	Pal. Inscr. M. J6; K5
53.	12.	*.181	Nebaj. Fenton vase, C5
64.	12.129?:	*?.57:240:48	Yax. L. 35, V6
65.	13.	*	Yax. L. 42, E3
84.	17?.	*:23 or 24	Pal. Inscr. W. N3
67.	89?:	*:23	P.N. 12, B21
63.	113:	*:23	Pal. Ruz 2, H5
89.	128:	*:23	Yax. var. of Gl. F
66.	142:	*	P.N. Thr. 1, K'4
83, 85.	679af:	*:23 or 24	Pal. Inscr. W. K9; O6
70, 79.	679af.	*:23 or 24	Pal. Sun, C10; Cross, C17
80, 81.	679af.	*:125	Pal. Cross, E13; U9
86.	747af.	*:255	Uaxac. sherd 3506
82.	numeral	*.125:24 or *:24:125	Form of Glyph D, lunar series at Pal.
61.		*:23 or 24	Pal. Inscr. W. K12
68.		*:23 or 24	Tuxtla shell, B7
90, 91.		*.122	Tik. 31, C22; E14
69.		*:125	Pal. T. 18, B13
76.		*.125:24	Pal. Fol. C5
78.		*.125:24?	Moral. 2, C8
75.		*:130?	Nar. 32, Z4
56–60, 62.		*:246	Pal. Cross, E17; R15; T13; T16; U2; Ruz 2, A4
2, 7.		*.181	Cop. Y, A2; 12, B10

87, 88.	*.181	S. José carved tripod jar (twice)
9, 11, 12, 19, 21, 26.	*.181:125	Pal. Cross, A17; E7; P5; Fol. B16; Sun, P13; H.S., A5
1, 3, 6, 8.	*.181:125	Cop. 6, D8; 7, B12; 12, B13; 3, A7
28.	*.181.125?	Cop. 7, F8
38–42.	*.181:125 or 126	Nar. 24, B13; 22, F6; G3; 10, A2; 12, B2
44.	*.181:125 or 126	Tonina 30, A4
4.	*.181:126	Cop. H.S. Gxii, i
30–37.	*.181:126	P.N. Thr. 1, Q1; K'4; 3, A8; D6; Alt. 2, A2; 36, C5; 8, A9; 1, B3
29.	*.181:126	Yax. L. 30, H1
47.	*.181:126	Uaxac. 7, C2
22, 24, 25, 49.	*.181:126	Pal. Sun, C1; Ruz 1, C4; S3; T. 18, C6
54.	*.181:126	Kuna L. 1, M2
72.	*.181:126	Tort. 7, B5
55.	*.181:126	Tik. 23, B4
50, 51.	*.181:126	Beyer 439, 440
46.	*.181:126	Moral. 2, B9
77.	*.181:126	Pusil. H, D14
93.	*.181:126	Carac. 3, B17a
27.	*.181:130	Pal. House D, Pier G
10, 13–18, 20, 23.	*.181:246	Pal. Cross, D2; P7; P11; P13; S4; S9; U7; Fol. N2; Inscr. W. E2
43.	*.181.246	Tonina 20, E4
45.	*.181:246?	Pestac 1, D4
52.	*.181:178?	Beyer 441
48.	*.181:?	Pal. Sarcoph. 3
92.	*:561.365.74	Tik. 31, F23

This glyph, which seems to represent a frog, has strong calendrical associations. It usually follows distance numbers or dates. In following C.R. and in taking the lunar postfix (181) it corresponds to the compound 516–181, and, accordingly, it seems quite possible that Glyph 740 is the personified form of Glyph 516. In that case these two closely parallel Glyph 513 and its personified form, the fish (738) when they function as the *xoc,* "count," element of the anterior and posterior date indicators (Thompson, 1950, 162–64). It is, I think, significant that when the count glyphs are present, Glyph 740 is not found.

The use of Glyph 740 at Palenque to record the age of the moon would suggest that it has the value day or night, and such a meaning would fit many of its uses, notably when it follows or precedes a C.R.

GLYPH 741 (Toad)
(36 Examples; Sheets 385, 386)

	a	b	c
31.		*	Personified form of uinal glyph
5, 6.		*	Pal. House C, Plat. H1; Ruz 2, B5
15.		*	P.N. 36, C2
29.		*	Yax. L. 13, D2
21.		*	Xcalum. N. build., Frag. B'
23.		*	Beyer 394
18.		*	Nar. H.S., P2
26.		*	Uaxac. sherd 3168
27.		*	Tort. 6, D6
25.	12.	*	Nebaj. Fenton vase, A2
22.	126.12:	*	Beyer 393
24.	61?:	*:23?	Xcalum. N. build., E. col.
16.	61?.	*:117	Nar. 24, C13
17.	122.?:	*?:117	Nar. 13, H10
10.	52.168:	*:178	Yax. L. 35, W7
12.	1000?.168?: 25?:	*?	Yax. 10, J1
14.	?.132?:	*	Yax. L. 10, E7
13.	188?.	*	Yax. L. 10, E7
2.	21.204:	*	Cop. T. 22, Step A12
4.	228.	*	Pal. House C, Plat. F1
8.	IV.288:	*	Cop. J, E. 13
30.	334:	*?	Carac. 16, B15
34.	XIX.355:	*?	Tik. 12, G6
35.	VI.?.25?:	*	Reversed. Seib. 7, support for personage

1.	*.23	Cop. 11, A5
9.	*:23	Yax. L. 31, I5
19, 20.	*:56	Xcalum. S. build., W. jamb II, A3; E. jamb II, A2
7.	*.59	Cop. carved brown. Long-year, 117a
3.	*:98	Pal. Ruz 1, G12
32.	*:102?	Cop. C', B2
11.	*:160?	Yax. L. 35, W7
33.	*.curled-up snake?	Tik. 13, A7
36.	*.220:116?: 125	Tort. 7, B2

Ideally the toad or frog is identifiable by the three circles arranged in a triangle on the forehead, which may be a conventionalized representation of the poison gland of the Middle American toad featured so prominently on plumbate effigy jars of toads. A curl at the back of the mouth is very characteristic, as are, also, a ring of circlets on the forehead, serrated teeth, and a typical upturned snub mouth and nostrils.

For further examples of Glyph 741, see under Glyphs 644, 683, and 688.

GLYPH 742 (Ocelot?)
(7 Examples; Sheet 387; Gates' Glyphs 207, 250; Zimmermann under Glyphs 710, 745)

7.	58:	*	La Mar 3, B12
5.	58:	*	M. 25d
6.	58:	*[281]	P. 23a
1.	1?.58:	*	Xcalum. W. build., Serp. Gl. 4
2.	12.58:	*	Bonam. 1, L. 1
4.	12.58:	*	El Cayo L. 1, H2
3.	110.58:	*	Bonam. 2, G4

The very tentative identification of this as the head of an ocelot is partly based on the presence of the *zac*, "white," affix (58). The Yucatecan name for the ocelot is *zac xicin*, "white ear." The animal is fierce, and the ear is rather prominent except in the example from Codex Madrid, where it is completely lacking.

[323]

GLYPH 743 (Turtle)

(85 Examples; Sheets 388–92; Gates' Glyphs 42, 213, 271; Zimmermann's Glyphs
723, 724)

85.		*	M. Cow shell disk
71.		*	M. 11b
8.		*	Cop. Rev. Stand, Gl. T
82–84.		*	Uaxac. mur. B7; C3; Q1
63.		*?	P.N. 36, D5
80.		*[281]	Pal. Sarcoph., S. side
68.		*[281]	Unique Kayab. D. 46c
75–78.	1.	*	M. 17a (4 times)
55.	12:	*	Yax. L. 10, F2
73.	12.?:	*	S. José carved tripod jar
41.	16:	*	Tik. L. 3, B4
39.	16?:	*	Nar. 12, C11
46.	16:82:	*:142	Quir. E, C14a
52.	12.16?:	*	Yax. L. 10, A8
16.	17.25?:	*:88	Pal. Inscr. E. M4
18, 19.	17.25?:	*:136	Pal. Inscr. M. C3; H2
20, 21.	511:24?.25:	*:136	Pal. Inscr. W. I4; K1
38.	?:25?:	*	Nar. 12, B10
46.	58.	*[202].181	Cop. N. A16
59.	59.	*:102?	Yax. L. 2, G1
1.	204?.61:	*:116	Cop. A, E3
4.	74:	*	Cop. Z, C3
17.	74:	*:178	Pal. Inscr. E. Q4
71, 72.	74:	*?	Cop. 13, E3; E7
47.	95:74:	*	Quir. E, C14b
43.	122.	*	Moral. 2, D2
13.	12.131?:	*	Pal. House C, I2
35, 36.	16.168:	*	Nar. 23, F20; E11
53.	16?:168:	*	Yax. L. 10, E3
22.	38?.168:	*	Pal. House C, Base. G3
29.	187:	*	P.N. 14, B14
10.	187:	*:12	Quir. F, D10
32.	1 or 11.187:	*	Bonam. 2, D4
33.	12?:187:	*	Bonam. mur. I.S.
28.	13.187:	*	Quir. G, QR1

27.	204.187:	*	Cop. A, C4
30.	220:102?.187:	*:279?	Bonam. 2, D6
74.	229.	*	P.N. 6, N1
31.	229.187:	*:12	Amel. 1, D3
3.	229.	*[528]:178	Pal. Fol. F2
50.	229.?:	*	Yax. L. 10, F4
49, 51.	248?:	*:53	Yax. L. 10, B6; C7
81.	310?:	*[281]	Pal. Sarcoph., N. side
2.	335:	*:335	Cop. A, A11
11.	341.	*.25	Pal. House A, E. corridor kin disk
23.	1.544?:	*	Yax. L. 31, K1
48.	12:626?:	*	Yax. L. 10, B3
76.	1010.	*[528]:178	Pal. T. 18, stucco
61.	?:	*	P.N. Thr. 1, D1
37.	?.	*	Nar. H.S., P2
12.	?.	*	Pal. Pal. House C, G2
25.	?.?:	*:57	Yax. 21, H2
65.	?.?:	*:?	P.N. 16, D7
79.	III.	*?.?	Kuna L. 1, I4
54.		*.12inv.:?	Yax. L. 10, D3
56.		*:53	Yax. L. 10, F8
66.		*[281]. or :57 :126	Kayab on monuments
40.		*:57?	Nar. 12, D9
42.		*?.?:60	Tik. 9, B2
26.		*:79	Yax. 21, H6
57.		*:102	Yax. L. 1, C1
72–74.		*.116	M. 11b; 88c (twice)
15.		*.116:57	Pal. Sun, D4
5.		*.116:	Cop. H, B2
7.		*:126	Cop. H.S. frag.
67.		*[281]:or.130	Kayab in codices
34.		*.181	Tuxtla Mus. shell, C8
69.		*[281].181: 130	D. 47f
58.		*.181:102?	Yax. L. 2, K1
70.		*[281].227	D. 49e
75.		*.593af	M. 19b
6.		*:?	Cop. H.S. frag.

Glyph 743 is differentiated from Glyph 744 by the absence of crest or markings around the eye. The curl at the corner of the mouth is sometimes absent. I have stated (Thompson, 1950, p. 116) reasons for identifying this glyph as that of the turtle rather than that of the macaw as Spinden has supposed. One might note that in several examples here given the *Yax* affixes (16 and 17) are used, whereas on Madrid 19b a turtle is depicted with a *Yax* symbol prominently engraved on his carapace.

For further examples of Glyph 743, see under Glyphs 501, 515, 595, 744, and 745.

GLYPH 744 (Macaw)
(63 Examples; Sheets 388–95; Gates' Glyph 225; Zimmermann's Glyph 734)

a   b

46–48.		*a	P.N., L. 3, U'1; 36, D5; 12, Capt.
36, 39, 41, 52.		*a	Pal. Fol. E8; House E corridor slab; Cross, Q5; T. 18, C18
30.		*a	Uaxac. I.S. vase
43.		*b	Yax. L. 18, D2b
7.		*b	Cop. B, back
29.		*a.*a	Beyer 435
25.		*a?	Pusil. H, D16
16.		*[528?]	Pal. Sarcoph. earplug
9.	16:	*a	Cop. H.S., Step M
11.	32?.17?:	*b	Cop. B', B1
6.	87?.	*b.280:?	Cop. T. 11, W. door, S. pan. B6
57, 58.	1000.58:	*a	Pal. Sarcoph. N. side; S. side
54.	87?:	*	Quir. G, S'2
22.	89?.	*	Calak. 51, G5
56.	103:	*b:280	Poptun sculpt. frag. 2
42.	109.44:	*b	Yax. L. 18, D2a
32.	124:	*a	P.N. 40, B11
60, 61.	150.	*b:?	Dos Pilas H.S. 2, A6; Sculpt. C, B6
1.	168:	*b.280	Cop. Q, A3
52.	168:	*b[528]	Cop. T. 11, W. door, S. pan. C1

62.	181?.359:	*?	Leyden Plate A8
12, 13.	74.184.	*a:142	Pal. 96, Gl. G4; J3
17.	74?:184:	*a:142?	Moral. 2, B10
35.	1010.74.184.	*a.23	Pal. Fol. LM7
2, 3.	184.16:	*b	Cop. Q, B5; F2
45.	291?.?:	*b	P.N., L. 3, N1
27.	333.3:	*b	Tik. L. 3, G7
34.	XII?.333.3:	*b	Tik. 5, C10
59.	229.528:	*a	Tort. 7, B4
14.	544:116.?:	*b	Yax. L. 3, F2
8.	115?:544:116: 764?.16:	*a	Cop. H.S. Gxiih
19.	128?.544?:116.	*b:260?	Moral. 2, E11
37.	671[544]:116.	*a.4	Pal. Sun, NO9
4.	68.671[544]. 116:16:	*b	Cop. 10, B9
5.	60:713[544]. 116.16:	*b	Cop. 11, AB6
38.	1010.	*a	Pal. Sun, O15–N16
10.	1010.?.?.	*b	Cop. 19, D10
63.	IV.	*	Ixkun 2, D12
24.	IV or III.16?:	*b	P.N. 40, C12
49.	IV.85:	*b	D. 40b
50.	IV.84:	*b	P. 6b
55.	IV?.	*a	P.N. 6, P1
51.		*?.85	M. 12a
53.	?.	*a	Lamb site, L. 1, D2
18.	?:	* or 743:?	Moral. 2, D12
31.	head.?:	*a	Tik. lint. in Amer. Mus. Nat. Hist.
20, 21.		*a:57 or 58	Pal. Sarcoph. Gl. 46; 48
28.		*a?.57?	Pal. Creation Stone, F2
23.		*b:75?	Seib. H.S., K2
33.		*a:142?	P.N. 32, A'2
40.		743 or *b.181: 148	Yax. L. 53, B2
44.		*b.280	P.N. Thr. 1, C1
26.		*b:280?	Nar. 29, G13

Glyph 744 (macaw) is differentiated from Glyph 743 (turtle) by the crest of feathers (744a) or the spots around the eye which correspond to the wrinkled black area around the eye of the macaw (744b). Most heads show both features. Those with the *yax* (green) affixes 16 and 17 may represent parrots. There is a possibility, too, that quetzals may be represented. The features of No. 28 are not typical, and may represent something quite different. No. 52 might be used as an affix.

Of much interest are the affixes and prefatory glyphs of the sun and the sun god with Nos. 2–5, 8, 10, 12, 13, 17, 19, 35, 37, and 38. I think the number four prefixed to Nos. 49 and 50 and probably to No. 24 should be read as solar symbols rather than as numerical, for the number four is well known to be the number of the sun god. The head of the sun god often substitutes for the number four, and logically one can expect the number four to substitute for the sun god. In the case of No. 9, the sun glyph follows the macaw.

It is known that the macaw was the guise of the sun god at Izamal and was worshiped under the name *Kinich Kakmo* "sun face fire macaw." The evidence of the glyph shows that the cult of the sun-macaw was widespread in the Classic period. The fire (*kak*) element in the name *Kinich Kakmo* is clarified by his custom of carrying torches and accompanying drought glyphs.

See also under Glyph 767.

GLYPH 745 (Pelican)
(13 Examples; Sheet 422)

11.		*	P.N., L. 2, G'3
5, 6.		*?	R. Amarillo Alt. 1, F1; I1
9.	12:	*	Cop. La Fundacion, frag.
10.	12.	*:130	Cop. brown ware. Long-year, 103d
13.	59.	*.2	M. 67a
1.	125.	*:246	Cop. K, M1
3.	142.	*	Cop. 7, D11
8.	142:	*:?	Cop. 7, F13
2.	142:	*.?:178	Cop. P, D9
4.	236?:	*	Cop. 12, back, B13
7.	?:	*.?	Kuna L. 1, D4
12.	?:	* or 743.?	Tik. 9, B2

Identification as the pelican is seriously open to doubt.

GLYPH 746 (Eagle)
(32 Examples; Sheets 423, 424)

9.		*	Personified katun glyph
16.		*	Quir. D, D17
23.		*	Chajcar box frag. Neg. 52.1.36
10.		*(full fig.)	Cop. W', I2
20.		*(full fig.)	P. 4d
4, 13.		*?	Cop. 2, A16; 12, D9
26.	59.68:42:	*	Cop. P, C4
21, 22.	49:	*:23	Huehuetenango vase (Brinton)
19.	126.	*	P.N., L. 3, U12
17.	150?.	*	Quir. P., Pan. A
2, 6.	126:181.	*:23	Cop. N, B6; H.S., Step Q
1.	178:181.	*:23	Cop. N, Ped. 10
25.	?:181.	*	Cop. J, W. Gl. 13
31.	187:236.	*[528]:87	Beyer 425
28.	115.279?:	*	P.N. 14, B13
32.	115.86:	*?	P.N. 8, X1
24.	288:529.	*	Cop. J, E. Gl. 22
8.	683.	*.23?	Cop. M, A7
18.	1000:1014?.	*:23	Yax. 10, H2
3.	118.IV:	*:23	Cop. A, G3
30.	V.229?:	*[528]:116	Cop. E, B10. Unusual 5 haab completed glyph
5, 7, 11.		*.23	Cop. Z, D1; H.S., Step S; Rev. Stand Z
12.		*?.23	Cop. Alt. of B
27.		*?:23	Cop. 7, B11
15.		*:121	Quir. G, I'2
29.		*.181	P. 8d
14.		*:342	Quir. J, A18

Nos. 1, 2, 6, and 8 are preceded by lunar glyphs and appear in clauses which involve a Yax-Baktun glyph and the glyph of God B, the long-nosed god. A fifth example undoubtedly occurred on Cop. H.S., Step T, but the presumed Glyph 746 is obliterated. No. 7 probably belongs in this group, for it is followed by the glyph

[329]

of the long-nosed god, but, again, the glyphs before it are missing. A lunar glyph is also prefaced to No. 25. The identification of the glyph as that of an eagle may not be correct. In some cases the bird has superimposed features reminiscent of those of God B. The headdresss commonly found with Glyph 746 resembles the Imix glyph (501), but this resemblance may well be fortuitous. A full-figure portrait in the codices has the Imix headdress and the features of God B (Zimmermann's Glyph 754). See also Glyph 1031 and under Glyphs 669 and 747.

GLYPH 747 (Vulture)
(167 Examples; Sheets 113, 425–32; Gates' Glyphs 221–223, 230; Zimmermann's
Glyphs 736, 750, 752, 753)

a   b

22–24, 96[1].	*a[1]	P.N., L. 2, B′3; D′3; F′3; L. 4, K3
8.	*a	Pal. stucco, Madrid
30.	*a	Tonina 8, Side B
143.	*ac	Form of day sign Ahau
7.	*ac	Cop. T. 26, outer chamber
68.	*b	Amel. 1, C3
59.	*b	Cop. carved brown, Longyear, 68e
161, 162.	*b	Yalloch cyl. jar (*ti* not certain)
55, 57.	*b	Beyer 433, 460
113–118.	*b	D. 8a; 11b; 17c; 19a; 36b; 38b
119–122.	*b	M. 38b; 67a; 87a; 108c
124.	*b[95]	D. 39c
123.	*[95]	D. 39c
89.	*[95]full fig.	D. 37c
132–134.	*b	P. 2b; 3c; 8b
13.	*bc	Yax. 11, D4
6.	*bc	Pal. Inscr. W. N12
56.	*bd	Beyer 434
9.	*c	Quir. J, D15
37.	*cd	Xcalum. N. build., Frag. n

4.		*d	Cop. 12, A12
12.		*e	Yax. 8, Gl. 2
152.		*	Muluch-Tzekal
92².		*	Pal. Ruz 1, D11
153.		*	Halal N. Lint., Gl. 7
75.		*	R. Amarillo Alt. 1, E2
154.		*	Labna round alt.
21.		*	P.N., L. 2, X7
139.		*	D. 23b
64–66.		*	Chajcar pottery boxes, Negs. 52–1–51; 53
125–131.		*	M. 10a; 19c; 22c; 25a?; 25b; 26c; 55b
100.		* full fig.	Quir. B, Block 17
148.		*? full fig.	Pal. Fol. N12
29.		*[1030]	Tik. 5, B13
76.		*[1030]	Quir. D, C21
71.		* or 746	Cop. 7, A12
36.	1.	*	Xcalum. N. build., Frag. h
145.	1:	*c:126	Quir. Str. 1, frag.
99.	1.	*c	Quir. F, C11
150.	1.	*:?	Pal. T. 18, sculpt. stone, C1
98².	1?.	*d:116?	Cop. 2, C8
86.	11.	*d	Pal. Cross, U8
25.	12.	*c:178?	Bonam. 2, F5
149.	12:	*	Pal. Ruz 2, H1
11.	13.	*bc:126	Quir. Str. 1, M1
72.	V.28:	*a.130:142	Pal. Fol. I1
85.	VP.28:	*	Pal. 96 Gl. L6
67.	1000?.28:	*ac	P.N. 3, F3
95².	?.28:	*c	P.N., L. 3, U10
83.	32:	*ac:126	Cop. H.S., Step F, Gl. D?
90.	36.	*:130	Yax. L. 53, H1
14.	36	*[1030].130	Yax. L. 26, O'1
16.	41?.	*[1030]:130	Yax. L. 46, I''
164.	45:	*	Dos Pilas H.S. 2, A5
39.	?:48:	*	Col. Esperanza ball crt., Gl. 18
87.	51:	*:188	Pal. 96 Gl. F3
40.	53:	*e	Tort. 6, A8
15², 94².	59.	*c:188	Yax. L. 2, E1; 3, A3
26².	59.	*:188	Chinikiha Thr. 1, A'1
165.	59:310.	*	Dos Pilas 2, D3

17.	1.59:	*d	P.N., L. 3, Q2
155.	60:	*.130?	Comal. tomb, E1
58.	74:	*:23	Nebaj. Fenton vase, C3
33.	57?.74:	*	Xcalum. I.S. build., rt. col., A3
74.	12.89:	*	R. Amarillo Alt. 1, I2
52.	115?.	*b	Cop. Md. 2, Step 1, I2
78.	117.	*?.181	Nar. 29, G17
82.	120?.	*:47	Xcalum. I.S. build., L. jamb, A1
62.	122.	*	Bonam. Rm. 1, bottom rt.
146.	122:	*c:24	Quir. Str. 1, frag.
141.	122.	*[95]full fig.	D. 73b
80.	122.	*?	Cop. T. 11, reused stone
5.	125.	*:130	Pal. Inscr. W. N12
88.	126.	*.87?:130	Pal. 96 Gl. I3
10.	131:	*:125	Quir. Alt. P, W1
34, 35.	150.	*	Xcalum. S. build., W. jamb, A5; E. col., A3
135.	164.	*	D. 35c
103–105, 108–112.	168:	*:130	Beyer 77; 79; 131; 138; 171–73; 175
106, 107.	168:	*.130	Beyer 132; 133
144.	36.168:	*:130	Bonam. 2, F6
32.	36?.168:	*	Pal. Sarcoph., Gl. 9
93[2].	40.168:	*ac	Yax. L. 41, E3
151.	131:168:	*	P.N. 12, A19
69[8].	204.	*b:126	Quir. J, E3
77.	200:[4]	*	Quir. F, B9
97.	204:	*d?	Cop. 2, D2
70[8].	205:	*b.126	Cop. H.S. Gxiiid
18.	229?.	*	P.N., L. 3, X4
44[2].	229?.	*:279?	Cop. T. 11, S. door, E. pan., B5
3.	238?.	*.130	Cop. T. 22, step, Gl. 11
157.	270.	*	Holmul sting ray
61.	279?.	*	Xcocha capital
166.	310.	*	Dos Pilas H.S. 2, E5
147.	310?.	*	Uxmal Tzompantli
156.	310?.265:	*	Pomona Tab. frag.
160.	549.	*	Yalloch cyl. jar
101, 102.	240:632:	*	Yax. L. 49, N2; L. 18, C3
91[2].	634:	*[501]?:142	Cop. K, Q2

84.	1015?.	*c:126	Cop. H.S., Step 11, Gl. D?
51.	IV.1010.	*a:130	Cop. T. 22, Step 22
137.	IV.	*b	P. 11d
136.	IV.	*bc	D. 56b
28.	VIII.	*b	Tik. 5, A9
63.	?.	*	Bonam. Rm. 1, L. B4
167.	?.	*a	Tik. jade, B3
19.	?.	*	P.N. 39, B10
1.	?.	*:116	Cop. N, Ped. 3
31.	?.	*d.117?:125	Jonuta 1, B1
45, 46.	?.	*.130	Cop. H.S. Gxiiib; c
73.	?:	*	Pal. Cross, O6
2.	?.	*.?	Cop. T. 22, Step 3
48.	?:	*:?	Cop. H.S., Step Q
49.	?.	*:?	Cop. H.S., Step S
159.	?.	*c	Yalloch tall cyl. jar
50.	?:	*.?	Cop. H.S., Step T
163.	Missing	*	B. Viejo. Cambridge Expedtn.
138.		*b:25	M. 107c
140.		*?:47	M. 54b
142.		*full fig.:59	D. 57b
60.		*.77	Cop. brown ware, Long-year, Fig. 103d
81.		*:103	Xcalum. I.S. build., L. lint., F
43.		*a:126	Cop. J, E14
41[2].		*a:130	Cop. K, R2
38.		*b[236].130	Xcalum. N. build., Serp. Gl. 14
79.		*b:130?	Nar. 23, F16
20.		*.130	P.N., L. 4, O6
47.		*.130	Cop. H.S. Gxii, i
42.		*:130	Cop. J, E26
27.		*[1000?]:130	Tik. L. 3, E4
55, 57.		*b.tumpline & load	Beyer 148; 149
158.		*.?	Slate mirror-back

1 Letters following the asterisks have these meanings: *a*, small Ahau on forehead; *b*, Affix 59 (*ti*) on forehead or before beak; *c*, wrinkled face; *d*, beak horizontal, and in some cases the glyph may represent some other bird; *e*, a crest is visible.

2 Eight examples thus marked follow katun glyphs with low coefficients. The ninth (No. 15) follows a five-tun anniversary glyph, and the tenth (No. 26) follows the seating of the haab glyph.

In addition, Nos. 52 and 98 precede katun glyphs with coefficients of three, and No. 99 precedes a personified baktun glyph.

³ Two rare examples of the anterior date indicator in which the vulture with ti on forehead serves as a personification of the *ti* affix (59).

⁴ Affix 200, placed here above Glyph 747, almost certainly belongs with Glyph 756, the preceding glyph, to which it is commonly postfixed.

In connection with the appearances noted above of Glyph 747 with katun glyphs with numerical coefficient, one should note apparent telescoping of the phrase. The katun affix (28) and on two occasions its numerical affix are transferred to the vulture glyph (Nos. 72, 85, 67, and 95). The substitution of the vulture for the more usual young god (Glyph 1000) to represent the day Ahau may have bearing on this matter.

In two cases (Nos. 83 and 84), the vulture seems to substitute for the more normal forms of Glyph D of the lunar series, a shift which may have its roots in mythology.

It is possible that the presence of the Ahau sign on the forehead indicates the king vulture; the *ti* sign, the ordinary John Crow or turkey buzzard. The vulture seems also to have a connection with human sacrifice and its symbol, the plucking out of the eye.

For further examples of Glyph 747, see under Glyphs 548, 632, 684, 740, and 769.

GLYPH 748 (Muan bird)
(32 Examples; Sheet 433; Gates' Glyph 40; Zimmermann's Glyph 735)

25, 26.		*	D. 53b; 55a
8–11.		*	Beyer 428–31
30.		*[24]	Month glyph Muan in D.
21.		*[217]	Form of baktun glyph on monuments
22–24.		*[217?]	Baktun glyph. D. 61a; 69f; 70c
19.		*[590]	Form of tun glyph on monuments
1.	59?.	*:165?	Quir. H, P2
4.	95?.	*	Nar. L. 1, F1
18.	110.	*:53	Yax. L. 18, A1
15–17.		*:110	Yax. L. 18, B2; B3; B4
14.	245.	*?	Pal. Inscr. W. H12

2.	?.	*	Yax. L. 14, A3
31.	IX.77.77:	*	Yax. L. 35, V5
27–29.	XIII.	*	D. 8b; 16c; 18b (name glyph of Muan)
5.		*:23	Pal. Sarcoph. jade earplug
20.		*:116	Month glyph Muan on monuments
32.		*.116	Bonam. 2, F2 (not month)
6, 7.		*:116	Beyer 426; 427
13.		*?.?:116	Nebaj. Fenton vase, B4
12.		*?:135?	On side. Beyer 461
3.		*?.?	Nar. 13, G5

A very unsatisfactory glyph on the monuments because of the difficulty of distinguishing it from some examples of Glyph 1030 and of Glyph 1023. The most distinguishing features are the tufts of hair on each side of the face, one of which appears before the forehead when the bird is shown in profile. There is good reason to believe that the Muan bird is the Yucatán screech owl (Thompson, 1950, pp. 114–15).

GLYPH 749 (Eagle on side)
(3 Examples; Sheet 434)

1.		*	Cop. T. 22, Step 3
3.		*	Carac. 3, A10
2.	110.134.	*.134	Cop. T. 22, Step 13

Tozzer and Allen (1910, p. 335) are inclined to identify this bird as the harpy eagle.

GLYPH 750 (large-beaked bird)
(15 Examples; Sheet 500)

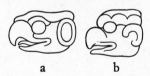

a   b

10.		*	P.N., L. 12, S2
8, 9.		*?	P.N. 36, C1; L. 2, X5
2.	35.?:	*:?	Seib. 7, A4

3.	36 or 35.?:	* :?	Seib. 7, B7
6.	121?.	* ?.130	P.N., L. 2, H'2
12.	353:	* .113	Pal. Fol. M1
11.	353?:	*	P.N., L. 3, X'
1.	103:353:	* :?	Pal. T. 18, detached stucco
4, 5.	565af:	* :125?	Nar. H.S., H1; P2
7.	?.?:	* ?	P.N. 8, C16
13.	V.	* :116	Pal. Inscr. W. D9
15.		* ?.181:217	Unusual tun completion. Tik. 12, E4
14.		* :?	La Mar 2, C1

Probably there is more than one cuckoo in this nest.

GLYPH 751 (Jaguar)
(159 Examples; Sheets 437–43)

a   b

102.		*	Quir. P, O2
131.		*	Carac. 16, D17
82, 84, 85.		*	P.N., L. 3, Z3; 1, J16; 8, C21
79.		*	Cop. Rev. Stand, A' (reversed)
78.		*	Jonuta 1, C2
153, 154.		*	Aguatec. 2, F2; 7, G2
9, 13.		*	Yax. 12, C5; L. 17, G1
128.		* [281?]	Pal. Sarcoph., Gl. 51
93.		* ?	Nar. 31, G5
94.		* ?	Tik. L. 3, B7
138.	1.?:	*	Xcalum. N. build., W. col., A4
144.	1?.	* :74?	Poco Uinik 3, B10
114, 115.	4.	*	P.N., L. 12, S1; Q1
62.	11:	* :25	Pal. Pal., House C, foundations, C1
73.	12:	*	Cop. K, K2
105.	12:	*	Yax. L. 37, T6

143.	16.	*:74	Poco Uinik 3, C20
119.	32[128?]:	*	Jonuta 2, A1
23.	44:	*[528].59	Yax. L. 21, C2
140¹, 141¹.	60:	*	Yax. L. 35, W3; 37, Q8
130.	60:	*	Xcocha capital
139.	60:	*	Kuna L. 1, C4
109, 113¹.	60?:	*	Yax. L. 22, A7; L. 46, G′ ′8
111.	60?:	*:142	Yax. L. 10, E2
76.	65:	*	Cop. N, Ped. Gl. 26
81.	65?:	*	Quir. P, Cart. 2
110.	92?:	*:117?	Yax. L. 10, D1
89.	125?.	*	Cop. J, E., Gl. 17
5–7, 10, 19, 28, 29, 31, 35, 38, 55, 57.	152:	*	Yax. L. 56, K2; L. 25, V2; L. 27, G1; 12, F3; Str. 44 Mid. Up Step D7; L. 26, B′ ′2; N′1; L. 32, A5; 20, C1; L. 44, L′4; 11, L3?; 7, D2
3, 8, 17, 18, 22, 34, 37, 44, 48, 52, 61.	152.	*	Yax. L. 25, A2; 12, A4; L. 53, D1; Str. 44. S.E. Up. Step X4; 11, I1; 20, A2; L. 52, H5; 15, A4; L. 1, G5; L. 46, G′ ′5; 13, E4
1.	152.	*	Pal. H.S., C3
134.	152.	*	Bonam. L. 2, D2
152.	152.	*:142	Dos Pilas 11, B2
158.	152:	*:142	Tamar. H.S. 2, AB5
4.	152:	*:142	Yax. L. 24, C′1
20, 27, 39.	152.	*:142	Yax. 21, G5; 18, E4; L. 58, E3
159.	152?.	*	Dos Pilas 3, D2
58.	152.116?:	*	Yax. 19, B1
32.	152:1010 or 1018:	*:142	Yax. 10, K2
121–124.	168:	*	Tort. 6, A3; B8; D8; F5
147.	174:	*	La Mar 3, B15
142.	213:	*	Variable element I.S. intro. gl. Pop.
2, 67, 75, 90.	213:	*	Cop. House off Fundación; 9, F9; E, B11; 9, D7
98.	213:	*	Xcalum. N. build., Frag. S
116.	213:	*	P.N., L. 3, X5
70.	213?:	*	Cop. reused stone, Md. 2

101.	213:	*:142	Quir. D, B23
74.	213?:	*:142	Pal. Ruz 1, L9
65.	213:	*:178	Cop. K, J1
66.	213:	*:255	Cop. 9, E5
72.	213:	*:?	Cop. 3, B8
71.	1.213:	*	Cop. 2, C1
69.	44:213?:	*	Cop. H.S., Step G
148.	228? or 229?.	*	La Mar 2, I2
100.	234.	*.?	Quir. E, A16
104.	125.236:	*	Yax. L. 37, Q2
11, 15, 24–26, 30, 36, 40, 42, 43, 45–47, 49–51, 53, 54, 59, 60, 107, 112, 146.	126.236:	*	Yax. L. 41, D4; L. 31, I1; L. 21, D7; L. 9, B4; 3, A4; L. 33, A7; L. 52, C2; L. 54, C4; L. 42, E4; L. 39, D2; L. 6, A7; L. 7, B4; L. 5, A3; L. 1, A5; L. 2, M1; L. 13, E3; L. 8, E2; 11, E5; 9, C2; L. 49, O2; L. 3, E1; 1, E10′; L. 17, B5
41.	236.126:	*	Yax. L. 43, B2
108.	236?.126?:	*	Yax. L. 22, C7
56, 63.	126:236:	*	Yax. 11, C′15; 6, C7
12.	126.236:	*:142	Yax. L. 16, F3
14, 16.	126.236.	*:142	Yax. L. 30, G2; L. 31, L1
21.	236[126]?:	*	Yax. 11, F1
33.	236[126]?.	*	Yax. 11, A′5
118.	236?:	*	Cop. K, O2
136.	236?:	*	Bonam. Rm. 2 judgment. 3rd batab
127.	281.	*	Pal. Sarcoph., Gl. 54
99.	282.60:	*.213	Pal. H.S., D2
96.	92.282.86:	*:140	Tik. T. 4, L. 4, D2
97.	92:282.86:	*	Tik. T. 4, L. 4, F12
151.	310?:	*	Tik. 31, C5
120.	323:	*	Jonuta 2, B3
133.	323:	*	Tort. 6, H7
83.	338?.176?:	*	P.N. 12, D11
106.	338.?:	*	Yax. L. 35, U4
156, 157.	544.116:	*	Aguatec. 1, A3; B5
95.	544.116.60:	*	Tik. T. 4, L. 2, B12
155.	544:116.	*	Aguatec. 2, F6
125.	III:?:	*	Tort. 6, C5

91.	?.	*	Nar. 22, H9
77.	?.	*	Cop. E, A12
103.	?.	*	Pal. stucco, unlocated
135.	?.	*	Bonam. L. 2, A8
149.	?.	*	Tik. 4, C4
92.	?.	*:?	Nar. 8, E7
64.	?.?:	*	P.N. 40, B12
117.		*[539].89	Tik. Alt. V, Gl. 35
145.	?.	*?	Quir. D, B24
87.		*:103	Caribe 1, B3
129.		*:140	Pal. Sarcoph., Gl. 24
126, 150.		*:142	Pal. Sarcoph. Gl. 26; E. side
137.		*:142	Kuna L. 1, F1
86.		*:142	Seib. H.S., K2
88.		*.145:188?	Amel. 1, B3
80.		*:150?	Quir. G, O2
68.		*.?:213?	Cop. H.S. Gxiiie
132.		*.?	Uaxac. sherd 3122

¹ In these examples the cord of the knot (Affix 60) passes through the jaguar's eye.

The few jaguar glyphs in the codices differ so markedly from Glyph 751 that it has seemed best to group them separately (Glyphs 800 and 801). The great numbers of jaguar glyphs at Yaxchilán occur in what seem to be variations on a single clause (Thompson, 1950, Fig. 46). The 126–236 arrangement seems to be favored when the next glyph is the moon compound (683:109), but these clauses need careful study.

The shield with Akbal (darkness) infix (Prefix 152) is of interest because the Akbal symbol and the water lily (Affix 213) are the special attributes of the jaguar as a deity of the underworld and symbol of the night sun (Thompson, 1950), pp. 74, 279).

Whether the bird affix (236) has a mythological significance or has a phonetic value is not at present obvious. I incline to the latter interpretation. It goes back to the earliest texts at Yaxchilán and survives to the end of the Classic period at that site.

In connection with the solar aspects of the jaguar, it should be noted that solar affixes or prefatory glyphs occur with Nos. 95–97, 99, and 155–157. A winged kin glyph (544:116) also precedes No. 100.

No. 23 is of particular interest because at the back of the head the jaguar's paw sustains a Cauac glyph.

See also under Glyph 609.

GLYPH 752
(9 Examples; Sheet 444)

5.		*?	Chama. Carey vase, B3
8.	1.	*[95]:?	Tik. 31, F7
7.	25.	*:139	Xcocha capital, front
6.	?:25.	*	Xcocha capital, right end
3.	115?:	*.	Pal. Ruz 1, D6
2.	168:	*	Pal. Inscr. W. J3
1.	113.168:	*	Pal. Inscr. E. K11
9.	74.184.	*?	Carac. 16, B18
4.		*:130	Personified form of Kankin

A menagerie which may contain more than one genus. The snout is prominent and may be spotted. All heads are hairy. The personified heads of Kankin seem to belong here, and if they can be accepted as representing the hairy dog, the link between Kankin and the glyph of the dog (559–568 compound) is more firmly established. No. 8 seems to link the series to the personified form of Kankin.

GLYPH 753 (Dog with torn ear)
(1 Example; Sheet 444)

1.	229.168:	*	Quir. Str. 1, U'

The dog with ears which are torn or eaten away is commonly represented in the art of central Mexico and in the Maya codices (Thompson, 1950, p. 79). This beautifully preserved example from Quiriguá with crenelated edge of its ear shows that the concept was present in the Maya area during the Classic period.

GLYPH 754
(13 Examples; Sheet 445)

10.		*[544]	I.S. intro. gl., Leiden plate
4, 6, 8, 13.		*[1073]	Tik. 13, B5; 7, B8; 3, C8; 26, B6
1.		*?	Alt. Sac. 4, D9
11, 12.		*?	Cop. A, C5; E4
2.	3.?	*	El Cayo L. 1, H2
3.	60?:	*	Tik. 4, C5
9.	197.168:	*:130	Beyer 621
5.		*:136	Beyer 92
7.		*?:?	Cop. H.S. Gxiil

A miscellaneous group. The examples from Tikal are homogeneous and with the rounded ends of their snouts may represent peccary, but the others are dubious. The bone awl (Affix 197) may pierce the eye of No. 9.

GLYPH 755 (Monkey)
(31 Examples; Sheet 446; Gates' Glyph 82 in part; Zimmermann's Glyphs 141, 142)

18.	*	Occasional day Ahau
27.	*	Occasional kin glyph
1, 2, 3.	*	P.N. 26, C1; 36, C6; 37, C10
6.	*	Nar. H.S., G1
29.	*	Kabah mur.
30.	*?	Uxmal tecali vase, D2
9.	*	Xcalum. S. build., W. front pan., C1
21.	*	P. 5c
26.	*	D. 69F
11.	*?	Tonina 31, Gl. 5
28.	*?	Yax. L. 14, A4

10.	33[59?].	*	Huehuetenango I.S. vase, C14
22.	70.	*	D. 17b
8.	125.	*:?	Tik. 12, B1
24.	70.	*	P. 11b
12.	129?109:	*.24	R. Hondo vase. Gann, 1918
25.	120.	*	P. 5b
7.	74.184.	*	Carac. 16, B18
31.	181?.?:	*	Tik. 31, E6
13.	220.	*	Nebaj. Fenton vase, D5
14.	220.	*	Huehuetenango I.S. vase, C3
20.	220.	*	Poctun homage vessel
15.	220.	*.?	R. Hondo blowgun plate, Gl. 12
16.	220.	*	Holmul tripod bowl, Gl. 14
17.	229?.	*:126	Xcalum. N. build., capital, A1
4.	291?.109:	*	El Cayo L. 1, N13
5.	317?:	*	Nar. H.S., M2
19.	III.87.	*	Cop. A, E5
23.		*:70	D. 11b

The 220.755 compound on various painted vessels suggests copying of the glyphs of one vessel by various artists, for these vessels appear to have no subject matter in common. No. 12 belongs with this group because a hand (Glyph 671) immediately precedes the monkey glyph. Bands of stylized heads each with a hand before it which are frequent in Copador pottery (e.g., Longyear, 1952, Fig. 104f) may represent copying and recopying of the 220.755 compound, but there is a rare deity with hand before his face. The "3" outline on the sides of the faces of several indicate that these represent spider monkeys (Thompson, 1939, p. 145). Others show crests.

Use of the monkey to represent the day sign Ahau is well illustrated at Palenque (Ruz 1, B13–14) and as a substitute for the normal kin sign on Lintel 48, Yaxchilán.

See also under Glyph 576.

GLYPH 756 (Bat)
(264 Examples; Sheets 447–58; Gates' Glyph 29; Zimmermann's Glyph 722)

	a	b	c	d

230.			*a¹	Month sign Zotz' on monuments
231.			*a[504]	Month sign Zotz' in Dresden
227.			*	Sayil Str. 3B1, Gl. 5
81.			*	Quir. P, E2
86.			*a	Yax. L. 10, A8
67.			*a	Cop. H.S. Gxiig
69.			*	Cop. H.S. Gxii, i
137, 255.			*a	P.N. 12, Capt., Gl. 50; 40, B15
261².			*	Chajcar carved vase. Dieseldorff, 1926–33
153.			*	Pal. T. 18, stucco
64, 12.			*[528]	Cop. M, B8; H.S. Gxiim
244.			*[544]	Pal. Inscr. E. Q1
217².	1.		*	Xculoc
253.	1.		*	P.N., L. 3, C′5
193–195.	1.		*:568	Beyer 150; 151; 162
196–201, 214.	1.		*.568:23	Beyer 152–57; 386
179.	1.		*:?	Xcalum. S. Build., E. inner pan., C2
97.	12.1:		*[568]	P.N. 15, C8
184.	12.		*	Kuna L. 1, N6
79.	16?:		*.116	Cop. T. 21a, G
91, 92.	19:		*	P.N., L. 3, Y′; F′
105.	21?.		*.177:?	Cop. 6, C4
151.	24:		*a[544]	Pal. stucco gl. in Mus.
68.	32[239]:		*a	Cop. H.S. Gxiif
65.	35:		*[528?]	Cop. 8, F3
8.	38.		*	Cop. M, B7
232.	38.		*[528]	Full fig. Cop. D, B7
39.	38?:		*:60?	R. Amarillo 1, E1
31.	38 or 40?.		*[528]:130	Cop. T. 11, Step 18

135.	58.	*	P.N. 12, Capt., Gl. 33
96.	58.60?.	*	P.N. 12, D3
88.	59:	*.177	Yax. L. 2, H1
224.	60 or 62.	*	Chajcar pottery frag. 52–1–51
178².	61:	*a	Xcalum. I.S. build., Lt. Col. A2.
168², 170.	61.	*	Nar. 12, H1; 14, G1
174, 175.	61.	*[568]	Calak. 51, F3; G4
176.	61.	*	Calak. 9, F1
119.	61.	*	Pal. death head, A1
133, 134, 139, 141, 235–238.	61.	*	P.N. 12, Capt., Gl. 9, 35; 13, E1; F1; 6, Gl. C; F; I1, J1
173, 240, 241.	61.	*	Motul 2, A1; D1; H
264.	61.	*[568]	Aguatec. 7, G1
127–132, 138, 234, 239, 154, 155.	61.	*[568]	P.N. 12, Capt., Gl. 1, 15, 24, 27, 39, 42; 15, C9; D1; 6, K1; Thr. 1, A1; F1
123, 124, 126.	61.	*[568]	Yax. L. 26, G'1; L. 45, U1; L. 46, H''
164.	61.	*[568]	Bonam. 1, H1
256, 257.	61:	*[568]	La Mar 1, D1; D8
117.	61:	*[568]	Cop. Z, C1
118.	61:	*[568]:136	Pal. 96 Gl. L4
140.	61:	*[568]	P.N. 13, E5
247.	61.	*[568]	Lacanhá 7, F1
142.	61.	*:568	P.N., L. 4, Z1
202.	61.	*:568	Beyer 158
120.	61:	*[568?]	Cop. R'', A1
166.	61.	*.1?	Amel. 1, B3
180.	61:	*.?	Xcalum. I.S. build., Lt. L. E.
191, 192.	61 or 62.	*	Beyer 148; 149
218².	61?	*	Xculoc Cent. lint. A
210³.	62.	*.7:7	Beyer 382
211³.	62:	*.7.7	Beyer 383
242.	65?:	*:130?	Cop. T. 21a, Gl. P
189.	74.	*	Beyer 146
243.	74?.	*	Halal main build., N. lint. E
253.	83?.1:	*	P.N., L. 3, C'2.
181, 182.	IV:84:	*[95]	Yax. L. 21, B7; C6

171.	Head.86:	*[?]	Tik. 5, D8
78.	95?.	*[528].?:?	Quir. M, C4
110–112.	95?.	*[528]:200	Quir. J, C14; D, A19; D19
113.	95:	*[528]	Quir. F, B9
114⁴.	95:	*a.117	Quir. B, Block 17
107.	59.102.	*.528	Cop. T. 11, Step 3
144, 146, 148.	109:	*a	Pal. Ruz 2, D2; E1; Scribe 2, A6
145, 147.	109:	*	Pal. Ruz 2, F4; G2
245, 246.	1?109:	*[281]	S. José carved tripod jar (twice)
150.	109:125:	*a	Pal. T. 18, stucco
90.	115:	*:2	Yax. 19, C2
143.	115.	*a[544]	Pal. Ruz 1, P13
149.	115?.	*[544]	Yax. 12, H3
43.	?.117:	*[528]	Quir. E, D17
93.	122.178:	*	P.N. shell plaque, K3
167.	125:	*:?	Nar. 12, C7
157.	125.	*.116	P.N., L. 3, Y4
122.	125.	*a[95].116	Yax. L. 18, A4
177.	125?.	*	Cop. T. 11, reused stone
158.	125.23:	*a	Bonam. 2, F1
252.	125.	*?a	Yax. L. 18, A4
116.	126:	*a	Cop. U, U5
172.	126:	*	Jonuta 2, A1
125.	126:	*a:23	Yax. L. 1, G4
169.	126.	*:?	Nar. 12, J1
42.	126:	*:?	Quir. Alt. O, S2
249.	126.	*[122?]	P.N. 40, B18
206, 207.	126.23:	*	Beyer 378; 379
208², 209.	126:23:	*	Beyer 380; 381
121.	126.	*[95?].116	Yax. 12, D4
250.	126.?:	*	P.N. 8, B15
136.	150.	*a	P.N. 12, Capt., Gl. 22
109.	155?.	*	Cop. 12, B14
29, 40.	168:	*	Cop. Rev. Stand, F′1; R′′, C2
38.	168:	*a	Cop. 9, C7
55.	168:	*	Quir. Alt. P, U2
159.	168:	*a.23	Bonam. 2, G5
59.	168:	*a.4:25	Yax. Str. 44, S.E. step Y7
60.	168:	*.4?:25	Yax. 18, A8
3, 11.	168:	*[528]	Cop. R, L2; Z, D2

45, 48.	168:	*[528]:126: 130	Quir. E, B15; B20
17², 18.	168:	*[528].130	Cop. U, H3; W1
37.	168?:	*[528].130	Cop. Alt. of I, Gl. G
28.	168?:	*.130	Cop. Rev. Stand J
7.	168:	*[528]:177	Cop. P, E4
52, 54.	168:	*.177?	Quir. G, F'3; P, Pan. 5
53.	168:	*:177?	Quir. P, D9
248.	168?:	*.177?	Cop. H.S. Frag. Gxiih
44, 47, 51.	168:	*[528]:200	Quir. E, B9; A20; G, X5
50.	168:	*[528]:200?	Quir. F, A13
56.	168:	*.200?	Quir. Alt. P, U1
82, 57.	168:	*:?	Quir. Alt. O, Z1; Str. 1, X'
160.	168?:	*.349.25	P.N., L. 2, Z3
19.	17.168?:	*[528]:130	Cop. U, R1
233.	23.168:	*a	Yax. 4, G7
30.	32:168:	*[528]	Cop. T. 21a, Gl. F
1, 2.	35.168:	*a	Cop. 9, F6; F10
33.	35.168:	*[528].130	Cop. B', B2
6.	35.168:	*.130?	Cop. 10, F6
5.	35:568.168:	*[528]:177	Cop. I, C6
23, 41.	36.168:	*[528]	Cop. A, H4; Md. 2, K2
26.	36.168:	*a[528]	Cop. H.S. Gxiiq
16.	36.168:	*[528].130: 141?	Cop. N, B8
15.	36?.168:	*[528]:130	Cop. N, Ped. Gl. 13
25.	36.168:	*.581:130	Cop. 11, A7
188.	38.168:	*a:130	Bonam. 1, N1
9, 10, 20.	38.168:	*[528]	Cop. 8, A5; E7; U, L4
27.	38:168:	*[528]	Cop. F', D4
24.	38.168:	*[528?]	Cop. G', B5
32².	38?.168:	*[528]	Cop. T, S. A4
21.	38?.168:	*[528?]	Cop. B, B13
49.	38.168:	*[528].130	Quir. J, G5
22.	38.168:	*[528]:130	Cop. A, E10
13, 34.	38?.168:	*[528]:130	Cop. H.S. Gxiic; C', E2
12.	38.168:	*[528]:177	Cop. 1, D4
4, 14.	38?.168:	*[528].177	Cop. K, Q1; 2, B10
36.	59?.168:	*	Cop. V, G1
61.	95.168:	*[528].177	Quir. A, D8
58.	126.168:	*a	Yax. L. 14, F4
183.	IV.168:	*:?	Alt. Sac. 12, D8
260.	?.168:	*[528].177	Cop. H.S. Gxiih

46.	?:168:	*[528]:200	Quir. E, A19
103.	74 or 60?:202:	*a	Cop. P, C8
102.	95.202:	*a	Cop. P, D8
156.	204?.	*:116	P.N., L. 3, A′1
203.	228.	*:568	Beyer 159
213.	228?.	*.?	Beyer 385
216².	232?.	*	Xculoc Center L., A
229.	322:	*	Tort. 6, G8
98.	12.344.	*[568]	P.N. 15, C16
165².	125:60:568.	*	Seib. H.S., R1
212.	738:	*	Beyer 384
95.	1010?.	*[528]	P.N., L. 3, Y2
220.	1030.	*a:595?	Nebaj. Fenton vase, F3
62, 77.	IV.	*[528]	Cop. G1, D3; U, G1
66.	IV?:	*:102	Cop. B, back
251.	XVI:	*[281]	Quir. F, A9
221.	?.	*	Uaxac. monkey & jaguar bowl
63.	?.	*	Cop. 7, B14
73.	?:	*a	Cop. H.S., Step G
74.	?:	*[528]:125	Cop. H.S., Step L
75.	?.	*[528]:125	Cop. H.S., Step S
87.	?:	*.177?	Yax. L. 2, L1
204.	?.	*.568	Beyer 160
205.	?.	*?.568	Beyer 161
263.	?.	*[568?]:136	Yalloch cyl. jar
108.	?.	*.missing	Cop. O′, F5
35.	?.	*:?	Cop. C′, B1
76.	?.	*.?:?	Cop. H.S., Step T
101.		*[528]:23?	Cop. P, F14
190.		*a:71	Beyer 147
225.		*.86?	Chiapa Stone D1
71.		*:87?	Cop. H.S. Gxiin
84.		*a:87?:126	Yax. Str. 44, S.E. Step W2
185–187.		*[544].116	Nar. 30, B10; 24, A14
94.		*:116?	P.N. 40, B16
152.		*?.4:116?	Yax. 18, F3
89.		*[528].125 or 126:?	Quir. Alt. O, O2
80.		*:126	Quir. G, S′2
106.		*[528].177?	Cop. Rev. Stand W
85².		*:25:178?: 177?	Yax. Str. 44, S.E. Step W3

258, 259.	*.181	Tabasco vase
228.	*:192?	Sayil Str. 3 B1, Gl. 10
83.	*[528?]:200	Quir. Alt. of O, L1
99, 100.	*:200	Cop. N, Ped.; 10, D9
222.	*a.219	Cop. carved brown vase, Longyear, 103d.
161–163.	*.349:25	P.N., L. 2, C′3; E′3; I′3
70.	*.568:350	Cop. H.S. Gxiip
262.	*[568?]:142	Yalloch cyl. jar
254.	*.568?	P.N., L. 3, B′8
223.	*.630:?	Pal. T. 4, N. sculpt. stone 1, C1
226.	*:670	Pal. T. 18, stucco
104.	*a[528?].?	Cop. P, C5
215.	*.?	Kuna L. 1, C5
219.	*:?	Iturbide stone, B2
115.	*:?	Quir. G, Q2

1 *a denotes the two-disk element, which is perhaps the same as Affix 7, and is distinguishable in these examples on cheek or on the prominent nose. In many examples it was surely once visible. I am inclined to think this is derived from the same source as the upper part of the Akbal (Glyph 504) sign and indicates darkness or night.

2 In these cases Glyph 568 precedes or follows the bat glyph.

3 These examples have an infix formed of a dot surrounded by circlets, as in Affix 315, on the cheek. It may represent Glyph 528.

4 It is uncertain that Affix 95 belongs with the bat glyph in this surrealist full-figure glyph block.

The role of Glyph 756, a reasonably naturalistic representation of the leaf-nosed vampire bat, is perplexing. Despite its ubiquity on the monuments, it appears in the codices only as the month sign Zotz', which means "bat" in most Maya languages and dialects.

There are two major associations of Glyph 756. One is with Glyph 568, the supposed glyph of sacrifice, and the other with Cauac glyphs (Glyph 528 and Affixes 177 and 200). The Affix 168 with associated Affixes 32 to 40 are often present.

Glyph 568 is rather widely accepted as the symbol of sacrifice. The bat has associations with darkness, the underworld, death and sacrifice; the first group because of its nocturnal habits and predilection for caves, the entrances to the underworld; the second, because of its blood-drinking habits. Seler (1902–23, IV, 464–67) calls attention to the fact that, in the *Popol Vuh*, Camazotz is the death bat who cuts off people's heads, and did that to the hero Hunahpu. In modern folklore the same story exists, but now the victim is Christ, who, like Hunahpu, is in prison awaiting his fate. As Seler notes, a bat god is shown cutting off the heads of victims in Codex Vatican B, p. 24, and Codex Borgia, p. 49, whereas in Codex Fejervary-Mayer, p. 41, the bat deity removes the heart of a sacrificial victim. Crescents (lunar?), crossbones, skulls, and circles adorn the wings of anthropomorphic bats in Mexican and Maya art. In present-day Guatemala the bat, as a blood sucker, is regarded as a sorcerer and is associated with sorcery.

The infixing of Glyph 568 might be explained on the grounds that it served to call attention to the sacrificial associations of the animal, but that explanation would hardly cover those cases in which Glyph 568 appears as a distinct glyph preceding or following Glyph 756.

With Prefix 61 and often with 568, the sacrificial glyph, infixed, the bat glyph commonly stands at the beginning of a subsidiary text, particularly in the case of small incised glyphs. In this respect it functions as does the compound 61–757.

At Copán and Quiriguá the Cauac signs modify the bat glyph, and at Copán, the addition of Affix 168 and its associated prefixes converts the whole into one of Berlin's city emblems. It is of interest to note that the importance of the bat in Copán is demonstrated not only in the hieroglyphic texts. Structure 20 at Copán seemingly was decorated with roof ornaments shaped as bats, perhaps an indication that that building was a shrine of the bat god, a bat personage is prominent on Altar T.

Finally, one may note that the principal god of the Cakchiquels was a bat god called Chamalcán, and the Tzotzil Maya of Chiapas obtained their name, according to a colonial writer, from the fact that they worshiped a bat deity of stone. The Náhuatl name of their chief town, Tzinacantlán, means "place of the bats."

Rare examples of 109–756 at Palenque would be red or great bats, and there are cases of infixing of Glyph 544, the sun glyph, a strange link for the bat, unless one supposes that the association is with the sun in the underworld. In one or two cases the bat sign follows the sun glyph, but I think the juxtaposition is fortuitous. On the other hand, the bat glyph frequently follows Glyph 1030 (e.g., Nos. 8, 14, 16, 44, 46, 49–51, 53, 76, and 78). This is particularly evident at Quiriguá. The bat and vulture glyphs are juxtaposed in a number of cases (69, 110, 113, 114, 148, 149, 159, 161, 162, and 222).

For further examples of Glyph 756, see under Glyphs 568, 630, 670, and 679.

GLYPH 757 (Jog with 281 infixed)
(185 Examples; Sheets 459–70; Gates' Glyph 31b and d [in part]; Zimmermann's
Glyph 708 [in part])

178.		*	Unique personified Muluc. Cop. H.S., Step L
34.		*	Cop. carved brown ware, Longyear, 117a
182.		*	Dos Pilas H.S. 2, D8
30.		*	Xcalum. S. build., E col., A4
103, 145.	1:	*	Cop. P, E12; Rev. Stand M
108–110.	1.	*:24?	Yax. 12, E1; L. 14, D1; G1
71, 148.	1.	*	Cop. I, C5; Court marker A2
79, 83.	1:	*	Yax. 11, H3; L. 32, C1
84, 179.	1.	*	P.N., L. 12, V1; L. 3, C'5
86.	1:	*	Pusil. E, D3
98.	1:	*	Calak. 51, C2
99.	1.	*	Calak. 9, G1
97.	1.	*	Moral. 1, I1
87, 91.	1.	*	Nar. 24, E7; 13, A5
35.	1.	*	Acanceh tomb mural
184.	1:	*:23	Tamar H.S. 2, G15
142–144.	1.	*:24	Yax. L. 15, C1; L. 17, A1; D1
155.	1.	*:88	Cop. 10, H3
139.	1.	*:88:126	Full fig. Cop. D'
53, 54, 58.	1.	*:106	Cop. U, S5; B, B8; O', H2
59, 73.	1.	*.106	Cop. R'', C3; Z, D3
55.	1:	*:106	Cop. A, C9
66.	1.	*:136	Caribe 1, A3
107.	1:	*:142	Yax. L. 24, D'1
94.	1.	*:142	Nar. 21, A3
60.	1.	*:279	Yax. 18, C2
93.	1.	*:?	Nar. 20, A3
82.	3.	*:136	Yax. L. 26, J'1
81.	11:	*	Pal. Cross, E3
181, 185.	11.	*	Dos Pilas 11, A1; 3, C1

172.	11.	*:103 or 102	Quir. Alt. P, T1
149.	12:	*	Cop. court marker, A3
56, 65.	13.	*	Alt. Sac. 4, C8; D5
85.	13.	*:23?	Seib. 7, B4
61.	13:	*:85	Cop. 10, F4
77.	13.	*.279?	Cop. H′′, A1
62.	1:24:	*:27?	Cop. 1, D1
64.	?.12:	*:60	Seib. 12, A4
146.	25.	*	Pal. I.S. pot, G3
147.	25:	*	Quir. J, D18
151.	25:	*	Pal. 96 Gl. J4
36.	60:	*	Pal. X site, 1, B1
124, 126.	60:	*	Yax. L. 10, B2; D1
118.	60?.	*	Quir. Alt. O, M1
136.	60:	*.181	Tik. L. 3, G5
183.	60:	*.181:142?	Carac. 3, D12b
130.	1.60:	*	Yax. L. 13, E1
132.	1.60:	*	P.N. 1, G10
133, 134, 89, 90, 92.	1.60:	*	Nar. 22, A3; 30, A3; 29, F16; 13, G1; 22, B1
138.	1.60:	*	Tik. Alt. VIII, A1
125, 131.	1:60:	*	Yax. L. 3, D1; 7, C6
95.	1.60:	*	Ixkun 1, K1
67.	1.60:	*	Nebaj. Fenton vase, B1
135.	1.60?:	*	Nar. 2, A1
28.	1.60?:	*	Xcalum. S. build., E. jamb, A6
119.	1:60:	*:142	Yax. L. 24, Y1
120.	1.60:	*:142	Yax. L. 53, E1
88.	1.60:	*.?	Nar. 24, E3
31.	1.60:	*.?:56	Xcalum. N. build., Frag. D′
152, 168.	1.60?:	*?	Bonam. Rm. 2 above chief; above Batab
123.	11.60:	*	Yax. 10, G1
127, 129.	13.60:	*	Yax. L. 1, E1; L. 2, F1
106.	13.60:	*:142	Cop. O′, A1
179.	13?.60:	*	La Mar 2, A1
117.	60.60:	*	Quir. J. D6
19.	113.60:	*	Pal. Ruz 1, A12
63.	135?.60:	*:27	Yax. 11, V1
170.	74.184.60:	*	Pal. 96 Gl. D6
121, 122.	204.60:	*	Yax. Str. 44, Mid. Step C13; L. 33, C1

137.	204.60:	*	Tik. 5, D5
18.	204.60:	*	Pal. Ruz. 1, C14
174.	204.60:	*[219?]	Pal. Creation, A2
80.	230.60:	*	Pal. Sun, C11
128.	1024.60:	*	Yax. L. 1, B2
72.	61?.	*:60	Sacchaná 2, C3
74.	65:	*.181	Cop. H.S., Step G
116.	1:65:	*:24	Quir. E, C18
70.	1.65 or 176?:	*	Cop. T. 11, S. door, E. pan., A4
69.	204.24?.65:	*:88?	Cop. 4, B8
105.	89?.	*?	Cop. T. 11, S. door, E. pan., D3
33.	90.	*:60	Beyer 387
13.	92.	*	Pal. Sun, M2
21, 22, 168.	92:	*	Pal. Ruz 2, A5; C2; T. 18, stucco
24.	92.	*.88	Pal. I.S. pot, H1
150.	1.92:	*?	Yax. 7, C8
7, 12, 20.	92.1:	*	Pal. Cross, S16; Fol. E4; H.S., A6
27.	92.1:	*?	Quir. G, E'4
1, 11.	92.11:	*	Pal. Cross, E8; Fol. N3
5, 8.	92.11?:	*	Pal. Cross, S6; U3
9.	92.11:	*[526?]	Pal. Cross U17
153.	92:60:	*	Pal. Ruz 1, Q6
14, 17, 25.	92.60:	*	Pal. Inscr. W. F4; Ruz 1, O19; frag.
26.	92.60:	*	Quir. J, F6
29.	92.60:	*	Xcalum. N. build., Frag. D'
15.	92.168?:60:	*	Pal. Inscr. W. T9
2–4, 6, 16.	92.204:	*	Pal. Cross, Q1; P8; P16; R12; Ruz 1, P2
10, 23.	92.?:	*	Pal. Cross, M1; House E mural, I''
32.	109?:	*	Xcalum. N. build., W. Col. A3
162[1].	112.	*[504]	M. 39a
163.	112.87:	*[504]	D. 10a
169.	121:	*	Pal. T. 18, stucco
154.	287?.122.	*	Nebaj. Fenton vase, D3
115.	168:	*	Pal. Ruz 2, D2

167.	168:	*	P.N., L. 3, O′
171.	74.184.	*:?	Chinikiha Thr. 1, B′1
104.	204:	*	Cop. P, E6
75.	204.	*	Cop. T. 22, Step 6
100.	204.	*	Calak. 9, C1
96.	204?.	*	Ixkun 1, C1
141.	204?.	*	Yax. L. 39, A4
78.	205.	*	Pal. Fol. G1
159.	234.	*	D. 9a
160, 161.	234.	*:140	D. 10b; 11b
156–158.	234.	*[504]	D. 3a; 8a; 36a
166.	234.	*[504]:?	D. 4b, on monster
112.	333.	*:126	Quir. J, H3
113.	333.	*:?	Quir. F, A12
114.	1.333:	*	Quir. F, C17
111.	333.513af:	*	Quir. E, B12
102.	513af:	*	Cop. B, B3
175, 176.	513.117.116:	*:116	Pal. T. 18, stucco
140.	?:669.	*	Full figure, Cop. W′, E1
57.	1000 full fig..?:	*:60	Cop. H.S., Step O
173.	?.?:	*	Cop. T, B4
76.	IX.?.	*	Cop. T. 22, Step 13
180.	1.XIII:	*	Cop. Ball Crt., marker Mid. lower
40.	XVIII:	*	Cop. A, C10
39.	XVIII:	*?	Nar. H.S., A2
51.	XVIII.1:	*	Cop. H, D3
46.	XVIII:1:	*	Quir. A, D10
41.	XVIII.1:	*:142?	Cop. 11, B4
48.	XVIII.1?:	*	Quir. J, G4
47.	122.XVIII:1:	*	Quir. E, B19
37.	1.122.XVIII:	*	Cop. B, B2
44.	122.XVIII:	*	Cop. H.S. frag.
38.	XVIII.122.	*	Cop. 4, B9
43.	122.XIII or XVIII:	*	Cop. H, D3
49, 50.	13.XVIII:	*	Quir. F, B12; E, A13
42.	XVIII.13.	*	Cop. 6, D6
45².	XV:204:	*	Cop. H.S., Step U
165.		*[504].25:585	D. 74a
68.		*.88:125	Cop. 6, D8
164.		*.103	D. 57b

| 101. | *.350 | Cop. K, K₁ |
| 177. | *:308? | Quir. Str. 1, Miscell. Gl. 13 |

¹ The infix of this and numbers 156–158, 160, 161, 163, and 165 is the top half of Glyph 504.
² The tread of the step may be worn so that three dots at the top may have been worn away.

Glyph 757 is distinguished from Glyphs 758–761 by the infixing of Affix 281 and, except for the few examples in Dresden codex, by the tongue hanging out of the mouth.

The identification of the animals represented in Glyphs 757–761 is very difficult. I am inclined to think that Glyph 757 represents a dog, an identification which the lolling tongue would support. Sometimes these glyphs approximate the standard Maya representation of the jaguar. Indeed, Tozzer and Allen (1910, Pl. 35, No. 6) say of an example of Glyph 757, "Glyph, probably of a jaguar head." Other small animals can also be claimed as the originals of these glyphs. In order not to prejudice future discussion, I use the term "jog," a combination of jaguar and dog, for ready identification.

Glyph 757 has Affix 1 prefixed to it more often than any other Maya glyph, and it will be noted that when a number is attached, the u-bracket, if present, may lie between number and main sign, something not encountered with calendrical glyphs. It appears probable that the u-bracket has a phonetic value—perhaps the first syllable of a word.

The 90–757 compounds appear in regular phrases at Palenque, usually following a 58–713 or 679–58–713 compound. The 60–757 compounds very frequently stand at the beginning of a section, in the same way as does the 60–756 (Bat) compound.

At Naranjo, Glyph 757 appears in clauses which usually include the 178–569 compound and/or Glyph I–606. This association with I–606 occurs also at Yaxchilán, Tikal, Palenque, and Pusilhá.

At Quiriguá, Glyph 757 occurs in combination with Glyph 1030, the long-nosed god.

The frequent appearances of Glyph 757 after a C.R. may be significant. All in all, this glyph offers possibilities for successful investigation.

See also under Glyph 712.

GLYPH 758 (Xul)

(201 Examples; Sheets 471–77; Gates' Glyph 31 [in part]; Zimmermann's Glyphs 707 and 708 [in part]).

	a	b	c
161.		*	M. 10c
110.		*	Alt. Sac. 13, D5
183.		*	Pal. Olvidado, stucco
38, 114, 115.		*[110]	Pal. death head, H1; T. 18, stucco, Y3; Z2
67–70.		*[110]	P.N. Alt. 2, B3; L. 3, S'2; U'2; 12, Capt. 25
76.		*[110]	Moral. 2, A10
80.		*[110]	Xcalum. N. build., W. corbel
199.		*[110]	Jade head, Br. Mus.
81.		*[110]	Huehuetenango I.S. vase, C2
128.		*[110?]	P.N. 8, A9
134.		*[110?]	Uaxac. I.S. vase, Gl. 15
201.		*[220]	Tort. 6, A10
135.	1:	*[110?]	Cop. O', C4
132.	1.	*[110?]	Chinkul. marker, Gl. 13
104^1.	1:	*?:24	Yax. L. 25, G1
92.	1:	*:24?	Quir. F, B8
52.	1.	*?:110	Cop. T. 21a, Gl. H
137.	1:	*:126	Quir. E, A10
48.	1:	*[110]:136	Yax. L. 10, D6
93.	1:	*:246	Quir. F, A13
102.	1?:	*:142?	Quir. D, B19
91^2.	1.?:	*:130?	Quir. J, C11
9.	3.	*[526]:126	Pal. 96 Gl. A3
131.	11.	*:103	Quir. Alt. P, T1
106^1.	12.	*:23	Yax. L. 13, C5
118.	12.?:	*	Sacchana 2, E2
158.	13.	*:103	D. 3a
11.	13.	*[526]:126	Pal. Creation, D2
13.	13.	*[526]:126	Quir. C, A15
18.	13.	*:130?	Quir. M, C2

[355]

2.	21.	*	Cop. 6, D1
83.	24.	*[110]	Nebaj vase, Neg. 42–9–626
151.	33.	*.181	D. 22b
47.	1?.60:	*[110?]	Yax. L. 10, D4
107.	60?:1:	*	Quir. F, B14
90.	61?.	*?:116	Nar. 21, A9
171.	62.	*	M. 72a
6.	79?.	*	Pal. Ruz 1, F19
74.	89:	*[110].89?	Tik. Alt. V, Gl. 4
7, 14, 19.	93.	*	Quir. D, D18; A23; H, P1
16, 20.	93:	*	Quir. F, C9; P, C5
23.	93.	*	Bonam. 3, B3
39.	109.	*:110	Pal. Creation, E1
200.	109.	*:110	Peto jaguar vase, Gl. 3
79.	109:	*[110]	Xcalum. I.S. build., Lt. lint., H
45.	109.	*:missing	Pal. T. 18, stucco
193, 194.	110.	*	Alt. Sac. 4, C8; D6
94.	110.	*[110]	R. Hondo blowgun bowl
99.	1.110:	*:142	Tort. 6, G2
182.	181:110:	*	P. 2c
56.	110?:	*:130	Pal. Sun, M3
149.	112.	*:?	P. 6d
162.	112.	*.?	M. 34d
144, 145.	112.87:	*	D. 19c; 49d
142, 143.	112.87:	*	P. 3b; 4b
146, 147.	87.112:	*	D. 47d; f
148.	87:	*:112	P. 2c
138.	118.	*	Cop. N, B3
29.	141:	*	Chama. Carey vase, E4
8.	153.	*:130	Pal. Sun, D16
159.	166.	*	M. 71b
141.	168:	*.110	D. 20b
133.	204.187:	*	Pal. Str. 18, stucco. Not Gl. B
117.	1.187:	*[110] or :110	Glyph B of lunar ser. Usual form
163.	190.	*	D. 2a
164–166.	190.	*	P. 2d; 8d; 11d
167.	190:	*	P. 5d
168.	190.	*?	M. 61c
123.	198?.	*:246.	Yax. L. 29, D4
10.	204.	*	Pal. H.S., C1

24.	204.	*	Nar. H.S., M2
25.	204.	*:126	Tik. T. 4, L. 3, C2
130.	204.	*:126	Sacchana 2, D3
12.	204.	*[526]:126	Quir. A, C3
98.	204.	*[110]:?	Cop. Md. 2, Step J1
28.	204?:	*:?	Cop. H.S. Gxiid
124.	213?.	*	Bonam. 1, O1
22.	229.	* ?:116 or 260?	Yax. 21, H8
108.	232.	*[526]:126	P.N., L. 3, V10
179.	234.	*	M. 93a
180.	234.	*?	M. 22c
181.	234.	*:?	P. 22a
172.	1?.234.	*:186	D. 22c
174–177.	283.	*	M. 43a; 46a; 80c (twice)
173.	283.	*.103	D. 29b
178.	1.283.	*	M. 43c
125.	125.323?.	*	Tonina T. 42
188.	542:671.	*:528	P. 2b
100.	565af.	*:188	Pal. 96 Gl. J1
126.	16:580:	*[181?]:25. 125?	Pal. Ruz 1, C10
129.	580.	*?	P.N., L. 3, F'
186, 187.	589.	*	D. 5b; 6b
26.	607.	*:126?	Beyer 592
27.	126.607:	* ?:246	Beyer 593
169.	?.736:	*:110	P. 10c
189–191.	1047.	*:186	P. 3b; 3d; 4c
84.	I:	*:110	Pal. T. 18, jamb A11
85.	I:	*:110	Quir. K, C2
87.	I:	*:110	Yax. 11, C'9
88.	I.	*:110	Yax. 1, F6
86.	I.	*[110]:110	Yax. L. 30, F5
89.	I.	*:missing	Pal. T. 4, N. stucco
72.	IV.	*:110	P.N. 12, C10
192.	228.V:	*?	Pal. Inscr. W. Q9
185.	IX.	*.59	M. 70b. Bolonyocte
195.	IX.32.	*	La Mar 1, B11
50.	?.	*[110]	Cop. 7, F8
97.	?.	*:110	Holmul tripod bowl, Gl. 13
196.	?.	*:110	Pal. T. 18, stucco
3.	?:	*	Cop. H.S., Step T
37.	?:	*	Pal. House C, D3

127.	?.	*	Pal. Ruz 2, F5
197.	?.	*	Tabasco vase, Villahermosa Mus.
4.	missing	*[110?]:126	Cop. H.S., Step P
109.	?:	*?	P.N. 39, B9
5.	?.?:	*	Cop. H.S., Step W
170.		*.96	M. 35d
103.		*?:65?	Moral. 2, E1
30, 31, 43, 44, 54, 55, 57, 61, 77, 78, 111, 112, 116.		*:110	Pal. Ruz 2, D4; F8; T. 18, stucco (twice); Fol. D5; G3; Inscr., M. 28; Ruz 1, E9; T. 18, Tab., A18; B13; Fol. jamb, B9; T. 18, stucco; incised shell
40.		*:110	R. Amarillo Alt. 1, H2
41, 46.		*:110	Yax. L. 56, I2; L. 45, U4
42, 49, 51.		*:110	Cop. U, E1; K, L2; W', E2
65, 66, 73.		*:110	P.N. Thr. 1, A'5; S1; 23, H7
75.		*:110	Jonuta 2, A4
95, 96.		*:110	Bonam. Rm. 1, attiring, 2nd batab; Rm. 2, above 3rd batab
82.		*:110	Chama. Carey vase, F3
17.		*:110?	Quir. G, R'2
136.		*:110	Nar. H.S., K3
32–36, 53, 58²–60, 62, 113.		*.110	Pal. House C, A3; B3; C3; E3; F3; Fol. C2; Ruz 1, C8; C17; E11; K8; Lt. scribe
152–157.		*.110	D. 20b (twice); 23a (4 times)
71.		*.110	P.N., L. 3, personal gl.
64.		*[110]:110	Yax. 7, D5
63².		*.188:110	Pal. Ruz 1, K13
184.		*.116	Month sign Xul on monuments
101.		*[526].126	Cop. T. 22, Step 3
15.		*[526?].126	Quir. D, D20
198.		*:126:181:?	Cop. G², A2
1.		*.130?	Cop. 6, D2
21.		*?.?:142	Quir. I, D7

139, 140.	*.181	D. 22b (twice)
120, 121.	*.181:47	D. 58e (twice)
150.	*.181:96	P. 8d
160.	*.181:251	D. 39b
122.	*[181?]:178?	Pal. House C, Eaves A2
119.	*:513af.	Cop. K, L1
105.	*[526]: missing?	Pal. detached stucco

¹ These examples have a protruding tongue.
² Glyph 526 follows, perhaps of significance in view of the examples (758b) with Caban infixed.

Infix 7, a very characteristic feature of Glyph 758 on the monuments, is not always visible. In many cases this is because of erosion, but in a few examples it probably never was carved. In almost all cases Glyph 758 can be distinguished from Glyph 757 by the absence of Infix 281 (Kan cross) and protruding tongue, and by the usual presence of Affix 7. Glyph 110, either as affix or infix, is very commonly added to Glyph 758, but is practically never found with Glyph 757. A rare exception is perhaps supplied by Glyph B on Quiriguá Stela E (east side), which is represented by Glyph 757, complete with protruding tongue and 281 (Kan cross) infix, but with Postfix 110. The glyph is thus drawn in Maudslay (1889–1902). Available photographs and a cast of the monument are not sufficiently clear to settle the point. If Maudslay's drawing is correct, this may supply an example of an error by the sculptor in copying the priest's drawing. There is a well-known error on the other face of this stela, where twelve tuns are recorded instead of thirteen tuns as demanded by the calculation.

In the codices the top part of the Akbal sign (Glyph 504) normally is painted on the animal's forehead, replacing Infix 7, and giving us a good indication that Affix 7 probably has the same meanings of darkness and night. That the change of infix does not alter the meaning can be deduced from the fact that that shift takes place in representations of the month sign Xul. In some cases the lower jaw is omitted. The identification of these "jog" heads in the codices is not easy; the grouping I have made is fallible.

For further examples of Glyph 758, see under Glyphs 539, 559, 560, 561, and 582.

GLYPH 759 (Jog with Etz'nab)
(70 Examples; Sheets 479, 480; Gates' Glyphs 126, 127; Zimmermann's Glyph 706)

a   b

69.		*	P.N. Thr. 1, E1
67, 68.		*	Holmul cyl. jar, Gl. 6; 12
1, 2.		*	P.N. 16, D5; L. 3, S'1
70.		*?	P.N. 12, Capt. 7
4.	1.	*	D. 14a
25.	1.	*:25	P. 11d
5.	1:	*:?	Carac. Stone 56
22–24.	10.	*	D. 14a (twice); 15a
10.	16.	*	Pal. Ruz 1, P3
3.	16:	*	Bonam. 2, I1
9, 11.	16.	*	Cop. H'', B1; 3, A7
14, 15.	16.	*?	Naachtun 8, A11; 9, E1
13.	16.	*?	Quir. H, M1
12.	16.	*:103	Quir. J, D8
7.	16:	*:103	Cop. A, E9
6.	35.125?:16.	*	Beyer 136
16.	126.16.	*	Beyer 135
18–20.	16.133:	*	Beyer 132–34
17.	16.133:	*:?	Beyer 137
21.	133.16:	*	Beyer 131
53, 54.	109:	*	D. 46b; 46c
55.	23.85:	*	D. 39c
56.	IV.85:	*	D. 40c
58, 60.	IV.85:	*	P. 3b; 7d
57.	IV.	*.85	D. 44a
59.	IV.	*.85	P. 7b
61.	IX.	*	D. 41c
62.	XII.?:	*	M. 91a
63, 64.	165.64:	*.165	D. 61a; 69f
66.	?.	*:?	Cop. 1, C4
26–52, 65.		*.181:25	D. 4a–10a (20 times; some obliterated); 4b–5b (7 times); P. 7b

The distinguishing features of the "jog" animal (see under Glyph 757) are hairs or fur behind the mouth. The Etz'nab infix may be set in the ear or at the back of the cheek or, in the cases of Nos. 67 and 68, around the eye; or, in the case of No. 69 and perhaps No. 70, in a sort of shield above the head. The wide distribution of examples with the yax (No. 16) prefix is of interest.

GLYPH 760 (Jog with fins)
(5 Examples)

5.		*	Chajcar carved vase. Diesel-dorff, 1926–33
1.	16.	*	P.N., L. 3, M'
2.	16.	*?:?	Cop. F, B7
3.	501.544:	*	P.N. Thr. 1, D'5
4.	501:544.	*:102	P.N. Thr. 1, Z3

The three examples from Piedras Negras almost certainly are highly conventionalized representations of fish with a fortuitous resemblance to the "jog" group of glyphs. The barbule on the face of No. 5 is very clear.

GLYPH 761 (Pseudo Jog)
(34 Examples; Sheets 481, 482)

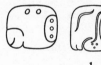

a   b

33.	44:	*	Cop. Q., beneath Fig. 12
25–27, 29.	44:	*:59	Quir. Str. 1, E'; R'; W'; D, C19
19.	44:	*:102	Cop. R, L2
30.	44?:	*?:102	Carac. Alt. 12, I7
11, 12, 15, 20, 23, 24.	115.44:	*:59	Quir. F, A14; G, Z2; I, B8; D, D22; P, Cart. 8; 12
14.	115.44?:	*:59	Quir. K, D7
21, 28.	115:44:	*:59	Quir. P, C7; Str. 1, Miscell. Gl. 3
22.	115?:44?:	*:59	Quir. P, E1

32.	501.44:	*?	Bonam. Rm. 2, smashing fingers
10.	115:	*:59	Quir. J, F7
1–5, 7, 18.	115.	*:59	Cop. U, K4; G', A5; 9, D7; 8, B3; L, E1; T, N. 10; bone ornament
13, 16.	115.	*:59?	Quir. P, Cart. 5; I, C4
6, 9.	115:	*:59?	Cop. Z, D2; R'', C2
17.	?:115:	*:59?	Quir. Str. 1, Miscell. Gl. 10
8.	115.?:	*?	Los Higos 1, C2
34.	115.1?:	*:?:59	Cop. O', C1
31.	126:	*?:?	Cop. H.S. Gxiil

Some examples are symbolic; others are personified. A distinguishing characteristic, only visible in the best-preserved examples is the oval containing three punctate marks on the extreme right of the glyph. Both at Quiriguá and at Copán, Glyph 761 generally follows Glyph 561 or a compound of which Glyph 561 is a component.

GLYPH 762
(26 Examples; Sheets 483, 484)

18.		*	Pal. H.S., A6
6.	184:	*	Pal. Fol. N17
12, 23.	184.	*	Pal. Inscr. E, T11; death head 7
24, 25.	184.	*:142	Pal. Fol. balustr. I1; Cross balustr. I1
1, 7, 13, 19, 27.	74.184.	*	Pal. Cross, O13; Fol. E5; Inscr. W. M2; H.S., C6; T. 4N. sculpt. stone 2, B1
2–5, 8–11, 14, 20, 21, 22.	74.184.	*:142	Pal. Fol. L9; M13; N4; N13; F5; Sun, N12; P9; N3; Inscr. W. S10; Pier f; Cross, I2; Sun shrine (Waldeck), B1
26.	74:184:	*:142	Pal. Fol. jamb, A10
16, 17.	74.184.60:	*:142	Pal. Ruz 1, R7; R17
15.	74.544:25?: 60?:	*:142	Pal. Ruz 1, M12

No. 18, one of the two examples which lack the 184 prefix, is preceded by Glyph 544, the kin sign, affording evidence that Affix 184 has the same value. This is confirmed by No. 15, which has the combination 74–544.

This creature which defies zoological classification appears in clauses, usually in immediate association with the compound 168–779 or 110–539. The glyph is confined to Palenque.

GLYPH 763
(1 Example; Gates' Glyph 212; Zimmermann's Glyph 715)

1.   *.62   D. 39c

GLYPH 764 (Chicchan snake)
(114 Examples; Sheets 487–93)

a   b

100.		*	Day Chicchan on monuments
36.	1:	*	Yax. L. 43, C3
76, 78.	1:	*:106	Yax. L. 25, A3; W1
81.	1:	*:106	Caribe 1, B2
27.	1:	*:106?	Yax. L. 26, M'1
95.	1.	*:108?	Bonam. 2, G2
30.	1.	*:150?	Yax. L. 33, H1
28.	1.?:	*	Yax. L. 33, A9
8.	4:	*	Yax. L. 15, E1
86.	4?:	*:?	Cop. 10, H4
93.	118?.4:	*	Cop. N, B2
103, 104.	11:	*	Dos Pilas H.S. 2, A4; B5
75.	13.	*.106	Cop. 6, D6
88.	25?.	*	Cop. H'', B3
46.	4.25:	*	Yax. L. 1, F2
82.	25.	* or 1030	Pal. Ruz 1, D10
9.	48:	*	Pal. Sarcoph., Gl. 12.

26.	12?:58.	*[188?]	Yax. L. 26, I′1
85.	93.117?:	*	Cop. U, N3
10.	228?.94?:	*	Yax. L. 13, F1
5, 11–13, 18, 20, 25, 31, 34, 40, 41, 47, 53, 55, 56, 61, 63, 65, 66.	1.108:	*	Yax. 12, E4; L. 53, C2; Str. 44, S.E. Up. Step Y3; Mid. Up. Step C5; 21, G7; 2, G9; 18, E3; L. 32, A6; 20, A1; 15, C1; L. 6, B4; L. 2, O1; L. 13, F1; L. 8, B1; 11, E3; 5, B2; 1, E11; 13, G1; 23, A13
70, 71.	1.108:	*	P.N., L. 4, N2; V1
1, 2, 4, 6, 14, 16, 21, 22, 24, 32, 48–51, 57, 58, 67.	1:108:	*	Yax. L. 56, L1; L. 27, H1; 12, C4; L. 41, D5; Str. 44 11, E2; I2; 3, A5; 10, L2; Mid. Up. Step D6; D5; L. 10, C3; C7; E4; B6; 7, C4; D4; 6, C7
108.	1.108:	*	Aguatec. 2, F5
113.	1.108:	*	Bonam. L. 2, D1
39.	1.108?	*	Yax. 15, B4
79.	1.108:	*:106	Yax. 11, Z6
80.	1:108:	*:106	Yax. 11, A′3
15, 54.	1.108:	*:106?	Yax. Str. 44, Mid. Up. Step C6; L. 46, F″7
77.	1.108?:	*:106	Yax. L. 24, C′1
109–112.	11:108:	*	Aguatec. 1, B5; A9; B13; D4
17, 19, 29, 35, 37, 43, 45, 64.	13.108:	*	Yax. 21, H5; G8; L. 33, A11; L. 54, D1; L. 42, G2; L. 3, G2; L. 1, A9; 1, E12
59.	122:108?:	*	Yax. Str. 44, Mid. Up. Step D4
23.	204.108:	*	Yax. L. 9, B5
52.	204:108:	*	Yax. L. 10, A3
33.	226.108:	*	Yax. 11, Y5
42, 44.	232.108:	*	Yax. L. 3, G1; L. 1, A7
3.	232.108:	*:106	Yax. 12, B4
101.	232:	*:23	Poptun Sculpt. Frag. 2
72.	116:	*:106	Cop. T. 22, Step 7
84.	122.	*.23	Cop. A, D9
83.	122.128:	*	Cop. A, C6

62.	122.?:	*?	Quir. L, Gl. 4
7.	168:	*	Yax. L. 16, E1
99.	25:36.168:	*:130	Cop. A., H5
69.	101.168:	*	P.N. 36, D2
68.	228:168:	*	Pal. Inscr. W. L10
102.	202?.	*	Samintaca vase
60.	204:	*:?	Yax. 19, C1
114.	204.?:	*	Calak. 9, D5
90–92, 98.	11.212:	*	Pal. Cross, F13; F17; P2; Pan., I1
89.	1.229?:	*	Cop. 3, A8
105.	831?:21.	*.17	Dos Pilas H.S. 2, D4
97.	II:	*?:178?	Xcalum. I.S. build., Rt. Col. A5
96.	IV:	*?:178?	Xcalum. I.S. build., Lt. Col. A8
94.	?:	*	Bonam. 2, I2
87.	?:	*	Cop. R, I2
106, 107.	?.?:		Dos Pilas H.S. 2, E6;
		*?	Sculpt. C, A6
38.	?.	*:350?	Quir. J, C18
73.		*:106	Cop. T. 22, Step 9
74.		*.106	Cop. 6, D3

Chicchan, corresponding to the Aztec Coatl, is the day of the snake, and the word survives among the Chorti as the name for certain snake deities of the rain. As the long-nosed god, God B, is derived from a snake and is a deity of rain, it is not surprising that weathered examples of Glyph 764 and of the portrait glyph of the long-nosed god (1030) are not always easily separated. The characteristics which distinguish the Chicchan glyph from Glyph 1030 are the hatched supra-orbital area, the shorter nose, the serrated teeth, and absence of earplug and hole in forehead. Glyph 764 is distinguished from Glyph 765 (black-spotted dog) by shape of nose, horizontal mouth, serrated teeth, and absence of ear.

The many examples of Glyph 764 at Yaxchilán appear in clauses which ring the changes on some eight glyphs (Thompson, 1950, Fig. 46, Nos. 10–17).

See also under Glyphs 683 and 744.

GLYPH 765 (Black-spotted Dog)
(80 Examples; Sheets 485, 486; Gates' Glyph 10; Zimmermann's Glyph 707)

	a		b	c	d

			c	d
1.		* or *[7]	Day sign Oc
71¹.		*[623]:130 or 23	variant for kin
18–27.	14.	*:103	D. 62c; e; f; 63a; b; c; 66a; 70b; c; d
46.	14.	*:135	D. 61c
60.	16:23.	*	D. 33c
36–41.	33.	*.103	D. 42c; 43c; 44c; 45a; 45c; 51a
42–45.	33.	*:135	D. 53b; 54a; 54b; 58a
17¹.	35?.	*:59:178?	Yax. L. 10, A4
63.	53.35:	*:135	Tik. T. 4, L. 3, D6
28.	58.	*:103	D. 65a
15¹.	109:	*:59	Yax. L. 10, D3
4.	113.	*:59	Pal. Sun, F2
3.	113.	*:188	Pal. Sun, Q16
2.	113.	*[7]:188	Pal. Sun, Q3
33–35.	115.	*:103	D. 24b; 24c; 33b
7.	115.	*:116 or 117	Tik. L. 3, C7
65, 66¹.	115.	*[544]:116	Pal. Inscr. M. H10; E. S6
6.	115.	*[544]:116	Quir. A, C11
5.	115.	*:59	Pal. Cross, Pan. E2
69.	115:	*[544?]	Nar. 13, D5
76.	1.115.	*.87:188	Yax. L. 25, H2
72¹–74¹.	122.	*[544?]:116	Nar. 23, H19; 30, B6; 21, F10
75¹.	122.	*:53?	Nar. 23, E15
29.	166.	*:103	D. 44a
54.	268.	*.103	D. 58b
59.	501:140.	*:103	D. 65a
64.	565a.	*[7]:188	Pal. Fol. G2
62.	589.	*	D. 5b
10.	679af.	*[7]:188	Pal. Sun., Q13
53.	1022.	*:103	D. 62B
48–50.	1027.	*:103	D. 61d; f; 62d

51, 52.	171.1027.	*:103	D. 61e; 62a
67, 68.	1051.	*[544]?	Beyer 389; 390
79, 80.	IV:	*	Pal. Inscr. W. S3; Sarcoph. Gl. 43
11, 12.	IX.	*:59	Bolonyocte. Pal. Inscr. W. P1; H.S., D5
78.	220.IX.	*:?	Tort. 7, C5
55.	IX.	*:59	P. 7d; 8b
56, 57.	IX.	*.59	D. 60a; 60b
58.	IX.33.	*:59	D. 68a
13[1].	IX.	*.138:59	Pal. House C, eaves
14[1].	IX.	*	Pal. Sarcoph., jade earplug
63[1].	IX.	*?	Uaxac. sherd 3982
77[1].	IX:	*[544]:116	Quir. F, A9
70.	?.?:	*?	Yax. 29, A2
16[1].		*:59	Yax. L. 10, A3
9.		*:59	Pal. Sun, P8
30, 31.		*:103	D. 58b; 66a
32.		*.103	D. 32b; 58e
61.		*.96:103	D. 65a
47.		*.181:96	P. 8d
8.		*.181:131?	Tuxtla Mus. carved shell

[1] Black orbital area not now recognizable.

This member of the "jog" family is distinguishable on the monuments from Glyph 764 by the absence of teeth, the upward sloping mouth, and the pointed nose. The characteristic feature, shared with Glyph 764, is the black (cross-hatched on the monuments) supraorbital area or, rarely, large spots on forehead or cheek. In some cases the hatched area is not now recognizable, and in a few cases probably was never present. This is particularly true of the 765–116 compound often with 544 infixed. Later investigation may assign these a new number. The jog with Infix 623 (crossed bones) in the eye, a form used to signify "day," seems to belong here, although the black area is absent. On the other hand, bones have the same symbolic value as black in denoting associations with the underworld (Thompson, 1950, pp. 168 and 280).

Nos. 78 to 80 are enclosed within cartouches, and so have the appearances of being day signs, but they do not function as such.

GLYPH 766
(11 Examples; Gates' Glyph 243.1; Zimmermann's Glyph 740)

| 1-8. | | * | D. 54a?; b; 55b; 56a?; b; 72b; c; 73c |
| 9-11. | IV. | * | D. 71c; 72a; 73a? |

GLYPH 767 (Water lily)
(4 Examples; Sheet 363)

a   b

1.	1:	*b	Tonina 30, A5
2.	744a.	*a	Pal. T. 18, C18
4.	744a.	*b	Pomona N. Md. frag.
3.		*a?	Pal. T. 18, C19

See also under Glyph 501.

GLYPH 768
(3 Examples)

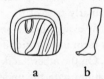

a   b

1.	1:248[552].	*a	Tik. T. 4, L. 3, F4
2.	204.248[552].	*a	Tik. T. 4, L. 3, F7
3.	228.	*b.?.23	Beyer 470

The examples from Tikal appear to represent human legs.

GLYPH 769 (Uayeb semblant)
(32 Examples; Sheets 355, 356)

a   b

	a	b	
4.	4.59?:	*.181	Cop. T. 11, W. door, S. pan., B5
5.	4?.59:	*	Cop. H.S., Frag. Gxiid
7.	65:	*:126	Cop. O', A2
24.	92?.4:65:	*	P.N. 40, C13
9.	65?.	*:246	Cop. Alt. O, E5
28.	65.119?:	*:178	Tik. 5, A13
14.	86:	*[580]:178	Quir. J, D17
15.	86:4:	*:178	Quir. F, B14
26.	95.86:	*:178?	Kuna L. 1, I5
13.	168?:95.86:	*:178	Quir. A, C9
8.	?.86:	*	Cop. 13, C2
25.	19.86?:	*:178?	P.N., L. 2, J1
22.	86?:168:	*:130	P.N. 12, D19
21.	86?:168?:	*[178]	P.N. 12, D10
18.	?:?:	*[178]:130	P.N. Thr. 1, B'5
16.	127?:	*?	Yax. L. 47, E6
3.	132:	*:125	Cop. 10, E8
31.	132?:	*	Cop. H.S. Gxiim
19.	168:	*:130	P.N. Thr. 1, S1
30.	168:	*.?	Pal. Inscr. tomb, jade earplug
23.	220?.168:	*:130?	P.N. 8, A15
20.	220?:168?:	*	P.N. 12, A14
27.	747baf.168?:	*	Amel. 1, C3
17.	1029.168:	*	Yax. L. 10, C6
11.	1.206?:	*:126	Cop. J, C5
6.	IV.1010.	*:548	Cop. H.S., Step 4.
29.	1014?.?:	*	Tik. 16, B2
10.	1019.	*:48?	Cop. Md. 2
12.	1019:58:	*:674?	Pal. House C, Found. D1
1.		*.126	Cop. A, H11
2.		*:126	Cop. A, G12
32.		*:130	Uxmal altar drum, rim

Glyph 769 resembles the better preserved examples of the Uayeb (157) affix (notably, that at S2, Ruz 1, Palenque) so closely that I believe it may be merely an enlarged version of the latter.

GLYPH 770
(1 Example)

1.	328.61.	*	Blowgun bowl (Blom)

GLYPH 771
(1 Example)

1.	74:	*:142	Xcalum. N. build., E col., A4

GLYPH 772
(2 Examples)

1.		*.19	Leyden Plate A8b
2.		*.357?:?	Leyden Plate A9b

GLYPH 773
(1 Example; Sheet 310)

1.	1.129:	*.24:56	Xcalum. N. build., W. col., A2

GLYPH 774
(13 Examples; Sheet 364)

1.	188?:	*:57	Yax. L. 37, S7
2.	316?.	*	Yax. L. 22, B7
5.	351:	*:184	Carac. 3, C18b
3, 4.	351:	*:184:74	Carac. 3, C13b; C16a
6.	351:	*.184:74	Carac. 3, C20b
8, 9.	351:	*.184.74	Nar. L. 1, B1; F4
10.	351:	*:184:74	Nar. H.S., V2
7.	351?:	*?:184?:74?	Carac. 3, F7
11, 12.	351:	*:?	Nar. H.S., C1; T2
13.	351:	*.?	Carac. 1, F3

Glyph 774 is not always easily distinguishable from Glyph 683, the moon glyph. The compound at Naranjo and Caracol supplies another link between those two sites.

GLYPH 775
(3 Examples; Sheet 364)

1, 2.		*	Cop. F', D2; D3
3.		*?	Quir. E, D17

GLYPH 776
(4 Examples; Sheet 361)

1, 2.	?:	*	Cop. H.S., Step C; Step L
4.		*?	Cop. H.S., Step J
3.		*?:130	Cop. H.S., Step C

GLYPH 777
(2 Examples; Sheet 367)

1.	45?.188:	*	Cop. F′, B3
2.	59.45?.86?:	*	Cop. F′, C3

Glyph 777 has the appearance of an affix rather than a main sign, but it is not recognizable elsewhere as an affix.

GLYPH 778
(7 Examples; Sheet 367)

4.	36.168:	*	Tik. 21, A1
1.	36?.168:	*:130[125]	Tik. 16, C1
5.	36.168:	*?	Dos Pilas 2, C6
2.	38?.168:	*	Tik. 5, D13
6.	38?.168:	*	Aguatec. 2, F7
3.	40.168:	*	Tik. T. 4, L. 3, C1
7.	?168?:	*?	Tik. 17, F9

In three cases Glyph 778 follows that of the long-nosed god; in the fourth example (No. 4) the preceding glyph is missing. No. 5 also follows the long-nosed god. Glyph 778 may be a variant of Glyph 716.

GLYPH 779
(1 Example)

1.	*	Uaxac. bowl. Morley, Petén, Pl. 178E

GLYPH 780

(11 Examples; Gates includes with Glyph 141; Zimmermann includes with Glyph 167)

1–2.	1.	*	M. 88b (twice)
3–6.	1.	*:*	M. 87b; 88b (thrice)
7–11.	667:	*	M. 38a (twice); 39a (thrice)

See under Glyph 667.

GLYPH 781
(1 Example)

1.	79:	*.181:24?	Cop. Alt. of St. 13

GLYPH 782
(1 Example)

1.	?:	*	Yax. L. 18, A2

GLYPH 783
(1 Example)

1.	544.*:330.	*.330	Carac. 6, E19

GLYPH 784
(1 Example)

1.   *   M. Cow shell disk

GLYPH 785
(12 Examples; Sheet 51a)

a   b

207.	122.84:	*	Uxmal Monjas capstone
1.	210?:	*	Pal. Cross, F14
2.	1:I:	*	Yax. L. 10, D4
206.	I:84:	*	Pal. Blom Tab. 1
201–205.	I.84:	*	Pal. Cross, C8; C16; Inscr. M. M9; Ruz 1, E10; H15
3.	1:II:	*	Yax. L. 10, B2
4.	V:	*:?	Yax. L. 10, C5
5.	VI:	*:88?	Yax. L. 10, E3

The examples from Yaxchilán show considerable variation. All six examples from Palenque precede Glyph 1011 (god with fish attributes).

GLYPH 786
(1 Example)

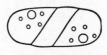

1.   44:   *   Cop. L, C1

The shape suggests an affix (cf. Affix 257, which it closely resembles), but the flattening may be due to spatial considerations as the glyph is beneath a seated figure.

GLYPH 787
(1 Example)

1.   *:59?:260?   Cop. H.S. Gxiif

This should be compared with rare symbolic forms of the day sign Eb (Thompson, 1950, Fig. 8, Nos. 58, 63).

GLYPH 788 (Jaguar with angular jaw)
(26 Examples)

9–12.	1.	*	Uaxac. mural, A1; C1; D1; E1
24, 26.	1:	*	Tik. 31, I1; M1
1–3.	3:	*	Uaxac. Tzakol stucco jar
4, 7, 8.	3.	*	Uaxac. Tzakol stucco jar; mural D1; G1
5.	11.	*	Uaxac. mural, lower part
13–21.	11?.	*	Uaxac. mural, A7; C1; D4; F1; H1; I1; J1; N1; P1
6.	60:	*	Uaxac. Tzakol stucco jar
22.	213.	*	Uaxac. mural C5
25.	?:	*	Tik. 4, B4
23.		*v	M. Cow celt, B6

All examples are of early Classic period. Conceivably the example on the celt is Olmec. The day sign, perhaps the local equivalent of Ix, on the Formative period stela at Kaminaljuyu belongs with this group. Heads are generally more naturalistic than in the illustration.

GLYPH 789

(2 Examples; Gates' Glyph 243.2; Zimmermann's Glyph 741)

1.	*	D. 47b
2.	*:?	D. 47a

Occurs with the Venus directional gods. Note Etz'nab infix as with Glyphs 759 and 766.

GLYPH 790 (Bird head)

(29 Examples; Gates' Glyphs 244, 245, 267; Zimmermann's Glyphs 743, 744, 1363b)

1–9.		*	D. 52b; 53a; 54a; b; 55a; b (twice); 57a; 61b
10, 11.		*	M. 20a; 34c
13.		*	P. 2b?
14.	48.	*	D. 54b
15.	49:510.	*	D. 52b
16.	49:510?.	*	M. 66a
17.	63:	*	P. 6b
18–21.	63:	*	M. 38a; 39a?; 87a; 88a
22, 23.	64:	*	M. 90a; 92d
24–27.	64:	*	D. 51b; 55b; 56a; 56a?
28.	207.	*	D. 61a
29.	281.	*	P. 5b
12.		*.23	D. 69c

Perhaps these should be treated as three glyphs, as Gates and Zimmermann have done. The black infixes, which all have, are the main reason for grouping all examples under one number.

GLYPH 791 (Upturned Snout 1)
(7 Examples; Zimmermann's Glyphs 730, 732, 733)

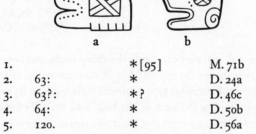

	a	b	c
3, 4.		*	M. 94c; 95c
7.		*?	D. 16c
6.		*.1	M. 11a
1, 2.	47	*:24	D. 17b; 17c
5.	91 or 90:	*	P. 6c

Nos. 1–4 are shown by their accompanying pictures to represent birds; whether Nos. 5–7 are of the same feather and should flock together is not certain.

GLYPH 792
(5 Examples; Gates' Glyphs 261.1, 262, 264; Zimmermann's Glyphs 720, 721)

	a	b	c
1.		*[95]	M. 71b
2.	63:	*	D. 24a
3.	63?:	*?	D. 46c
4.	64:	*	D. 50b
5.	120.	*	D. 56a

In No. 2 the second stroke of the St. Andrew's cross in the eye is not visible.

GLYPH 793 (Upturned Snout 3)
(38 Examples; Sheets 495, 496)

	a	b
38.		*a Cop. 7, A10
34.		*a Pal. T. 18 Tab., A15
37.		*a? Variants I.S. intro. gl. Zac & Cumku

36.	1.	*b(vert.)	Pal. Inscr. E. N10
15, 27, 30.	74:	*a	Pal. Inscr. E. M5; Ruz 1, Q7; Ruz 2, C4
28.	142:	*a:23	Pal. 96 Gl. C6
24.	36[43].168:	*a	Pal. Ruz 1, H7
5, 8, 11.	37.168:	*a	Pal. Cross, O15; Fol. L14; K1
9, 14, 20, 21, 31.	38.168:	*a	Pal. Fol. O4; Sun, D13; Inscr. M. L2; W. I6; Cross, W. jamb, I7
10.	38.168:	*a:142	Pal. Fol. F6
22, 32.	38?.168:	*a	Pal. Ruz 1, C13; House E mural, L'
25, 26.	38[43].168:	*a	Pal. Ruz 1, N12; O12
12.	40.168:	*a	Pal. Sun, O12
4, 7.	40.168:	*a:130	Pal. Cross, E15; Fol. M9
35.	?.168:	*a:140	Pal. Pal. sculpt. frag.
1–3, 6, 13, 16–19, 29, 33.	348:	*b	Pal. Cross, C1; F3; F8; Fol. D10; Sun, C13; Inscr. E. O1; O5; R6; R8; Pal. House A, over door; T. 18 Tab., C12
23.		*b:?	Pal. Ruz 1, C9

Form b lacks the curl at corner of mouth, the sharp teeth, and lower jaw. Instead, it has the peculiar elements in the mouth. Affixes vary according to type, for almost all of type b have Affix 348, whereas type a attracts Affix 168 and its associates. However the finlike projections at the back of the head and barbules behind the mouth make it evident that both types represent the same aquatic creature.

For a variant form of Glyph 793, see under Glyph 575.

GLYPH 794
(8 Examples; Gates' Glyph 251; Zimmermann's Glyph 719)

1–6.		*a	D. 43b; 44b; 45b (thrice); 68a
7, 8.	190.	*b	D. 71a; 72a

The so-called Mars beast, but almost certainly a symbol of meteorological conditions (Thompson, 1950, p. 258).

GLYPH 795 (Deer haunch)
(9 Examples; Gates' Glyphs 291 and 4.31; Zimmermann's Glyph 761)

1–4.		*	D. 23b; 29a (picture); 35a (picture); 41c
5.		*	M. 106b
6.		*:103	M. 105b
7.		*:103:135	D. 28c
8.		*:103:135	M. 8c
9.		*:506	D. 30b

GLYPH 796 (Deer)
(5 Examples; Gates' Glyph 4.31, 201c; Zimmermann's Glyphs 711, 712, 717)

1.		*	P. 10b
2.		*	M. 92d
3.	96.	*?	P. 17b
4, 5.		*:506	M. 77d; 78e

GLYPH 797
(2 Examples; Gates' Glyphs 394, 395)

| 1. | | * | M. 36, B17 |
| 2. | 25: | * | M. 36, C17 |

This probably represents a fish tail. The affix with the second example may belong with the previous glyph.

GLYPH 798
(3 Examples; Gates' Glyph 293.4; Zimmermann's Glyph 763)

1.		*:*.*	D. 27c
2.	VII.	*:*.*	D. 26b
3.		*:109.544	D. 25c

An unidentified sacrificial food.

GLYPH 799 (Iguana)
(12 Examples; Gates' Glyph 280; Zimmermann's Glyph 760)

1.	*	M. 3b
2.	*:24?	P. 8d
3–5.	*:506	D. 29b; 29c (picture); 30b; 43c (picture)
7.	*:506	P. 16b
8.	*:506	M. 107b
9.	*:506:103	M. 77
10.	*:506?:103?	M. 78
11.	*:506:686	M. 6a
6.	*:506:686	D. 43c (picture)
12.	*:686	M. 105c

GLYPH 800 (Jaguar)
(10 Examples; Gates' Glyphs 201, 202; Zimmermann's Glyph 710)

1.		*	P. 2c
2, 3.	109.	*	D. 8a; 47e
4.	109.	*	M. 41a
5.	109:	*	M. 14b

6.	109:	*	P. 7c
7, 8.	172.109:	*	D. 24c; 26b
10, 11.	IV.	*	M. 40c (twice)

Black spots are prominent, but there are no tusks and lower jaw is poorly made or absent.

GLYPH 801 (black-spotted dog)
(4 Examples; Gates' Glyphs 201d, 204, 206; Zimmermann's Glyphs 709, 713)

1, 2.		*	M. 2a; 91d
3.	I.	*	P. 24
4.		* ?	M. 2b

Note in this connection the form of Xul in the codices with black marking around the eye.

GLYPH 802
(5 Examples; Gates' Glyph 50.2; Zimmermann's Glyphs 124, 716, 727)

1.		*	D. 56a
4.		*	M. 52a
2.		* :533	D. 66a
3.	548.	*	D. 51b
5.	?.	* ?	M. 26a

Distinguished by the unusual eye marking. The features of No. 2 differ in other respects markedly from the others.

GLYPH 803
(2 Examples; Gates' Glyphs 247, 248; Zimmermann's Glyph 746)

1.	*[584?]	P. 4d
2.	*[679]	D. 70c

No. 2 probably serves as a numerical coefficient, perhaps 5 or 13, of the katun sign immediately below it.

GLYPH 804
(2 Examples; Sheet 404; Gates' unassigned; Zimmermann's unassigned)

1.	544:	*.612af	D. 51b
2.	IX.511:	*?	Beyer 476

GLYPH 805
(2 Examples; Sheet 361)

1, 2.	*.1	Chajcar pottery boxes

GLYPH 806
(2 Examples; Gates' Glyph 266; Zimmermann's Glyph 1363c)

1.	1.23:	*	D. 57b
2.	181.	*	M. 86c

Distinguished by the unusual eye markings.

GLYPH 807
(2 Examples; Sheets 402, 403)

1.	VIII:84:	*.23	Quir. E, B21
2.	59.IX:	*:23	Yax. 18, C6

These are suggestive of symbols for completion, but that does not seem to be their function.

GLYPH 808
(1 Example; Gates' Glyph 371)

| 1. | ?.233: | * | P. 5, B2 |

GLYPH 809
(1 Example; Gates' Glyph 369)

| 1. | | * | P. 4, B7 |

The right element is here drawn as a kin, but there is a certain doubt about this.

GLYPH 810
(1 Example; Gates' Glyph 389)

| 1. | 84: | * | M. 37, B15 |

GLYPH 811
(1 Example)

1.		*:276?	M. 35d

GLYPH 812
(11 Examples; Gates' Glyph 355; Zimmermann's Glyph 730a)

1.		*	M. 20c
2.	1.	*:47	M. 20c
3, 4.	25.	*:47	M. 92c (twice)
5.		*.1	M. 111c
6.		*.181?	M. 111c
7–11.		*.181:47	M. 83b (thrice); 102b (twice)

GLYPH 813
(2 Examples)

1.		*:25	Uaxac. Str. BXIII mural, lower part
2.		*:?	Uaxac. Str. BXVIII mural, lower part

GLYPH 814
(1 Example)

1.	116:	*	Cop. T. 11, E. door, N. pan., C3

[384]

GLYPH 815
(2 Examples)

1.	116.59:25:	*:125	Pal. Tower Scribe 2, E4
2.	116.109?:25:	*:125	Pal. Tower Scribe 1, A4

GLYPH 816
(1 Example)

1.	130:	*:129	Cop. tripod jar, Longyear, 1171i''

GLYPH 817
(1 Example)

1.	233v	*	Uaxac. sherd, R. E. Smith, Fig. 81s

GLYPH 818
(1 Example; Sheet 405)

1.	*.116.	Bonam. Rm. 1, bottom right of 3 batabs

GLYPH 819 (Eye)
(6 Examples; Sheet 501)

6.	88:	*:229	Carac. 3, C12a
5.	88?.154.	*:?	Pomona frag.
1.	154.	*.88	Cop. 6, C1
2.	154.	*:145	Pal. Tower Scribe Tab. 2, B1
3.	154.	*P:12?	Carac. 19, Frame 5
4.	237:	*	Cop. T. 11, S. door, E. pan., D2

Affix 154 forms an inseparable part of the compound. The two picture an extruded eye. It should be noted that there are other examples of the plucked-out eye, notably in the lunar series of Copán N and Ruz 1. These are discussed by Thompson (1952, p. 62). Affix 237 variant is certainly closely related to the concept of the extruded eye, for it represents a vulture pecking out an eye. There is a Maya term, *"col ich,"* "pull out an eye," and a term *"colop u ich kin"* is common in the books of Chilam Balam, perhaps a name for the sun god. No. 4 is in a horizontal position. Glyphs D1 and C3, before and after it, are heads of death gods.

GLYPH 820 (blood offering)
(7 Examples; Sheet 407)

1–3.		*	Yax. L. 13; L. 14; L. 25, in bowls held by priests
7.	122.	*?	Arenal polychrome jar
4.	132?:	*	Yax. L. 14, G2
5.	III.132?:	*	Yax. L. 13, F3
6.	?	*?	Yax. L. 25, Gl. B

No. 3 is partly obscured by the blood-spattered papers in the bowl. No. 6 may be Glyph 568 (sacrifice). It is very difficult to make out details of this glyph, and some of the details in the drawing may be incorrect.

GLYPH 821
(3 Examples; Sheets 406, 415)

3.	229.	*:126:130?	Xculoc, N. lint., E
1.	?:	*:125	Xcochkax jamb frag.
2.		*.9:125	Xcochkax jamb frag.

GLYPH 822
(1 Example; Sheet 405)

| 1. | | * | Xcocha frag. in milpa |

The fret may be an affix in this unusually rectangular glyph.

GLYPH 823
(1 Example; Sheet 417)

| 1. | ?.64: | *:142 | Pal. T. 18 Tab., C4 |

GLYPH 824
(2 Examples)

| 1. | 340:315: | * | Pal. Sarcoph., Gl. 12 |
| 2. | | *?:23 | M. Cow shell disk |

GLYPH 825
(4 Examples; Sheet 420)

1.	92?.XII or XI:	*	Cop. 13, E9
2.		*?.116	Cop. 7, D12
3, 4.		*?:116	Cop. 13, E3; E7

Detail of the interior of this glyph is not entirely clear.

GLYPH 826
(1 Example)

1.	IX.	*:295v	Iturbide capstone, Seler

This appears to be a name-glyph of God K. It appears at the back of a portrait of God K on a painted capstone photographed many years ago by T. Maler. See Glyph 707.

GLYPH 827 (Bird)
(1 Example; Sheet 430)

1.	32.	*	Xcocha frag. in milpa

Distinguished by the flare at the back of the eye. This occurs also with Glyph 802 and very rarely with Glyph 743.

GLYPH 828
(1 Example; Sheet 432)

1.	125.343:	*	Yax. L. 18, C3

GLYPH 829
(10 Examples; Gates' Glyph 31e; Zimmermann's Glyph 718)

| 1–9. | 90. | * | M. 22b; 23b; 89d (4 times); 90d (thrice) |
| 10[1]. | 90. | * | M. 22b |

[1] Face downwards.

This glyph serves as the action glyph of an almanac.

GLYPH 830
(1 Example)

| 1. | 501. | * | Yax. L. 18, D2 |

GLYPH 831
(2 Examples)

| 1. | | * | Quir. E, D20 |
| 2. | III.125: | * | Pal. Cross, E4 |

For a dubious example of Glyph 831, see under Glyph 764.

GLYPH 832 (headless jaguar)
(5 Examples; Sheet 358)

4.	59.339?:	*	Yax. L. 32, E1
1.		*:302v	Pal. Sun, D2
2, 3.		*:339	Yax. L. 47, H3; 18, B1
5.		*:339?	Tik. 3, D3

GLYPH 833
(1 Example)

1.   354.1:   *.58   Cop. 11, A4

GLYPH 834
(1 Example)

1.   11.   *   Pal. Fol. M3

GLYPH 835
(1 Example; Gates' Glyph 387)

1.   *   M. 8d

Somewhat similar elements in Mexican art suggest this may represent falling rain.

GLYPH 836
(1 Example; Gates' Glyph 366)

1.   *:23   P. 6b

GLYPH 837
(1 Example)

1.	177	*:?	M. 34c16

GLYPH 838
(1 Example)

1.		*:2	Arenal polychrome jar

GLYPH 839 (Turkey)
(10 Examples; Gates' Glyph 292; Zimmermann's Glyph 762)

1.	*	M. 109b
8.	*:506	M. 105b
2.	*:506	D. 30b
7.	*:506:506	M. 104b
3.	*.506	D. 41c
10.	*:506:686	D. 28c
4.	*.506vert.	M. 107b
5.	*:686	M. 8
6.	*:?	D. 23b
9.	*:?	M. 106c

In these cases which for the most part appear in pictures, turkey is being offered as sacrificial food either alone or in preparations served with maize, such as tamales, as the presence of Glyph 506 makes clear. In some cases the dish in which the food is served is indicated (Glyph 686).

GLYPH 840
(1 Example)

1.	*.220:?	Pomona Br. Honduras jade earplug

GLYPH 841
(1 Example)

1.	*	Cop. Ball Crt. I.S. intro. gl.

A unique form of the I.S. introductory glyph. Unfortunately, there is no information on the uinal with which it is associated. The glyph is reminiscent of the 712[504] glyph.

GLYPH 842
(1 Example)

1.	?.44:	*	Tula shell plaque

GLYPH 843 (step)
(5 Examples)

1.	32.	*	Tik. 31, E5
57.	45.	*:126	Xcalum. I.S. build., lt. col.
49.	197.	*	Beyer 625
46.	614:115.	*	Beyer 563
47.	614:115.	*.59?	Beyer 562

Except for No. 1, all examples give the appearance of being exaggerated forms of Glyph 515. Indeed, the associated affixes support that attribution.

GLYPH 844
(6 Examples)

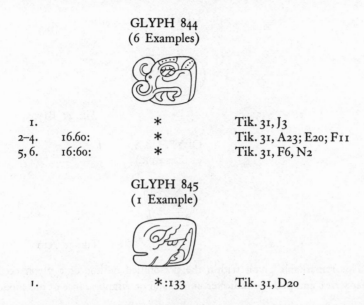

1.		*	Tik. 31, J3
2–4.	16.60:	*	Tik. 31, A23; E20; F11
5, 6.	16:60:	*	Tik. 31, F6, N2

GLYPH 845
(1 Example)

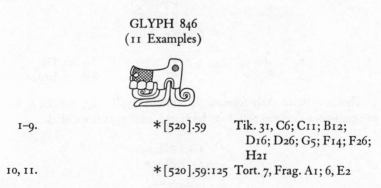

1.		*:133	Tik. 31, D20

The lightly incised details which distinguish this glyph are visible only on the excellently preserved Stela 31; other examples may elude identification because of weathering.

GLYPH 846
(11 Examples)

1–9.		*[520].59	Tik. 31, C6; C11; B12; D16; D26; G5; F14; F26; H21
10, 11.		*[520].59:125	Tort. 7, Frag. A1; 6, E2

This glyph appears to have calendric significance, for all its appearances (except G5 and Nos. 10 and 11, where the preceding glyphs are missing) follow Cauac glyphs or the tun and katun signs. The infixing of the uinal sign reinforces this conclusion. In the case of the example at F14, two glyphs intervene between the count of the year glyph (513–528) and Glyph 846. No. 10 precedes a C.R. date; No. 11 immediately follows one.

GLYPH 847
(1 Example)

1.   233:   *   Tik. 31, B17

GLYPH 848
(1 Example)

1.   1.   *   Tik. 31, A10

This remarkable glyph within the personified outline of a glyph occurs in a lunar series, and perhaps indicates new moon or disappearance of old moon.

GLYPH 849
(2 Examples)

1.   168:59.   *   Tik. 31, D6
2.   ?.359:   *   Tik. 31, E10

This may be an early form of the vulture glyph (747) for the *ti* affix (59) is present in one case and both have hachured areas to indicate black.

GLYPH 850
(1 Example)

1.   VII.359:   *   Tik. 31, E17

GLYPH 851
(1 Example)

1.   60:   *   Tik. 31, G23

GLYPH 852
(1 Example)

1.   VIII: *:125   Tik. 31, E7

The presence of a cartouche and Postfix 125 as well as an attached number suggest that this is a day sign. If that is the case, the day sign involved is not at present identifiable.

GLYPH 853
(2 Examples)

1, 2.   44:   *   Tik. 31, C14, C24

The upper part of the sign closely resembles Affix 109, but this resemblance may be fortuitous.

GLYPH 854
(1 Example)

1.   366:   *   Tik. 31, O1

The lower part of the glyph is an inverted sky (561) sign.

[395]

GLYPH 855 (Katun substitute)
(1 Example)

| 1. | 1.XVIII: | * | Aguatec. 1, B2 |

This glyph follows a record of 11 Ahau 18 Mac, which ends the eighteenth katun. In view of its position, the presence of a numerical coefficient of 18, and the absence of any regular period-ending glyph, the conclusion appears inescapable that the compound is to be read as "eighteenth katun."

GLYPH 856
(3 Examples)

1.	16?:	*	Aguatec. 2, G7
2.	17.115?.VII.	*	Aguatec. 1. D8
	511:		
3.	59:	*:140	Aguatec. 1, D10

Glyph 576 might be a variant of Glyph 856.

UNIDENTIFIED MAIN SIGNS

1300-1347

Many of the signs in this group, numbered 1300 onwards, are too indistinct to be identified with certainty or to be drawn. Others are of a nondescript nature, but have been included because of rare affixes attached to them. Glyph 1333 looks Maya (see Glyphs 679 and 561), but the jade figure on which it is incised most definitely is not Maya. Most of these glyphs are placed in this sort of purgatory in the hope that eventually they may be fully identified through the unearthing of better-preserved examples, and thereby promoted to full rank in the catalog with new numbers in the 800's.

173:	1300:178	Cop. B, A13	Sheet 406
?.1:173:	1301	Cop. S, Gl. F	406
?.	1302.?:89	Nar. L. 1, C2; E4	407
101.168:	1303	P.N. drum frag.	407
101.168:	1303.130?	P.N. drum frag.	407
	1304	Beyer 120. Monkey?	
	1305:23	Nar. 23, G5; G6	408
	1306:?	Nar. 13, E11	408
1.	1307:23	Ixkun 2, C2	408
VIII.?:	1308:23?	Alt. Sac. 4, A9; D8	408
VIII.?:	1309:102	Ixlu Alt. of 2, D2	408
	1310	Pal. H.S., D2	409
	1311:119?	Yax. L. 25, U2	410
	1312:136	Yax. L. 15, G3, rt. half	410

53.	1313:142	Pal. Inscr. W. C9	411
74?:	1314.181:246	P.N. 8, B19	316
229.	1315	P.N., L. 2, E′2	414
XVII.?:	1316	P.N., L. 3, B′′1	420
XVII.	1317:116	Nar. 23, F11	420
?:	1318	Cop. Rev. Stand Gl. T	420
11.XVIII?:	1319	Xultun 18, A4	421
1000.	1320:533	Pal. 96 Gl. J8	
?.116.86:	1321	P.N. 3, C4	
86:	1322.184	Tik. 5, A7	
333:	1323:?	Beyer 622	
	1324	M. 28c3. A crow?	
XVI.	1325	P.N. 40, A16	420
228.	1326:103:126	Chama bat vase, Seler, B1	
229.	1327:25	Chama bat vase, Seler, A1	
103?.	1328:136	Chama bat vase, Seler, B2	
307.	1329:?	M. 22d3	
336:	1330:130	Beyer 137	
356:	1331.181	Tik. 12, D2	
347.	1332.87	Yax. L. 18, D1	
	1333	Seville jade. Perhaps Olmec gl.	
68:	1334.59	Jade head, Br. Mus.	
IV?.	1335	Mayapán shell, Gl. 1	
II.	1336	Mayapán shell, Gl. 3	
60.	1337:23	Yalloch cyl. vase	
154?.	1338.?	Hondo jar, Gl. D. Seler Fig. 27	
32:	1339.181	Tik. 31, C21	
203.?:	1340.?:23	Tik. 31, K1	
V:	1341	Cop. 7, A13	503
1.	1342	Covarrubias *sub judice*, B2	
367.	1343	Covarrubias *sub judice*, A3	
?.539:	1344 (affix)	Covarrubias *sub judice*, A4	
12.?:	1345	Kuna L. 1, N4. Variant of 544??	
	1346:130?	Kuna L. 1, N3b	
17?:	1347	Aguatec. 2, G3	

CONCORDANCE WITH ZIMMERMANN'S GLYPH NUMBERS

AFFIXES

("Z" designates Zimmermann's numbers; "T," those used in this book)

Z	T	Z	T
1	1	20	109
1a	10	21	58
2	13	22	95
3	15	23	281
4	172	24	17
5	234	25	12
6	115	26	207
7	137	27	166
8	286	28	238
9	194	29	277
10	15	30	33
11	X	31	112
12	14	32	110
13	152	33	190
14	147	35	90
15	171	36	146
16	164	37	51
17	70	38	122
18	336 & 298	40	42

Z	T	Z	T
41	63	64	138
42	168	65	136
43	239	70a	186
43a	31	70b	163
44	69	71	96
44a	73	72	59
45	124	73	62
46	145	74	126 & 47
47	233	75	74
48	296	76	130
49	49	77	85
50	287	78	136
51	155	79	23
52	159	80	24
53	66	81	25
54	256	82	87
55	162	83	114
56	266	84	140 & 251
57	285	85	93
58	60	85a	327
59	62	86	99
60	181	87	120
61	104	88	326
62	116	90	20
63	140	91	19

MAIN SIGNS

100	227	114	1056
101	542	115	1025
102	680	116	1014
103	702	117	1014
104	301	118	1030[614]
105	1059	119	1065
106	1003	120	1047
107	1014	121	1063
108	1027	122	1060
109	1026	123	1055
110	1028	124	802
111	1005	125	1030
112	1050	126	1006
113	731	127	1038a

Z	T	Z	T
128	1038b	707	765
129	1053	708	758
130	1037	709	801
131	1016	710	800
132	1053	711	796
133	1039	712	796
134	1039	713	801
135	1064	715	763
136	1024	716	802
137	1022	717	796
138	1022	718	829
139	1062	719	794
140	1010	720	792
141	755	721	792
142	755	722	756
143	1054	723	743
144	1058	724	743
145	1057	725	743
146	1009	726	626
147	682	727	802
148	1047	728	none
149	1048	729	737
150	1049	730	791
151	736	730a	812
152	736	731	613
153	509	731a	612
154	1052	732	791
160	671	733	791
161	670	734	744
162	1028	735	748
163	713	736	747
164	221	737	970
166	669	740	766
167	667	741	789
169	668	742	1020
700	734	743	790
701	735	744	790
702	588	745	742
703	684	746	803
704	731	750	747
705	648	751	236
706	759	752	747

Z	T	Z	T
753	747	1324	506
754	746	1325	726
755	78	1328	510
756	608	1329	511
757	210	1330	567
758	738	1331	521
759	737	1331a	299:521
760	799	1333	584
761	795	1333a	679
762	839	1334	524
763	798	1336	525[578]
1300	717	1337	526
1300a	568	1338	527
1301	582	1339	528
1302	604	1340	548
1303	586	1340a	549
1304	625	1340b	561g
1305	593	1341	544
1306	192	1341a	544
1306a	614	1342a	537
1307	572	1342b	542
1308	581	1343	585
1308a	580	1343a	727
1308b	516	1344	17
1308c	730	1345	561a
1309	632	1346	561d
1310	19	1347	561c
1310a	21	1348	563
1310b	19	1349	551
1311	577	1350	552 & 304
1312	595	1350a	552v
1313	268	1351	565c
1314	724	1352	565b
1315	676	1353	153
1316	687	1354	568
1317	663	1355	559
1318	572	1356	609
1319	573	1357	563
1320	533	1358	564
1321	501	1359	283
1322	503	1360	558
1323	504	1361	557

Concordance with Zimmermann's Glyph Numbers

Z	T	Z	T
1362	507	1371	591
1363	601	1372	623
1363a	515	1373	98
1363b	790	1374	570[109]
1363c	806	1375	250
1368	109	1376	728
1369	589	1377	725
1370	136		

SOURCES OF TEXTS

WHEREVER ALL OR MANY of the texts of a site are discussed in a single publication, such as Morley, 1920, and Morley, 1937–38, with full bibliographical citations, it has seemed unnecessary to cite earlier sources. That citation stands for the whole site unless important material on its hieroglyphic texts has been published since Morley's book or better illustrations have been published than those available to Morley. In such cases the new citations are also given. Sites without legible non-calendric glyphs are excluded.

"C.I.W." is the abbreviation used for the Carnegie Institution of Washington, whose negative file is now lodged in the Peabody Museum of Archaeology and Ethnology, Harvard University.

Acanceh mural	Seler, 1902–23, Vol. V
Aguas Calientes	Morley, 1937–38, Vol. II
Aguateca	Photographs of Ian Graham; G. L. Vinson, 1960
Altar de Sacrificios	Morley, 1937–38, Vol. II; Morley, 1945; Willey, Smith, Bullard, and Graham
Arenal pottery	Gann, 1928
Balakbal	Morley, 1937–38, Vol. I; Thompson, 1940a

Benque Viejo   Morley, 1937–38, Vol. II; Gann, 1925, p. 64; Thompson, 1940; Cambridge Expedtn. 1960 sherds

Blowgun bowl   Blom, 1950
Bonampak   Ruppert, Thompson, and Proskouriakoff, 1955
Calakmul   Ruppert and Denison, 1943; C.I.W. album of rubbings and photographs
Cancuén   Morley, 1937–38, Vol. II
Caracol   Satterthwaite, 1951; 1954; Univ. Mus. negative file; H. Anderson photograph
Chajcar   Dieseldorff, 1926–33. C.I.W. negative file
Chama pottery   Dieseldorff, 1904; 1904a; 1926–33; Gordon and Mason, 1925–28
Chiapa, stone of   Morley, 1937–38, Vol. II
Chichén Itzá   Ricketson, 1927; Beyer, 1937; Thompson, 1937
Chilib squash vessel   Mérida Mus.; Brainerd, 1958, Fig. 90c
Chinikihá   Maler, 1901
Chinkultic   Blom and La Farge, 1926–27; C.I.W. negative file; ball court marker (really from Colonia la Esperanza). Kelemen, 1943, Pl. 82c
Chipoc pottery   R. E. Smith, 1952
Cobá   Thompson, Pollock, and Charlot, 1932; Andrews, 1938
Codex Dresden   *See* bibliographical references
Codex Madrid   *See* bibliographical references
Codex Paris   *See* bibliographical references
Comalcalo   Blom and La Farge, 1926–27
Comitán   Blom and La Farge, 1926–27
Copán   Gordon, 1902; Morley, 1920; 1939; Thompson, 1944a; Strömsvik, 1952; Andrews, 1958; C.I.W. negative file
 pottery   Longyear, 1952; Gordon and Mason, 1925–28
Covarrubias *sub judice* Covarrubias, 1957, Fig. 94c. Authenticity not yet settled
Dos Pilas   P. Ivanoff photographs; G. L. Vinson, 1960
Doz Pozos   Another name for Dos Pilas
Dzibilchaltun   Andrews, 1959; unpublished photographs by Andrews

Dzibilnocac	*See* Iturbide
El Amparo	Palacios, 1928
El Caribe	Morley, 1937–38, Vol. II
El Cayo	Maler, 1903
El Encanto	Morley, 1937–38, Vol. II
El Pabellon	Morley, 1937–38, Vol. II
El Palmar	C.I.W. negative file; Thompson, field notes
El Quiché pottery	Lothrop, 1936a
El Retiro	Berlin, 1955
Etzna	Ruz, 1945; C.I.W. negative file
Flores	Morley, 1937–38, Vol. III
Halakal	Beyer, 1937
Hatzcap Ceel	*See* Mountain Cow
Holactún	*See* Xcalumkin
Holmul pottery	Merwin and Vaillant, 1932
Huehuetenango pottery	Brinton, 1895; Gordon and Mason, 1925–28
Ichpaatún	Gann, 1926; Pavón Abreu, 1945a; Drawing by Hipólito Sánchez Vera, Campeche
Ikil	García Maldonado, 1955; photographs of E. W. Andrews, Middle American Research Institute
Itsimte	Morley, 1937–38, Vol. II
Iturbide	Seler, 1916; C.I.W. negative file
Ixkun	Morley, 1937–38, Vol. II
Ixlu	Morley, 1937–38, Vol. II; Thompson, 1956
Jade head, Br. Mus.	Maudslay 1889–1902, 1, Pl. 32; Br. Mus. photograph
Jaina	C.I.W. negative file
Jonuta	
1	Kelemen, 1943, Pl. 78*b*
2	Photograph of H. Von Wissing
Kabah	
jambs	Roys, 1943, Fig. 11; C.I.W. negative file
mural	Brinton, 1895
square altar	Photographs of Dr. Philip Phillipps
jambs	Amer. Mus. Nat. Hist.
Kuna	Photographs of Robert Bruce and Wolfgang Cordan; Bruce, 1956; Cordan, 1959
La Amelia	Morley, 1937–38, Vol. II
La Florida	Thompson, 1950, Fig. 49, 5

La Honradez	Morley, 1937–38, Vol. I
La Mar	Maler, 1903
Stela 3	Photographs and drawing of José L. Franco
Labná trunk of façade mask	Beyer, 1935; C.I.W. negative file
Lacanhá	Giles G. Healey photographs; Blom and Duby, 1955; Pavón Abreu, 1949
La Esperanza	*Listed under* Chinkultic
La Milpa, Br. Honduras	Thompson field notes, 1938; C.I.W. negative file
La Muñeca	Ruppert and Denison, 1943
Laguna Perdida	Morley, 1937–38, Vol. II
Lamb site	Photograph of Ginger Lamb
Leyden plate	Morley, 1937–38, Vol. I
Los Higos	Morley, 1920
Lubaantun	Morley, 1937–38, Vol. IV
Machaquilá	*See* Poptún
Macuspana	*See* Tortuguero
Managua	Berlin, 1955
Mayapán shell	Shook and Irving, 1955, Fig. 6*q*
Mexicanos	Lothrop, 1936
Michol	*See* Río Michol
Miraflores, Chis.	Berlin, 1955
Morales	
Stela 1	Andrews, 1943
Stelae 2, 3, altars	Pavón Abreu, 1945
Stelae 4, 5	Instituto Nacional de Antrop. e Hist., photographs
Motul de San José	Morley, 1937–38, Vol. III
Mountain Cow	Thompson, 1931
Moxviquil, Chis.	F. Blom, San Cristóbal de las Casas, negative file
Muluch Tsekal	C.I.W. negative file
Naachtún	Morley, 1937–38, Vol. III
Nakum	Morley, 1937–38, Vol. II
Naranjo	Morley, 1937–38, Vol. II; Thompson, 1943, 1956
Nebaj	
pottery	Dieseldorff, 1926–33; C.I.W. negative file
stucco	Smith and Kidder, 1951
Fenton vase	Joyce, 1914

Ocosingo jades   Brinton, 1895
Ojos de Agua   Blom and Duby, 1955–57
Oxkintok   Shook, 1940; C.I.W. negative file
Oxlahuntun   Healey, 1948; Thompson, 1950, Fig. 59
Oxpemul   Ruppert and Denison, 1943
Palenque
  Temples of Cross, Foliated   Maudslay, 1889–1902
    Cross, Sun, Inscriptions,
    Palace, and Death head
  Blom Tablet (Sun)   Blom and La Farge, 1926–27
  Creation Stone   Palacios, 1937
  engraved shell   Ruz, 1958a
  Hieroglyphic Stairway   Maudslay, 1889–1902; Thompson, 1954a
  incised obsidian   Ruz, 1958a
  Initial Series pot   Ruz, 1952a
  jade earplugs   Ruz, 1954a
  Madrid tablets 1 and 2   Lothrop, 1929
  96 Glyphs tablet   Palacios, 1937; Thompson, 1950
  Palace House A   Beyer, 1936; Berlin, 1945; Thompson, 1954
  Palace House C   Beyer, 1935b
  Palace mural   Seler, 1915; Beyer, 1938
  Palace sculptured stone   Ruz, 1958c
    fragments
  Peñafiel tablet   Saville, 1928
  Ruz 1 (Tablero de El Palacio)   Ruz, 1952; Thompson, 1952
  Ruz 2 (Tablero de los esclavos)   Ruz, 1952a
  Sarcophagus   Ruz, 1954a; 1958
  Scribe 1 and 2 (Tower)   Palacios, 1937
  Scribe 3 (Temple 21)   Ruz, 1958a
  subterranean altar (Palace)   Ruz, 1952b
  Tablet 4 (missing)   Saville, 1928
  Temples 3 and 4   Blom and La Farge, 1926–27; Ruz, 1958b;
                            1958c
  Temple 18 stucco glyphs   Blom and La Farge, 1926–27; Fernández and
                            Berlin, 1954; Ruz, 1958a
    tablets   Ruz, 1958a; Lizardi, 1956
    sculptured stone   Ruz, 1958a
  Temple 21 sculptured stone   Ruz, 1958b
    fragments
  Temple of Cross balustrades   Ruz, 1958

Temple of Cross stucco glyphs	Ruz, 1958b
Temple of Foliated Cross balustrades	Sáenz, 1956; Ruz, 1958a
Temple of Foliated Cross sculptured stone	Ruz, 1958
Temple of Inscriptions	Thompson, 1932; Berlin, 1951b
Temple of Sun	*See* Blom Tablet *under* Palenque
El Templo Olvidado	Berlin, 1944
El Templo del Conde	Blom and La Farge, 1926–27
Palenque X (unlocated site near Palenque	José L. Franco photographs and drawings
Papa, Alta Verapaz	Dieseldorff, 1926–33, Vol. III, Fig. 85
Pestac	Blom, 1935
Peto vase	Spinden, 1913, Fig. 185; Gordon and Mason
Piedras Negras	Morley, 1937–38; Beyer, 1939; 1940; 1945; Andrews, 1942; Thompson, 1943; 1944a; Satterthwaite, 1943; W. R. Coe, 1959; Butler, 1935; Berlin, 1951a
Poco Uinic	Palacios, 1928; Thompson, 1942; 1944b; Middle American Research Institute photographs and drawings
Poctún	*See* Poptún
Pomona, Br. Honduras	Kidder and Ekholm, 1951
Pomona, Tabasco	Photographs Instituto Nacional de Antropol. e Hist.
Poptún	Shook and Smith, 1950; Anon., 1958. The sculptured stone listed as from Poptún actually comes from Machaquilá, a new site, about 30 km. to the west.
Pusilhá	Morley, 1937–38
pottery, etc.	Joyce, 1929; Br. Mus. exhibits
Quen Santo	*See* Sacchaná
Quintana Roo blowgun bowl	Blom, 1950
Quiriguá	Morley, 1937–38
Str. 1 unpublished	C.I.W. negative file
Alt. O	Thompson, 1945
Río Amarillo	Morley, 1920
Río Hondo, Br. Honduras, pottery	Gann, 1918; Gordon and Mason
Río Hondo, Guatemala, pottery	Seler, 1904; Gordon and Mason
Río Michol	Berlin, 1955

Rossbach Collection	Lothrop, 1936a
Sacchaná	Seler, 1901
San Agustín Acasaguastlán	Smith and Kidder, 1943
San José pottery	Thompson, 1939
San Pedro Carcha	C.I.W. negative file
Sanimtaca	McDougall, 1943
Santa Elena Poco Uinic	*See* Poco Uinic
Santa Rita	Gann, 1900
Santa Rosa Xlabpak or Xtampak	C.I.W. negative file; photographs of Lawrence Roys
Santo Ton	Blom and Duby, 1955–57; Middle American Research Institute negative file
Sayil	C.I.W. negative file
Seibal	Morley, 1937–38, Vol. II
Seville jade	Joyce, 1929–30; Kelemen, 1943, Pl. 246a
Silan	Gann, 1924
Sisilhá, Campeche	C.I.W. negative file
Slate mirror-back	Photograph in possession of R. H. Thompson
Tabasco vase	C. Cook de Leonard, 1954
Tabi	Gann, 1924; Andrews, 1939
Tamarandito	Photographs of G. L. Vinson
Tayasal	Morley, 1937–38, Vol. III
Tenam	Blom and La Farge, 1926–27
Tikal	Morley, 1937–38, Vol. I; Long, 1940; Beyer, 1943; Thompson, 1950, Fig. 5, 53 caption; Berlin, 1951; Coe and Broman, 1958; Satterthwaite, 1956; 1958; Shook, 1958; Univ. Mus. negative file
Tila	
Stelae A. B	Beyer, 1927
Stela C	Thompson, 1950, Fig. 56, 3
Tohcok, Campeche	C.I.W. negative file
Tonina	Blom and La Farge, 1926–27; Beyer, 1938a; Thompson, 1942; 1944; C.I.W. negative file; Blom and Duby, 1955–57
Tortuguero	Blom and La Farge, 1926–27; C.I.W. negative file
Stela 6	Photographs and drawings of José L. Franco
Tula	Peñafiel, 1890
Tulum	Lothrop, 1924; Gann, 1924

Tzendales	Spinden, 1913, Fig. 232
Tzibanche wood ceiling	Gann, 1928a
jade	Beyer, 1932
Uaxactún	Morley, 1937–38, Vol. I; Kidder, 1947; Thompson, 1956
mural	A. L. Smith, 1950
pottery	A. L. Smith, 1932; R. E. Smith, 1955
Ucanal	Morley, 1937–38, Vol. I
Ulua carved brown	Lothrop, 1936
Uolantun	Morley, 1937–38, Vol. I
Uxmal	
columnar altar	Holmes, 1895–97, Pl. 7
Monjas capstones	Blom, 1934; Thompson, 1941, p. 107; Morley, 1920
ball court markers	Ruz, 1958d
stelae	Blom, 1934; Middle American Research Institute negative file
tecali vase	Ruz, 1954
Uxul	Ruppert and Denison, 1943
Xcalumkin	Maler, 1920; Thompson, 1937; Ruz, 1945; C.I.W. negative file
Xcocha	C.I.W. negative file; Pavón Abreu, 1942
Xcochkax	C.I.W. negative file
Xculoc	C.I.W. negative file; Pavón Abreu, 1942
Xkichmook	E. H. Thompson, 1898
Xultún	Morley, 1937–38, Vol. I
Xunantunich	*See* Benque Viejo
Yalloch pottery	Gann, 1918; Gordon and Mason
Yaxchilán	Morley, 1937–38, Vol. II; Beyer, 1935a; Thompson, 1936; 1946; 1952a
Yula	Beyer, 1937

REFERENCES

BELOW ARE GIVEN THE PRINCIPAL SOURCES for hieroglyphic texts used in preparing this catalog other than those listed in Morley, 1936–37, together with citations of reasonably acceptable decipherments of non-calendrical hieroglyphs published since 1950. Papers on the structure of the Maya calendar, on Maya astronomy, and such subjects not directly related to the compilation of the catalog are omitted. For earlier papers on these subjects see Morley, 1936–37, and Thompson, 1950.

ANDREWS, E. W.

1938   "Some new material from Cobá, Quintana Roo," *Ethnos*, 3:33–46. Stockholm.

1939   "A group of related sculptures from Yucatán," *Carnegie Inst. Wash. Pub. 509*, Contrib. 26. Washington.

1942   "The inscription on Stela 38, Piedras Negras, El Petén, Guatemala," *Amer. Antiquity*, 7:364–68. Menasha.

1943   "The archaeology of southwestern Campeche," *Carnegie Inst. Wash. Pub. 546*, Contrib. 40. Washington.

1958   "A revision of some dates on the hieroglyphic stairway, Copán, Honduras," *Middle Amer. Res. Ser. Pub. 26*, pp. 1–8. New Orleans.

1959   "Dzibilchaltún, lost city of the Maya," *Nat. Geog. Mag.*, 115:90–109. Washington.

References

ANON.

1958   *"Nuevas adquisiciones,"* Antropol. e Hist. de Guatemala, Vol. X, No. 2, p. 67. Guatemala.

BARTHEL, T. S.

1952   *"Der Morgensternkult in den Darstellungen der Dresdener Maya-handschrift,"* Ethnos, 17:73–112. Stockholm.

1953   *"Regionen des Regensgottes. Zur Deutung der unteren Teile der Seiten 65–69 in der Dresdener,"* Ethnos, 18:86–105. Stockholm.

1954   "Maya epigraphy: some remarks on the affix 'al,' " Proc. 30th Int. Cong. Amer. (Cambridge), pp. 45–49. London.

1955   *"Maya-Palaeographik: die Hieroglyphe Strafe,"* Ethnos, 20:146–51. Stockholm.

1955a   *"Versuch über die Inschriften von Chichén Itzá viejo,"* Baessler Archiv., n.s., 3:5–33. Berlin.

BERLIN, H.

1943   "Notes on Glyph C of the lunar series at Palenque," Carnegie Inst. Wash., Dept. Archaeol., Notes on Middle Amer. Archaeol. and Ethnol., No. 24. Cambridge.

1944   *"Un templo olvidado en Palenque,"* Rev. Mex. de Estudios Antropol., 6:62–90. Mexico.

1945   "A critique of dates at Palenque," Amer. Antiquity, 10:340–47. Menasha.

1951   *"El templo de las Inscripciones—VI—de Tikal,"* Antropol. e Hist. de Guatemala, Vol. III, No. 1, pp. 33–54. Guatemala.

1951a   *"Breves estudios arqueológicos, El Petén, Guatemala,"* Antropol. e Hist. de Guatemala, Vol. III, No. 2, pp. 1–9. Guatemala.

1951b   *"La Inscripción del Templo de las Leyes en Palenque,"* Soc. de Geog. e Hist. de Guatemala, Anales, 25:120–29. Guatemala.

1953   "Archaeological reconnaissance in Tabasco," Carnegie Inst. Wash., Dept. Archaeol., Current Reports, No. 7. Cambridge.

1955   "News from the Maya world," Ethnos, 20:201–209. Stockholm.

1957   "A new inscription from the Temple of the Foliated Cross at Palenque," Carnegie Inst. Wash., Dept. Archaeol., Notes on Middle Amer. Archaeol. and Ethnol., No. 130. Cambridge.

1958   *"El glifo 'emblema' en las inscripciones Mayas,"* Jour. Soc. des Amer. de Paris, 47:111–19. Paris.

BEYER, H.

1926   *"Apuntes sobre el jeroglífico maya Muluc,"* Mem. Soc. Cient. "Antonio Alzate," 45:143–46. Mexico.

1926a   *"Die Verdopplung in der Hieroglyphenschrift der Maya,"* Anthropos, 21:580–82. St. Gabriel-Mödling bei Wien.

1927   *"Las dos estelas mayas de Tila, Chis,"* Mem. Soc. Cient. *"Antonio Alzate,"* 47:123–43. Mexico.

1928   "El origen del jeroglífico maya Akbal," *Rev. Mex. de Estudios Hist.,* 2:5–9. Mexico.

1932   "An Ahau date with a katun and a katun ending glyph," *Middle Amer. Res. Ser. Pub. 4,* pp. 131–36. New Orleans.

1933   "A discussion of the Gates classification of Maya hieroglyphs," *Amer. Anthropol.,* 35:659–94. Menasha.

1934   "The position of the affixes in Maya writing," *Maya Res.,* 1:20–29; 101–108. New York.

1935   "The date on the long-nosed mask of Labna," *Maya Res.,* 2:184–88. New York.

1935a   "The dates on Lintel 10 of Yaxchilán," *Maya Res.,* 2:394–97. New York.

1935b   "The date on the cornice of House C of the palace at Palenque," *El México Antiguo,* Vol. III, Nos. 9–10, pp. 53–55. Mexico.

1936   "Decipherment of a greatly damaged inscription at Palenque," *El México Antiguo,* 4:1–6. Mexico.

1936a   "The position of the affixes in Maya writing, III," *Maya Res.,* 3:102–104. New York.

1937   "Studies on the inscriptions of Chichén Itzá," *Carnegie Inst. Wash. Pub. 483,* Contrib. 21. Washington.

1938   "Two high period series at Palenque," *El México Antiguo,* 4:145–54. Mexico.

1938a   *"Die Tagesdaten auf dem Maya-Altar des Mexikanischen National Museums,"* Zeit. f. Ethnol., 70:88–93. Berlin.

1939   "Elucidation of a secondary series on Lintel 2 of Piedras Negras," *El México Antiguo,* 4:289–92. Mexico.

1940   "Rectification of a date on Stela 12 of Piedras Negras," *El México Antiguo,* 5:7–8. Mexico.

1943   *"Algunos datos sobre los dinteles mayas de Tikal en el Museo Etnográfico de Basilea,"* Proc. 27th Int. Cong. Amer., 1:338–43. Mexico.

1945   "An incised Maya inscription in the Metropolitan Museum of Art, New York," *Middle Amer. Res. Records,* Vol. I, No. 7. New Orleans.

BLOM, F.

1934   "Short summary of recent explorations in the ruins of Uxmal, Yucatán," *Proc. 24th Int. Cong. Amer.,* pp. 55–59. Hamburg.

1935   "The Pestac stela," *Maya Res.,* 2:190–91. New York.

1950   "A polychrome Maya plate from Quintana Roo," *Carnegie Inst. Wash., Dept. Archaeol., Notes on Middle Amer. Archaeol. and Ethnol.,* No. 98. Cambridge.

References

——— AND G. DUBY

1955–57   *La selva lacandona.* 2 vols. Mexico.

——— AND O. LA FARGE

1926–27   *Tribes and temples. Middle Amer. Res. Ser.,* Vol. I. 2 vols. New Orleans.

BRAINERD, G. W.

1958   "The archaeological ceramics of Yucatán," *Univ. of Cal. Pub., Anthropol. Records,* 19. Berkeley and Los Angeles.

BRINTON, D. G.

1895   "A primer of Maya hieroglyphics," *Univ. Pa. Ser. in Philol., Lit., and Archaeol.,* Vol. III, No. 2. Philadelphia.

BUSHNELL, G. H. S. AND A. DIGBY

1955   *Ancient American pottery.* London.

BUTLER, M.

1935   "Piedras Negras pottery," *Univ. Mus., P.N. Prelim. Papers,* 4. Philadelphia.

CASO, A.

1928   *"Las estelas zapotecas," Mus. Nac. de Arqueol., Hist., y Etnograf. Monografías.* Mexico.

1934   *"Sobre una figurilla de hueso del antiguo imperio maya," Anales del Mus. Nac. de Arqueol., Hist., y Etnograf.,* Epoca 5, 1:11–16. Mexico.

1947   *"Calendario y escritura de las antiguas culturas de Monte Albán,"* in *Obras completas de Miguel Othón de Mendizabal.* Mexico.

CHILAM BALAM OF CHUMAYEL

See Roys, 1933.

CODEX DRESDEN

1880   *Die Maya-Handschrift der Königlichen Bibliothek zu Dresden; herausgegeben von* Prof. Dr. E. Förstemann. Leipzig (2nd ed., 1892).

See Gates, 1932b.

CODEX MADRID (Cortesiano Section)

1892   *Códice Maya denominado Cortesiano que se conserva en el Museo Arqueológico Nacional (Madrid).* Reproducción fotocromolitográfica. Madrid.

CODEX MADRID (Troano Section)

1869–70   *Manuscrit Troano. Etudes sur le système grafique et la langue des Mayas.* By C. E. Brasseur de Bourbourg. 2 vols. Paris.

CODEX PARIS

1887   *Codex Peresianus, manuscrit hiératique des anciens indiens de l'Amérique Central conservé à la Bibliothèque Nationale de Paris, avec une introduction par Léon de Rosny.* Paris.

1949   *Codex Paris.* Infra-red photographs by Giles G. Healey. Set in hands of author. Paris.

CoE, W. R.

1959   "Piedras Negras archaeology: artifacts, caches, and burials," *Mus. Monographs.* Philadelphia.

—— AND V. L. BROMAN

1958   "Tikal Report No. 2. Excavations in the Stela 23 Group," *Mus. Monographs. Tikal Reports,* No. 2. Philadelphia.

COOK DE LEONARD, C.

1954   *"Dos extraordinarias vasijas del Museo de Villa Hermosa (Tabasco),"* Yan, No. 3, pp. 83–104. Mexico.

CORDAN, W.

1959   *Geheimis im Urwald.* Berlin.

COVARRUBIAS, M.

1957   *Indian art of Mexico and Central America.* New York.

DIESELDORFF, E. P.

1904   "A pottery vase with figure painting from a grave in Chama," *U.S. Bur. Amer. Ethnol. Bull. 28,* pp. 639–44. Washington.

1904a   "A clay vessel with a picture of a vampire-headed deity," *U.S. Bur. Amer. Ethnol. Bull. 28,* pp. 665–66. Washington.

1926–33   *Kunst und Religion der Mayavölker im alten und heutigen Mittelamerika.* 3 vols. Berlin and Hamburg.

DIRINGER, D.

1948   *The alphabet. A key to the history of mankind.* London.

FERNÁNDEZ, M. A. AND H. BERLIN

1954   "Drawings of glyphs of Structure XVIII, Palenque," *Carnegie Inst. Wash., Dept. Archaeol., Notes on Middle Amer. Archaeol. and Ethnol.,* No. 119. Cambridge.

GANN, T. W. F.

1900   "Mounds in northern Honduras," *Bur. Amer. Ethnol. 19th Ann. Rept.,* Pt. 2, pp. 655–92. Washington.

1918   "The Maya Indians of southern Yucatán and northern British Honduras," *Bur. Amer. Ethnol. Bull. 64.* Washington.

1924   *In an unknown land.* London and New York.

1925   *Mystery cities.* London and New York.

1926   "A new Maya stela with Initial Series date," *Man,* Vol. XXVI, No. 37. London.

1928   *Discoveries and adventures in Central America.* London and New York.

1928a   "Recently discovered Maya temples in Yucatán with date sculptured on wooden lintel," *Man,* Vol. XXVIII, No. 5. London.

References

García Maldonado, A.
1955   *"Las ruinas de Iki," El Diario del Sureste.* Mérida.

Gates, W.
1931   *An outline dictionary of Maya glyphs. Maya Soc. Pub. 1.* Baltimore.
1931a   "Glyph studies," *Maya Soc. Quart.,* 1:32–33. Baltimore.
1932   "Glyph studies," *Maya Soc. Quart.,* 1:68–70. Baltimore.
1932a   "Glyph studies," *Maya Soc. Quart.,* 1:153–82. Baltimore.
1932b   *The Dresden Codex. Reproduced from tracings of the original. Colorings finished by hand. Maya Soc. Pub. 2.* Baltimore. (Edition of 75 copies.)

Gordon, G. B.
1896   "Prehistoric ruins of Copán, Honduras," *Mem. Peabody Mus. Harvard Univ.,* Vol. I, No. 1. Cambridge.
1902   "The hieroglyphic stairway, ruins of Copán," *Mem. Peabody Mus. Harvard Univ.,* Vol. I, No. 6. Cambridge.

——, and J. A. Mason
1925–28   *Examples of Maya pottery in the Museum and other collections.* University Mus. Philadelphia.

Healey, G. G.
1948   "Oxlahuntun," *Archaeology,* 1:129–33. New York.

Holmes, W. H.
1895–97   "Archaeological studies among the ancient cities of Mexico," *Chicago Nat. Hist. Mus., Anthropol. Ser.,* Vol. I. Chicago.

Joyce, T. A.
1914   *Mexican archaeology.* London and New York.
1929   "Report on the British Museum Expedition to British Honduras, 1929," *Jour. Royal Anthropol. Inst.,* 59:439–59. London.
1929–30   "A Maya jadeite carving from Central America," *Br. Mus. Quart.,* 4:51. London.

Kelemen, P.
1943   *Mediaeval American art.* New York.

Kidder, A. V.
1947   *The artifacts of Uaxactún, Guatemala, Carnegie Inst. Wash. Pub. 576.* Washington.

—— and G. F. Ekholm
1951   "Some archaeological specimens from Pomona, British Honduras," *Carnegie Inst. Wash., Dept. Archaeol., Notes on Middle Amer. Archaeol. and Ethnol.,* No. 102. Cambridge.

Knorozov, Y. V.
1958   "The problem of the study of the Maya hieroglyphic writing," *Amer.*

Antiquity, 23:284–91. Salt Lake City. (Contains references to earlier papers of this author.)

LIZARDI R., C.

1941   *"El glifo B y la sincronología Maya-cristiana,"* in *Los Mayas Antiguos*, pp. 243–69. Mexico.

1949   *"Mas fechas mayas,"* El *México Antiguo*, 7:238–60. Mexico.

1956   *"Otras inscripciones palencanas,"* appendix to Sáenz, *Exploraciones en la pirámide de la Cruz Foliada.*

LONG, R. C. E.

1940   "The dates on Altar 5 at Tikal," *Amer. Antiquity*, 5:283–86. Menasha.

LONGYEAR, J. M.

1952   *Copán ceramics. A study of southeastern Maya pottery, Carnegie Inst. Wash. Pub. 597.* Washington.

LOTHROP, S. K.

1924   *Tulum. An archaeological study of the east coast of Yucatán, Carnegie Inst. Wash. Pub. 335.* Washington.

1929   "Sculptured fragments from Palenque," *Jour. Royal Anthropol. Inst.*, 59:53–63. London.

1936   "Sculptured pottery of the Maya and Pipil," *Maya Res.*, 3:140–52. New Orleans.

1936a   *Zacualpa. A study of ancient Quiché artifacts, Carnegie Inst. Wash. Pub. 472.* Washington.

———, W. F. FOSHAG, AND J. MAHLER

1957   *Pre-Columbian art. Robert Woods Bliss collection.* London and New York.

MALER, T.

1901   "Researches in the central portion of the Usumatsintla Valley (Piedras Negras, Chinikiha, etc.)," *Mem. Peabody Mus. Harvard Univ.*, Vol. II, No. 1. Cambridge.

1902   *"Yukatekische Forschungen,"* Globus, 82:197–230. Brunswick.

1903   "Researches in the central portion of the Usumatsintla Valley (Yaxchilán, El Cayo, etc.)," *Mem. Peabody Mus. Harvard Univ.*, Vol. 2, No. 2. Cambridge.

MAUDSLAY, A. P.

1889–1902 *Archaeology Biologia Centrali-Americana.* 5 vols. London.

McDOUGALL, E.

1943   "A vase from Sanimtaca, Alta Verapaz, Guatemala," *Carnegie Inst. Wash., Dept. Archaeol., Notes on Middle Amer. Archaeol. and Ethnol.*, No. 30. Cambridge.

References

MERWIN, R. E., AND G. C. VAILLANT

1932   "The ruins of Holmul, Guatemala," *Mem. Peabody Mus. Harvard Univ.*, Vol. III, No. 2. Cambridge.

MORLEY, S. G.

1920   *The inscriptions at Copán, Carnegie Inst. Wash. Pub. 219.* Washington.

1937–38   *The inscriptions of Petén, Carnegie Inst. Wash. Pub. 437.* 5 vols. Washington.

1939   "Recent epigraphic discoveries at the ruins of Copán, Honduras," in *So live the works of men*, pp. 277–93. Albuquerque.

1945   "The Initial and Supplementary Series of Stela 5 at Altar de Sacrificios," *Carnegie Inst. Wash., Dept. Archaeol., Notes on Middle Amer. Archaeol. and Ethnol.*, No. 58. Cambridge.

MOTUL DICTIONARY

1929   *Diccionario de Motul, maya-español, atribuido a Fray Antonio de Ciudad Real y Arte de la lengua maya por Fray Juan Coronel.* J. Martínez Hernández, ed. Mérida.

PALACIOS, E. J.

1928   *En los confines de la selva lacandona. Exploraciones en el estado de Chiapas, 1926. Secretaría de Educación Pública.* Mexico.

1937   "Mas gemas del arte maya en Palenque," *Anales del Mus. Nac. de Arqueol. Hist. y Etnog.*, Epoca 5, Vol. II, pp. 193–225. Mexico.

PAVON ABREU, R.

1945   *"Morales, una importante ciudad arqueológica en Tabasco," Mus. Arqueol. Etnog. e Hist. Campeche*, Cuaderno No. 6. Campeche.

1945a   *"La estela número 1 de Ichpaatun, su data cronológica," Yikal Maya Than*, 6:147–51. Mérida.

1949   *"Nuevas fechas mayas," Aulas*, pp. 371–78. Campeche.

PEÑAFIEL, A.

1890   *Monumentos del arte mexicano antiguo.* 5 vols. Berlin.

PROSKOURIAKOFF, T.

1944   "An inscription on a jade probably carved at Piedras Negras," *Carnegie Inst. Wash., Dept. of Archaeol., Notes on Middle Amer. Archaeol. and Ethnol.*, No. 47. Cambridge.

———, AND J. E. S. THOMPSON

1947   "Maya calendar round dates such as 9 Ahau 17 Mol," *Carnegie Inst. Wash., Dept. of Archaeol., Notes on Middle Amer. Archaeol. and Ethnol.*, No. 79. Cambridge.

RICKETSON, E. B.

1927   "Sixteen carved panels from Chichén Itzá, Yucatán," *Art and Archaeol.*, 23:11–15. Washington.

Roys, R. L.

1933   *The book of Chilam Balam of Chumayel, Carnegie Inst. Wash. Pub. 438.* Washington.

1943   *The Indian background of colonial Yucatán, Carnegie Inst. Wash. Pub. 548.* Washington.

Ruppert, K., and J. H. Denison

1943   *Archaeological reconnaissance in Campeche, Quintana Roo, and Petén. Carnegie Inst. Wash. Pub. 543.* Washington.

Ruppert, K., J. E. S. Thompson, and T. Proskouriakoff

1955   *Bonampak, Chiapas, Mexico. Carnegie Inst. Wash. Pub. 602.* Washington.

Ruz L., A.

1945   *"Campeche en la arqueología maya," Acta Anthropológica,* Vol. I, Nos. 2–3. Mexico.

1952   *"Exploraciones arqueológicas en Palenque (1949)," Anales Instituto Nac. de Antropol. e Hist.,* 4:49–61. Mexico.

1952a   *"Exploraciones en Palenque: 1950," Anales Instituto Nac. de Antropol. e Hist.,* 5:25–45. Mexico.

1952b   *"Exploraciones en Palenque: 1951," Anales Instituto Nac. de Antropol. e Hist.,* 5:47–66, Mexico.

1954   *"Uxmal: temporada de trabajos 1951–1952," Anales Instituto Nac. de Antropol. e Hist.,* 6:49–67. Mexico.

1954a   *"Exploraciones en Palenque: 1952," Anales Instituto Nac. de Antropol. e Hist.,* 6:79–110. Mexico.

1958   *"Exploraciones arqueológicas en Palenque: 1953," Anales Instituto Nac. de Antropol. e Hist.,* 10:69–116. Mexico.

1958a   *"Exploraciones arqueológicas en Palenque: 1954," Anales Instituto Nac. de Antropol. e Hist.,* 10:117–84. Mexico.

1958b   *"Exploraciones arqueológicas en Palenque: 1955," Anales Instituto Nac. de Antropol e Hist.,* 10:185–240. Mexico.

1958c   *"Exploraciones arqueológicas en Palenque: 1956," Anales Instituto Nac. de Antropol. e Hist.,* 10:241–99. Mexico.

1958d   *"El juego de pelota de Uxmal,"* in *Miscellanea Paul Rivet,* pp. 635–67. Mexico.

Sáenz, C. A.

1956   *Exploraciones en la pirámide de la Cruz Foliada, Instituto Nac. de Antrop. e Hist., Informes,* No. 5. Mexico.

Satterthwaite, L.

1938   *"Maya dating by hieroglyphic styles," Amer. Anthrop.,* 40:416–28. Menasha.

References

1940   "Another Piedras Negras stela," *Univ. Mus. Bull.*, Vol. VIII, No. 4, pp. 24–27. Philadelphia.

1943   "New photographs and the date of Stela 14, Piedras Negras," *Carnegie Inst. Wash., Dept. of Archaeol., Notes on Middle Amer. Archaeol. and Ethnol.*, No. 28. Cambridge.

1950   "Reconnaissance in British Honduras," *Univ. Mus. Bull.*, Vol. XVI, No. 1, pp. 21–36. Philadelphia.

1954   "Sculptured monuments from Caracol, British Honduras," *Univ. Mus. Bull.*, Vol. XVIII, Nos. 1–2, pp. 2–45. Philadelphia.

1956   "Maya dates on stelae in Tikal 'enclosures,'" *Univ. Mus. Bull.*, Vol. XX, No. 4, pp. 25–40. Philadelphia.

1958   "Five newly discovered carved monuments at Tikal and new data on four others," *Mus. Monographs, Tikal Reports*, No. 4. Philadelphia.

SAVILLE, M. H.

1928   "Bibliographic notes on Palenque, Chiapas," *Mus. Amer. Indian, Heye Foundation, Indian Notes and Monographs*, Vol. VI, No. 5. New York.

SELER, E.

1901   *Die alten Ansiedelungen von Chacula.* Berlin.

1902–23   *Gesammelte Abhandlungen zur Amerikanischen Sprach- und Alterthumskunde.* 5 vols. Berlin.

1904   "Antiquities of Guatemala," *U.S. Bur. Amer. Ethnol. Bull. 28*, pp. 75–121. Washington.

1915   *"Beobachtungen und Studien in den Ruinen von Palenque,"* from *Abhandlungen der Königl. Preuss. Akademie der Wissenschaften, Jahrgang*, 1915. *Phil. Hist. Klasse*, Nr. 5. Berlin.

1916   *"Die Quetzalcouatl-Fassaden Yukatekischer Bauten,"* from *Abhandlungen der Königl. Preuss. Akademie der Wissenschaften, Jahrgang*, 1916. *Phil. Hist. Klasse*, Nr. 2. Berlin.

SHOOK, E. M.

1940   "Exploration in the ruins of Oxkintok, Yucatán," *Revista Mex. de Estudios Antropol.*, 4:165–71. Mexico.

1958   "Field director's report: the 1956 and 1957 seasons," *Mus. Monographs, Tikal Reports*, No. 1. Philadelphia.

——, AND W. N. IRVING

1955   "Colonnaded buildings at Mayapán," *Carnegie Inst. Wash., Dept. Archaeol., Current Reports*, No. 22. Cambridge.

——, AND R. E. SMITH

1950   *"Descubrimientos arqueológicos en Poptun,"* *Antropol. e Hist. de Guatemala*, Vol. II, No. 2, pp. 3–15. Guatemala.

SMITH, A. L.

1932 "Two ceramic finds at Uaxactún," *Carnegie Inst. Wash. Pub. 436,* Contrib. 5. Washington.

1950 *Uaxactun, Guatemala: Excavations of 1931–1937, Carnegie Inst. Wash. Pub. 588.* Washington.

———, AND A. V. KIDDER

1943 "Explorations in the Motagua Valley, Guatemala," *Carnegie Inst. Wash. Pub. 546,* Contrib. 41. Washington.

1951 *Excavations at Nebaj, Guatemala, Carnegie Inst. Wash. Pub. 594.* Washington.

SMITH, R. E.

1952 "Pottery from Chipoc, Alta Verapaz, Guatemala," *Carnegie Inst. Wash. Pub. 596,* Contrib. 56. Washington.

1955 *Ceramic sequence at Uaxactún, Guatemala, Middle Amer. Res. Inst., Tulane Univ. Pub. 20.* 2 vols. New Orleans.

SPINDEN, H. J.

1913 "A study of Maya art. Its subject matter and historical development," *Mem. Peabody Mus. Harvard Univ.,* Vol. VI. Cambridge.

STRÖMSVIK, G.

1952 "The ball courts at Copán. With notes on courts at La Unión, Quiriguá, San Pedro Pinula, and Asunción Mita," *Carnegie Inst. Wash. Pub. 596,* Contrib. 55. Washington.

THOMPSON, E. H.

1898 "Ruins of Xkichmook, Yucatán," *Chicago Nat. Hist. Mus. Anthropol. Ser.,* 2:209–29. Chicago.

THOMPSON, J. E. S.

1931 "Archaeological investigations in the southern Cayo District, British Honduras," *Chicago Nat. Hist. Mus., Anthropol. Ser.,* Vol. XVII, No. 3. Chicago.

1932 "The solar year of the Mayas at Quiriguá," *Chicago Nat. Hist. Mus., Anthropol. Ser.,* Vol. XVII, No. 4. Chicago.

1936 "The dates of the Temple of the Cross, Palenque," *Maya Res.,* 3: 287–93. New Orleans.

1936a "Lunar inscriptions in the Usumacintla Valley," *El México Antiguo,* 4:69–73. Mexico.

1937 "A new method of deciphering Yucatecan dates with special reference to Chichén Itzá," *Carnegie Inst. Wash. Pub. 483,* Contrib. 22. Washington.

1939 *Excavations at San José, British Honduras, Carnegie Inst. Wash. Pub. 506.* Washington.

References

1940 "Late ceramic horizons at Benque Viejo, British Honduras," *Carnegie Inst. Wash. Pub. 528*, Contrib. 35. Washington.

1940a *"Apuntes sobre la estela número 5 de Balakbal, Q.R.," Rev. Mex. de Estudios Antropol.*, 4:5–9. Mexico, D.F.

1941 "A co-ordination of the history of Chichén Itzá with ceramic sequences in Central Mexico," *Rev. Mex. de Estudios Antropol.*, 5:97–111. Mexico.

1942 "Observations on Glyph G of the lunar series," *Carnegie Inst. Wash., Dept. Archaeol., Notes on Middle Amer. Archaeol. and Ethnol.*, No. 7. Cambridge.

1943 "The Initial Series of Stela 14, Piedras Negras and a date on Stela 19, Naranjo, Guatemala," *Carnegie Inst. Wash., Dept. Archaeol., Notes on Middle Amer. Archaeol. and Ethnol.*, No. 18. Cambridge.

1944 "Jottings on inscriptions at Copán," *Carnegie Inst. Wash., Dept. Archaeol., Notes on Middle Amer. Archaeol. and Ethnol.*, No. 38. Cambridge.

1944a "The dating of seven monuments at Piedras Negras," *Carnegie Inst. Wash., Dept. Archaeol., Notes on Middle Amer. Archaeol. and Ethnol.*, No. 39. Cambridge.

1944b "Variant methods of date recordings in the Jatate drainage, Chiapas," *Carnegie Inst. Wash., Dept. Archaeol., Notes on Middle Amer. Archaeol. and Ethnol.*, No. 45. Cambridge.

1945 "The inscription on the altar of Zoomorph O, Quiriguá," *Carnegie Inst. Wash., Dept. Archaeol., Notes on Middle Amer. Archaeol. and Ethnol.*, No. 56. Cambridge.

1946 "The dating of Structure 44, Yaxchilán, and its bearing on the sequence of texts at that site," *Carnegie Inst. Wash., Dept. Archaeol., Notes on Middle Amer. Archaeol. and Ethnol.*, No. 71. Cambridge.

1950 *Maya hieroglyphic writing: introduction, Carnegie Inst. Wash. Pub. 589.* Washington. (2nd ed., Univ. of Oklahoma Press, Norman, 1960.)

1951 "Aquatic symbols common to various centers of the classic period in Meso-america," *Proc. 29th Int. Cong. Amer.* (New York), 1:31–36. Chicago.

1952 "The introduction of Puuc style of dating at Yaxchilán," *Carnegie Inst. Wash., Dept. Archaeol., Notes on Middle Amer. Archaeol. and Ethnol.*, No. 110. Cambridge.

1952a *"La inscripción jeroglífica del Tablero de El Palacio, Palenque," Anales Inst. Nac. de Antropol. e Hist.*, 4:61–68. Mexico.

1954   *The rise and fall of Maya civilization.* Univ. of Oklahoma Press, Norman.

1954a   "Memoranda on some dates at Palenque, Chiapas," *Carnegie Inst. Wash., Dept. Archaeol., Notes on Middle Amer. Archaeol. and Ethnol.,* No. 120. Cambridge.

1956   "Chronological decipherments from Uaxactún, Naranjo, and Ixlu, Petén," *Carnegie Inst. Wash., Dept. Archaeol., Notes on Middle Amer. Archaeol. and Ethnol.,* No. 127. Cambridge.

1958   "Symbols, glyphs, and divinatory almanacs for diseases in the Maya Dresden and Madrid codices," *Amer. Antiquity,* 23:297–308. Salt Lake City.

1959   "Systems of hieroglyphic writing in Middle America and methods of deciphering them," *Amer. Antiquity,* 24:349–64. Salt Lake City.

————, H. E. D. POLLOCK, AND J. CHARLOT

1932   *A preliminary study of the ruins of Cobá, Quintana Roo. Carnegie Inst. Wash. Pub. 424.* Washington.

THOMPSON, R. H.

1958   "Modern Yucatecan Maya pottery making," *Soc. Amer. Archaeol. Mem. 15.* Salt Lake City.

TOZZER, A. M., AND G. ALLEN

1910   "Animal figures in the Maya codices," *Papers Peabody Mus., Harvard Univ.,* Vol. IV, No. 3. Cambridge.

VINSON, G. L.

1960   "Two important recent archaeological discoveries in Esso concessions, Guatemala," *Exploration News Letter, Standard Oil Company (N. J.).* New York.

WILLEY, G. R., A. L. SMITH, W. R. BULLARD, AND J. A. GRAHAM

1959   "Altar de Sacrificios, 1959. A preliminary report," *(mimeographed), Peabody Mus., Harvard Univ.* Cambridge.

ZIMMERMANN, G.

1953   *Kurze Formen- und Begriffssystematik der Hieroglyphen der Maya-handschriften. Beiträge zur mittelamerikanischen Völkerkunde, I.* Hamburg.

1956   *Die Hieroglyphen der Maya-Handschriften, Universität Hamburg Abhandlungen aus dem Gebiet der Auslandskunde,* Vol. LXVII— *Reihe B (Völkerkunde, Kulturgeschichte, und Sprachen Band 34).* Hamburg.

PLATES

Plate 1

Lintel 35, Yaxchilán, Chiapas. Early glyphs beautifully carved in a fluid style which later disappears. About A.D. 530. (*Courtesy British Museum.*)

Plate 2

Front of Stela 31, Tikal, Petén. Text, except for large introductory glyph, on the back of a stela purposely buried by the Mayas. It is closer to the standard presentation of Central area than is the previous text, although it was carved between half a century and a century earlier. (*Courtesy University Museum, Philadelphia.*)

Plate 3

Middle Panel, Temple of Inscriptions, Palenque. Part of a long inscription in the temple above the great burial chamber at Palenque. Glyphs drawn by Miss Annie Hunter, who had a genius for recovering eroded lines on weathered texts. Probably A.D. 692. *(Courtesy British Museum.)*

Plate 4

Glyphs in Stucco, Palenque. Stucco glyphs recovered in disorder in the debris of Temple XVIII, having fallen from a wall. Perhaps A.D. 721.

Lintel 41, Yaxchilán, Chiapas. A superb example of Usumacinta carving of figures and glyphs. Note the pleasant disposition of the glyphs. Perhaps A.D. 756. (*Courtesy British Museum.*)

Plate 6

Stela 7, Yaxchilán, Chiapas. A badly smashed and incomplete stela with typical Yaxchilán clause in glyph panel. No calendric glyphs on surviving fragments. About A.D. 750. *(Courtesy Peabody Museum, Harvard University.)*

Plate 7

Altar W′, Copán. Four sides of a small altar. The back carried full-figure glyphs, the only known sequence of these in a text without Initial Series. Unfortunately, they are badly smashed, perhaps purposely. A.D. 755. (*Courtesy Peabody Museum, Harvard University.*)

Plate 8

Stela A, Copán. The front displays a human figure. The text opens with an Initial Series on one of the sides before passing to the back, here shown. It is in a state of remarkable preservation as the monument has been exposed since its dedication in A.D. 731. *(Courtesy British Museum.)*

Plate 9

Stela D, Quiriguá (side view). Front and back are carved with human figures. The tips of their feather headdresses gracefully frame the panel of full-figure glyphs which is almost twenty feet high. A.D. 766. (*Courtesy School of American Research.*)

Plate 10

Sculpture G, Quiriguá. This remarkable celestial monster with jaguar features is two-headed. A human head is set in each open mouth; large areas of each flank are filled with glyphs. A.D. 775. (*Courtesy School of American Research.*)

Plate 11

Stela 3, La Mar, Usumacinta Valley. The scene of a chief seizing a pris-
oner and the delineation of some of the glyphs accord with the late date
of this newly discovered piece. A.D. 795.

Plate 12

Stela 6, Tortuguero (Macuspana), Tabasco. Tortuguero, the western-most site, except Comalcalco, with Maya hieroglyphic texts, lies on the borders of the Zoque, a non-Maya group. Yet these glyphs reveal strong influences from Palenque. Probably A.D. 667.

Plate 13

Texts from the Northern Maya Area. Top: Typical glyphs from Chi-´
chén Itzá, Lintel 2, Temple of Three Lintels. Probably A.D. 889. Below:
Columns of North Building, Xcalumkin. Probably A.D. 771. The glyph
style is very distinct from that of the Central area. (*Courtesy Peabody
Museum, Harvard University.*)

Plate 14

Weathered Text, Stela 71, Calakmul, Campeche. An example of the appearance of very many Maya texts. Because of checks and the known mechanism of the Initial Series, the date of this inscription—9.14.0.0.0, 6 Ahau 13 Muan (A.D. 711)—is perfectly clear, but not a single non-calendric glyph can be identified and entered in the glyph catalog.

Plate 15

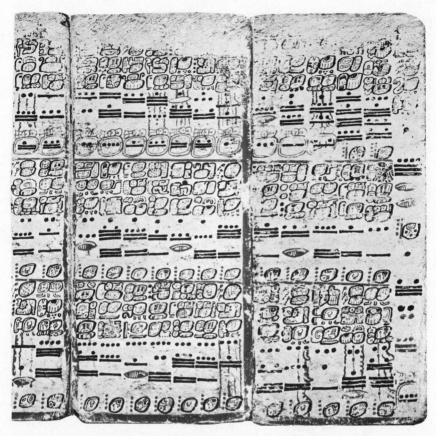

Farmer's Almanac, Codex Dresden. Right part of page 71 and pages 72 and 73. Days on which rainy periods and drought may be expected to begin are indicated. Because the subjects treated differ from those of the stone monuments, the glyphs also are different. *(Photos from Förstemann 1892 edition.)*

Plate 16

Almanacs, Codex Madrid. Pages 10 and 11 of the codex, which also deals with drought and rain, scorching weather, planting, etc. This codex also called Tro-cortesianus. *(Photos from de Rosny 1883 edition.)*

DRAWINGS OF GLYPHS

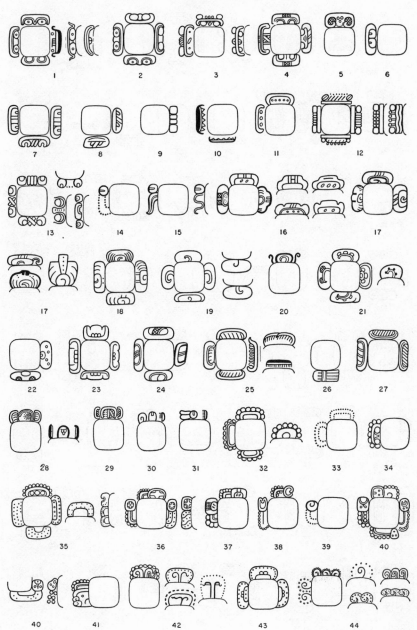

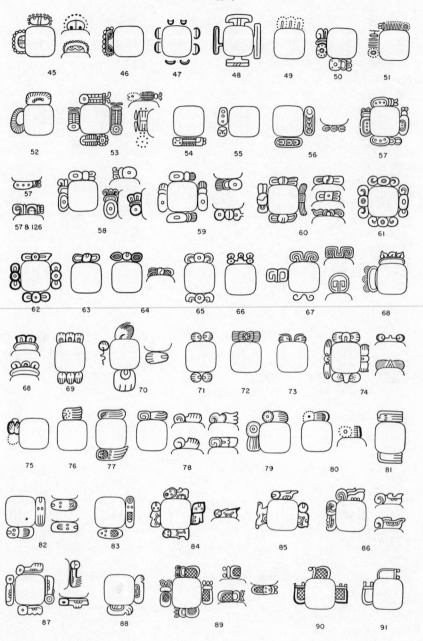

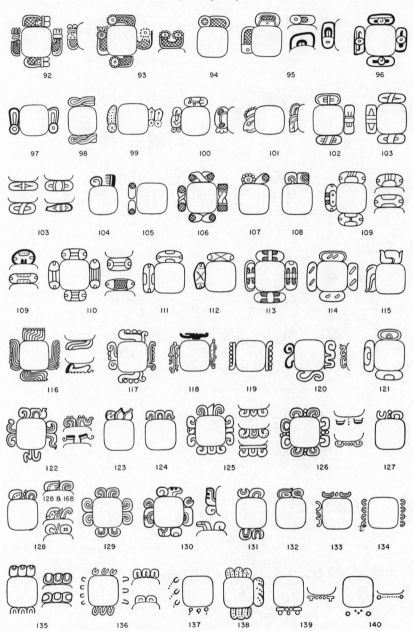

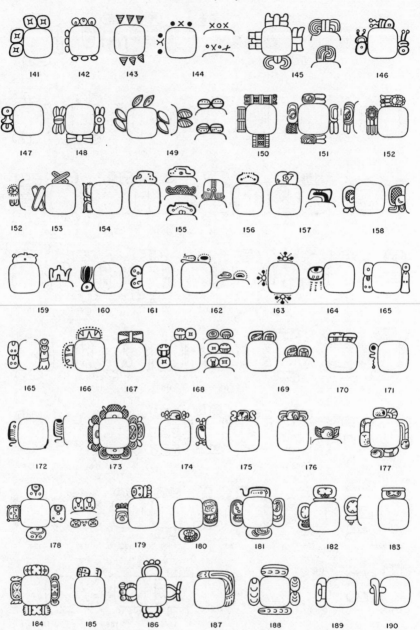

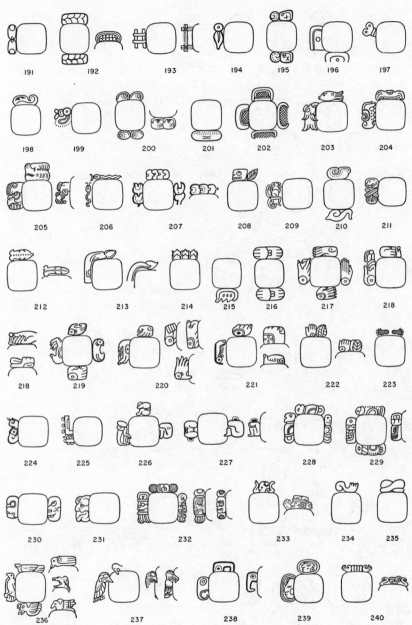

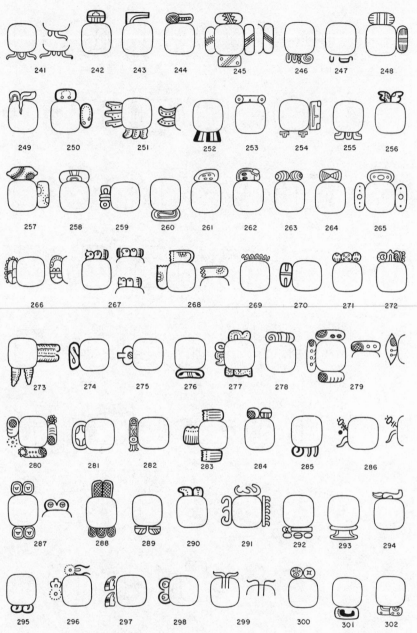

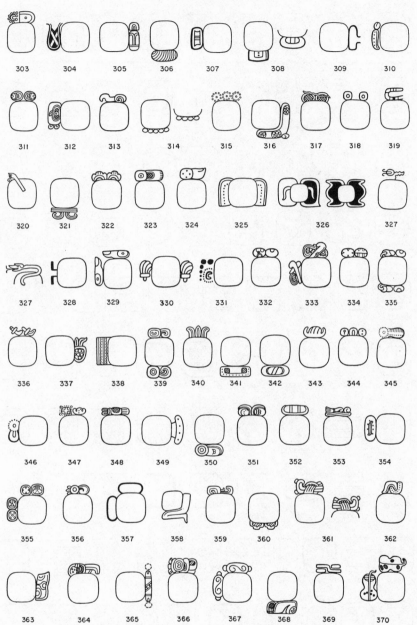

303   304   305   306   307   308   309   310

311   312   313   314   315   316   317   318   319

320   321   322   323   324   325   326   327

327   328   329   330   331   332   333   334   335

336   337   338   339   340   341   342   343   344   345

346   347   348   349   350   351   352   353   354

355   356   357   358   359   360   361   362

363   364   365   366   367   368   369   370

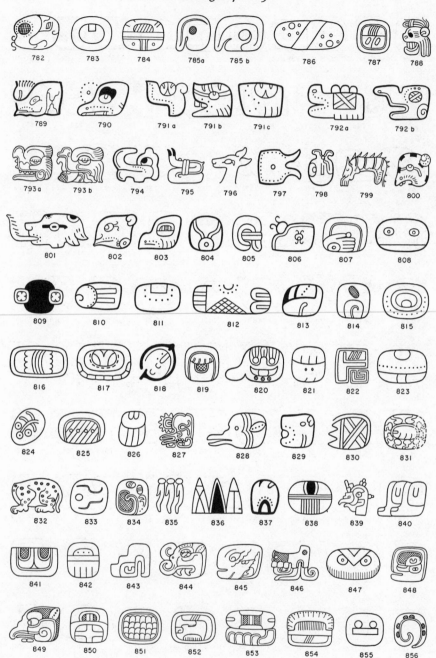

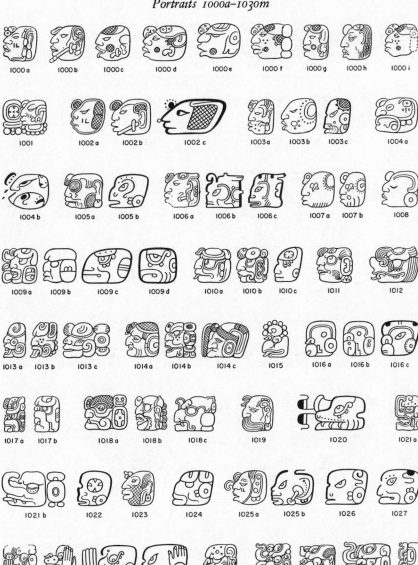

1000 a   1000 b   1000 c   1000 d   1000 e   1000 f   1000 g   1000 h   1000 i

1001   1002 a   1002 b   1002 c   1003 a   1003 b   1003 c   1004 a

1004 b   1005 a   1005 b   1006 a   1006 b   1006 c   1007 a   1007 b   1008

1009 a   1009 b   1009 c   1009 d   1010 a   1010 b   1010 c   1011   1012

1013 a   1013 b   1013 c   1014 a   1014 b   1014 c   1015   1016 a   1016 b   1016 c

1017 a   1017 b   1018 a   1018 b   1018 c   1019   1020   1021 a

1021 b   1022   1023   1024   1025 a   1025 b   1026   1027

1028 a   1028 b   1028 c   1028 d   1029   1030 a   1030 b   1030 c   1030 d

1030 e   1030 f   1030 g   1030 h   1030 i   1030 j   1030 k   1030 l   1030 m

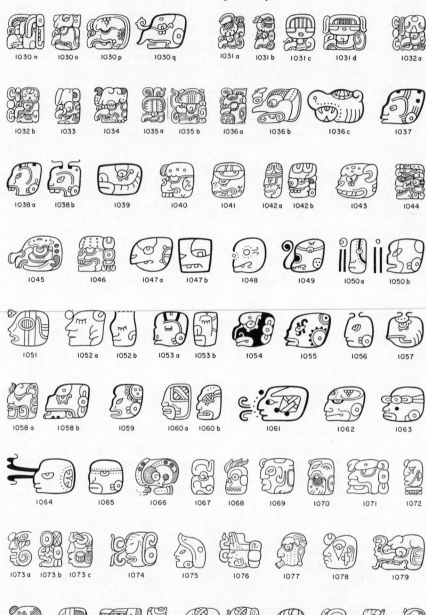

1030 n 1030 o 1030 p 1030 q 1031 a 1031 b 1031 c 1031 d 1032 a

1032 b 1033 1034 1035 a 1035 b 1036 a 1036 b 1036 c 1037

1038 a 1038 b 1039 1040 1041 1042 a 1042 b 1043 1044

1045 1046 1047 a 1047 b 1048 1049 1050 a 1050 b

1051 1052 a 1052 b 1053 a 1053 b 1054 1055 1056 1057

1058 a 1058 b 1059 1060 a 1060 b 1061 1062 1063

1064 1065 1066 1067 1068 1069 1070 1071 1072

1073 a 1073 b 1073 c 1074 1075 1076 1077 1078 1079

1080 1081 1082 a 1082 b 1083 a 1083 b 1084 1085 1086 1087